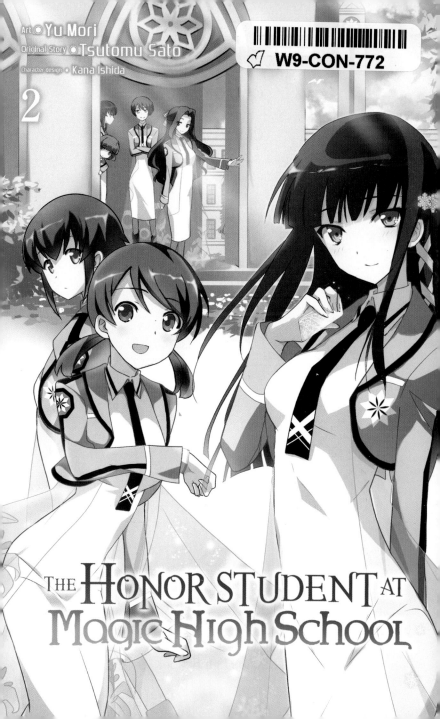

Art ● Yu Mori
Original Story ● Tsutomu Sato
Character design ● Kana Ishida

W9-CON-772

2

THE HONOR STUDENT AT Magic High School

CONTENTS

The Honor Student
at Magic High School

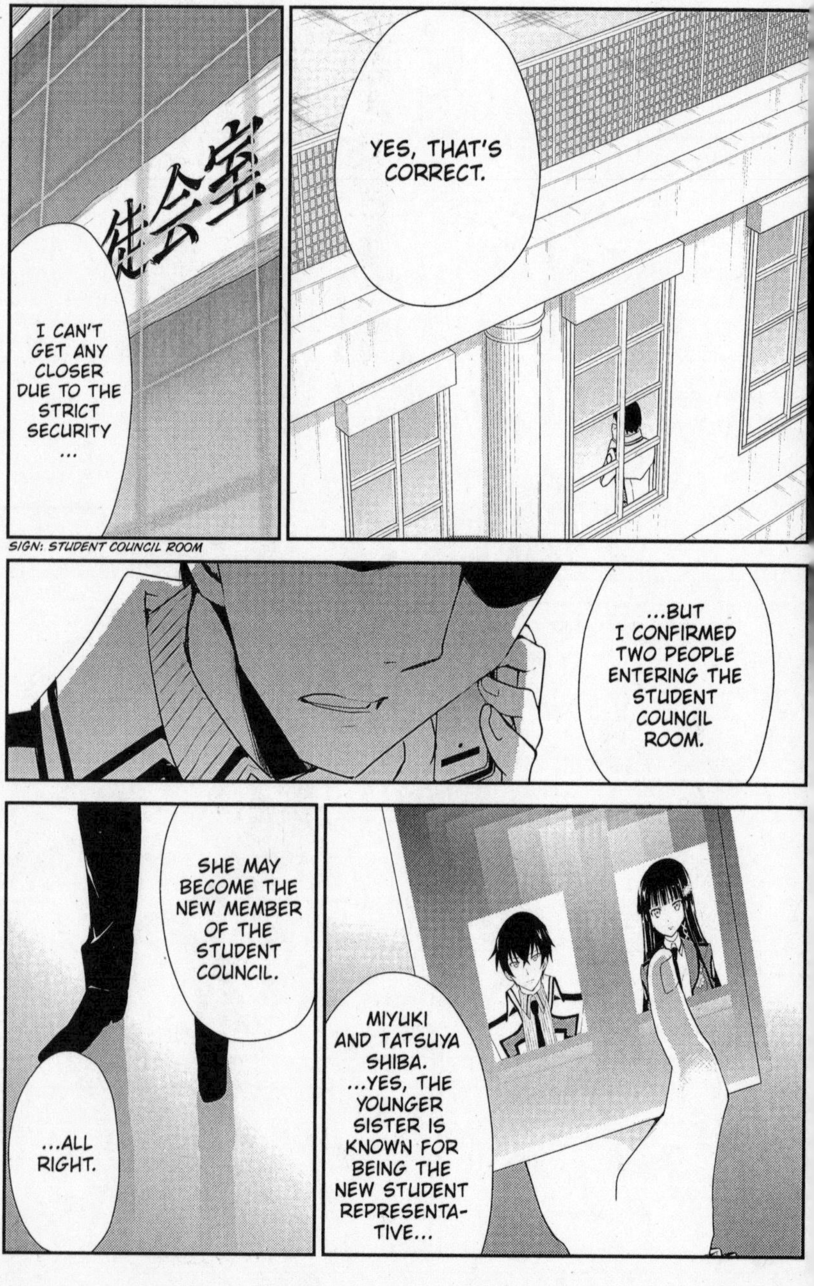
YES, THAT'S CORRECT.
I CAN'T GET ANY CLOSER DUE TO THE STRICT SECURITY ...
SIGN: STUDENT COUNCIL ROOM
...BUT I CONFIRMED TWO PEOPLE ENTERING THE STUDENT COUNCIL ROOM.
MIYUKI AND TATSUYA SHIBA. ...YES, THE YOUNGER SISTER IS KNOWN FOR BEING THE NEW STUDENT REPRESENTA-TIVE...
SHE MAY BECOME THE NEW MEMBER OF THE STUDENT COUNCIL.
...ALL RIGHT.

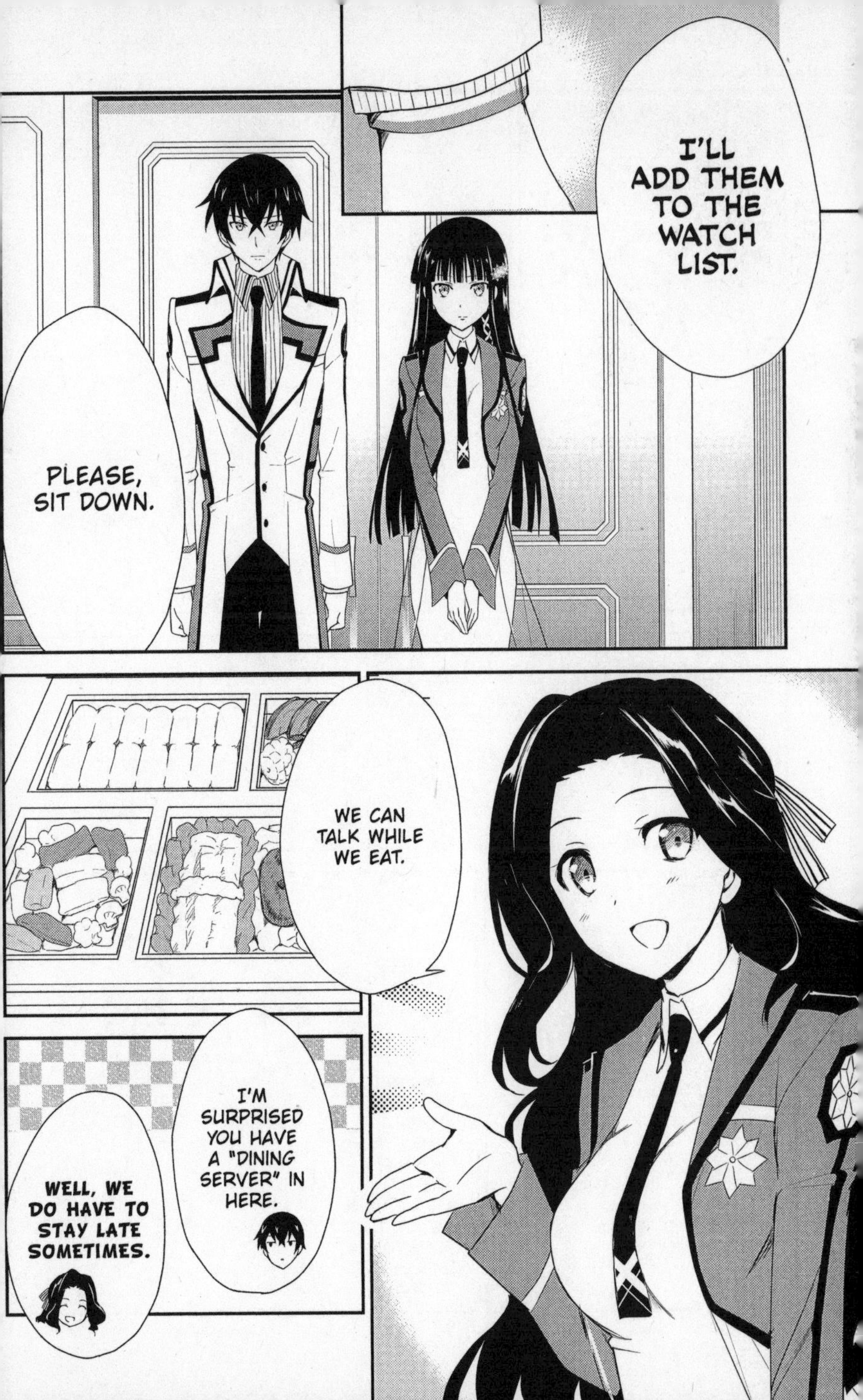
I'LL ADD THEM TO THE WATCH LIST.
PLEASE, SIT DOWN.
WE CAN TALK WHILE WE EAT.
I'M SURPRISED YOU HAVE A "DINING SERVER" IN HERE.
WELL, WE DO HAVE TO STAY LATE SOMETIMES.

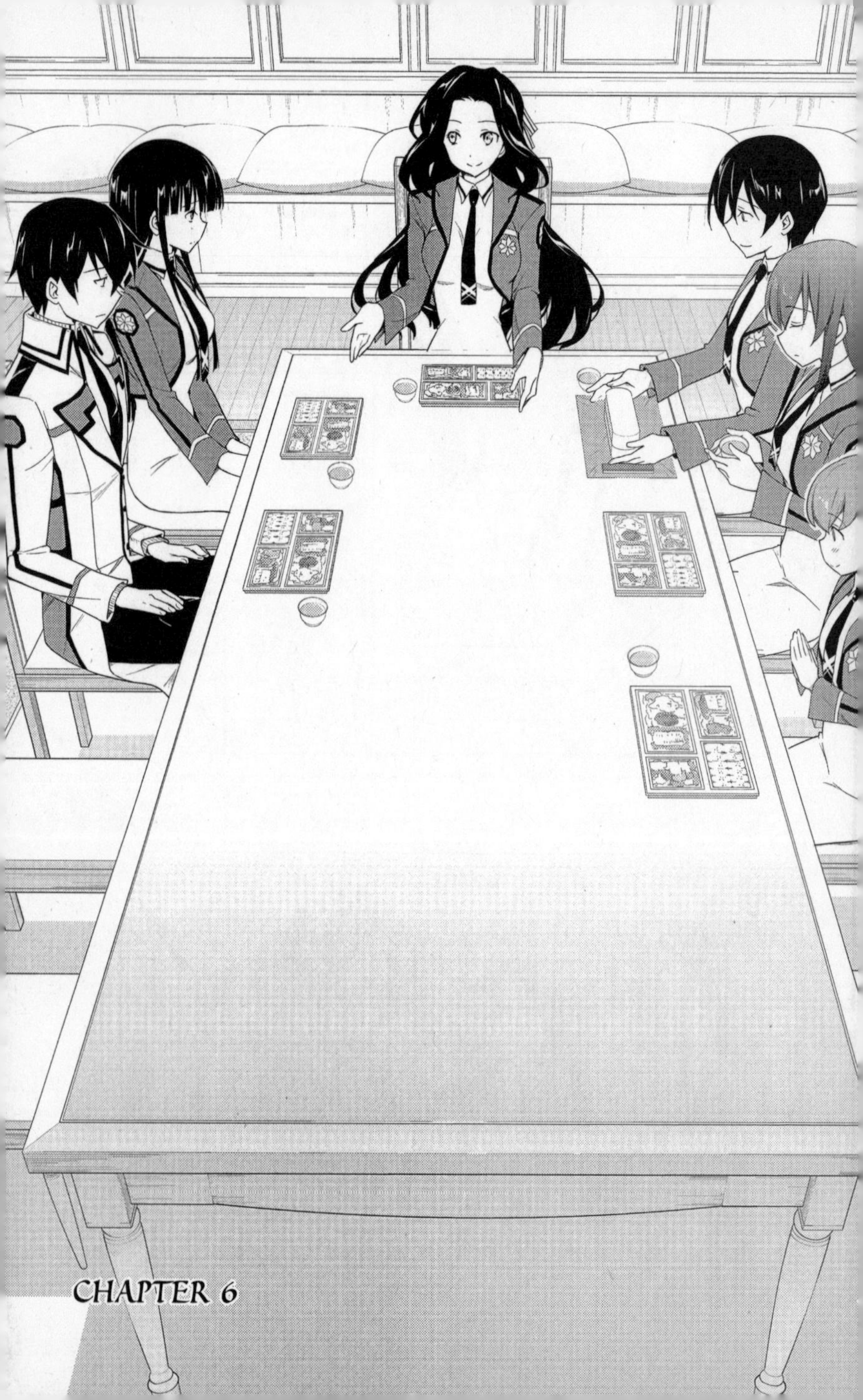
CHAPTER 6

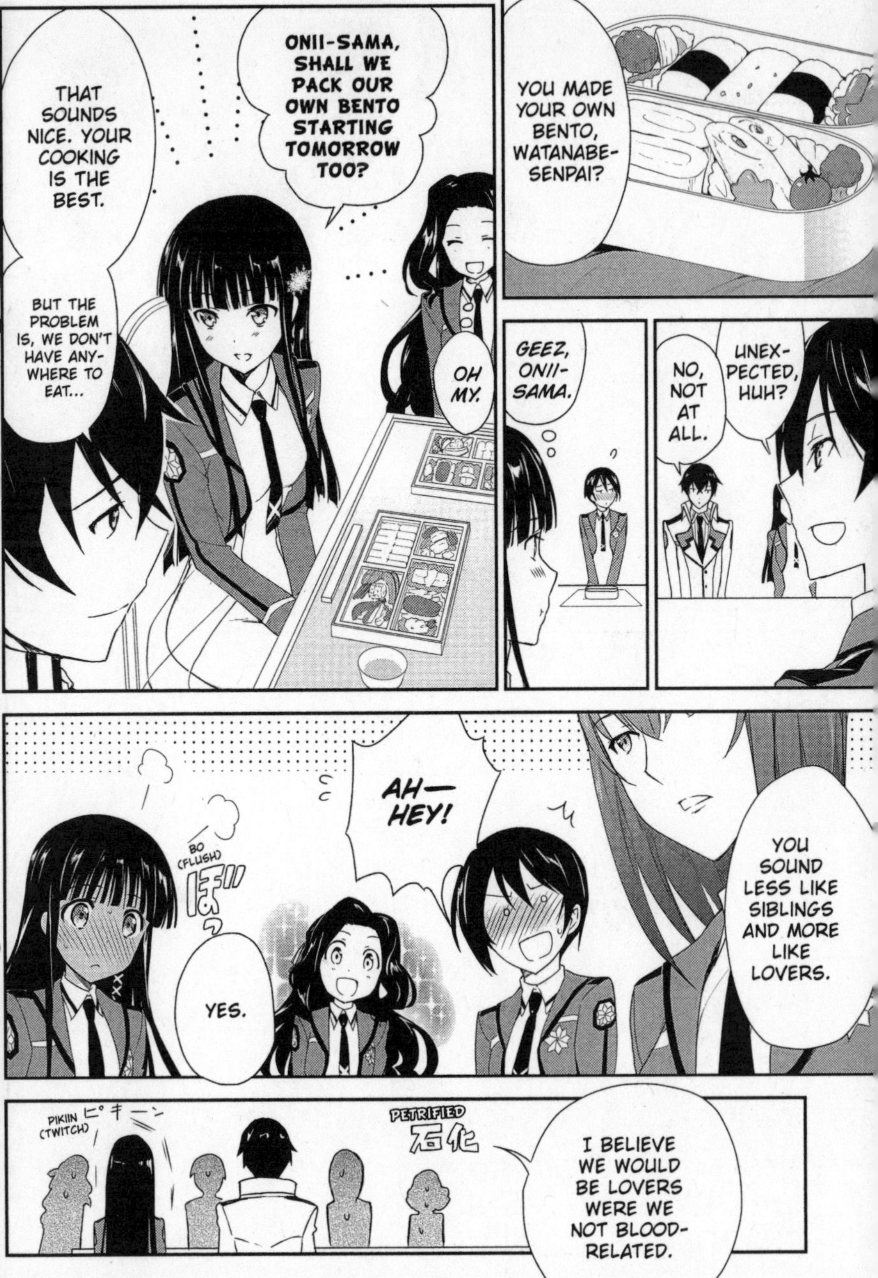
YOU MADE YOUR OWN BENTO, WATANABE-SENPAI?
UNEX-PECTED, HUH?
NO, NOT AT ALL.
GEEZ, ONII-SAMA.
ONII-SAMA, SHALL WE PACK OUR OWN BENTO STARTING TOMORROW TOO?
THAT SOUNDS NICE. YOUR COOKING IS THE BEST.
OH MY.
BUT THE PROBLEM IS, WE DON'T HAVE ANY-WHERE TO EAT...
YOU SOUND LESS LIKE SIBLINGS AND MORE LIKE LOVERS.
AH— HEY!
BO (FLUSH)
ぼっ
YES.
I BELIEVE WE WOULD BE LOVERS WERE WE NOT BLOOD-RELATED.
PETRIFIED
石化
PIKIIN (TWITCH)
ピキーン

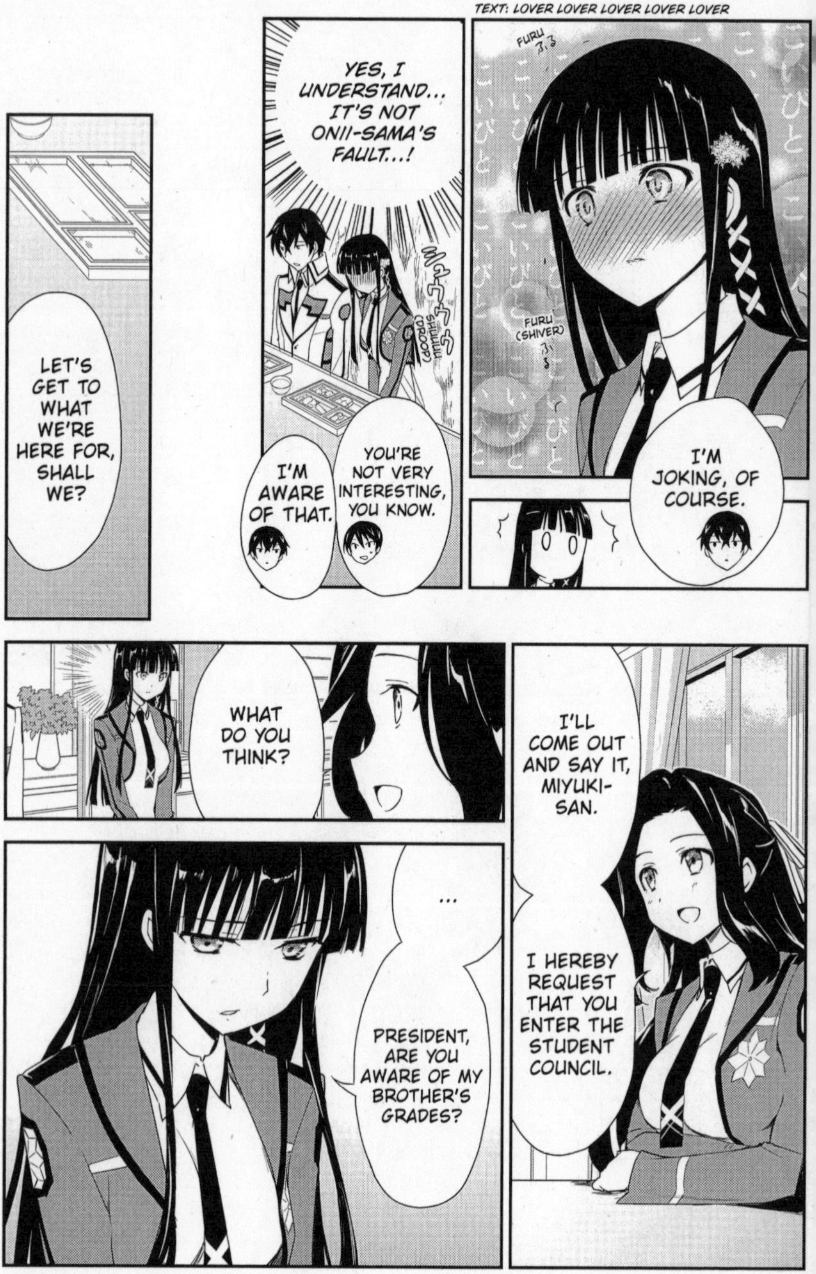
TEXT: LOVER LOVER LOVER LOVER LOVER
FURU
FURU (SHIVER)
I'M JOKING, OF COURSE.
YES, I UNDERSTAND... IT'S NOT ONII-SAMA'S FAULT...!
SHUUUU (DROOP)
YOU'RE NOT VERY INTERESTING, YOU KNOW.
I'M AWARE OF THAT.
LET'S GET TO WHAT WE'RE HERE FOR, SHALL WE?
I'LL COME OUT AND SAY IT, MIYUKI-SAN.
I HEREBY REQUEST THAT YOU ENTER THE STUDENT COUNCIL.
WHAT DO YOU THINK?
...
PRESIDENT, ARE YOU AWARE OF MY BROTHER'S GRADES?

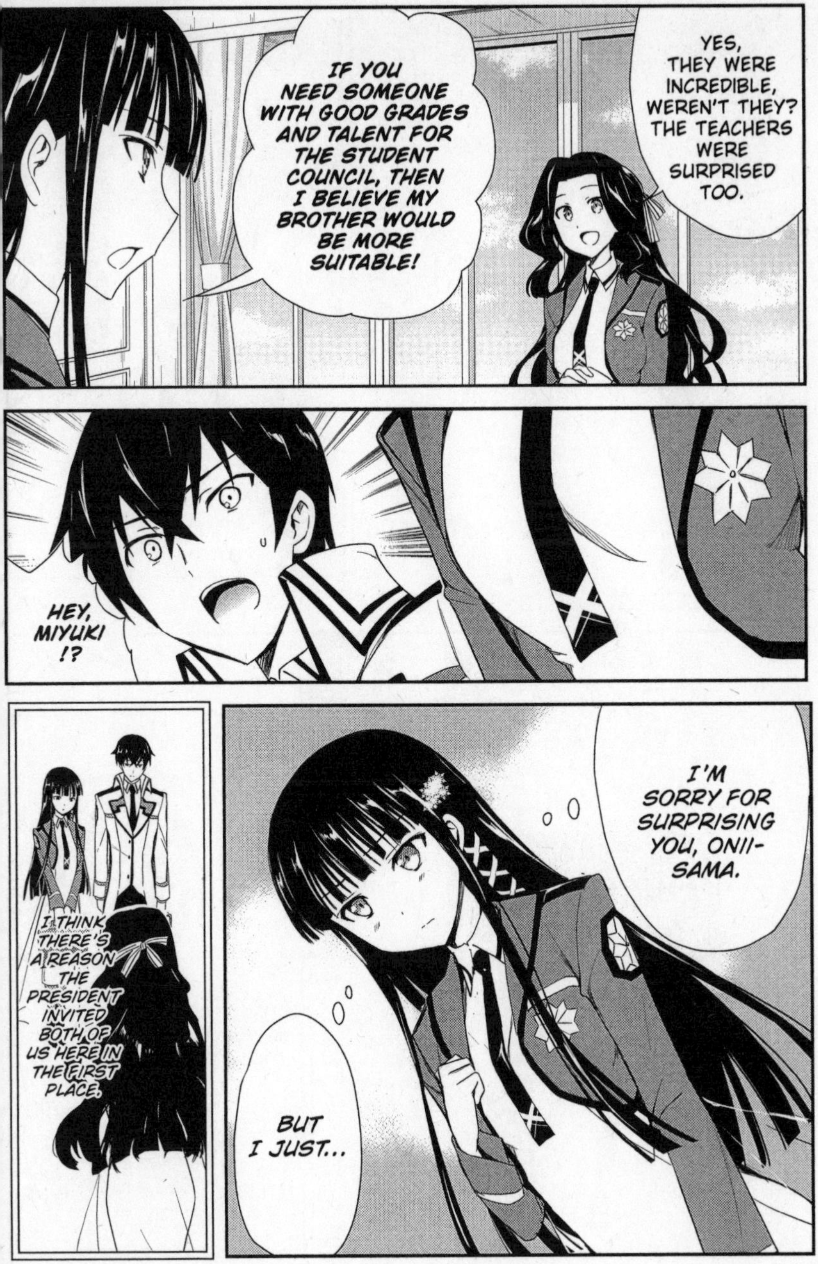
YES, THEY WERE INCREDIBLE, WEREN'T THEY? THE TEACHERS WERE SURPRISED TOO.
IF YOU NEED SOMEONE WITH GOOD GRADES AND TALENT FOR THE STUDENT COUNCIL, THEN I BELIEVE MY BROTHER WOULD BE MORE SUITABLE!
HEY, MIYUKI !?
I'M SORRY FOR SURPRISING YOU, ONII-SAMA.
BUT I JUST...
I THINK THERE'S A REASON THE PRESIDENT INVITED BOTH OF US HERE IN THE FIRST PLACE.

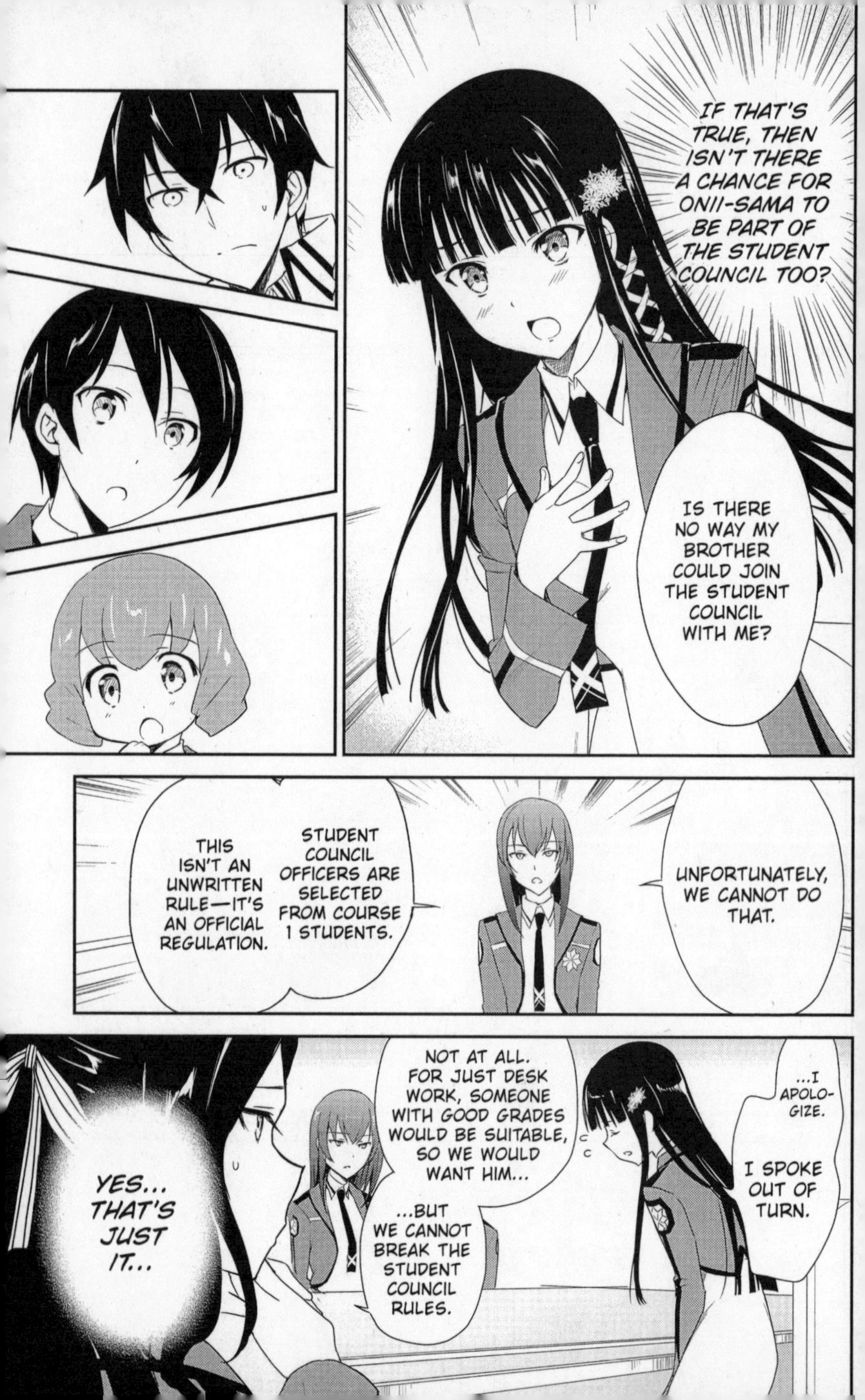
IF THAT'S TRUE, THEN ISN'T THERE A CHANCE FOR ONII-SAMA TO BE PART OF THE STUDENT COUNCIL TOO?
IS THERE NO WAY MY BROTHER COULD JOIN THE STUDENT COUNCIL WITH ME?
UNFORTUNATELY, WE CANNOT DO THAT.
STUDENT COUNCIL OFFICERS ARE SELECTED FROM COURSE 1 STUDENTS.
THIS ISN'T AN UNWRITTEN RULE—IT'S AN OFFICIAL REGULATION.
...I APOLOGIZE.
I SPOKE OUT OF TURN.
NOT AT ALL. FOR JUST DESK WORK, SOMEONE WITH GOOD GRADES WOULD BE SUITABLE, SO WE WOULD WANT HIM...
...BUT WE CANNOT BREAK THE STUDENT COUNCIL RULES.
YES... THAT'S JUST IT...

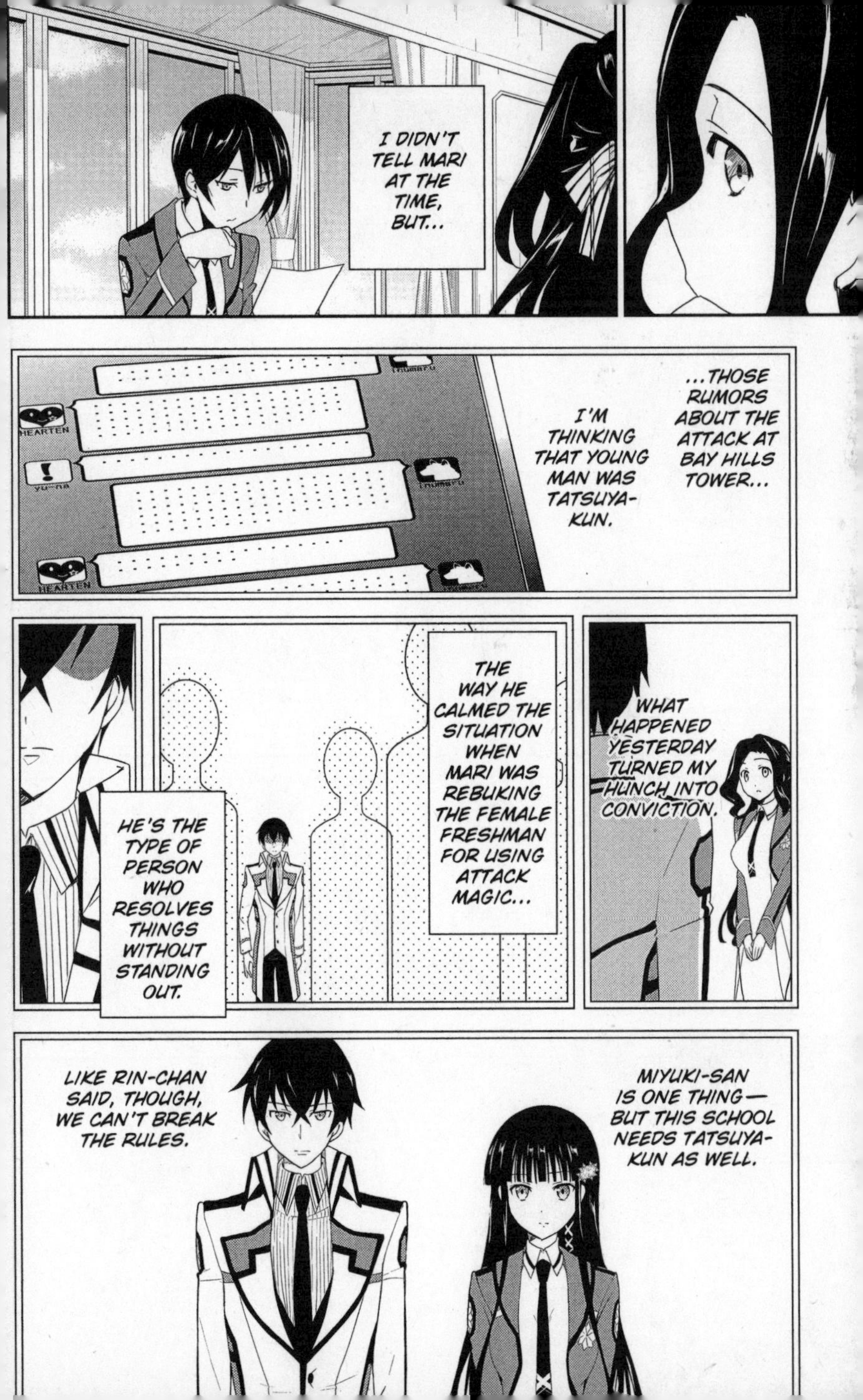
I DIDN'T TELL MARI AT THE TIME, BUT...
...THOSE RUMORS ABOUT THE ATTACK AT BAY HILLS TOWER...
I'M THINKING THAT YOUNG MAN WAS TATSUYA-KUN.
HEARTEN
yu~na
HEARTEN
WHAT HAPPENED YESTERDAY TURNED MY HUNCH INTO CONVICTION.
THE WAY HE CALMED THE SITUATION WHEN MARI WAS REBUKING THE FEMALE FRESHMAN FOR USING ATTACK MAGIC...
HE'S THE TYPE OF PERSON WHO RESOLVES THINGS WITHOUT STANDING OUT.
MIYUKI-SAN IS ONE THING— BUT THIS SCHOOL NEEDS TATSUYA-KUN AS WELL.
LIKE RIN-CHAN SAID, THOUGH, WE CAN'T BREAK THE RULES.

SIGN: HIGH ACHIEVERS

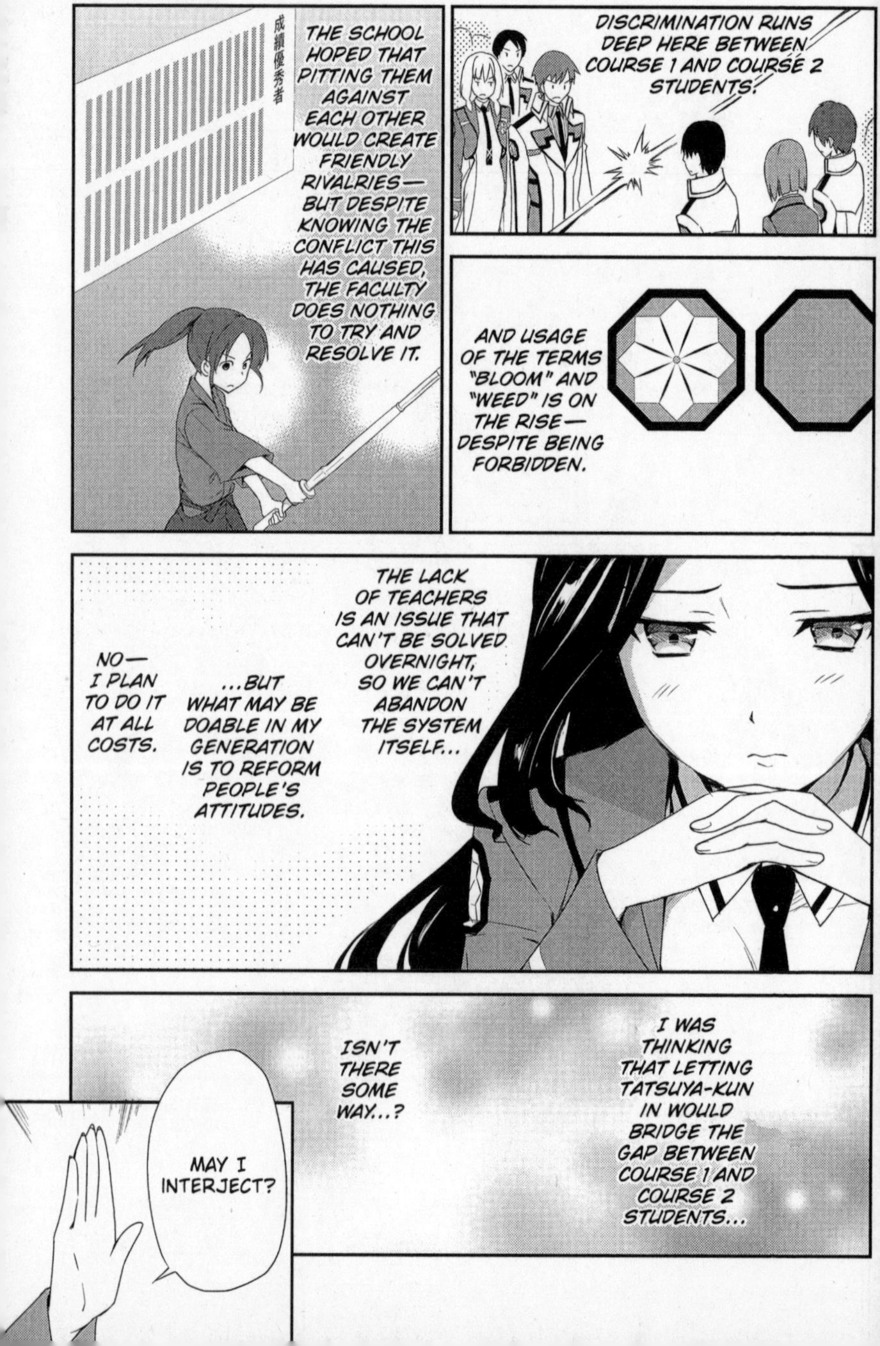
DISCRIMINATION RUNS DEEP HERE BETWEEN COURSE 1 AND COURSE 2 STUDENTS.
AND USAGE OF THE TERMS "BLOOM" AND "WEED" IS ON THE RISE—DESPITE BEING FORBIDDEN.
成績優秀者
THE SCHOOL HOPED THAT PITTING THEM AGAINST EACH OTHER WOULD CREATE FRIENDLY RIVALRIES—BUT DESPITE KNOWING THE CONFLICT THIS HAS CAUSED, THE FACULTY DOES NOTHING TO TRY AND RESOLVE IT.
THE LACK OF TEACHERS IS AN ISSUE THAT CAN'T BE SOLVED OVERNIGHT, SO WE CAN'T ABANDON THE SYSTEM ITSELF...
...BUT WHAT MAY BE DOABLE IN MY GENERATION IS TO REFORM PEOPLE'S ATTITUDES.
NO—I PLAN TO DO IT AT ALL COSTS.
I WAS THINKING THAT LETTING TATSUYA-KUN IN WOULD BRIDGE THE GAP BETWEEN COURSE 1 AND COURSE 2 STUDENTS...
ISN'T THERE SOME WAY...?
MAY I INTERJECT?

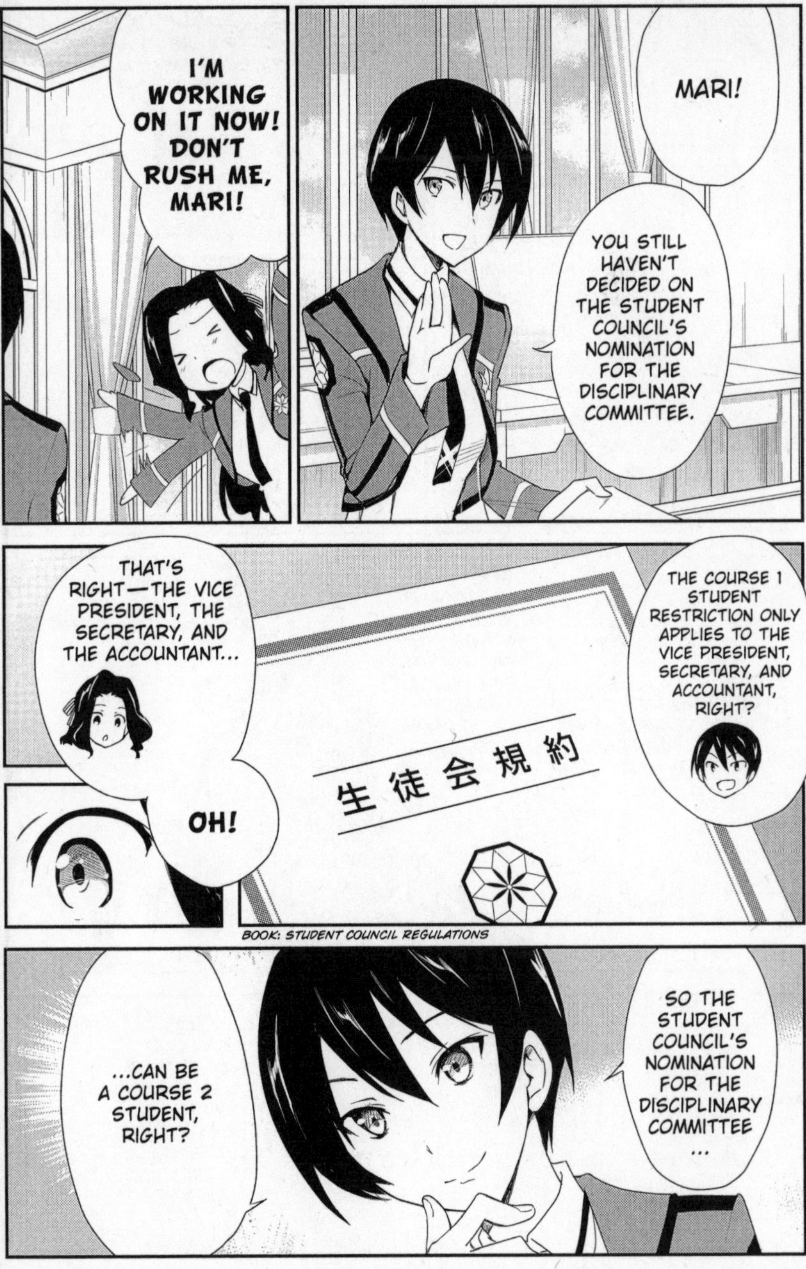
MARI!
YOU STILL HAVEN'T DECIDED ON THE STUDENT COUNCIL'S NOMINATION FOR THE DISCIPLINARY COMMITTEE.
I'M WORKING ON IT NOW! DON'T RUSH ME, MARI!
THE COURSE 1 STUDENT RESTRICTION ONLY APPLIES TO THE VICE PRESIDENT, SECRETARY, AND ACCOUNTANT, RIGHT?
生徒会規約
THAT'S RIGHT—THE VICE PRESIDENT, THE SECRETARY, AND THE ACCOUNTANT...
OH!
BOOK: STUDENT COUNCIL REGULATIONS
SO THE STUDENT COUNCIL'S NOMINATION FOR THE DISCIPLINARY COMMITTEE...
...CAN BE A COURSE 2 STUDENT, RIGHT?

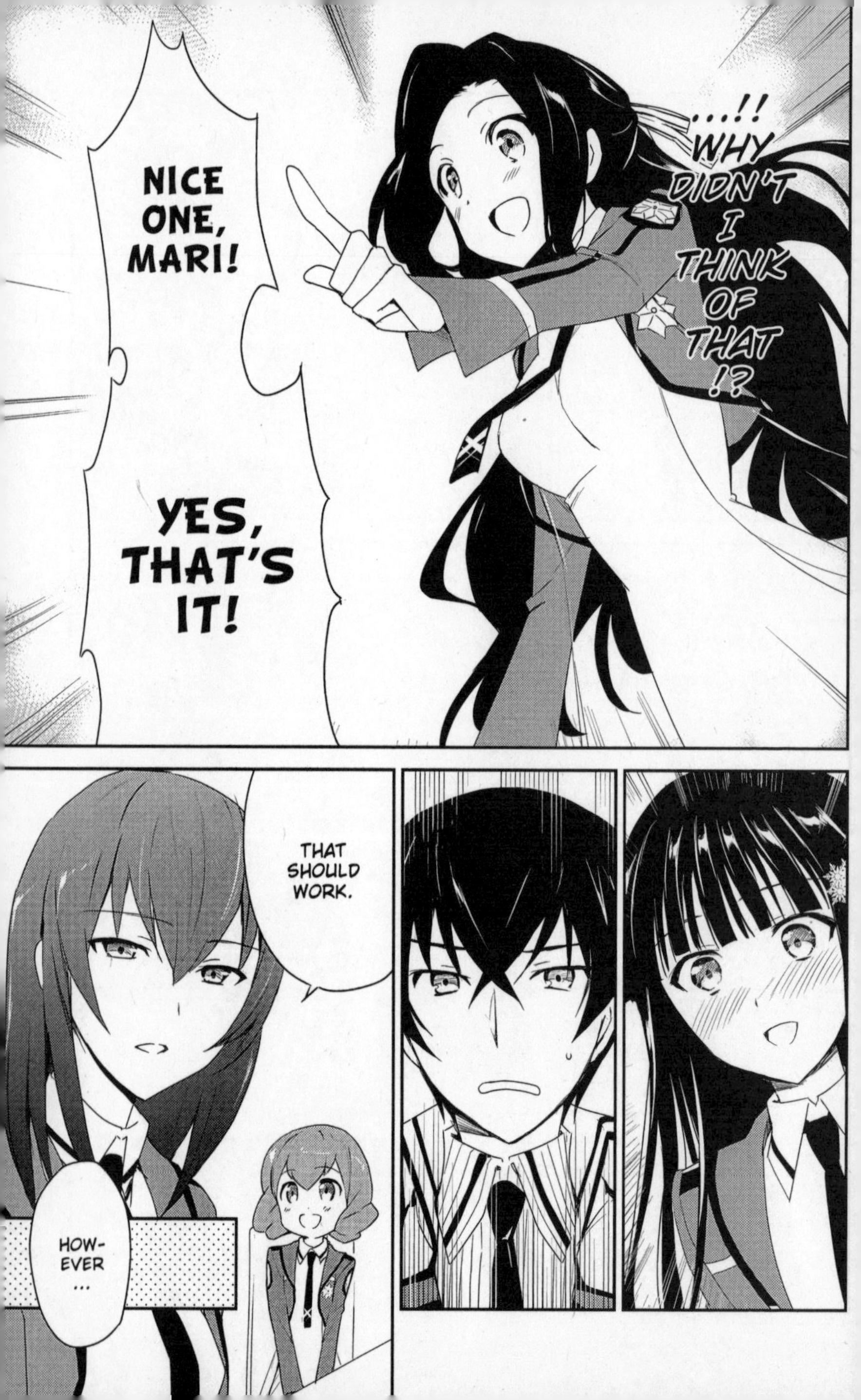
...!! WHY DIDN'T I THINK OF THAT!?
NICE ONE, MARI!
YES, THAT'S IT!
THAT SHOULD WORK.
HOW-EVER...

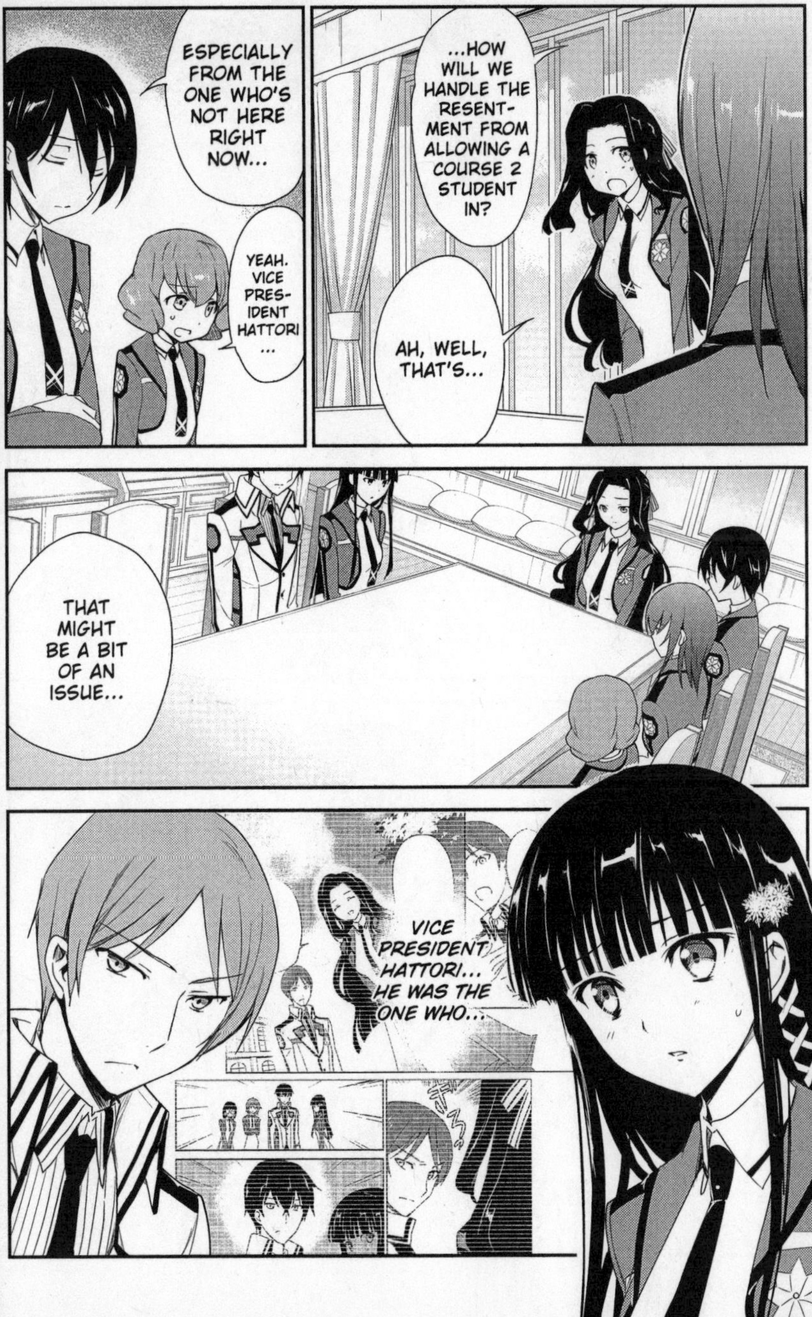
...HOW WILL WE HANDLE THE RESENT-MENT FROM ALLOWING A COURSE 2 STUDENT IN?
AH, WELL, THAT'S...
ESPECIALLY FROM THE ONE WHO'S NOT HERE RIGHT NOW...
YEAH. VICE PRES-IDENT HATTORI...
THAT MIGHT BE A BIT OF AN ISSUE...
VICE PRESIDENT HATTORI... HE WAS THE ONE WHO...

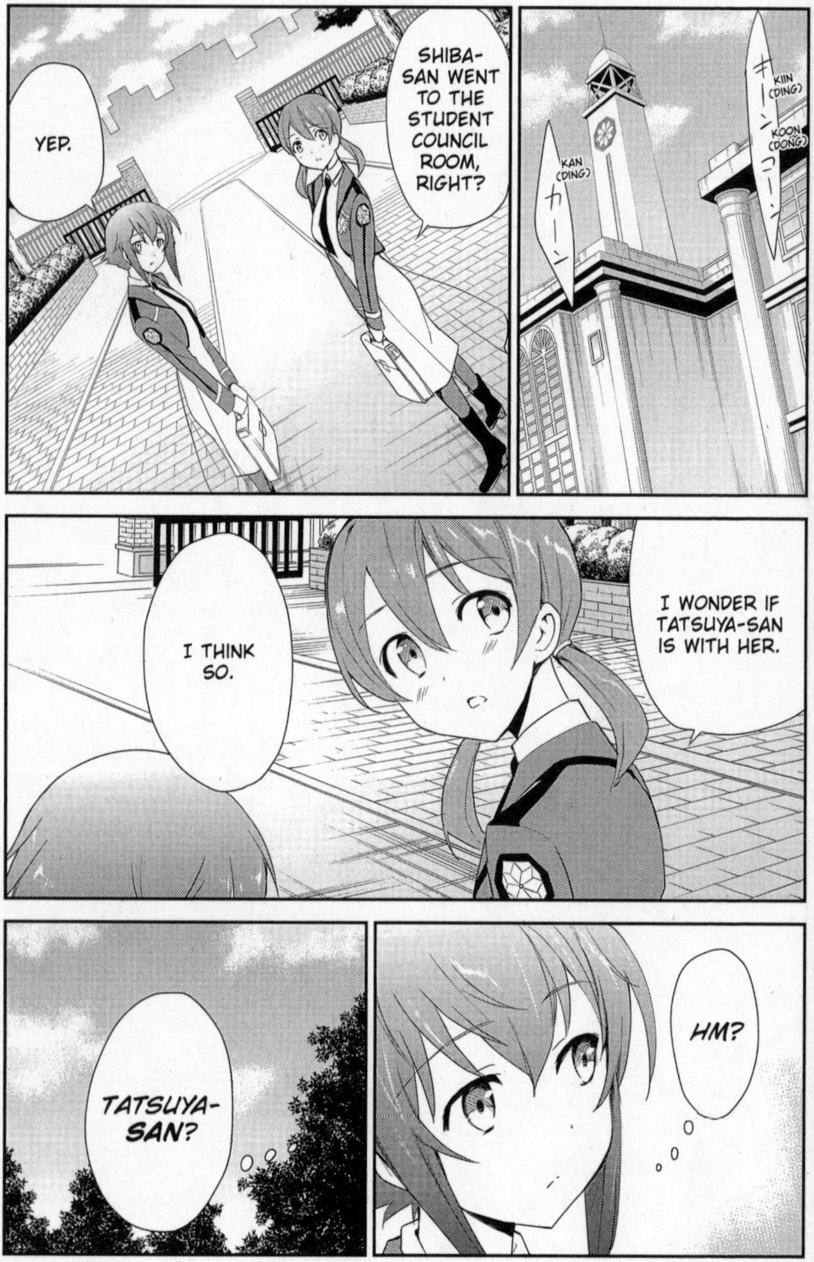
キーン
KIIN (DING)
コーン
KOON (DONG)
カーン
KAN (DING)
SHIBA-SAN WENT TO THE STUDENT COUNCIL ROOM, RIGHT?
YEP.
I WONDER IF TATSUYA-SAN IS WITH HER.
I THINK SO.
HM?
TATSUYA-SAN?

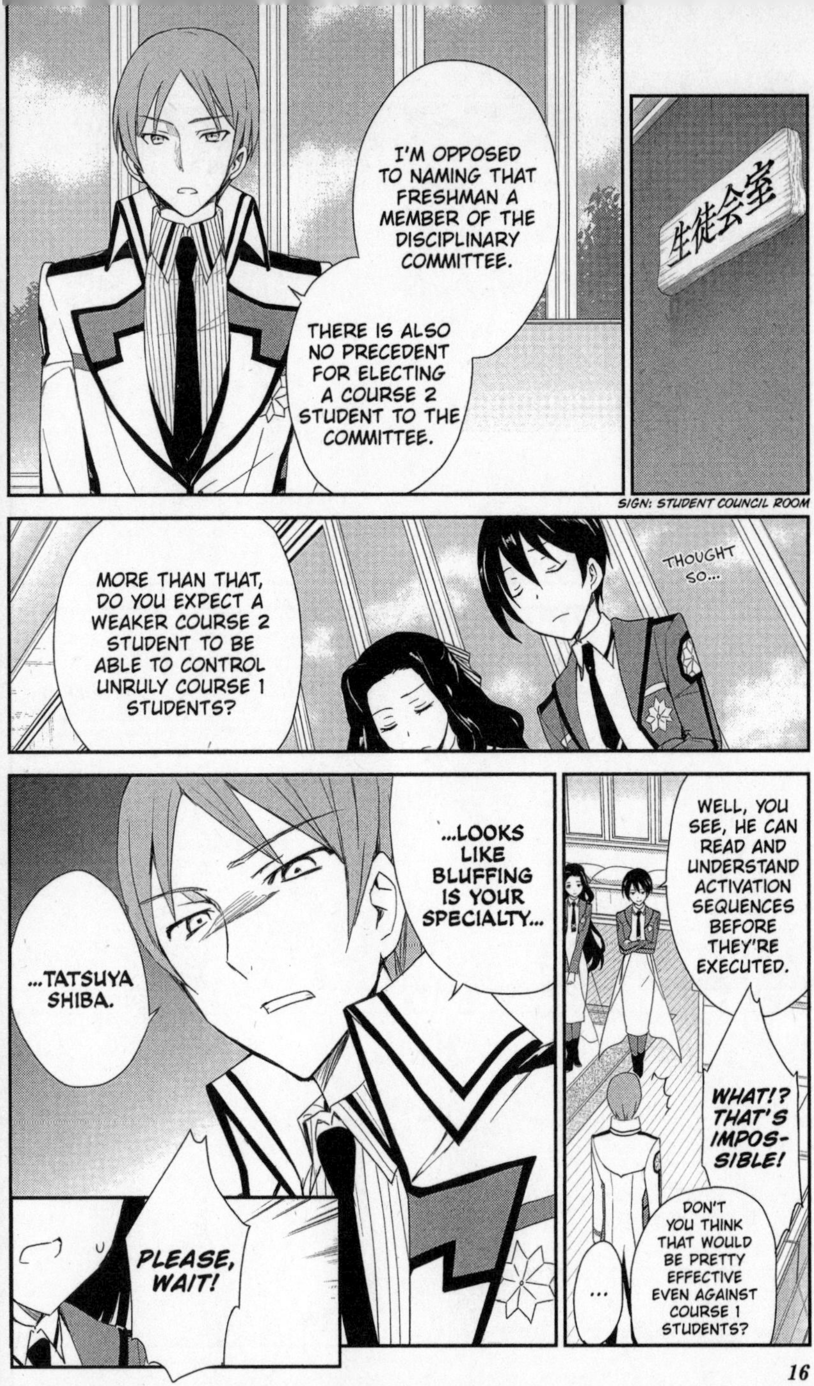
生徒会室
SIGN: STUDENT COUNCIL ROOM
I'M OPPOSED TO NAMING THAT FRESHMAN A MEMBER OF THE DISCIPLINARY COMMITTEE.
THERE IS ALSO NO PRECEDENT FOR ELECTING A COURSE 2 STUDENT TO THE COMMITTEE.
MORE THAN THAT, DO YOU EXPECT A WEAKER COURSE 2 STUDENT TO BE ABLE TO CONTROL UNRULY COURSE 1 STUDENTS?
THOUGHT SO...
WELL, YOU SEE, HE CAN READ AND UNDERSTAND ACTIVATION SEQUENCES BEFORE THEY'RE EXECUTED.
WHAT!? THAT'S IMPOS-SIBLE!
DON'T YOU THINK THAT WOULD BE PRETTY EFFECTIVE EVEN AGAINST COURSE 1 STUDENTS?
...
...LOOKS LIKE BLUFFING IS YOUR SPECIALTY...
...TATSUYA SHIBA.
PLEASE, WAIT!

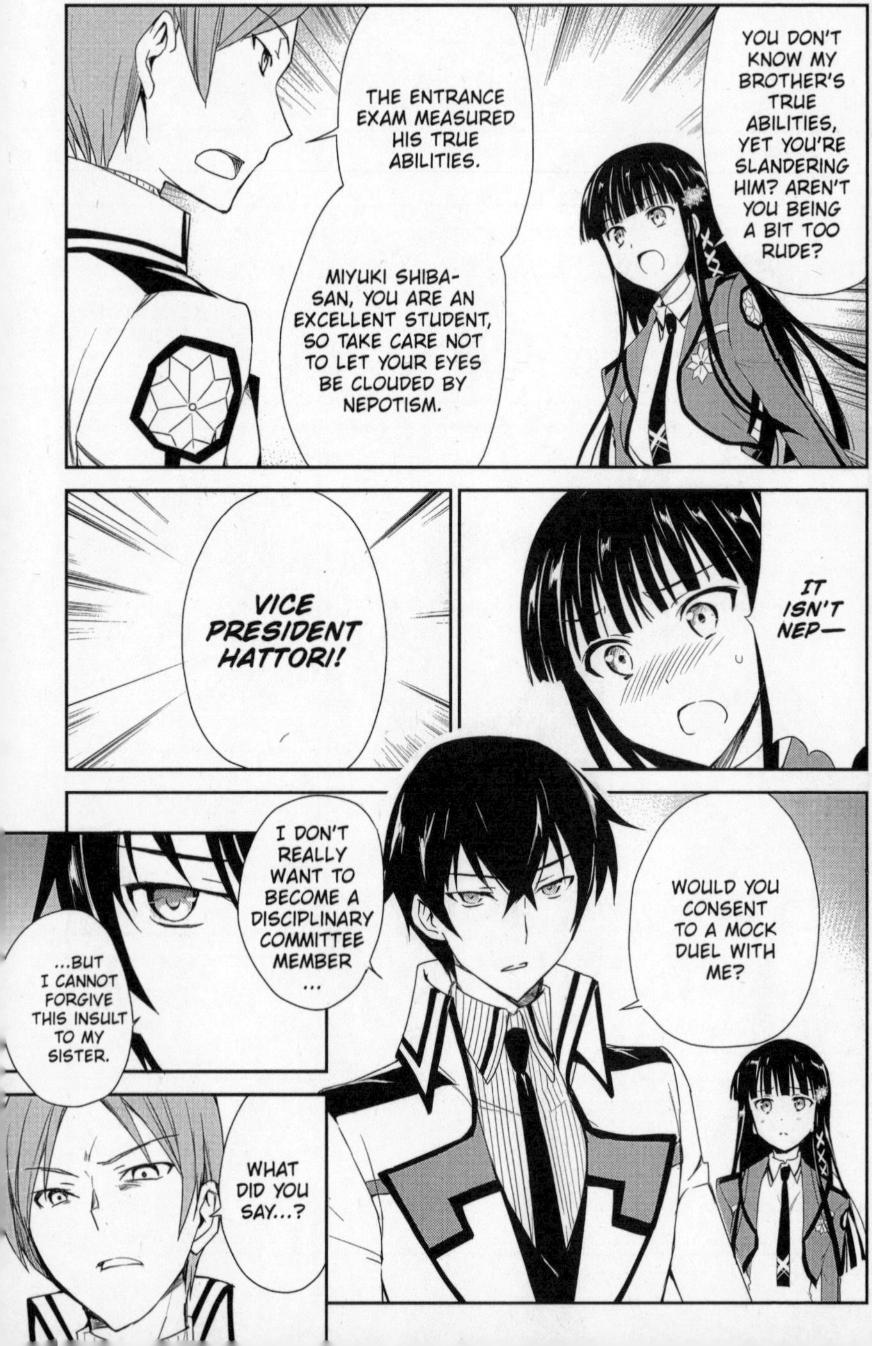
YOU DON'T KNOW MY BROTHER'S TRUE ABILITIES, YET YOU'RE SLANDERING HIM? AREN'T YOU BEING A BIT TOO RUDE?
THE ENTRANCE EXAM MEASURED HIS TRUE ABILITIES.
MIYUKI SHIBA-SAN, YOU ARE AN EXCELLENT STUDENT, SO TAKE CARE NOT TO LET YOUR EYES BE CLOUDED BY NEPOTISM.
IT ISN'T NEP—
VICE PRESIDENT HATTORI!
I DON'T REALLY WANT TO BECOME A DISCIPLINARY COMMITTEE MEMBER ...
...BUT I CANNOT FORGIVE THIS INSULT TO MY SISTER.
WHAT DID YOU SAY...?
WOULD YOU CONSENT TO A MOCK DUEL WITH ME?

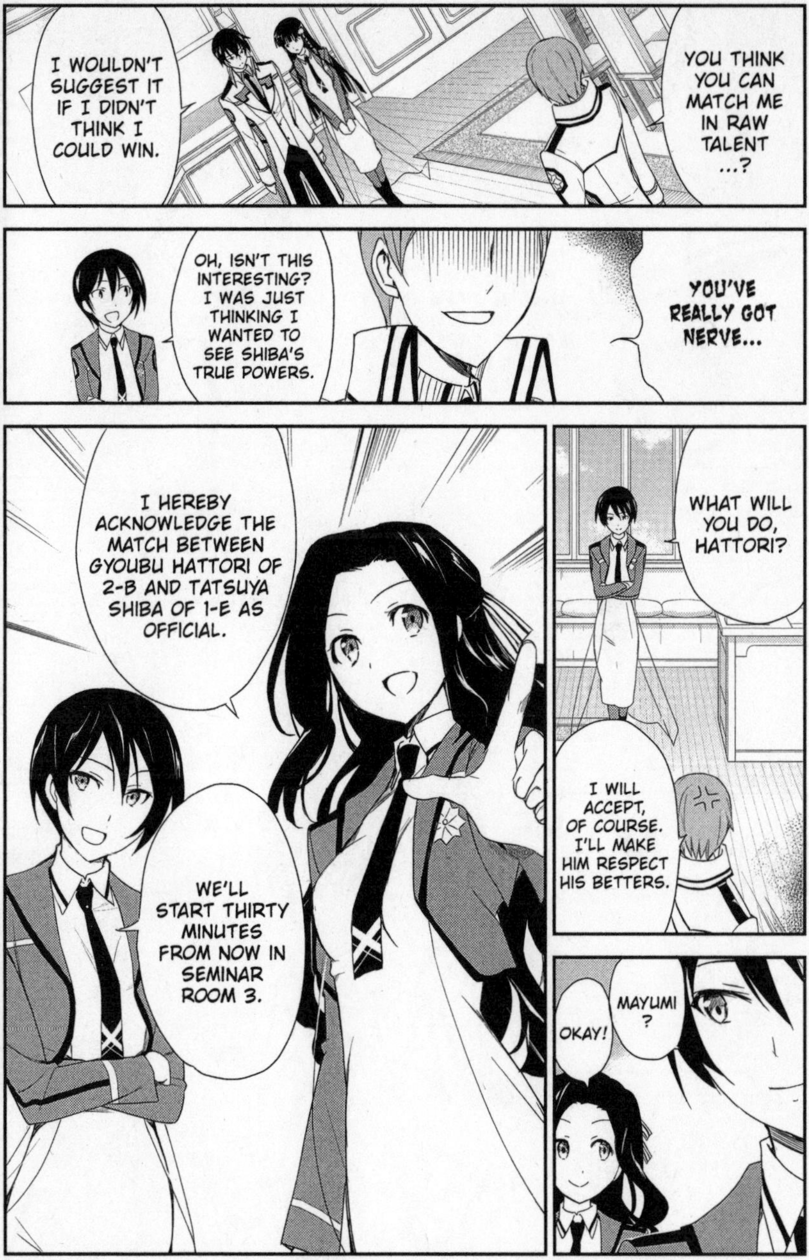
YOU THINK YOU CAN MATCH ME IN RAW TALENT ...?
I WOULDN'T SUGGEST IT IF I DIDN'T THINK I COULD WIN.
YOU'VE REALLY GOT NERVE...
OH, ISN'T THIS INTERESTING? I WAS JUST THINKING I WANTED TO SEE SHIBA'S TRUE POWERS.
WHAT WILL YOU DO, HATTORI?
I WILL ACCEPT, OF COURSE. I'LL MAKE HIM RESPECT HIS BETTERS.
MAYUMI ?
OKAY!
I HEREBY ACKNOWLEDGE THE MATCH BETWEEN GYOUBU HATTORI OF 2-B AND TATSUYA SHIBA OF 1-E AS OFFICIAL.
WE'LL START THIRTY MINUTES FROM NOW IN SEMINAR ROOM 3.

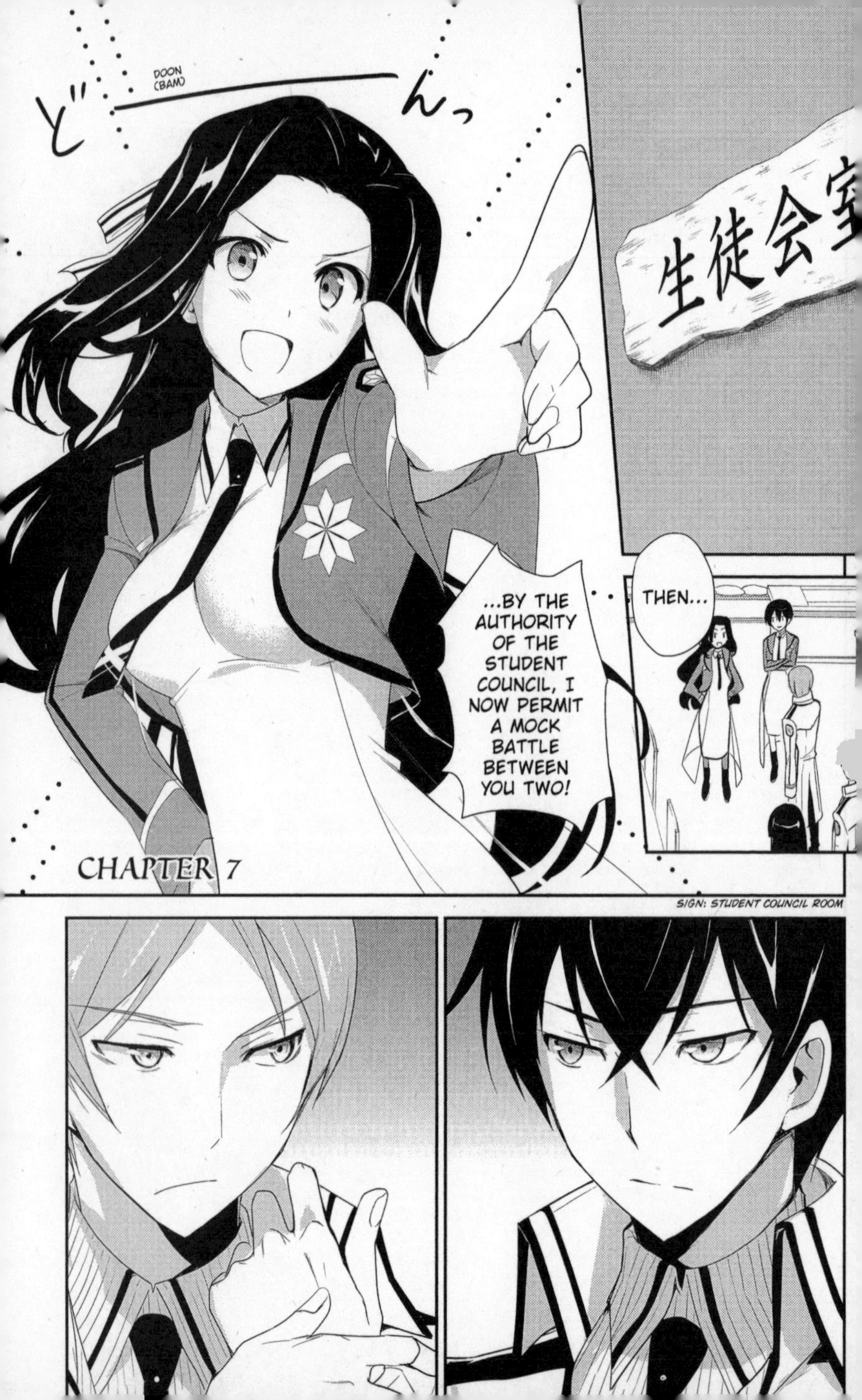

生徒会室
SIGN: STUDENT COUNCIL ROOM
THEN...
...BY THE AUTHORITY OF THE STUDENT COUNCIL, I NOW PERMIT A MOCK BATTLE BETWEEN YOU TWO!
ど――んっ
DOON (BAM)
CHAPTER 7

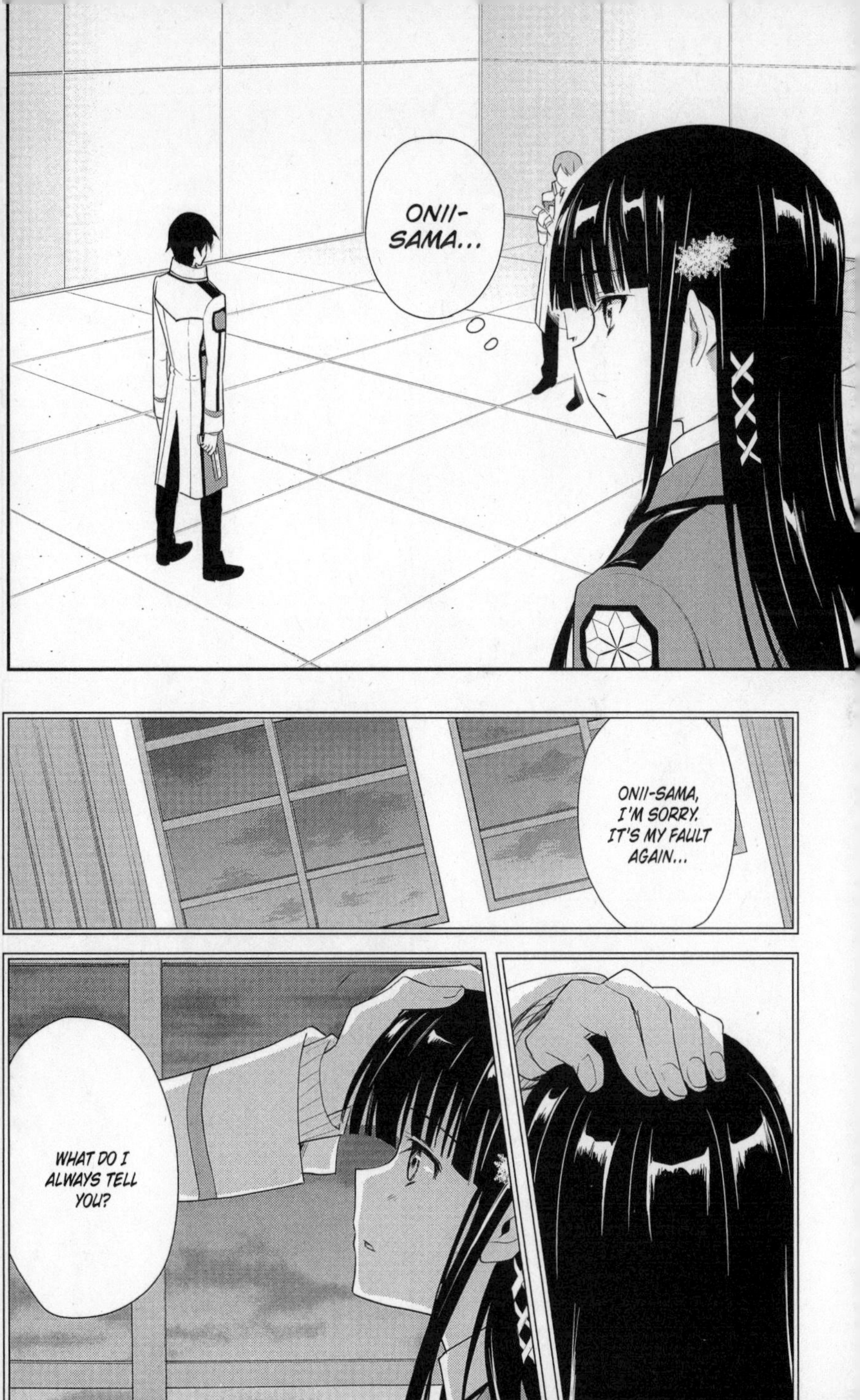
ONII-SAMA...
ONII-SAMA, I'M SORRY. IT'S MY FAULT AGAIN...
WHAT DO I ALWAYS TELL YOU?

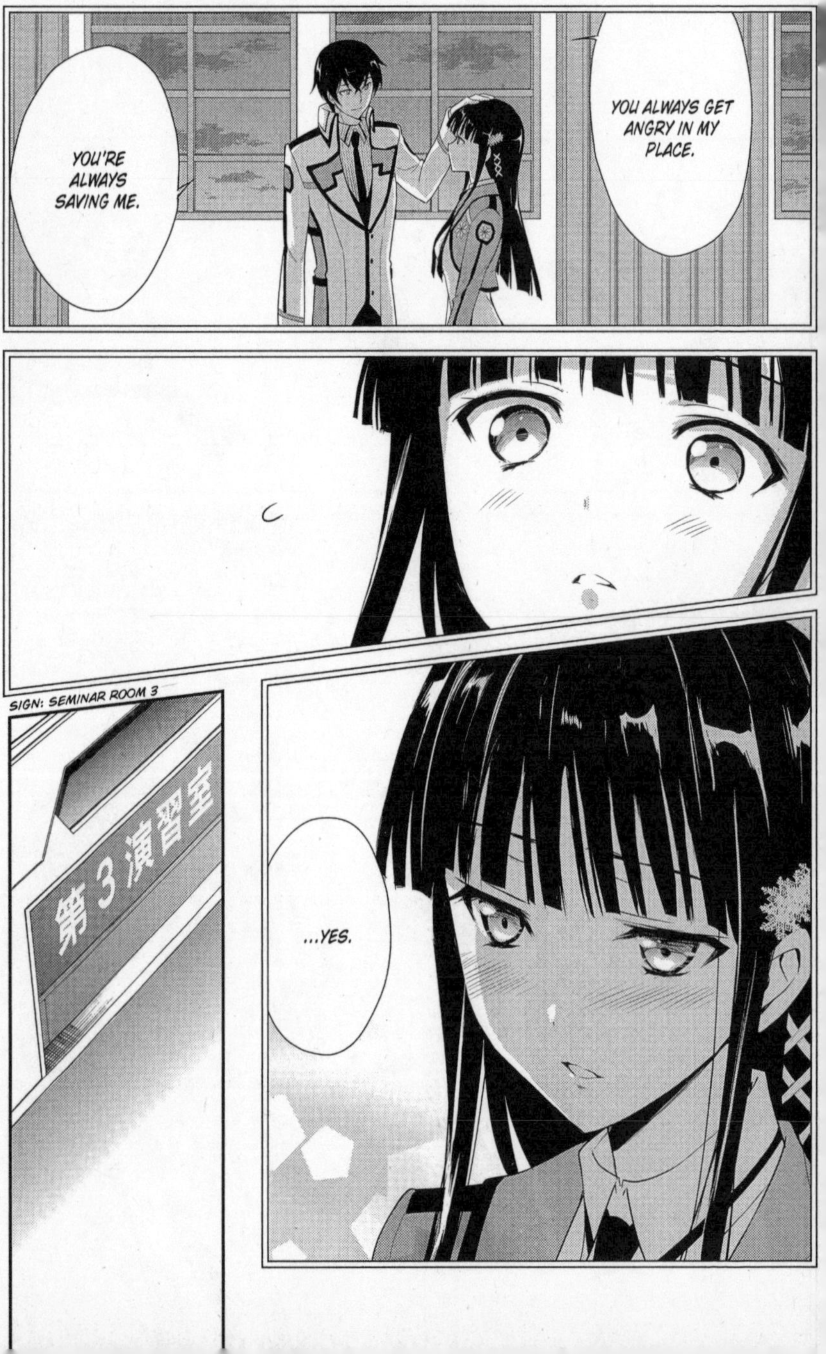
YOU ALWAYS GET ANGRY IN MY PLACE.
YOU'RE ALWAYS SAVING ME.
...YES.
SIGN: SEMINAR ROOM 3
第3演習室

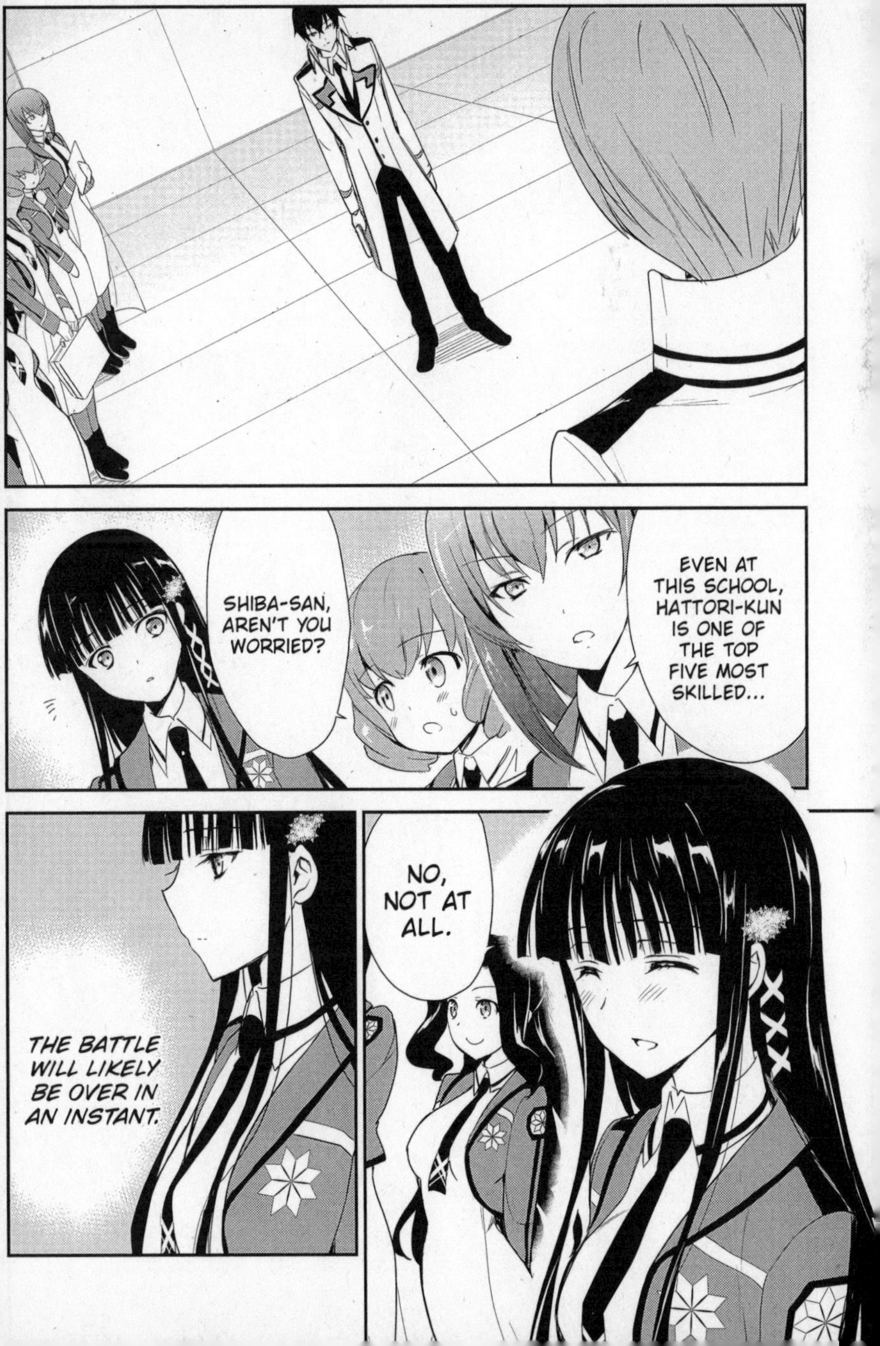
EVEN AT THIS SCHOOL, HATTORI-KUN IS ONE OF THE TOP FIVE MOST SKILLED...
SHIBA-SAN, AREN'T YOU WORRIED?
NO, NOT AT ALL.
THE BATTLE WILL LIKELY BE OVER IN AN INSTANT.

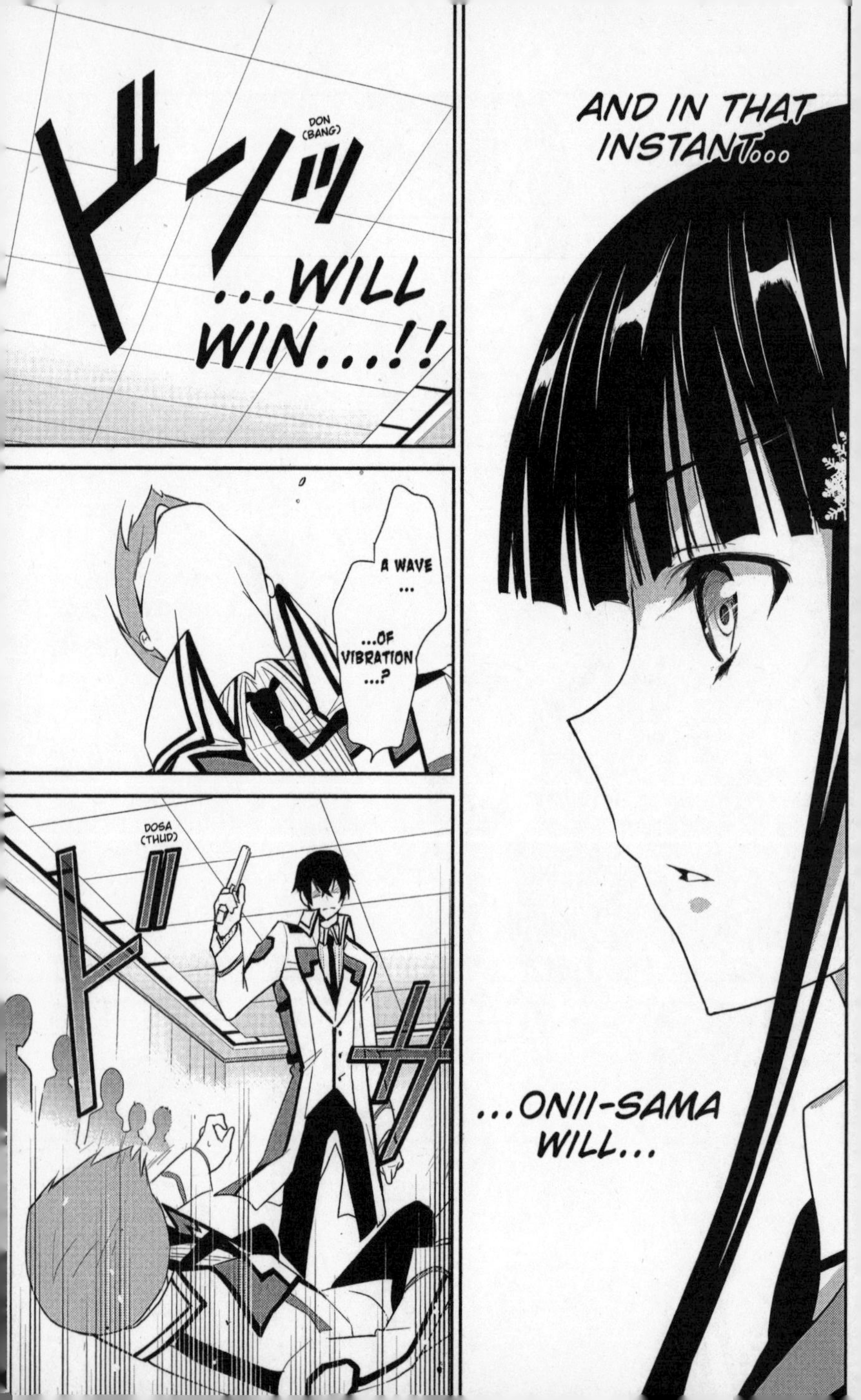
AND IN THAT INSTANT...
...ONII-SAMA WILL...
ドンッ
DON (BANG)
...WILL WIN...!!
A WAVE ...
...OF VIBRATION ...?
ドサ
DOSA (THUD)

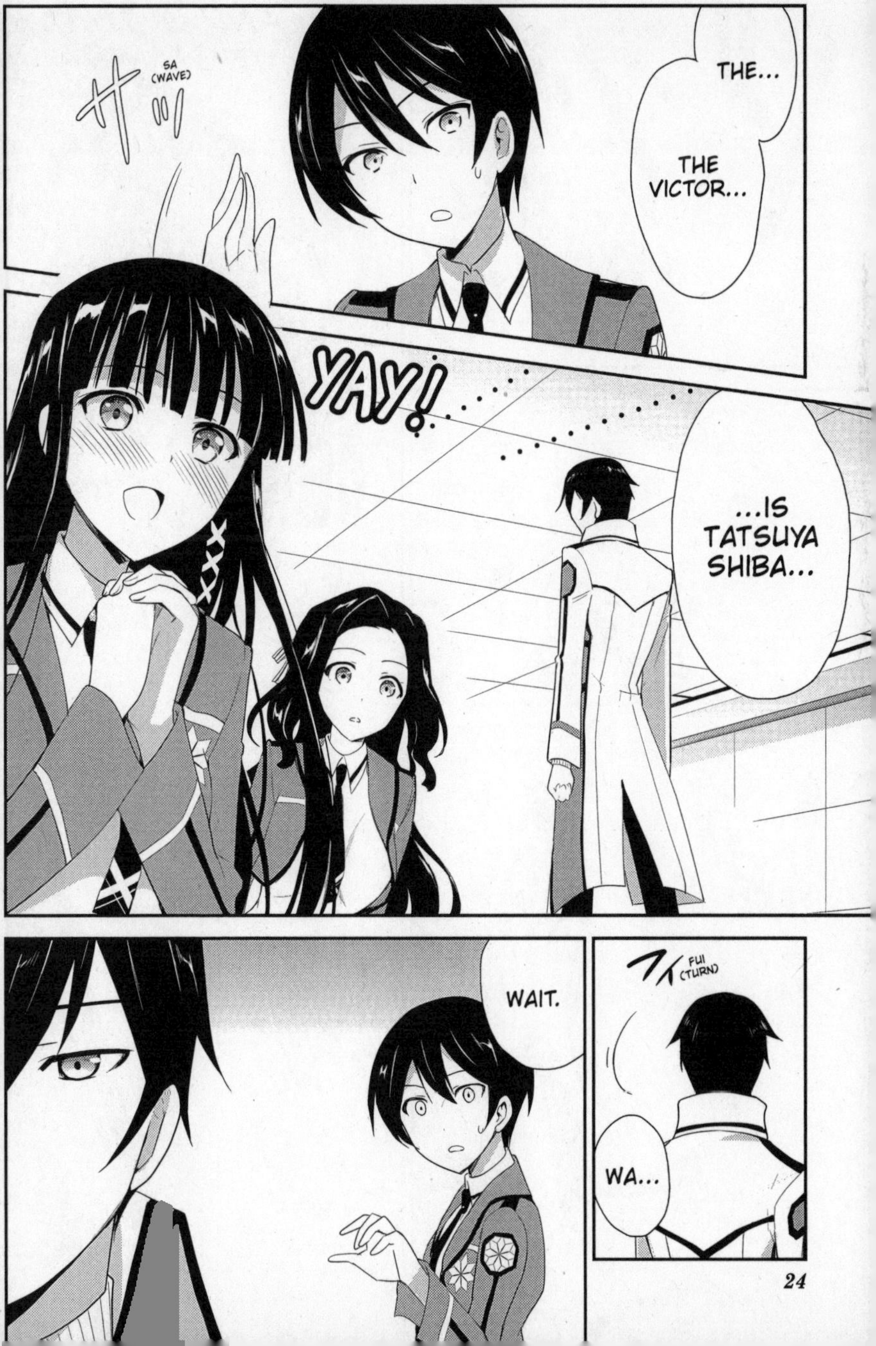
THE...
THE VICTOR...
SA (WAVE)
...IS TATSUYA SHIBA...
YAY!
FUI (TURN)
WA...
WAIT.

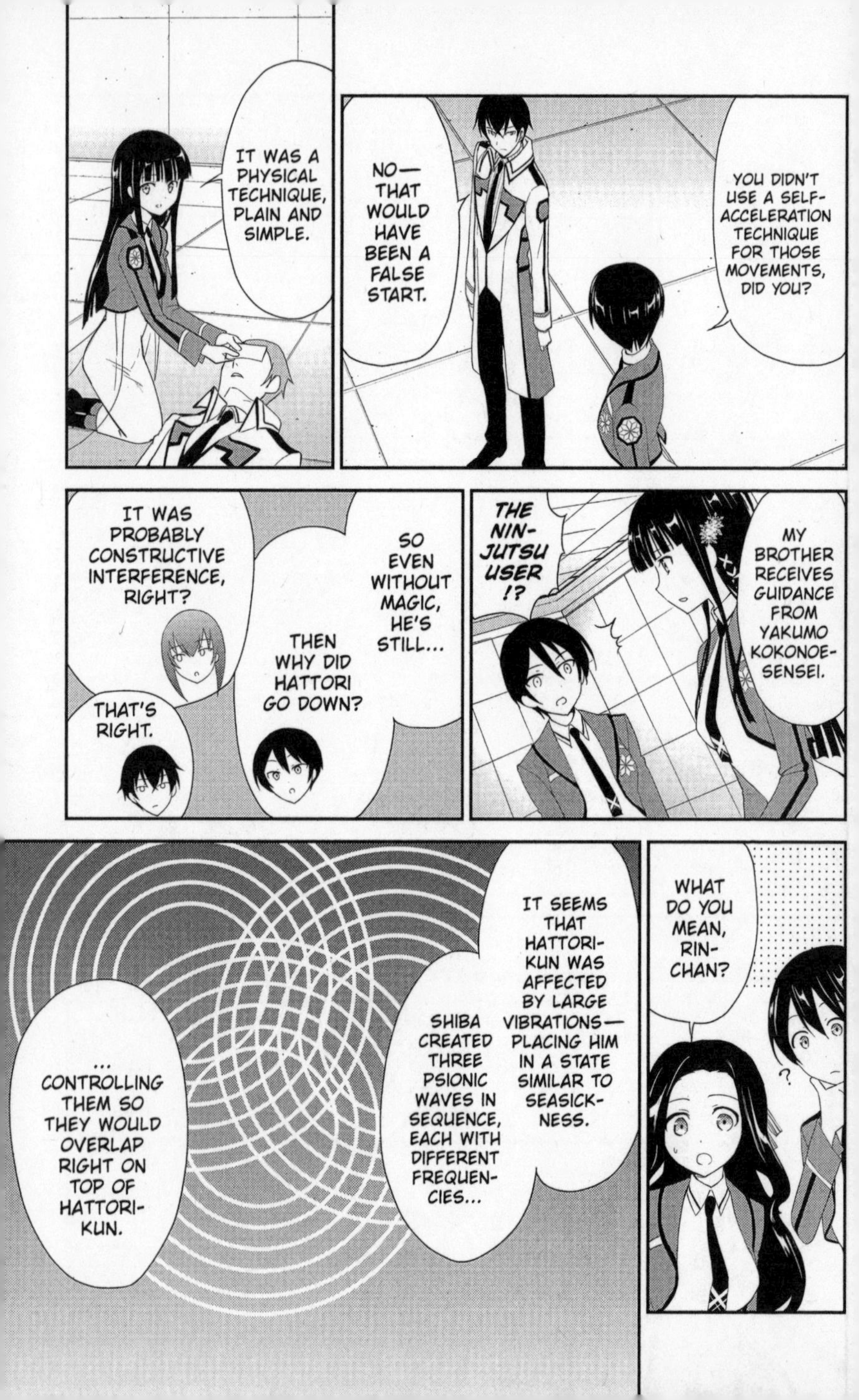
YOU DIDN'T USE A SELF-ACCELERATION TECHNIQUE FOR THOSE MOVEMENTS, DID YOU?
NO— THAT WOULD HAVE BEEN A FALSE START.
IT WAS A PHYSICAL TECHNIQUE, PLAIN AND SIMPLE.
MY BROTHER RECEIVES GUIDANCE FROM YAKUMO KOKONOE-SENSEI.
THE NINJUTSU USER!?
SO EVEN WITHOUT MAGIC, HE'S STILL...
IT WAS PROBABLY CONSTRUCTIVE INTERFERENCE, RIGHT?
THEN WHY DID HATTORI GO DOWN?
THAT'S RIGHT.
WHAT DO YOU MEAN, RIN-CHAN?
IT SEEMS THAT HATTORI-KUN WAS AFFECTED BY LARGE VIBRATIONS—PLACING HIM IN A STATE SIMILAR TO SEASICKNESS.
SHIBA CREATED THREE PSIONIC WAVES IN SEQUENCE, EACH WITH DIFFERENT FREQUENCIES...
...CONTROLLING THEM SO THEY WOULD OVERLAP RIGHT ON TOP OF HATTORI-KUN.

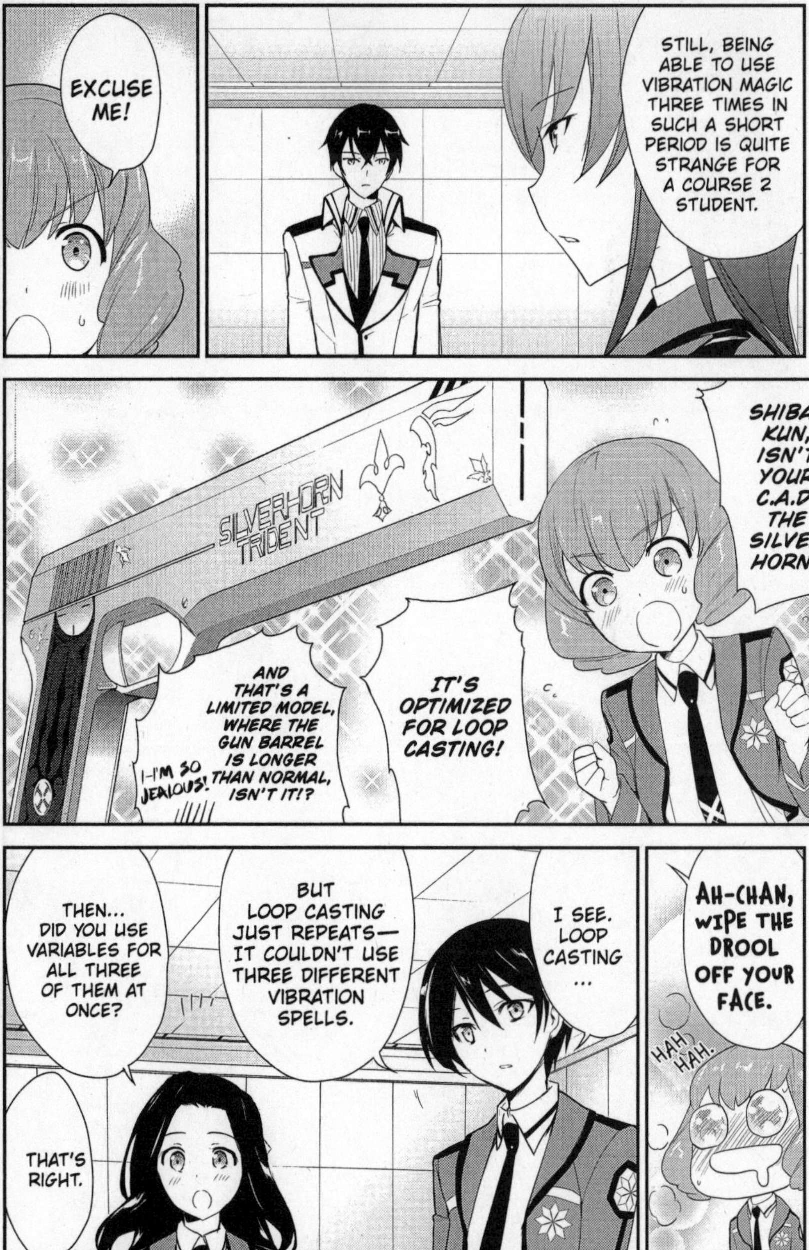
STILL, BEING ABLE TO USE VIBRATION MAGIC THREE TIMES IN SUCH A SHORT PERIOD IS QUITE STRANGE FOR A COURSE 2 STUDENT.
EXCUSE ME!
SHIBA-KUN, ISN'T YOUR C.A.D. THE SILVER HORN?
IT'S OPTIMIZED FOR LOOP CASTING!
AND THAT'S A LIMITED MODEL, WHERE THE GUN BARREL IS LONGER THAN NORMAL, ISN'T IT!?
SILVERHORN TRIDENT
I-I'M SO JEALOUS!
AH-CHAN, WIPE THE DROOL OFF YOUR FACE.
HAH HAH.
I SEE. LOOP CASTING...
BUT LOOP CASTING JUST REPEATS—IT COULDN'T USE THREE DIFFERENT VIBRATION SPELLS.
THEN... DID YOU USE VARIABLES FOR ALL THREE OF THEM AT ONCE?
THAT'S RIGHT.

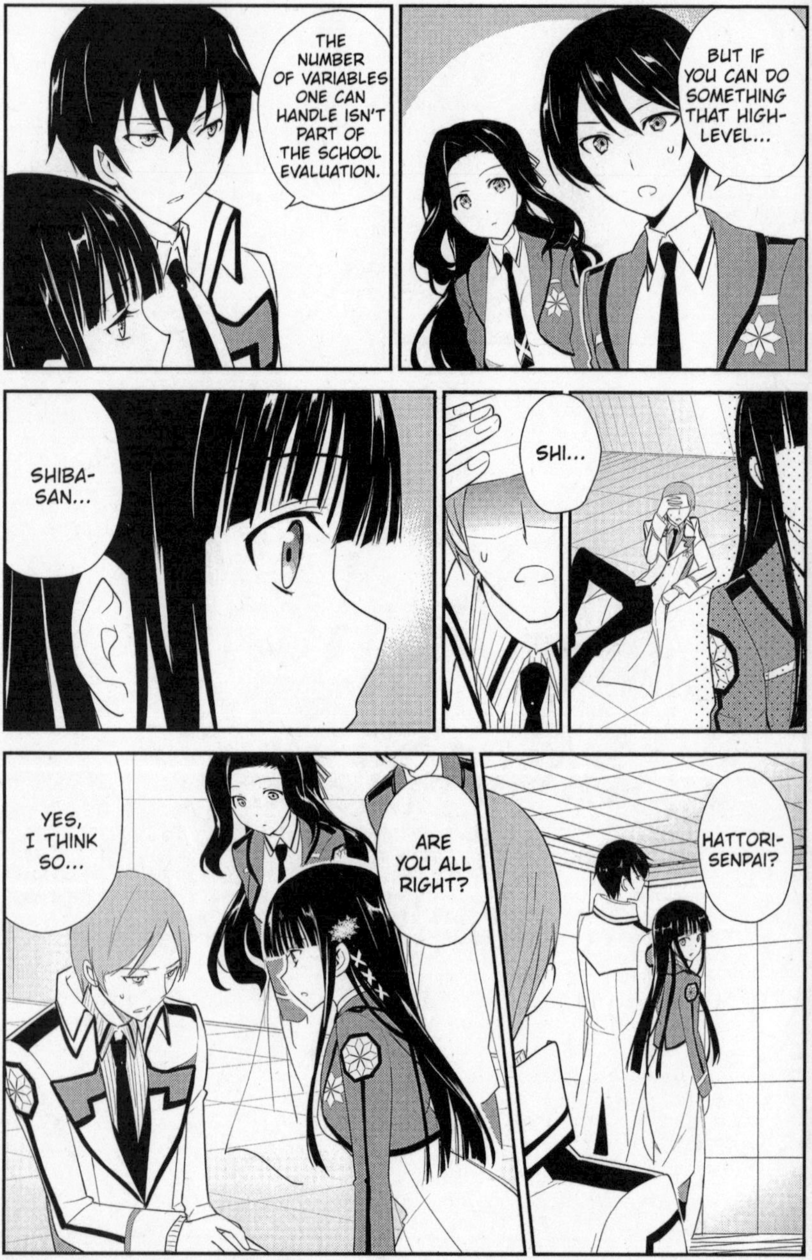
BUT IF YOU CAN DO SOMETHING THAT HIGH-LEVEL...
THE NUMBER OF VARIABLES ONE CAN HANDLE ISN'T PART OF THE SCHOOL EVALUATION.
SHI...
SHIBA-SAN...
HATTORI-SENPAI?
ARE YOU ALL RIGHT?
YES, I THINK SO...

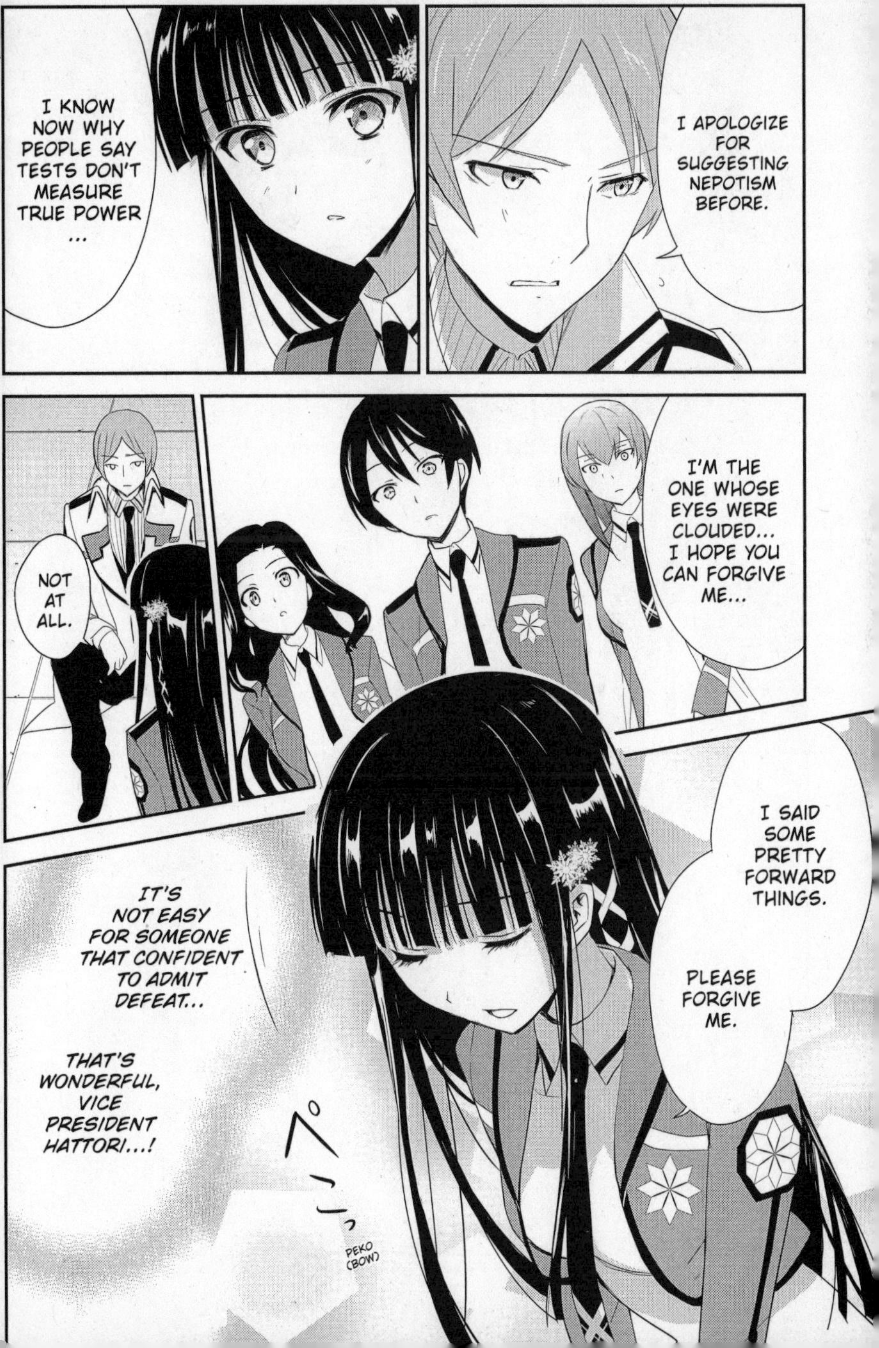
I APOLOGIZE FOR SUGGESTING NEPOTISM BEFORE.
I KNOW NOW WHY PEOPLE SAY TESTS DON'T MEASURE TRUE POWER ...
I'M THE ONE WHOSE EYES WERE CLOUDED... I HOPE YOU CAN FORGIVE ME...
NOT AT ALL.
I SAID SOME PRETTY FORWARD THINGS.
PLEASE FORGIVE ME.
IT'S NOT EASY FOR SOMEONE THAT CONFIDENT TO ADMIT DEFEAT...
THAT'S WONDERFUL, VICE PRESIDENT HATTORI...!
PEKO (BOW)

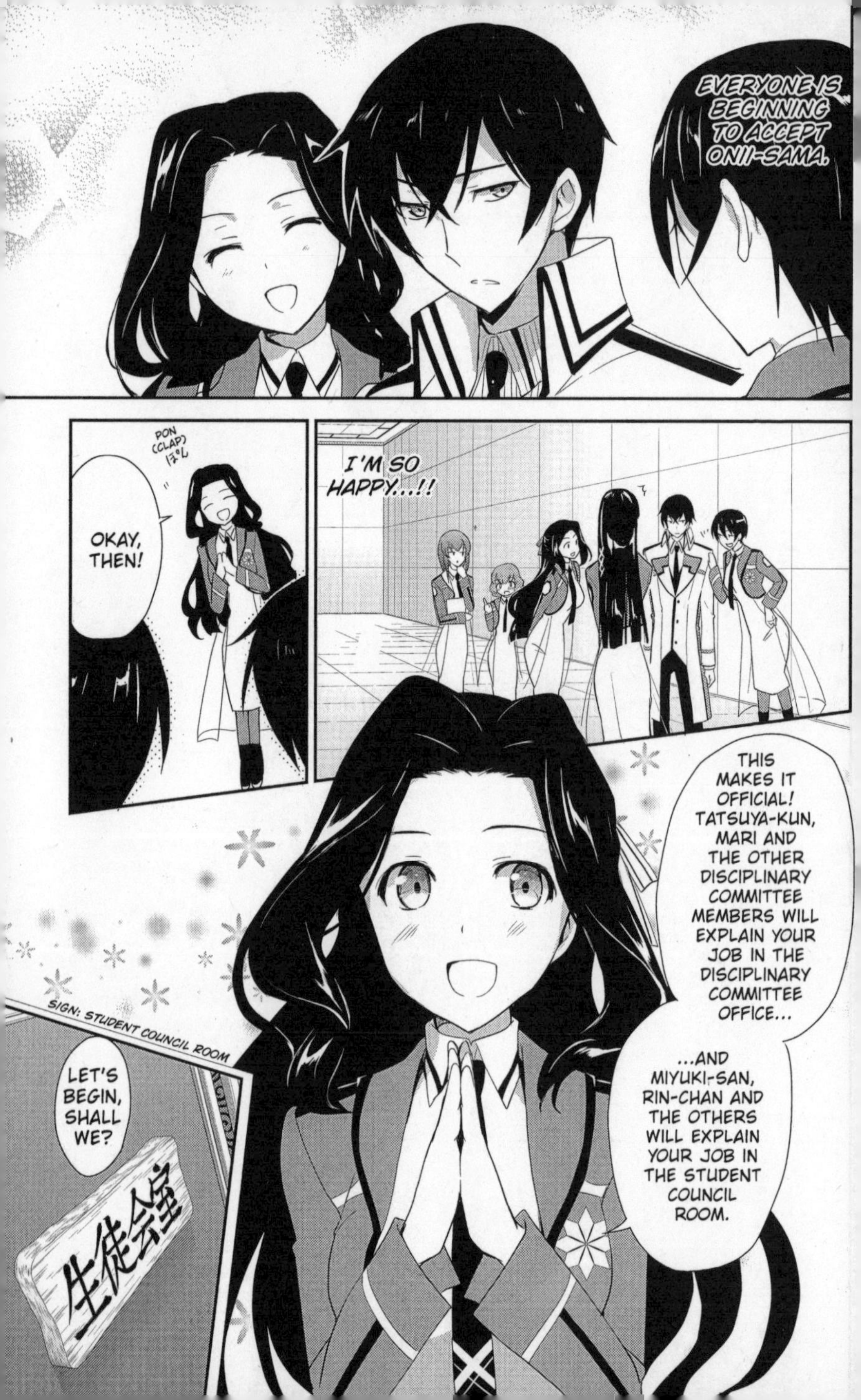
EVERYONE IS BEGINNING TO ACCEPT ONII-SAMA.
I'M SO HAPPY...!!
PON (CLAP) ぽん
OKAY, THEN!
THIS MAKES IT OFFICIAL! TATSUYA-KUN, MARI AND THE OTHER DISCIPLINARY COMMITTEE MEMBERS WILL EXPLAIN YOUR JOB IN THE DISCIPLINARY COMMITTEE OFFICE...
...AND MIYUKI-SAN, RIN-CHAN AND THE OTHERS WILL EXPLAIN YOUR JOB IN THE STUDENT COUNCIL ROOM.
LET'S BEGIN, SHALL WE?
SIGN: STUDENT COUNCIL ROOM
生徒会室

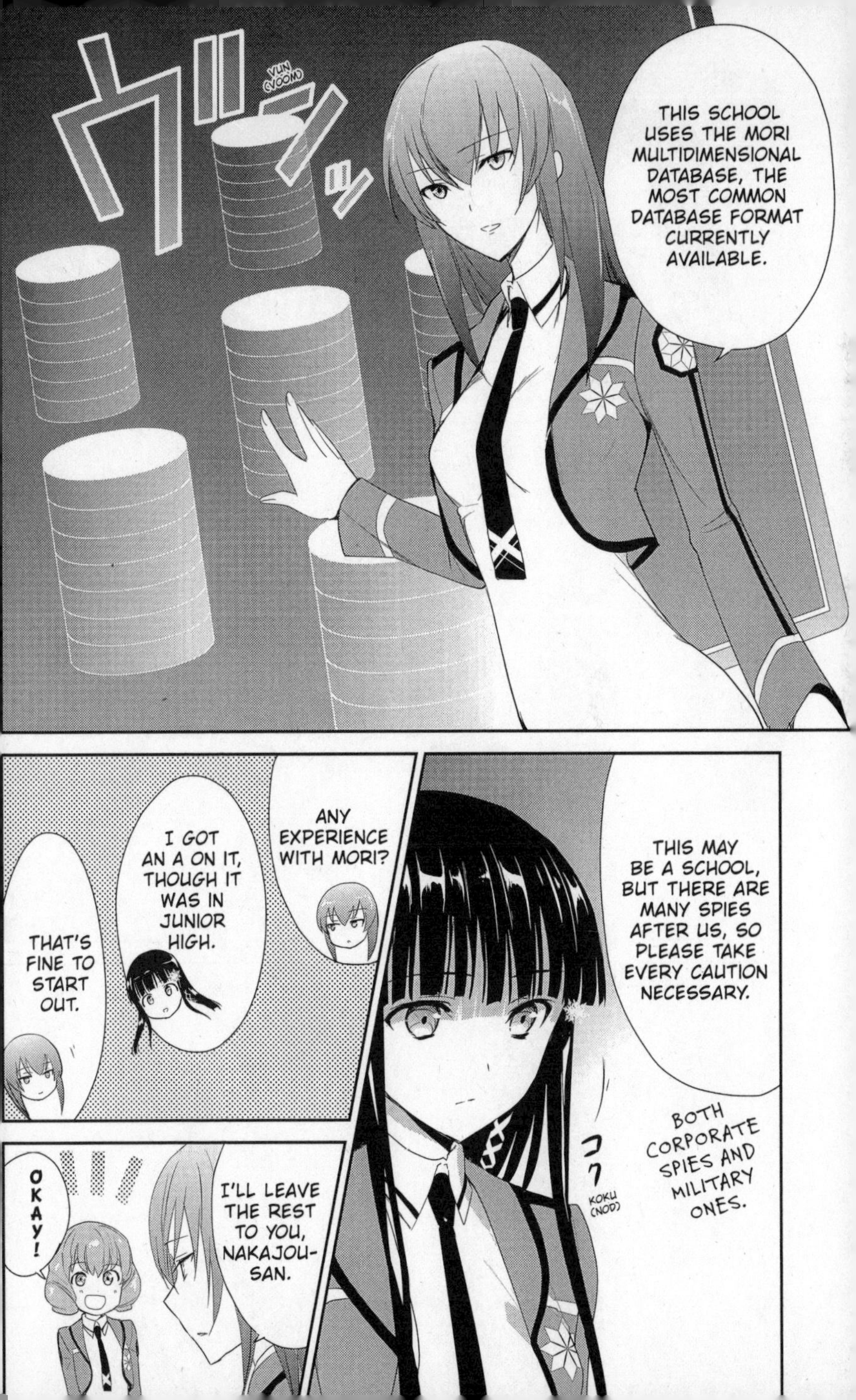
THIS SCHOOL USES THE MORI MULTIDIMENSIONAL DATABASE, THE MOST COMMON DATABASE FORMAT CURRENTLY AVAILABLE.
ウヴーンッ
VUN (VOOM)
THIS MAY BE A SCHOOL, BUT THERE ARE MANY SPIES AFTER US, SO PLEASE TAKE EVERY CAUTION NECESSARY.
BOTH CORPORATE SPIES AND MILITARY ONES.
コク
KOKU (NOD)
ANY EXPERIENCE WITH MORI?
I GOT AN A ON IT, THOUGH IT WAS IN JUNIOR HIGH.
THAT'S FINE TO START OUT.
I'LL LEAVE THE REST TO YOU, NAKAJOU-SAN.
OKAY!

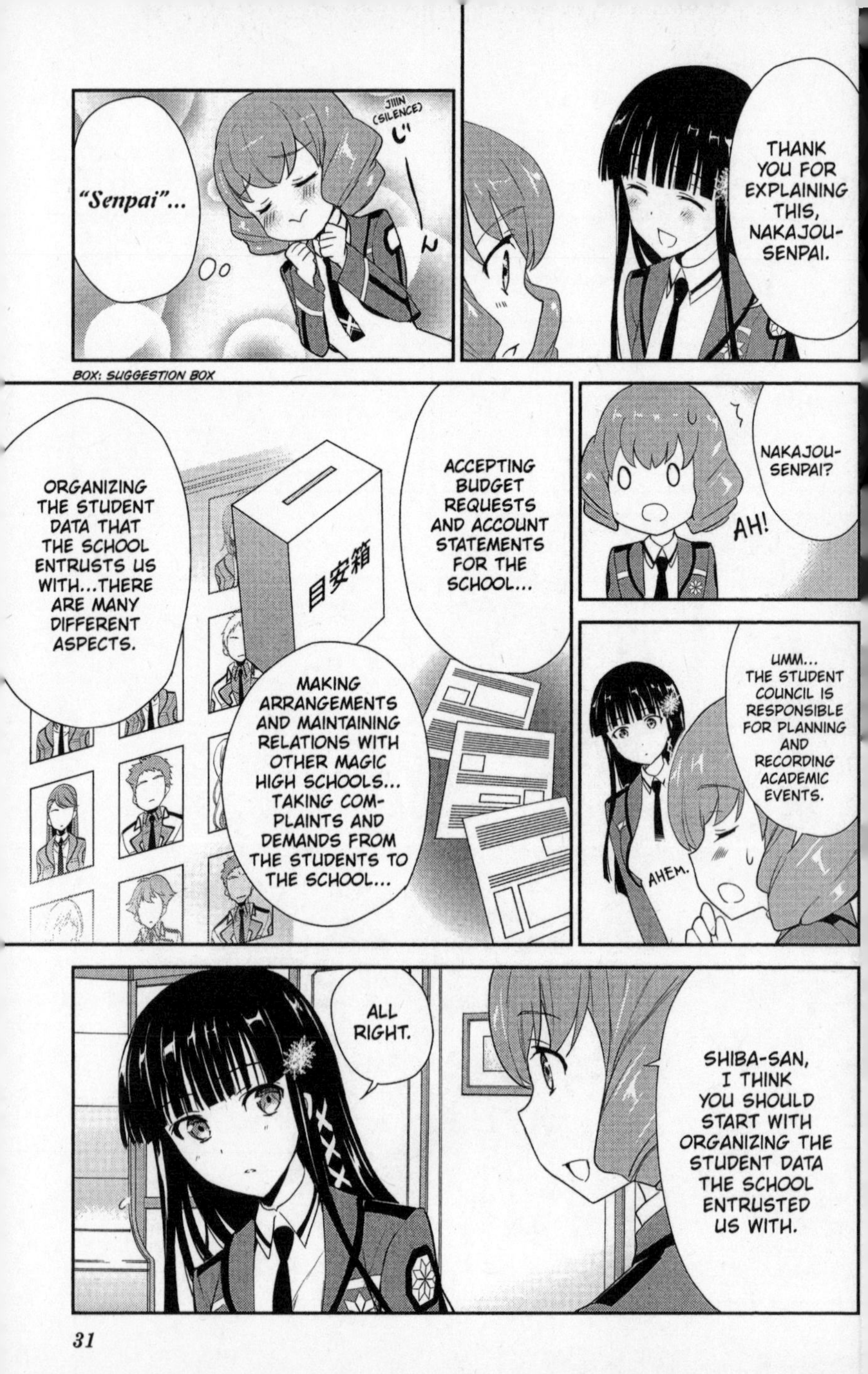
THANK YOU FOR EXPLAINING THIS, NAKAJOU-SENPAI.
JIIIN (SILENCE)
じ~ん
"Senpai"...
BOX: SUGGESTION BOX
NAKAJOU-SENPAI?
AH!
UMM... THE STUDENT COUNCIL IS RESPONSIBLE FOR PLANNING AND RECORDING ACADEMIC EVENTS.
AHEM.
ACCEPTING BUDGET REQUESTS AND ACCOUNT STATEMENTS FOR THE SCHOOL...
ORGANIZING THE STUDENT DATA THAT THE SCHOOL ENTRUSTS US WITH...THERE ARE MANY DIFFERENT ASPECTS.
目安箱
MAKING ARRANGEMENTS AND MAINTAINING RELATIONS WITH OTHER MAGIC HIGH SCHOOLS... TAKING COM-PLAINTS AND DEMANDS FROM THE STUDENTS TO THE SCHOOL...
SHIBA-SAN, I THINK YOU SHOULD START WITH ORGANIZING THE STUDENT DATA THE SCHOOL ENTRUSTED US WITH.
ALL RIGHT.

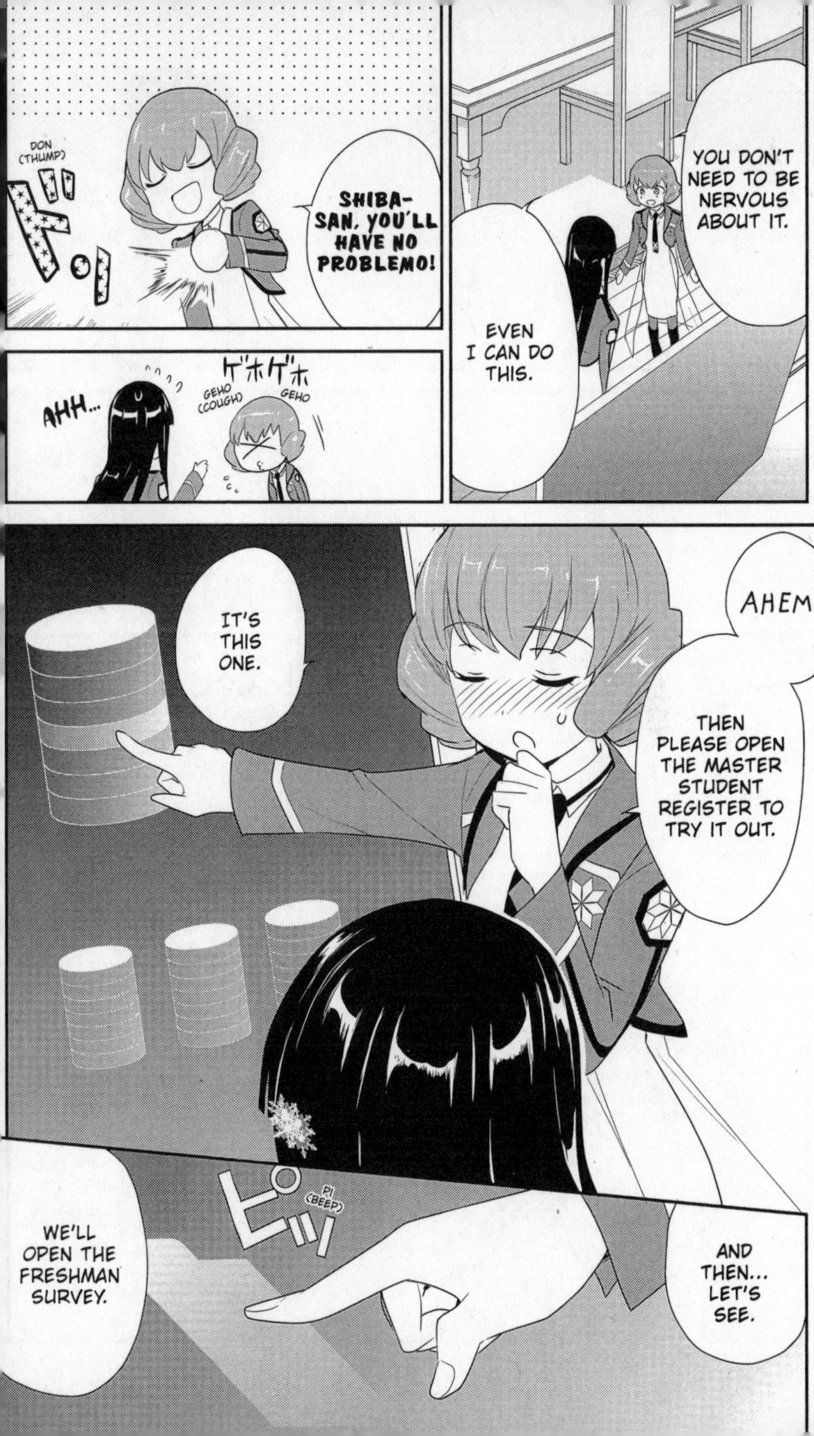

YOU DON'T NEED TO BE NERVOUS ABOUT IT.
EVEN I CAN DO THIS.
ドッ
DON (THUMP)
SHIBA-SAN, YOU'LL HAVE NO PROBLEMO!
ゲホゲホ
GEHO (COUGH) GEHO
AHH...
AHEM.
THEN PLEASE OPEN THE MASTER STUDENT REGISTER TO TRY IT OUT.
IT'S THIS ONE.
AND THEN... LET'S SEE.
ピッ
PI (BEEP)
WE'LL OPEN THE FRESHMAN SURVEY.

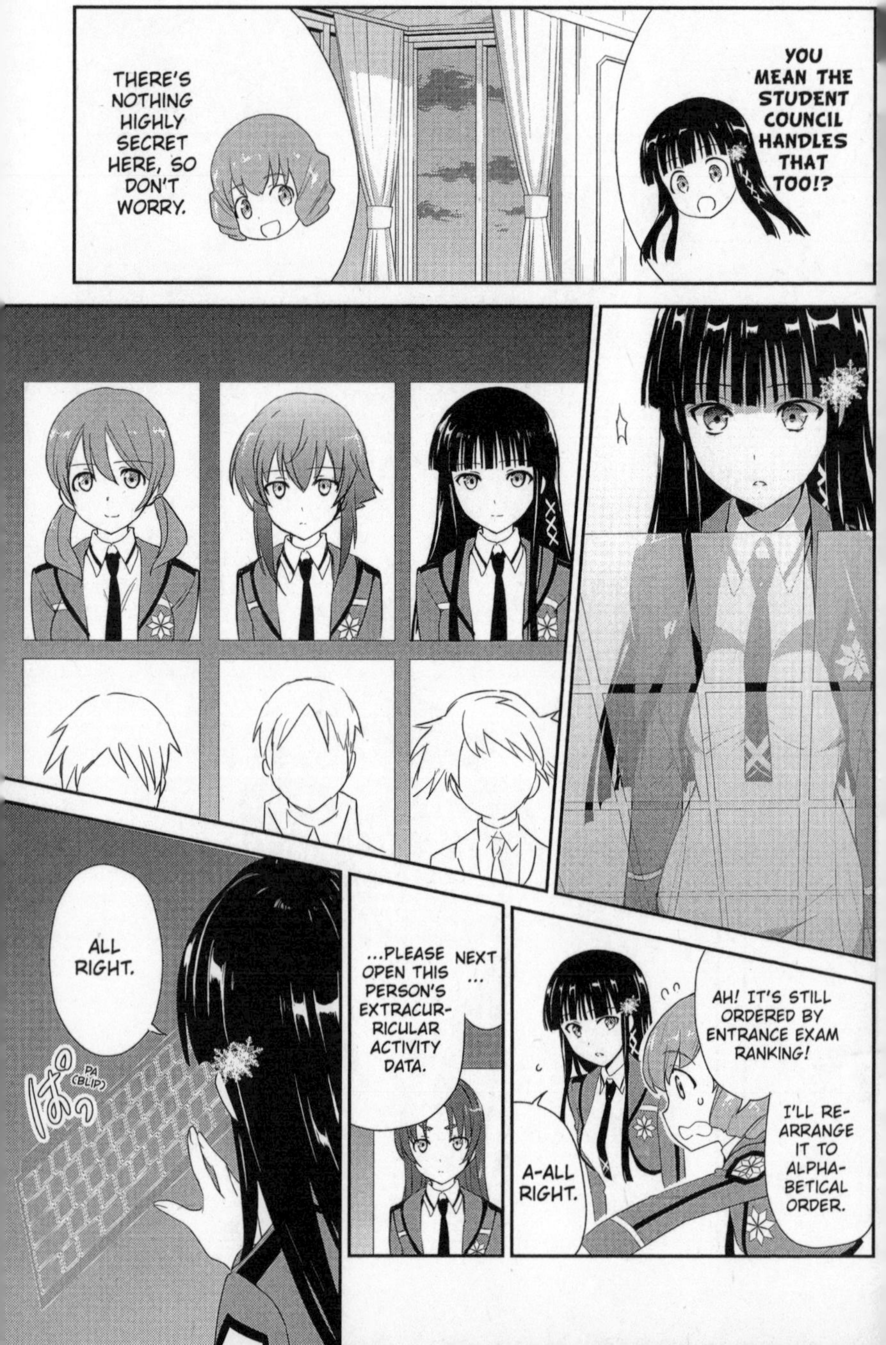
YOU MEAN THE STUDENT COUNCIL HANDLES THAT TOO!?
THERE'S NOTHING HIGHLY SECRET HERE, SO DON'T WORRY.
AH! IT'S STILL ORDERED BY ENTRANCE EXAM RANKING!
I'LL RE-ARRANGE IT TO ALPHA-BETICAL ORDER.
A-ALL RIGHT.
NEXT...
...PLEASE OPEN THIS PERSON'S EXTRACUR-RICULAR ACTIVITY DATA.
ALL RIGHT.
ぱっ
PA (BLIP)

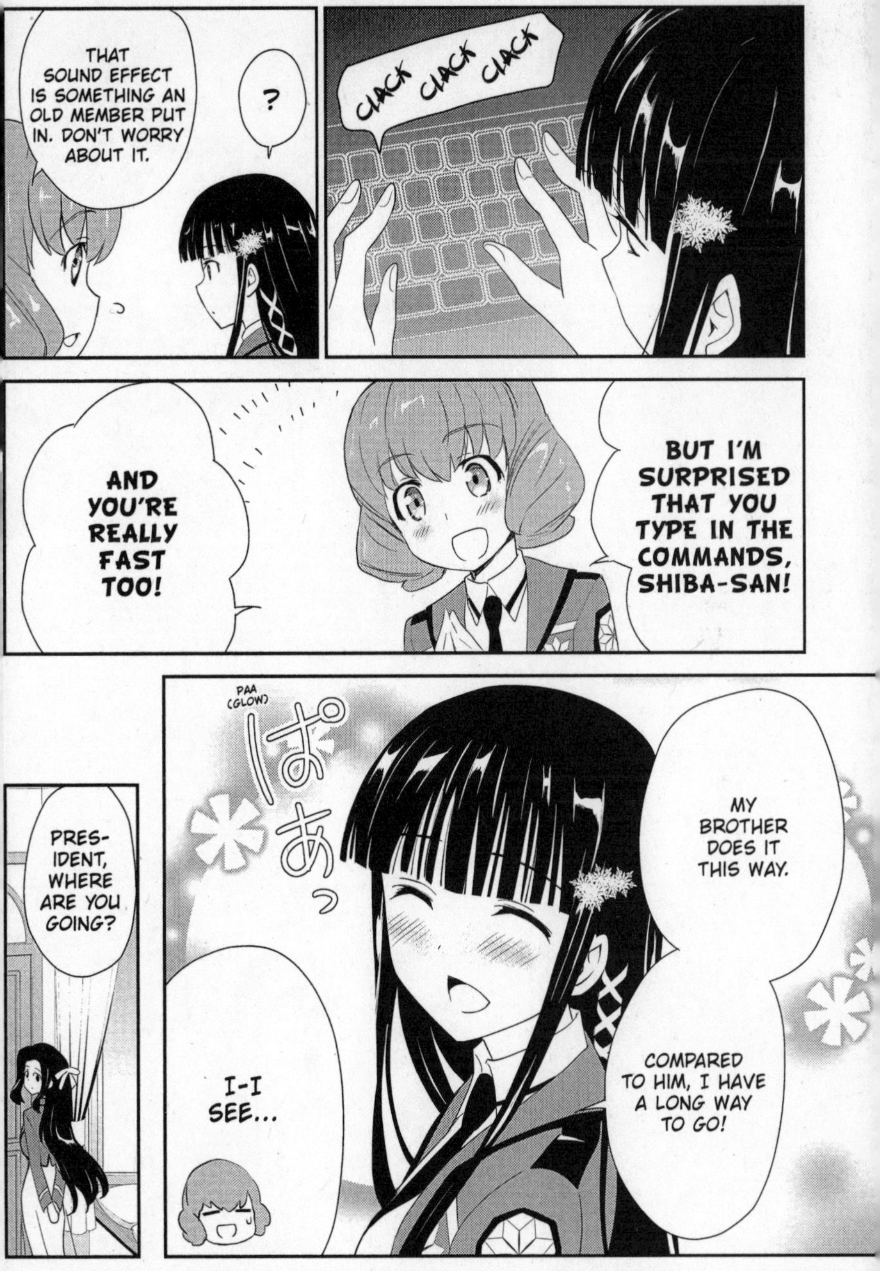
CLACK CLACK CLACK
?
THAT SOUND EFFECT IS SOMETHING AN OLD MEMBER PUT IN. DON'T WORRY ABOUT IT.
BUT I'M SURPRISED THAT YOU TYPE IN THE COMMANDS, SHIBA-SAN!
AND YOU'RE REALLY FAST TOO!
PAA (GLOW)
ぱあっ
MY BROTHER DOES IT THIS WAY.
COMPARED TO HIM, I HAVE A LONG WAY TO GO!
I-I SEE...
PRES-IDENT, WHERE ARE YOU GOING?

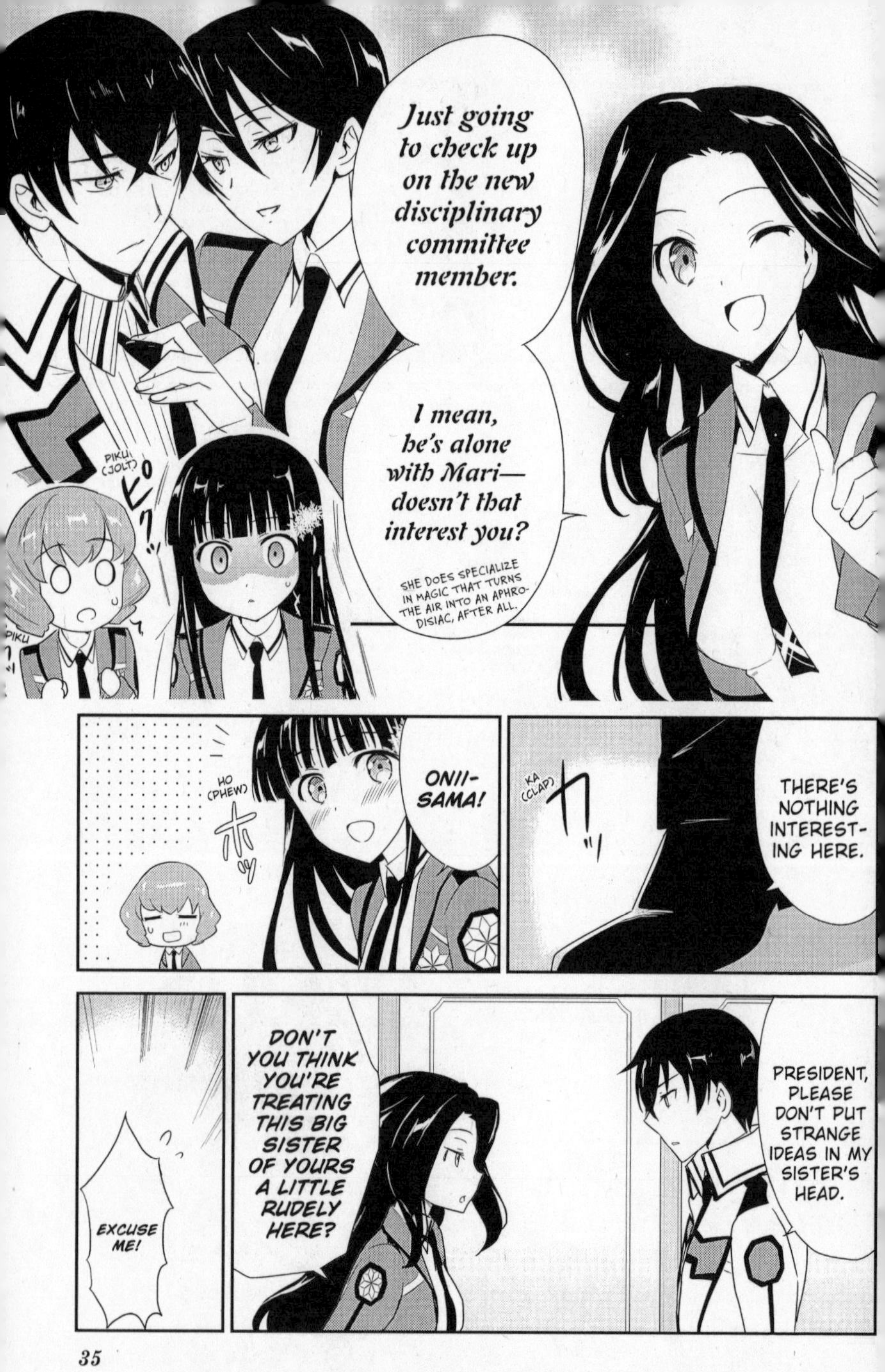
Just going to check up on the new disciplinary committee member.
I mean, he's alone with Mari— doesn't that interest you?
SHE DOES SPECIALIZE IN MAGIC THAT TURNS THE AIR INTO AN APHRODISIAC, AFTER ALL.
PIKU (JOLT)
PIKU
THERE'S NOTHING INTERESTING HERE.
KA (CLAP)
ONII-SAMA!
HO (PHEW)
PRESIDENT, PLEASE DON'T PUT STRANGE IDEAS IN MY SISTER'S HEAD.
DON'T YOU THINK YOU'RE TREATING THIS BIG SISTER OF YOURS A LITTLE RUDELY HERE?
EXCUSE ME!

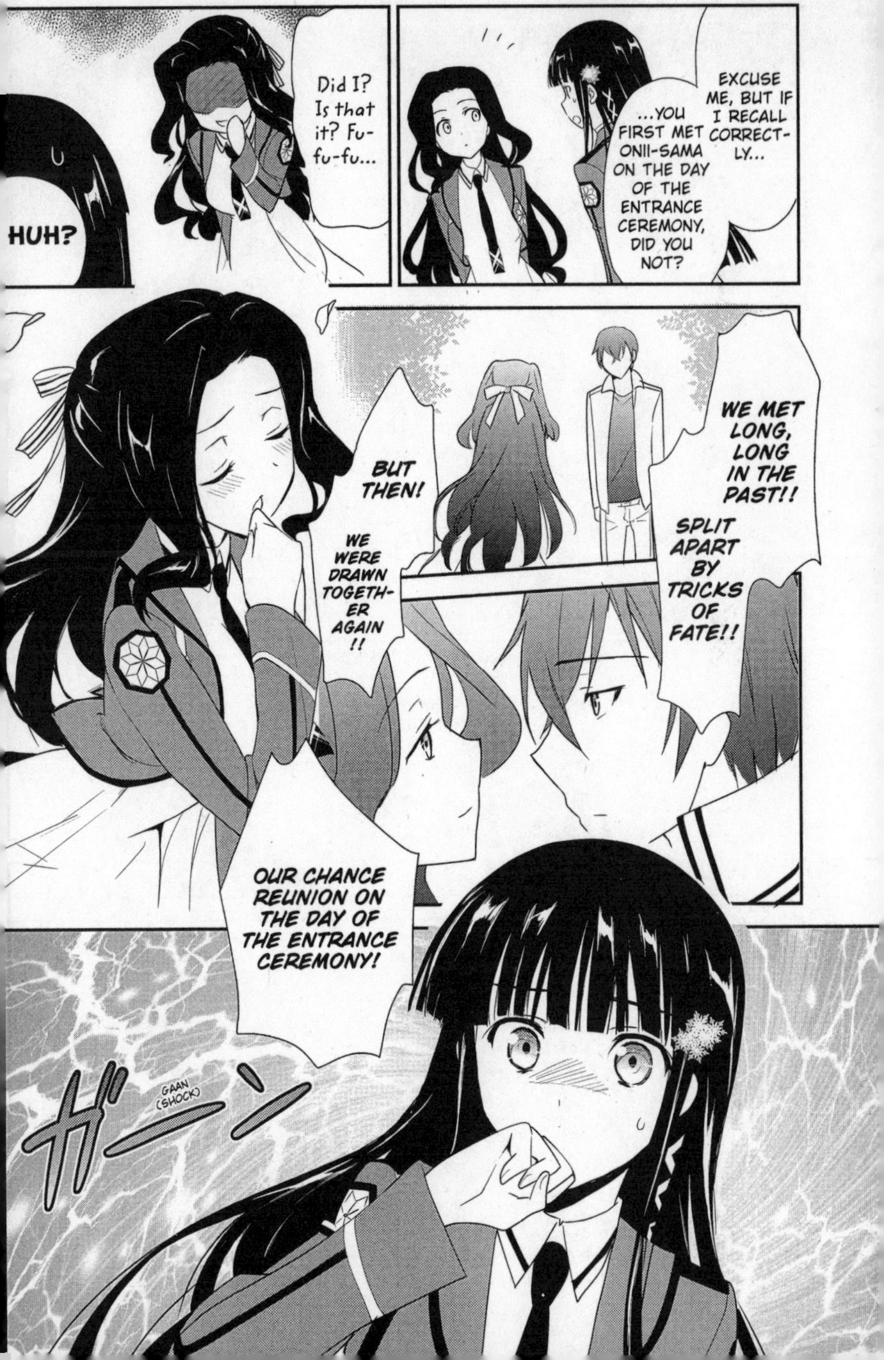
EXCUSE ME, BUT IF I RECALL CORRECTLY...
...YOU FIRST MET ONII-SAMA ON THE DAY OF THE ENTRANCE CEREMONY, DID YOU NOT?
Did I? Is that it? Fu-fu-fu...
HUH?
WE MET LONG, LONG IN THE PAST!!
SPLIT APART BY TRICKS OF FATE!!
BUT THEN!
WE WERE DRAWN TOGETHER AGAIN!!
OUR CHANCE REUNION ON THE DAY OF THE ENTRANCE CEREMONY!
ガーン
GAAN (SHOCK)

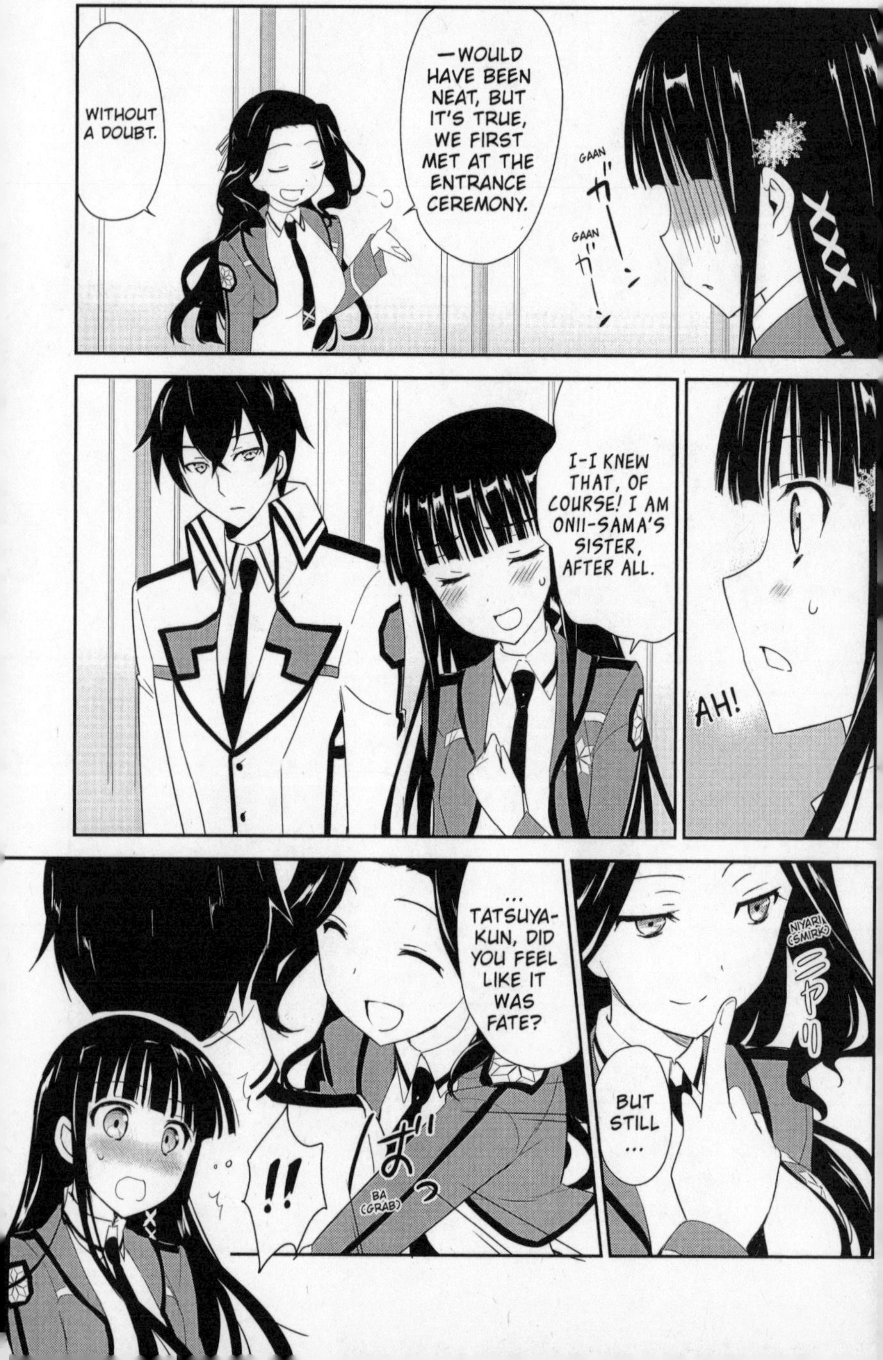
GAAN
ガーン
GAAN
ガーン
—WOULD HAVE BEEN NEAT, BUT IT'S TRUE, WE FIRST MET AT THE ENTRANCE CEREMONY.
WITHOUT A DOUBT.
AH!
I-I KNEW THAT, OF COURSE! I AM ONII-SAMA'S SISTER, AFTER ALL.
NIYARI (SMIRK)
ニヤリ
BUT STILL ...
... TATSUYA-KUN, DID YOU FEEL LIKE IT WAS FATE?
BA (GRAB)
ばっ
!!

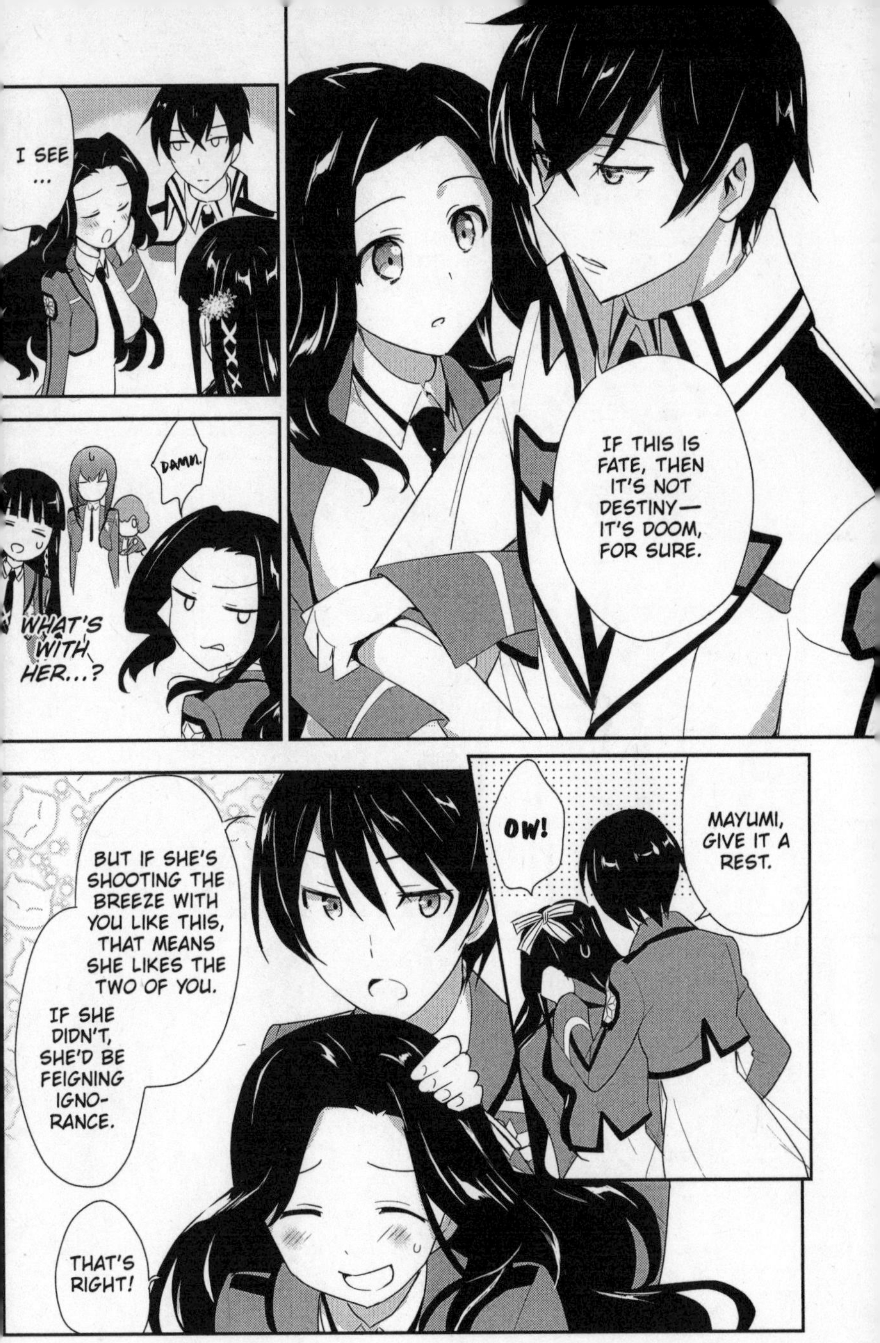
IF THIS IS FATE, THEN IT'S NOT DESTINY—IT'S DOOM, FOR SURE.
I SEE ...
DAMN.
WHAT'S WITH HER...?
MAYUMI, GIVE IT A REST.
OW!
BUT IF SHE'S SHOOTING THE BREEZE WITH YOU LIKE THIS, THAT MEANS SHE LIKES THE TWO OF YOU.
IF SHE DIDN'T, SHE'D BE FEIGNING IGNO-RANCE.
THAT'S RIGHT!

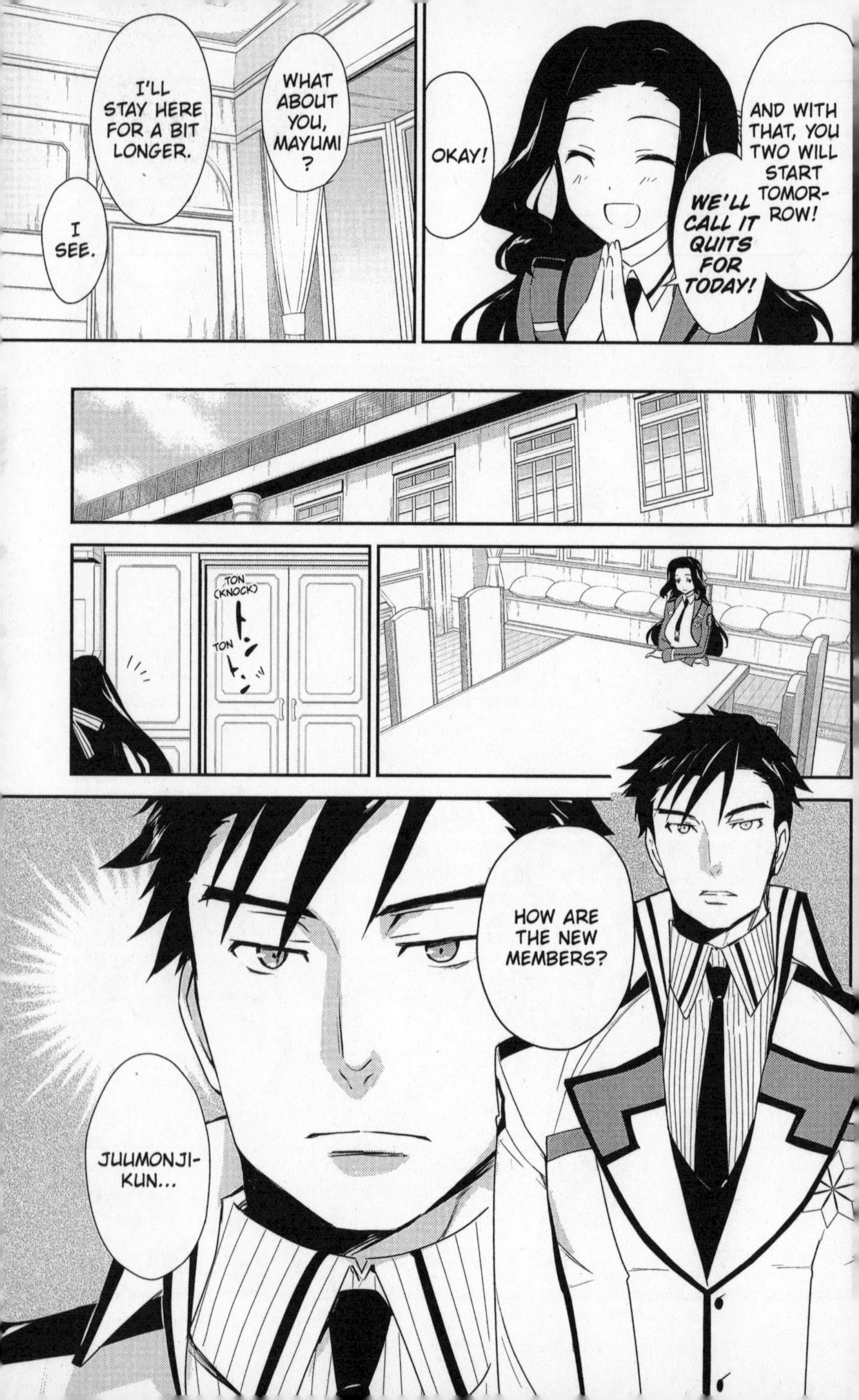
AND WITH THAT, YOU TWO WILL START TOMORROW!
WE'LL CALL IT QUITS FOR TODAY!
OKAY!
WHAT ABOUT YOU, MAYUMI?
I'LL STAY HERE FOR A BIT LONGER.
I SEE.
TON (KNOCK)
TON
HOW ARE THE NEW MEMBERS?
JUUMONJI-KUN...

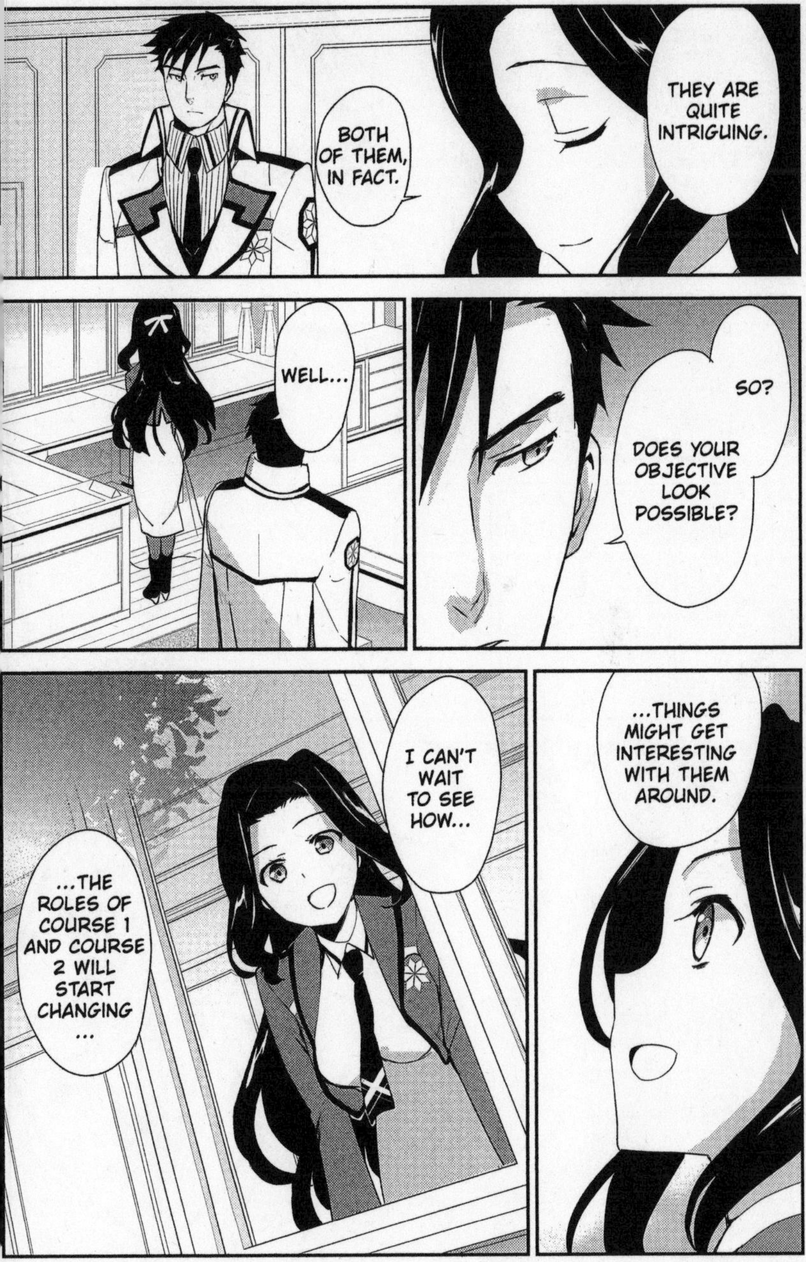
THEY ARE QUITE INTRIGUING.
BOTH OF THEM, IN FACT.
SO?
DOES YOUR OBJECTIVE LOOK POSSIBLE?
WELL...
...THINGS MIGHT GET INTERESTING WITH THEM AROUND.
I CAN'T WAIT TO SEE HOW...
...THE ROLES OF COURSE 1 AND COURSE 2 WILL START CHANGING...

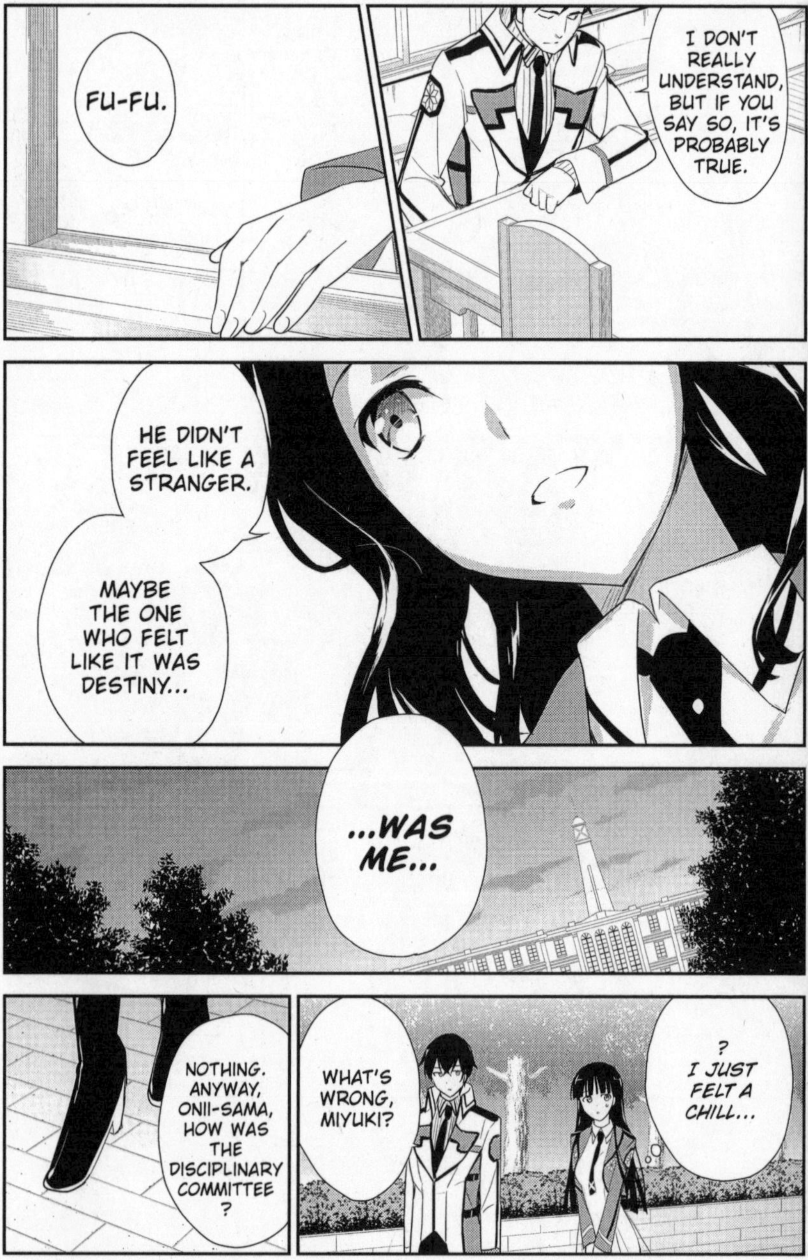
I DON'T REALLY UNDERSTAND, BUT IF YOU SAY SO, IT'S PROBABLY TRUE.
FU-FU.
HE DIDN'T FEEL LIKE A STRANGER.
MAYBE THE ONE WHO FELT LIKE IT WAS DESTINY...
...WAS ME...
? I JUST FELT A CHILL...
WHAT'S WRONG, MIYUKI?
NOTHING. ANYWAY, ONII-SAMA, HOW WAS THE DISCIPLINARY COMMITTEE ?

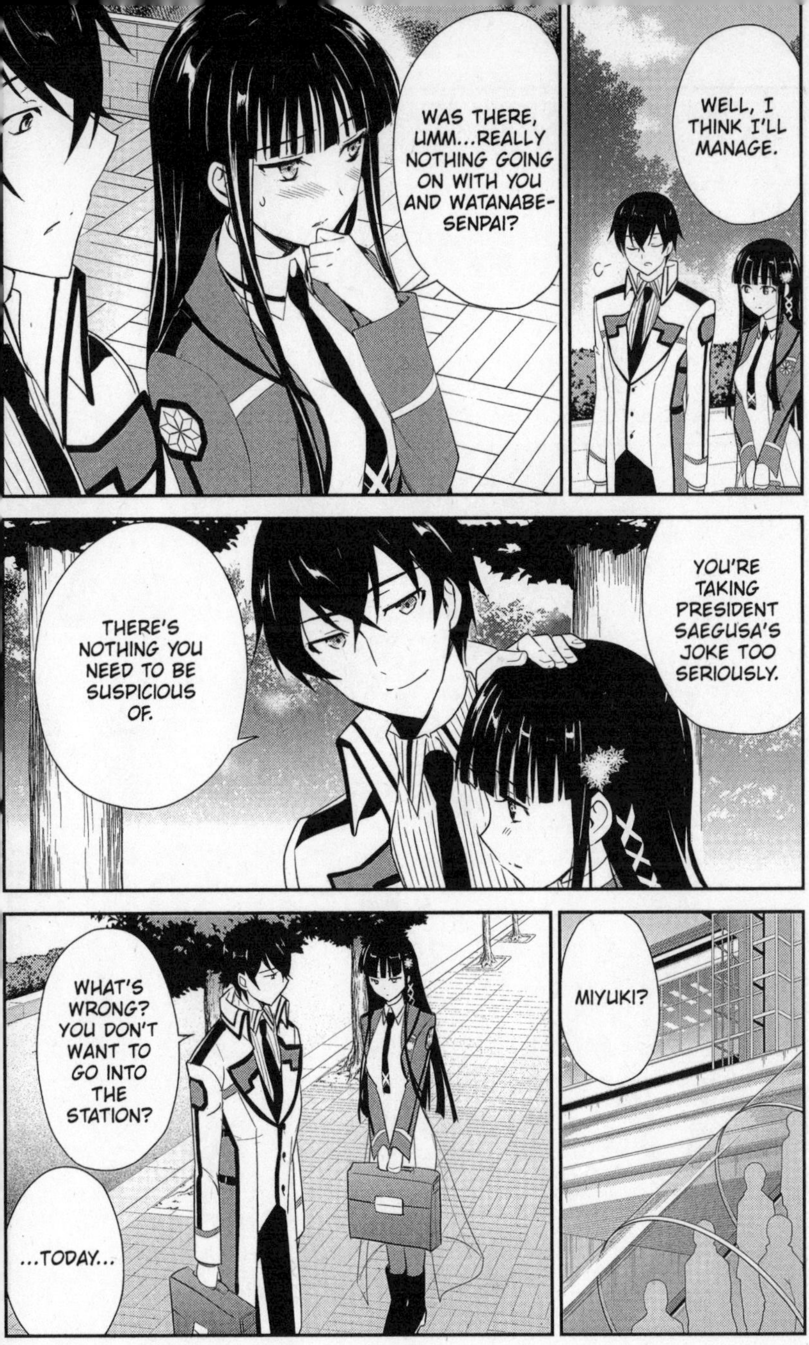
WELL, I THINK I'LL MANAGE.
WAS THERE, UMM...REALLY NOTHING GOING ON WITH YOU AND WATANABE-SENPAI?
YOU'RE TAKING PRESIDENT SAEGUSA'S JOKE TOO SERIOUSLY.
THERE'S NOTHING YOU NEED TO BE SUSPICIOUS OF.
MIYUKI?
WHAT'S WRONG? YOU DON'T WANT TO GO INTO THE STATION?
...TODAY...

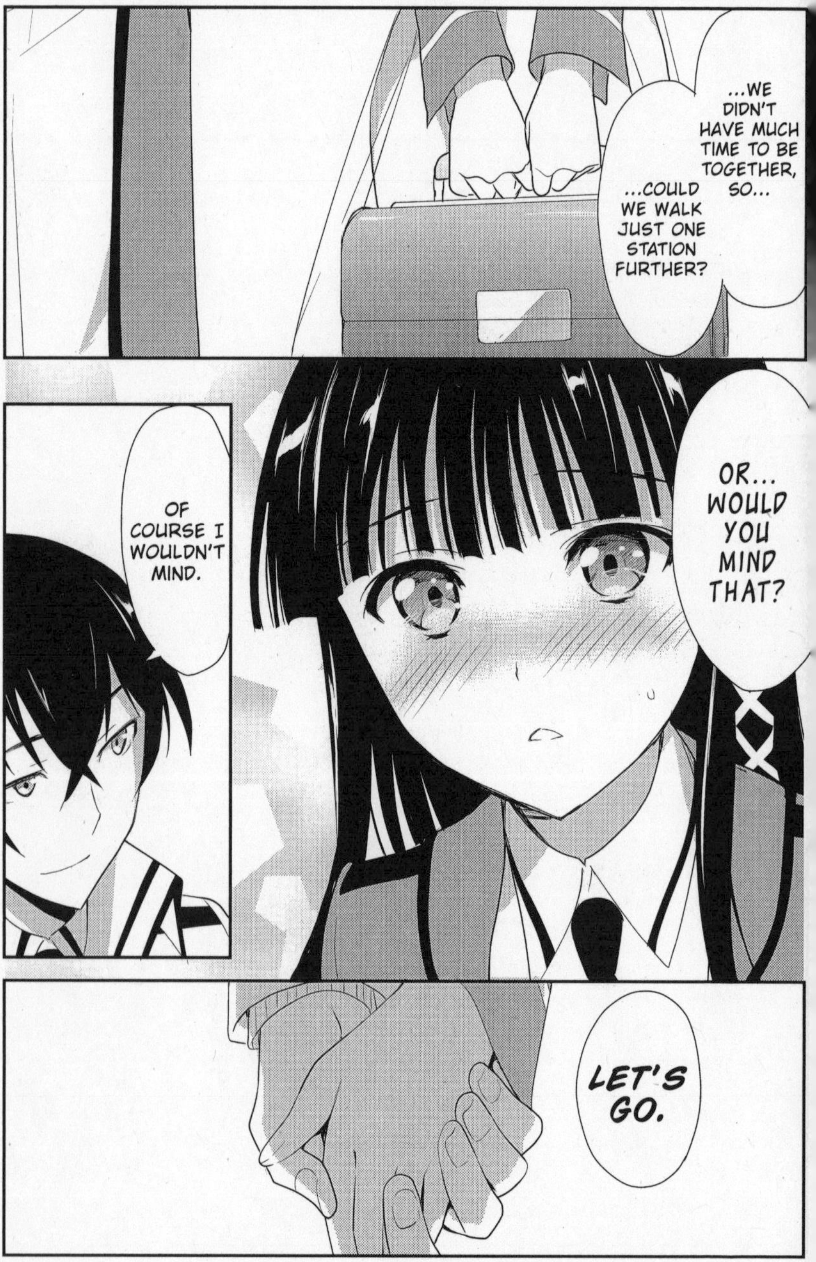
...WE DIDN'T HAVE MUCH TIME TO BE TOGETHER, SO...
...COULD WE WALK JUST ONE STATION FURTHER?
OR... WOULD YOU MIND THAT?
OF COURSE I WOULDN'T MIND.
LET'S GO.

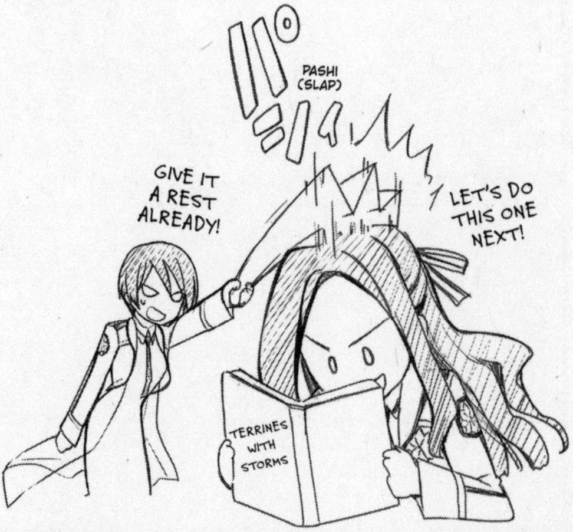
LET'S DO THIS ONE NEXT!
PASHI (SLAP)
GIVE IT A REST ALREADY!
TERRINES WITH STORMS

CHAPTER 8

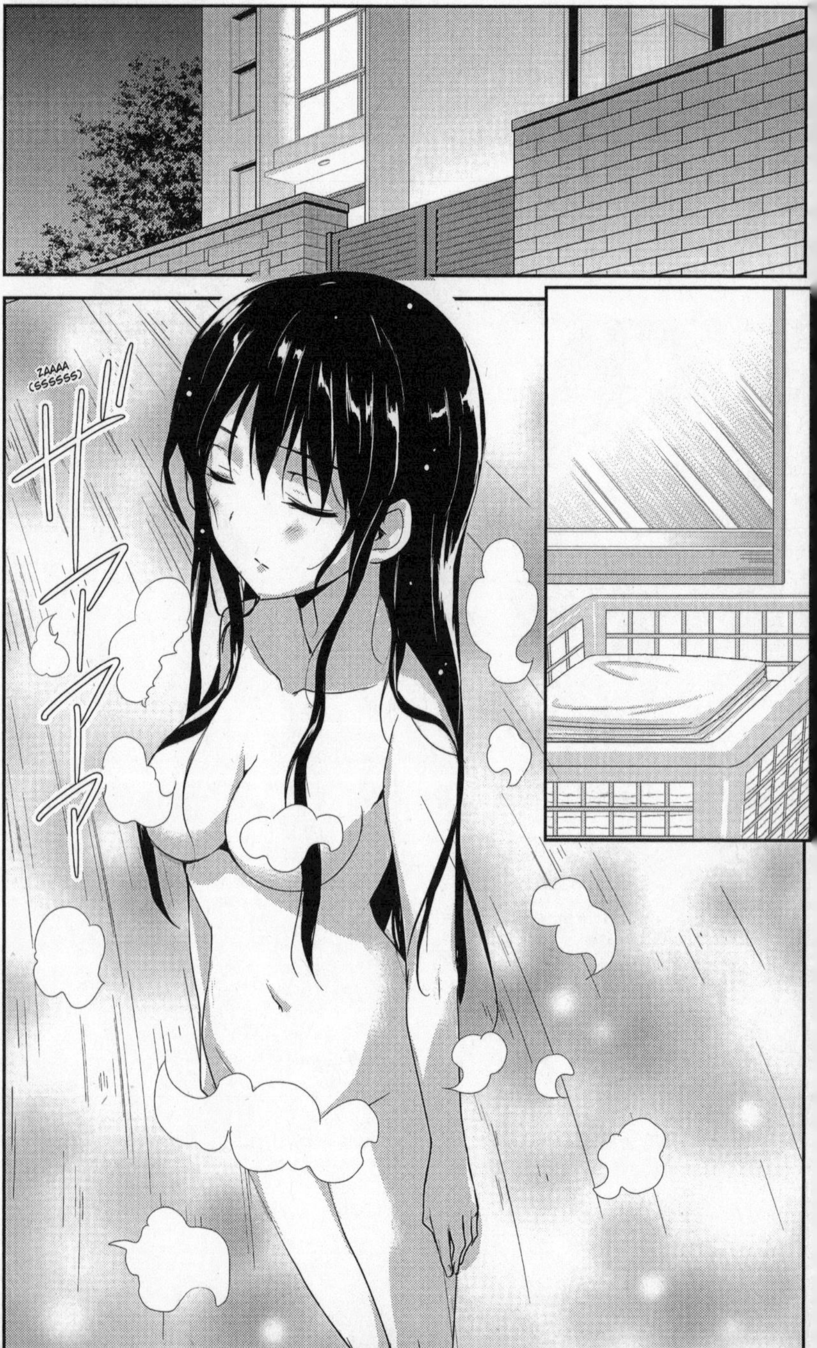
ZAAAA (SSSSSS)

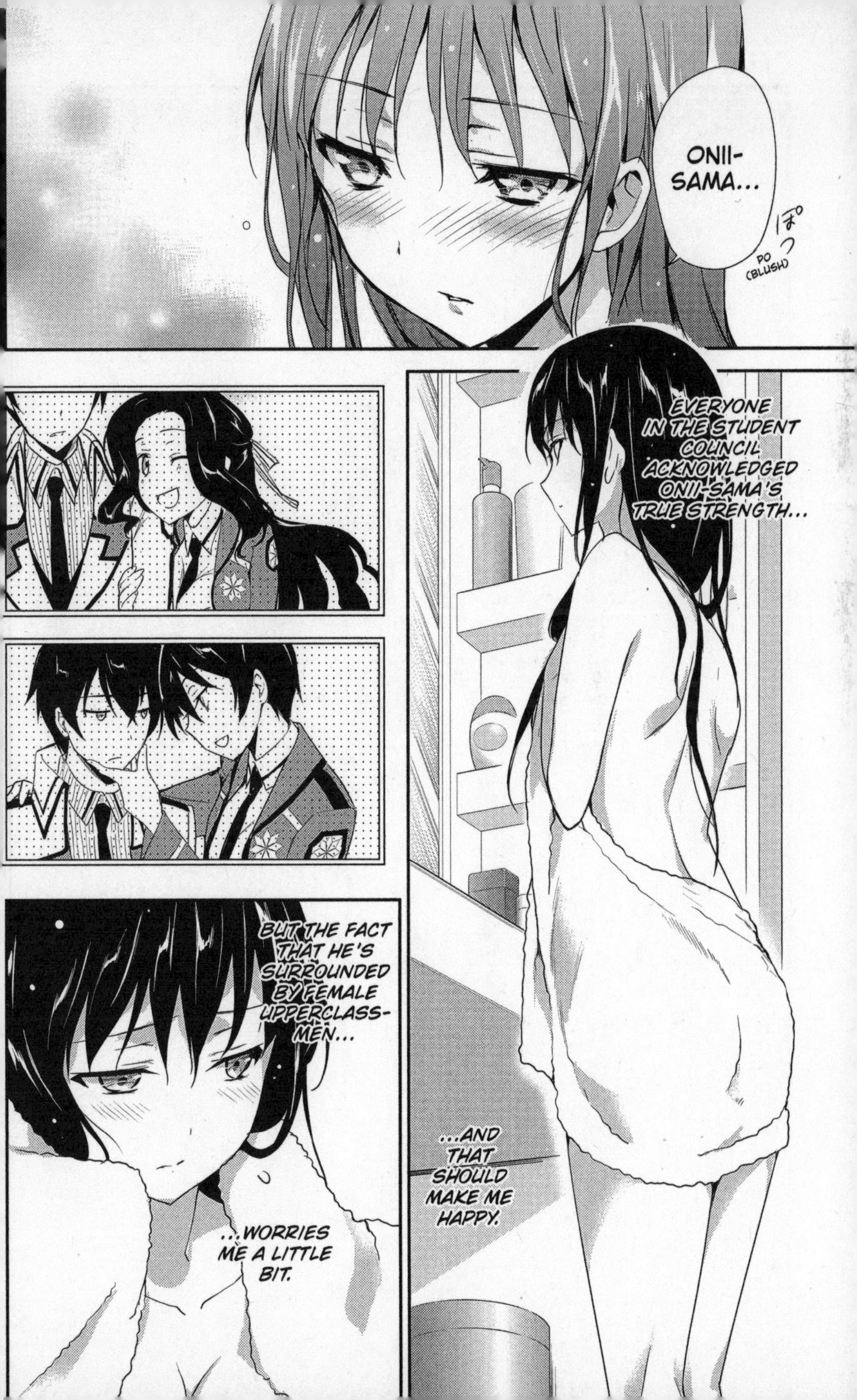
ONII-SAMA...
ぽっ
PO (BLUSH)
EVERYONE IN THE STUDENT COUNCIL ACKNOWLEDGED ONII-SAMA'S TRUE STRENGTH...
...AND THAT SHOULD MAKE ME HAPPY.
BUT THE FACT THAT HE'S SURROUNDED BY FEMALE UPPERCLASS-MEN...
...WORRIES ME A LITTLE BIT.

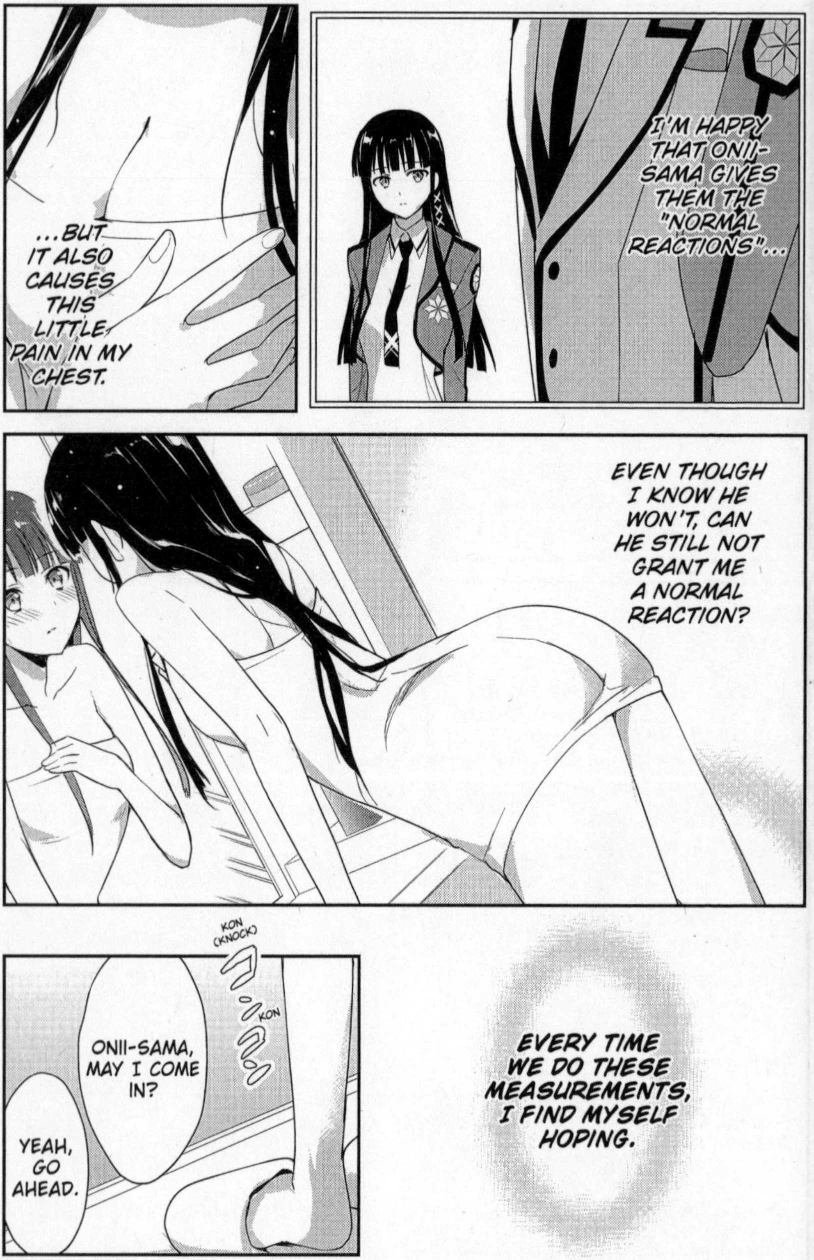
I'M HAPPY THAT ONII-SAMA GIVES THEM THE "NORMAL REACTIONS"...
...BUT IT ALSO CAUSES THIS LITTLE PAIN IN MY CHEST.
EVEN THOUGH I KNOW HE WON'T, CAN HE STILL NOT GRANT ME A NORMAL REACTION?
EVERY TIME WE DO THESE MEASUREMENTS, I FIND MYSELF HOPING.
KON (KNOCK)
KON
ONII-SAMA, MAY I COME IN?
YEAH, GO AHEAD.

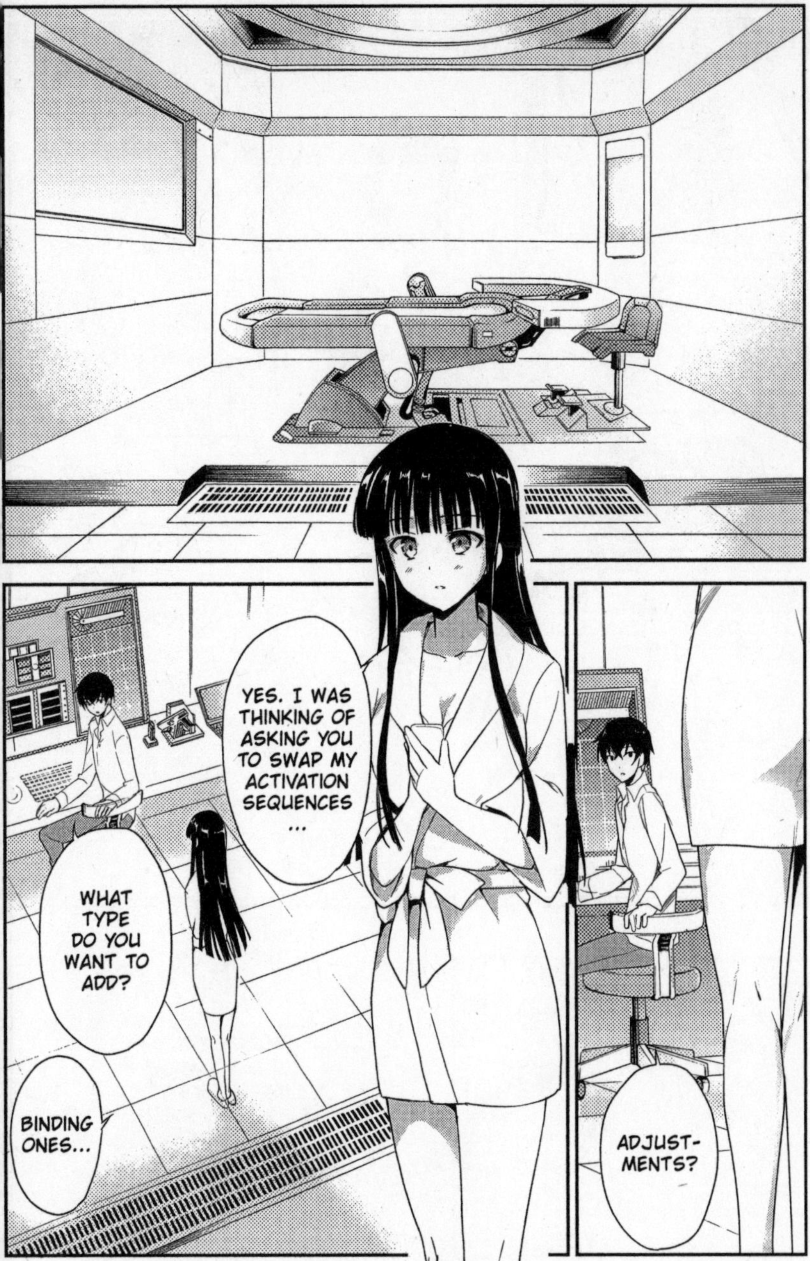
ADJUST-MENTS?
YES. I WAS THINKING OF ASKING YOU TO SWAP MY ACTIVATION SEQUENCES ...
WHAT TYPE DO YOU WANT TO ADD?
BINDING ONES...

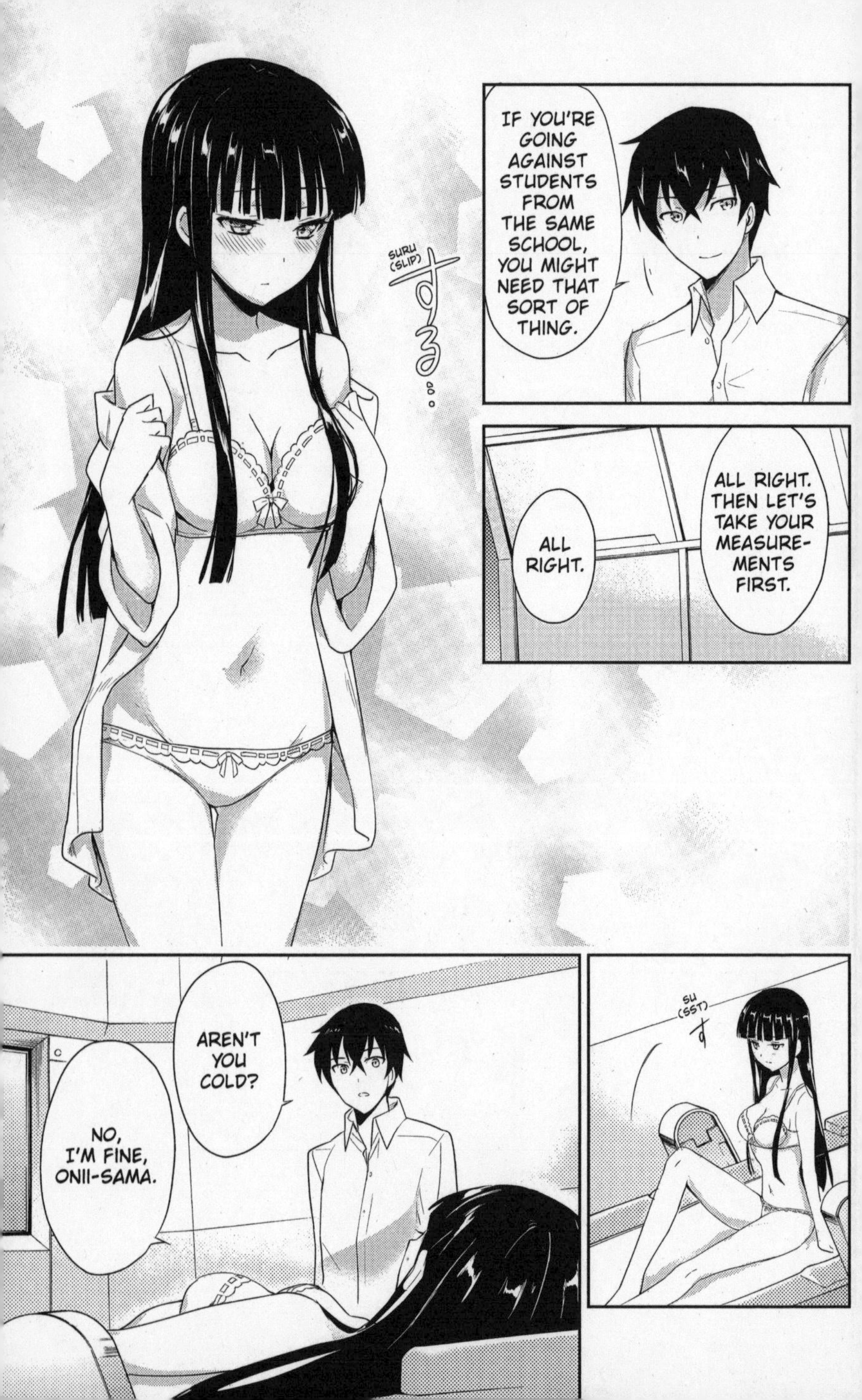
IF YOU'RE GOING AGAINST STUDENTS FROM THE SAME SCHOOL, YOU MIGHT NEED THAT SORT OF THING.
ALL RIGHT. THEN LET'S TAKE YOUR MEASUREMENTS FIRST.
ALL RIGHT.
SURU (SLIP)
SU (SST)
AREN'T YOU COLD?
NO, I'M FINE, ONII-SAMA.

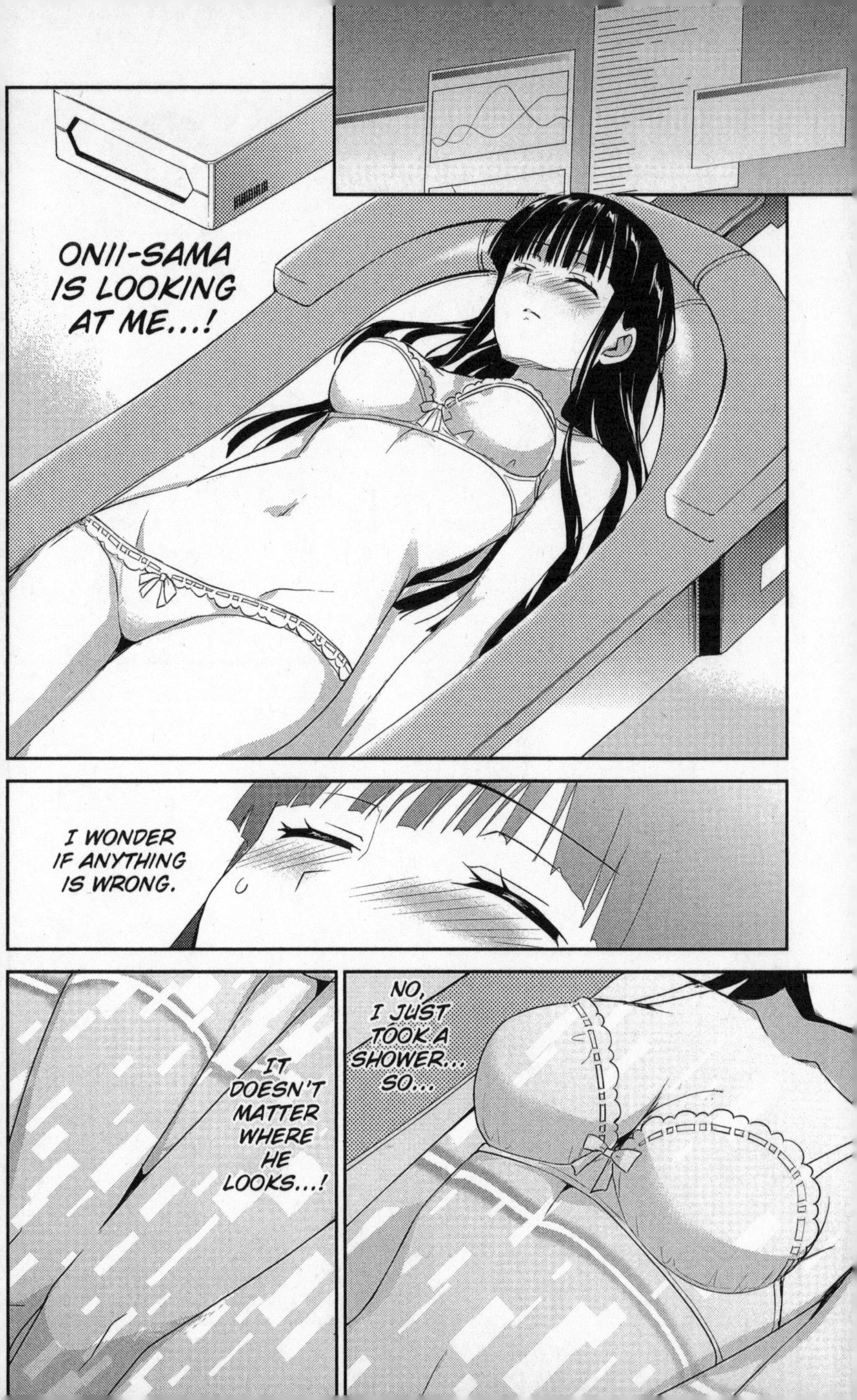
ONII-SAMA IS LOOKING AT ME...!
I WONDER IF ANYTHING IS WRONG.
NO, I JUST TOOK A SHOWER... SO...
IT DOESN'T MATTER WHERE HE LOOKS...!

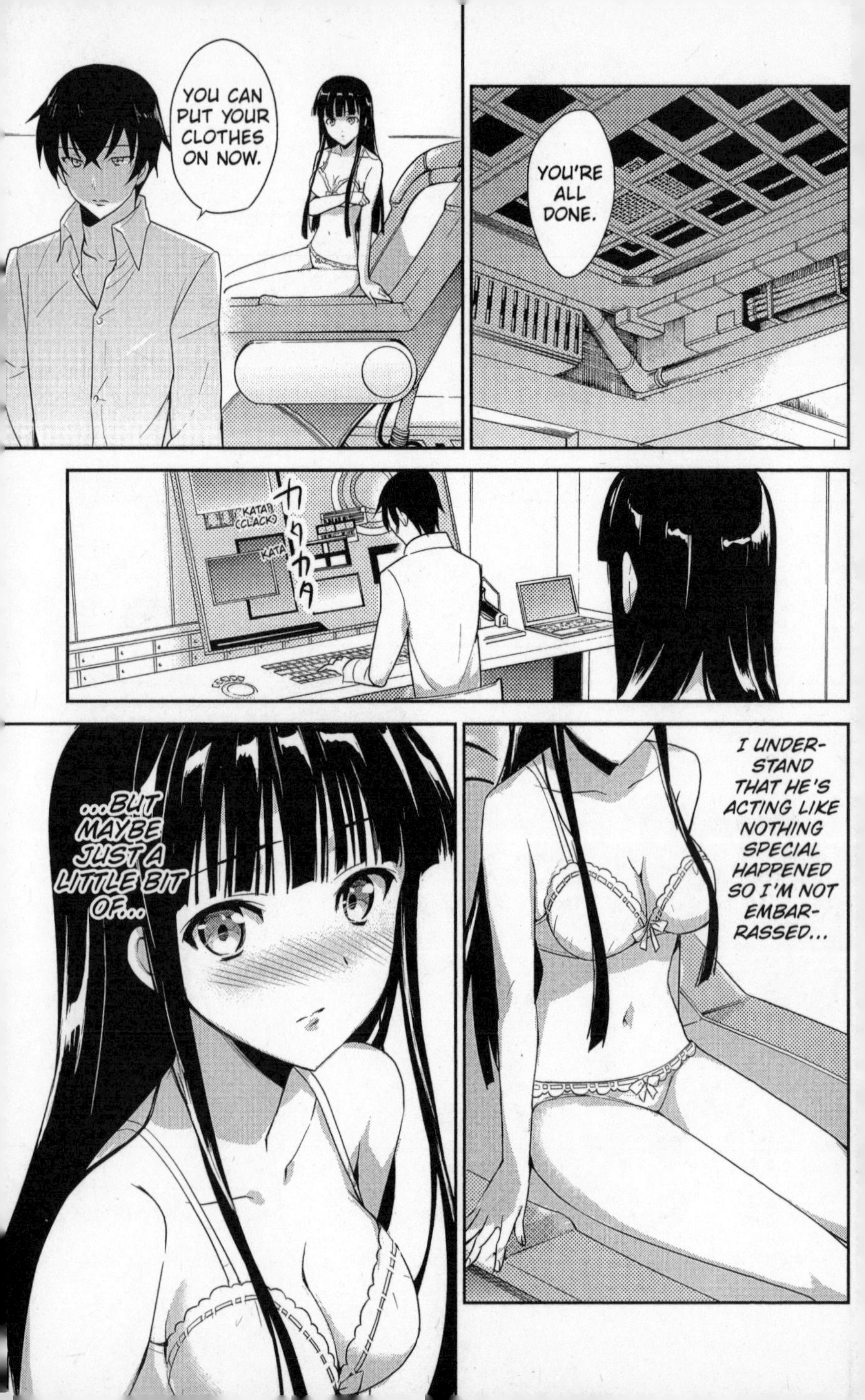
YOU'RE ALL DONE.
YOU CAN PUT YOUR CLOTHES ON NOW.
カタカタ
KATA (CLACK) KATA
I UNDER-STAND THAT HE'S ACTING LIKE NOTHING SPECIAL HAPPENED SO I'M NOT EMBAR-RASSED...
...BUT MAYBE JUST A LITTLE BIT OF...

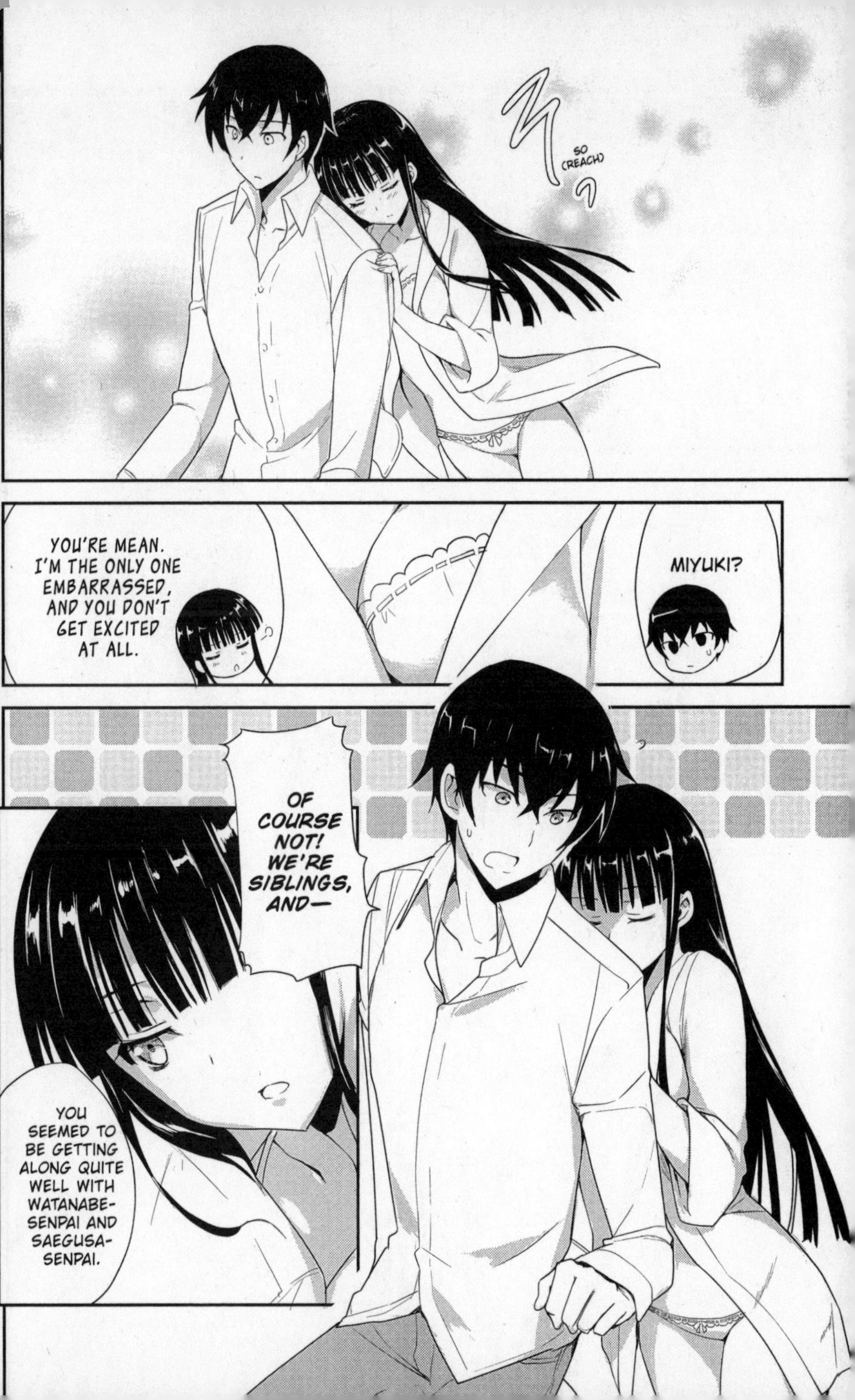
SO (REACH)
MIYUKI?
YOU'RE MEAN. I'M THE ONLY ONE EMBARRASSED, AND YOU DON'T GET EXCITED AT ALL.
OF COURSE NOT! WE'RE SIBLINGS, AND—
YOU SEEMED TO BE GETTING ALONG QUITE WELL WITH WATANABE-SENPAI AND SAEGUSA-SENPAI.

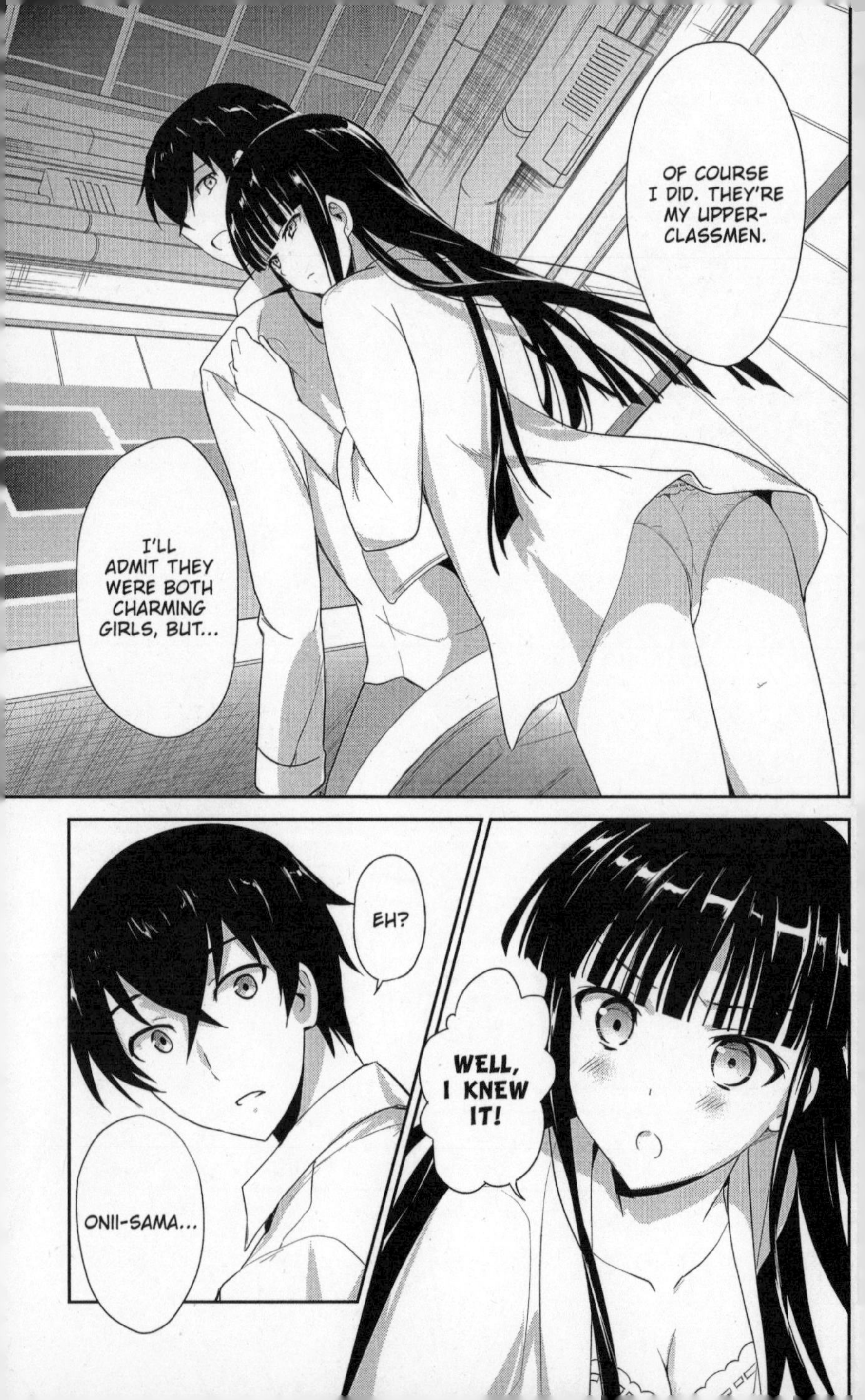
OF COURSE I DID. THEY'RE MY UPPER-CLASSMEN.
I'LL ADMIT THEY WERE BOTH CHARMING GIRLS, BUT...
WELL, I KNEW IT!
EH?
ONII-SAMA...

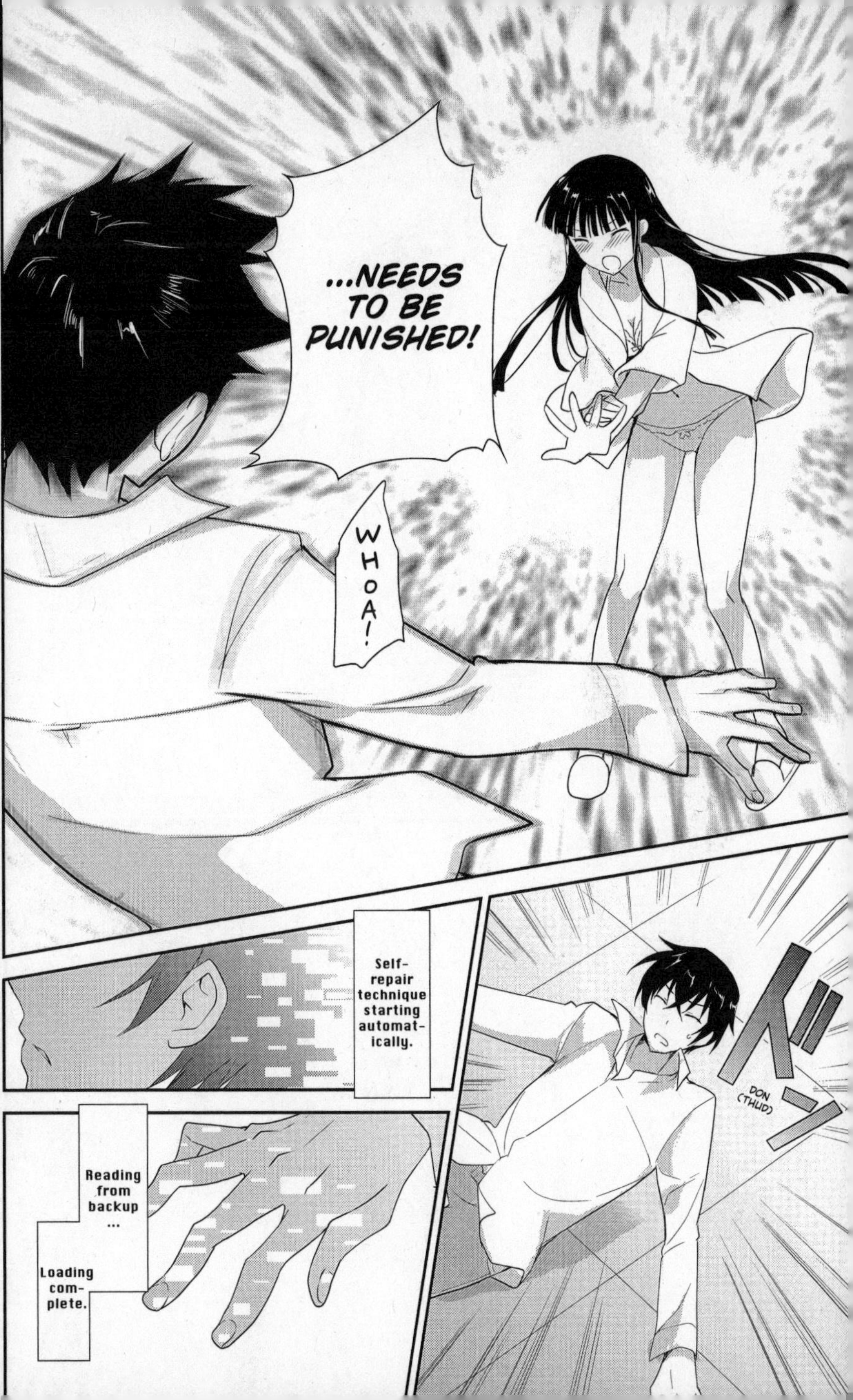
...NEEDS TO BE PUNISHED!
WHOA!
DON (THUD)
Self-repair technique starting automatically.
Reading from backup ...
Loading complete.

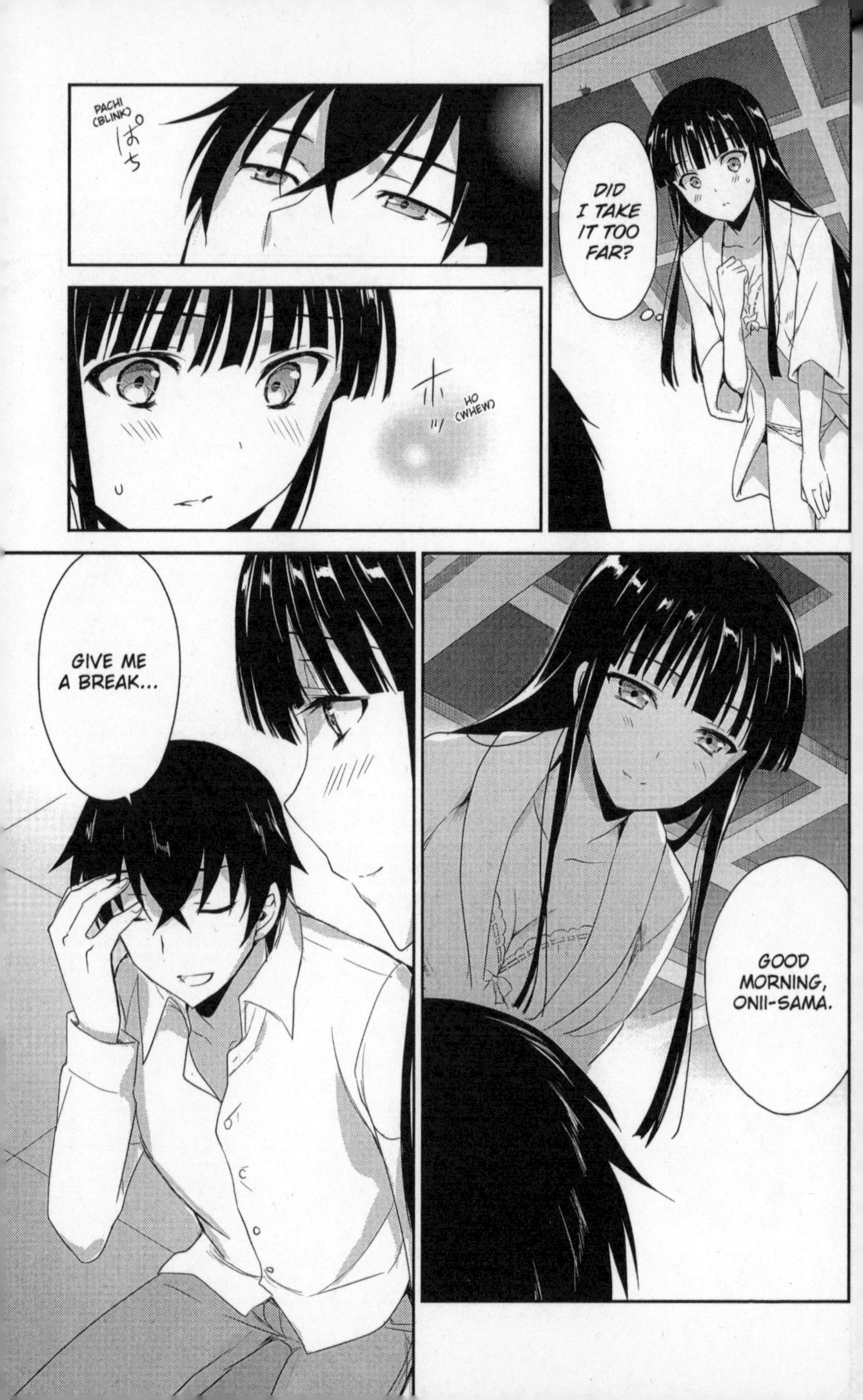
DID I TAKE IT TOO FAR?
ぱち
PACHI (BLINK)
ホッ
HO (WHEW)
GOOD MORNING, ONII-SAMA.
GIVE ME A BREAK...

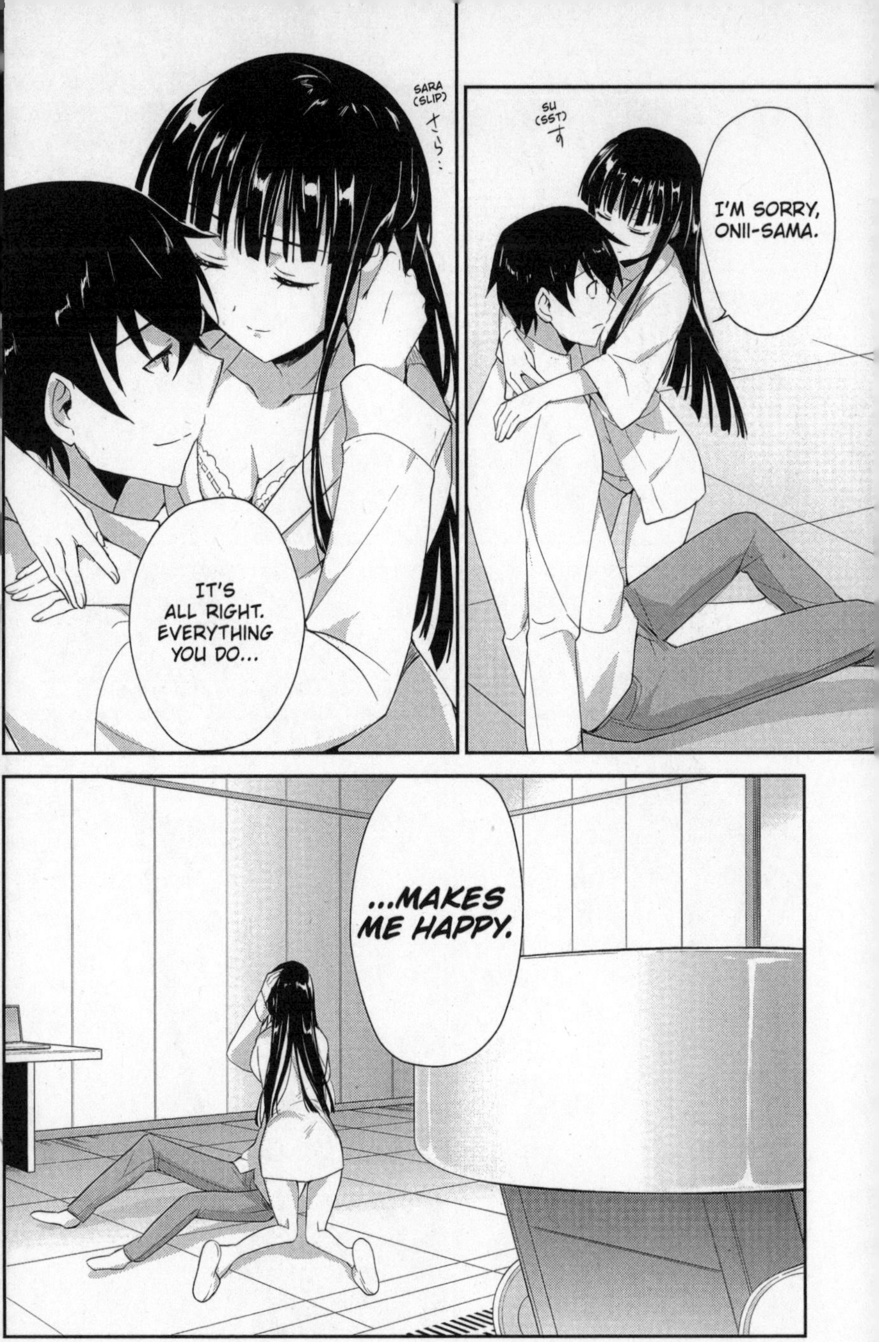
SU (SST)
す
I'M SORRY, ONII-SAMA.
SARA (SLIP)
さら…
IT'S ALL RIGHT. EVERYTHING YOU DO...
...MAKES ME HAPPY.

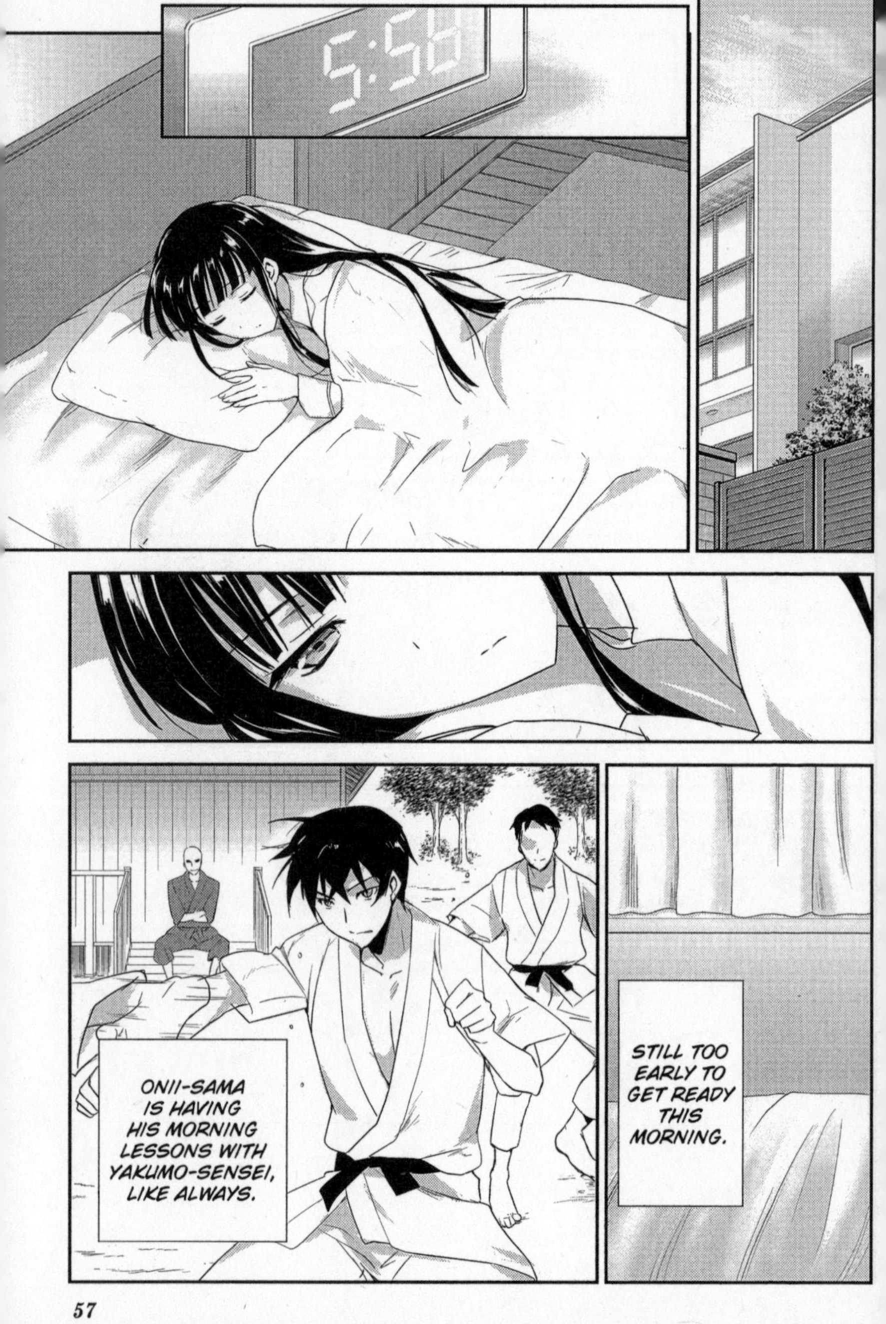
5:58
STILL TOO EARLY TO GET READY THIS MORNING.
ONII-SAMA IS HAVING HIS MORNING LESSONS WITH YAKUMO-SENSEI, LIKE ALWAYS.

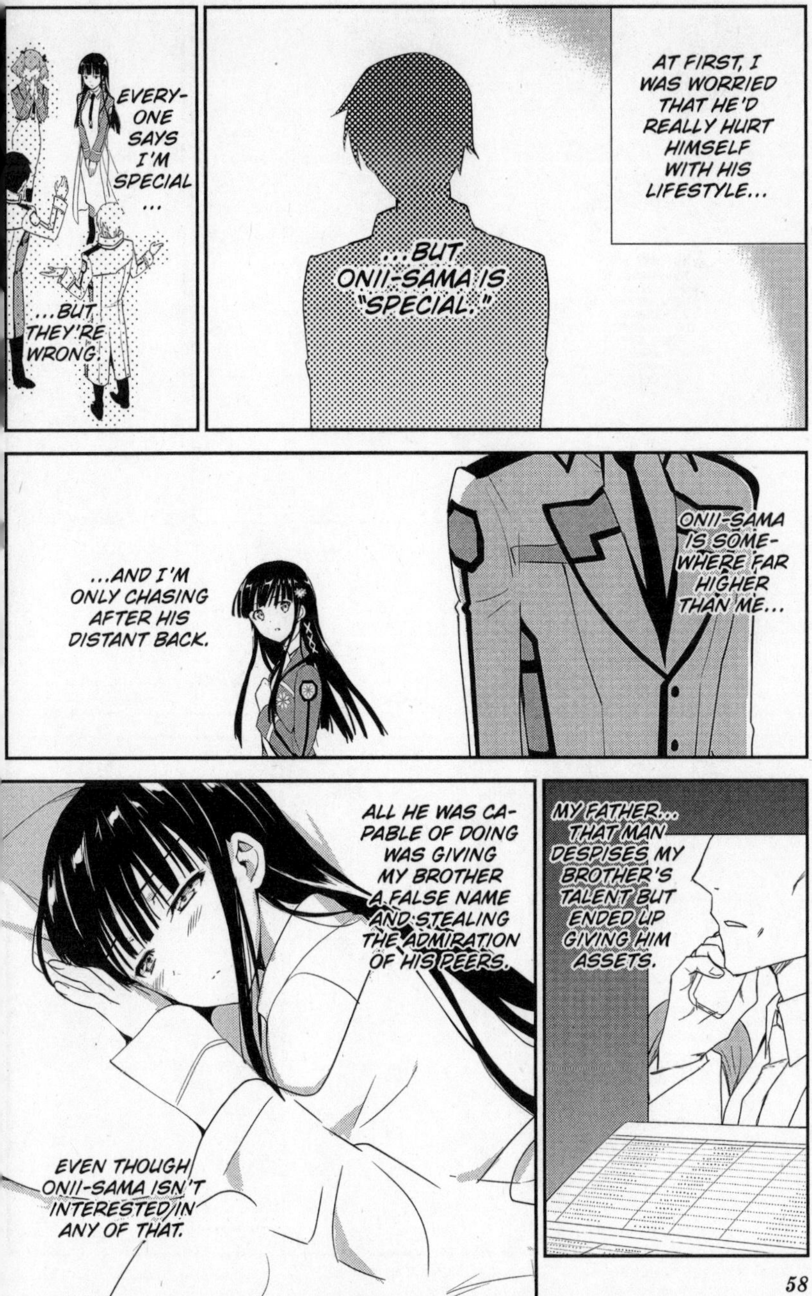
AT FIRST, I WAS WORRIED THAT HE'D REALLY HURT HIMSELF WITH HIS LIFESTYLE...
...BUT ONII-SAMA IS "SPECIAL."
EVERY-ONE SAYS I'M SPECIAL...
...BUT THEY'RE WRONG.
ONII-SAMA IS SOME-WHERE FAR HIGHER THAN ME...
...AND I'M ONLY CHASING AFTER HIS DISTANT BACK.
MY FATHER... THAT MAN DESPISES MY BROTHER'S TALENT BUT ENDED UP GIVING HIM ASSETS.
ALL HE WAS CA-PABLE OF DOING WAS GIVING MY BROTHER A FALSE NAME AND STEALING THE ADMIRATION OF HIS PEERS.
EVEN THOUGH ONII-SAMA ISN'T INTERESTED IN ANY OF THAT.

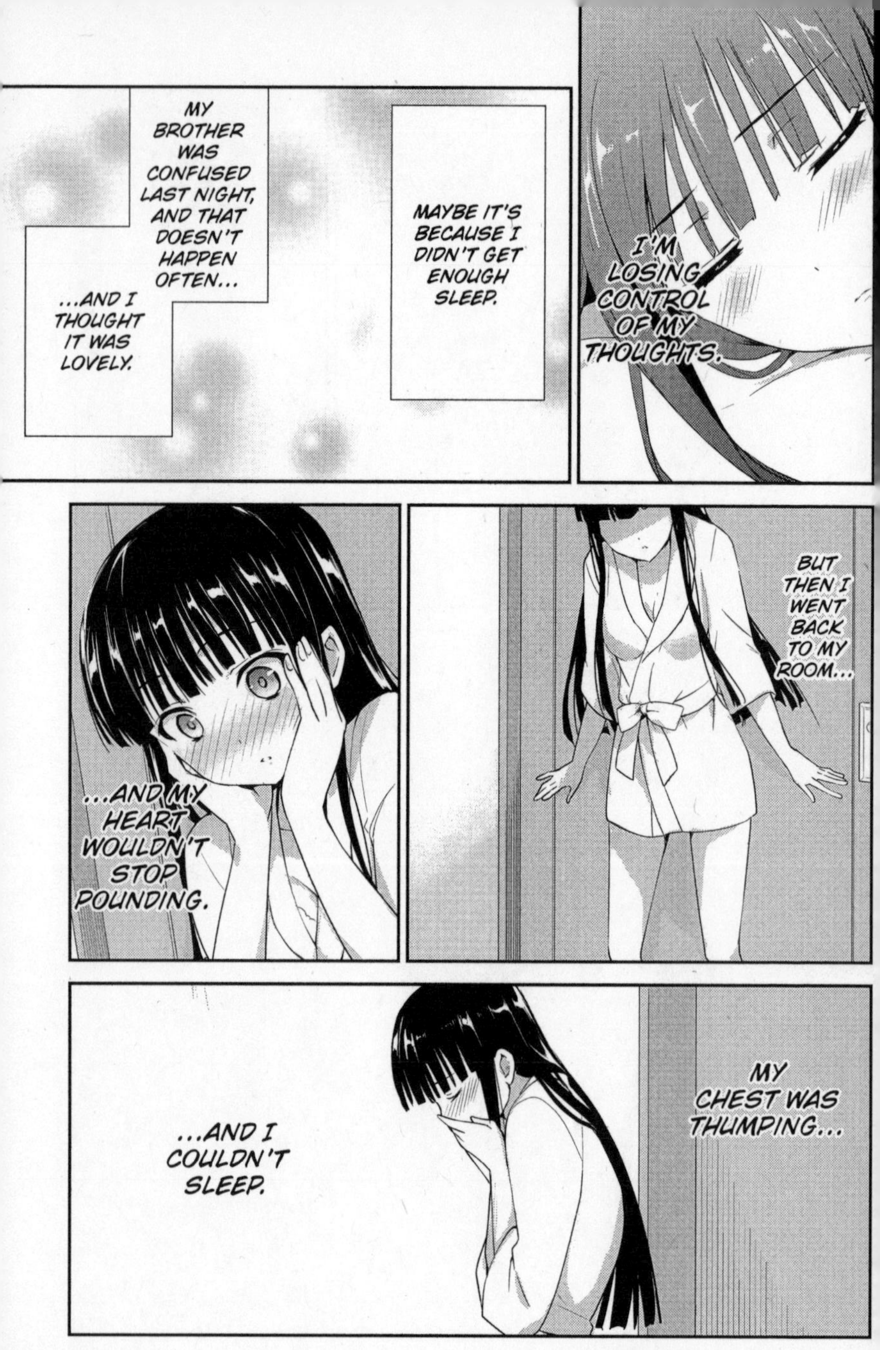
I'M LOSING CONTROL OF MY THOUGHTS.
MAYBE IT'S BECAUSE I DIDN'T GET ENOUGH SLEEP.
MY BROTHER WAS CONFUSED LAST NIGHT, AND THAT DOESN'T HAPPEN OFTEN...
...AND I THOUGHT IT WAS LOVELY.
BUT THEN I WENT BACK TO MY ROOM...
...AND MY HEART WOULDN'T STOP POUNDING.
MY CHEST WAS THUMPING...
...AND I COULDN'T SLEEP.

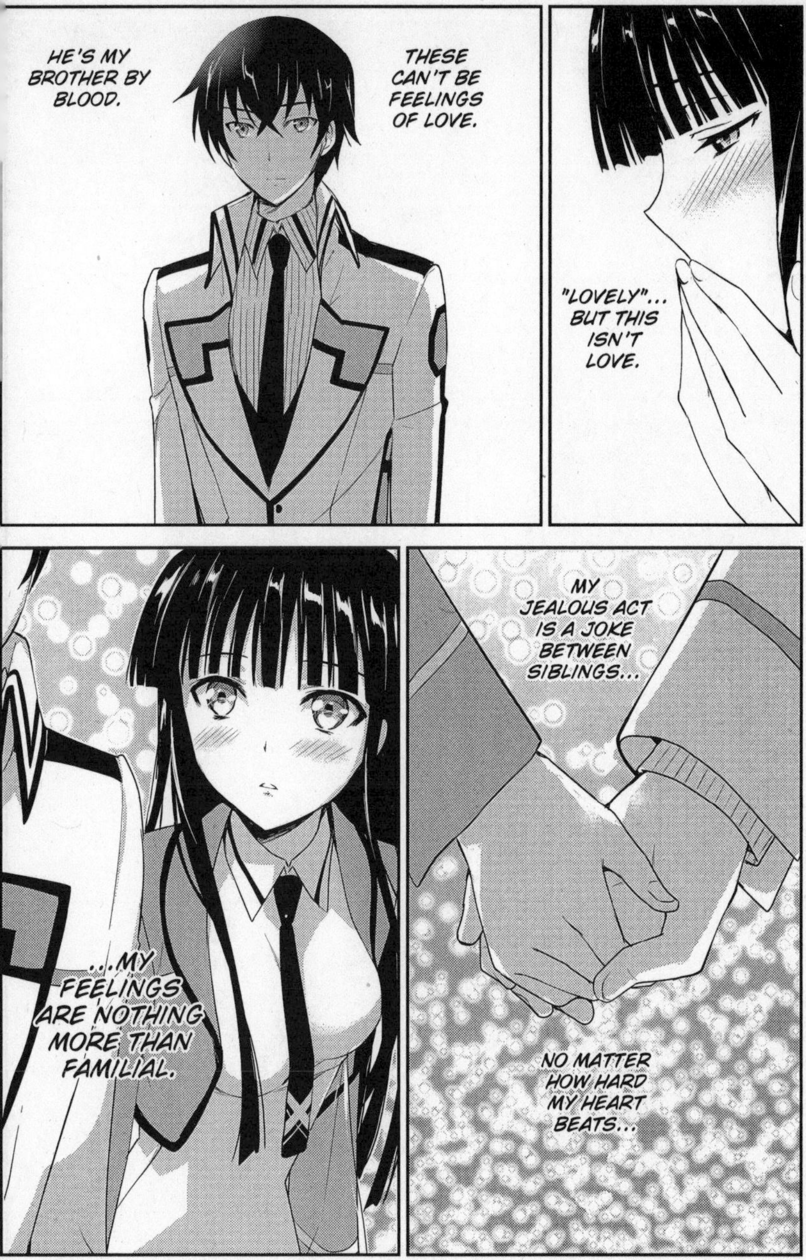
"LOVELY"... BUT THIS ISN'T LOVE.
THESE CAN'T BE FEELINGS OF LOVE.
HE'S MY BROTHER BY BLOOD.
MY JEALOUS ACT IS A JOKE BETWEEN SIBLINGS...
NO MATTER HOW HARD MY HEART BEATS...
...MY FEELINGS ARE NOTHING MORE THAN FAMILIAL.

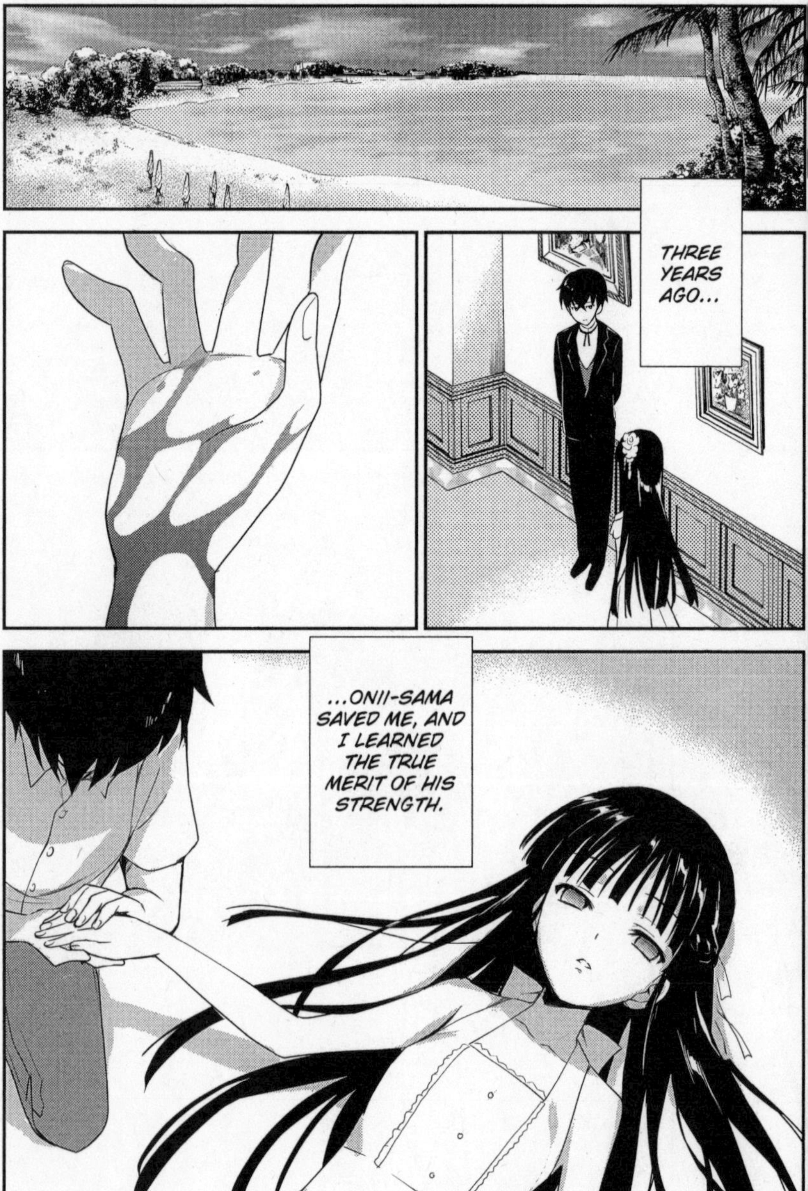
THREE YEARS AGO...
...ONII-SAMA SAVED ME, AND I LEARNED THE TRUE MERIT OF HIS STRENGTH.

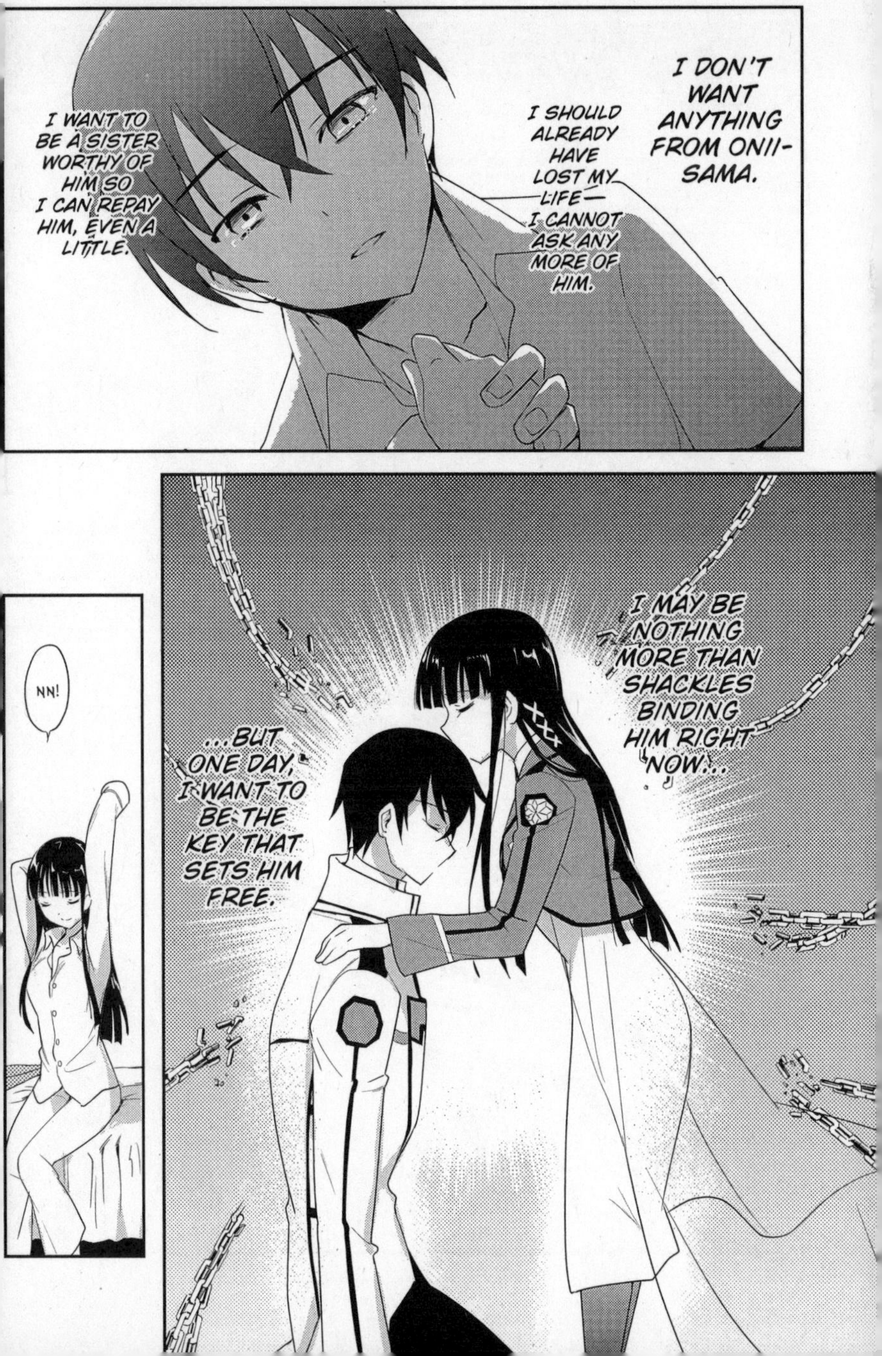
I DON'T WANT ANYTHING FROM ONII-SAMA.
I SHOULD ALREADY HAVE LOST MY LIFE— I CANNOT ASK ANY MORE OF HIM.
I WANT TO BE A SISTER WORTHY OF HIM SO I CAN REPAY HIM, EVEN A LITTLE.
I MAY BE NOTHING MORE THAN SHACKLES BINDING HIM RIGHT NOW...
...BUT ONE DAY, I WANT TO BE THE KEY THAT SETS HIM FREE.
NN!

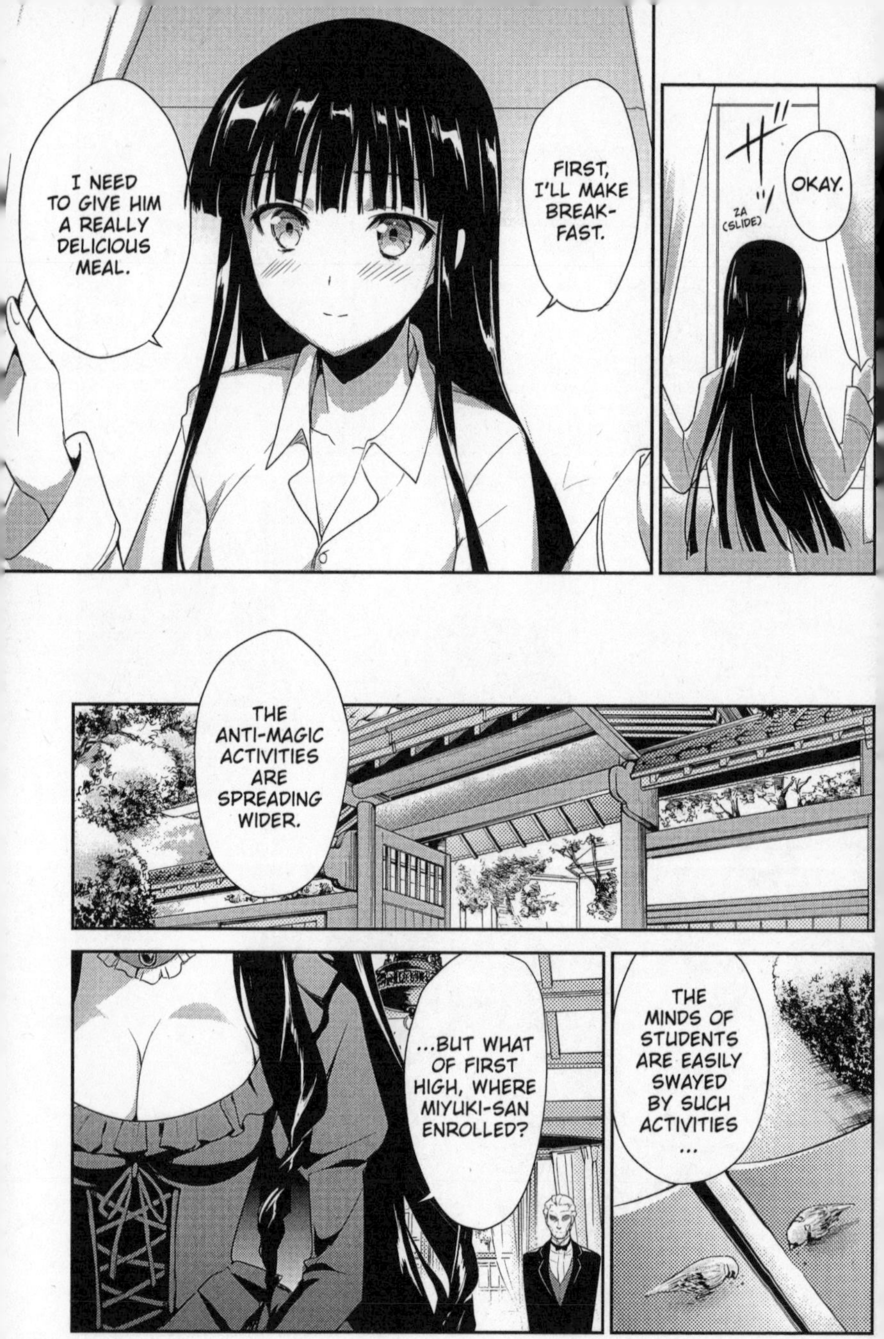
OKAY.
ZA (SLIDE)
FIRST, I'LL MAKE BREAK-FAST.
I NEED TO GIVE HIM A REALLY DELICIOUS MEAL.
THE ANTI-MAGIC ACTIVITIES ARE SPREADING WIDER.
THE MINDS OF STUDENTS ARE EASILY SWAYED BY SUCH ACTIVITIES ...
...BUT WHAT OF FIRST HIGH, WHERE MIYUKI-SAN ENROLLED?

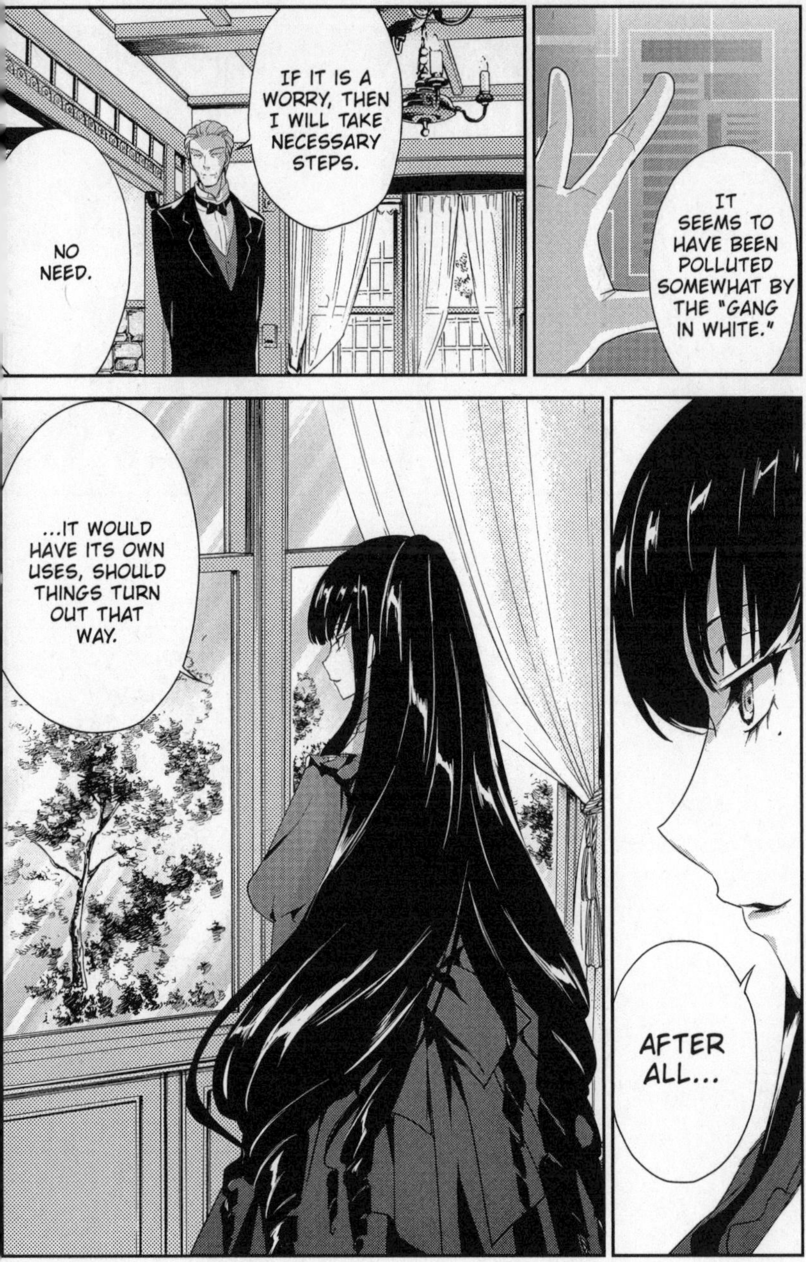
IT SEEMS TO HAVE BEEN POLLUTED SOMEWHAT BY THE "GANG IN WHITE."
IF IT IS A WORRY, THEN I WILL TAKE NECESSARY STEPS.
NO NEED.
AFTER ALL...
...IT WOULD HAVE ITS OWN USES, SHOULD THINGS TURN OUT THAT WAY.

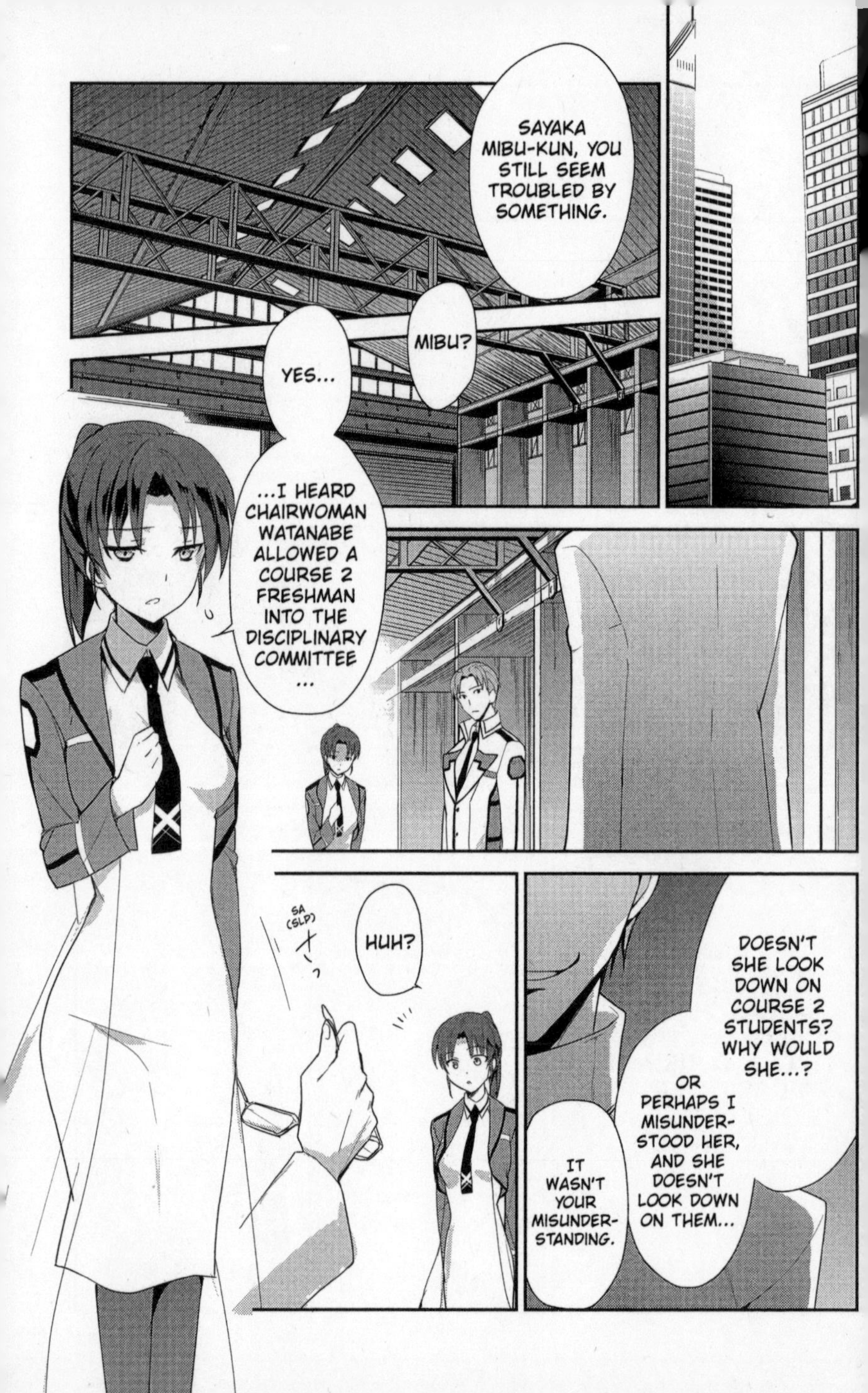
SAYAKA MIBU-KUN, YOU STILL SEEM TROUBLED BY SOMETHING.
MIBU?
YES...
...I HEARD CHAIRWOMAN WATANABE ALLOWED A COURSE 2 FRESHMAN INTO THE DISCIPLINARY COMMITTEE ...
DOESN'T SHE LOOK DOWN ON COURSE 2 STUDENTS? WHY WOULD SHE...?
OR PERHAPS I MISUNDER-STOOD HER, AND SHE DOESN'T LOOK DOWN ON THEM...
IT WASN'T YOUR MISUNDER-STANDING.
HUH?
SA (SLP)

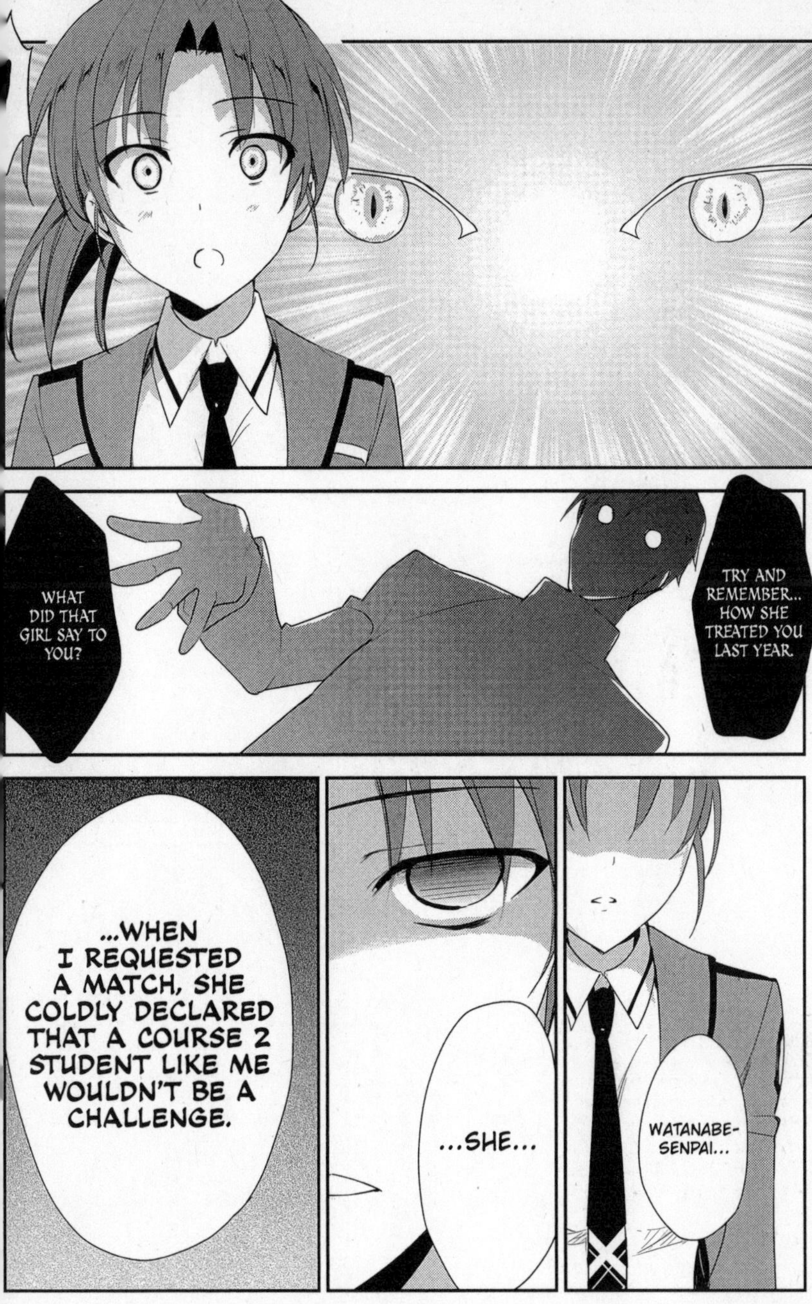
TRY AND REMEMBER... HOW SHE TREATED YOU LAST YEAR.
WHAT DID THAT GIRL SAY TO YOU?
WATANABE-SENPAI...
...SHE...
...WHEN I REQUESTED A MATCH, SHE COLDLY DECLARED THAT A COURSE 2 STUDENT LIKE ME WOULDN'T BE A CHALLENGE.

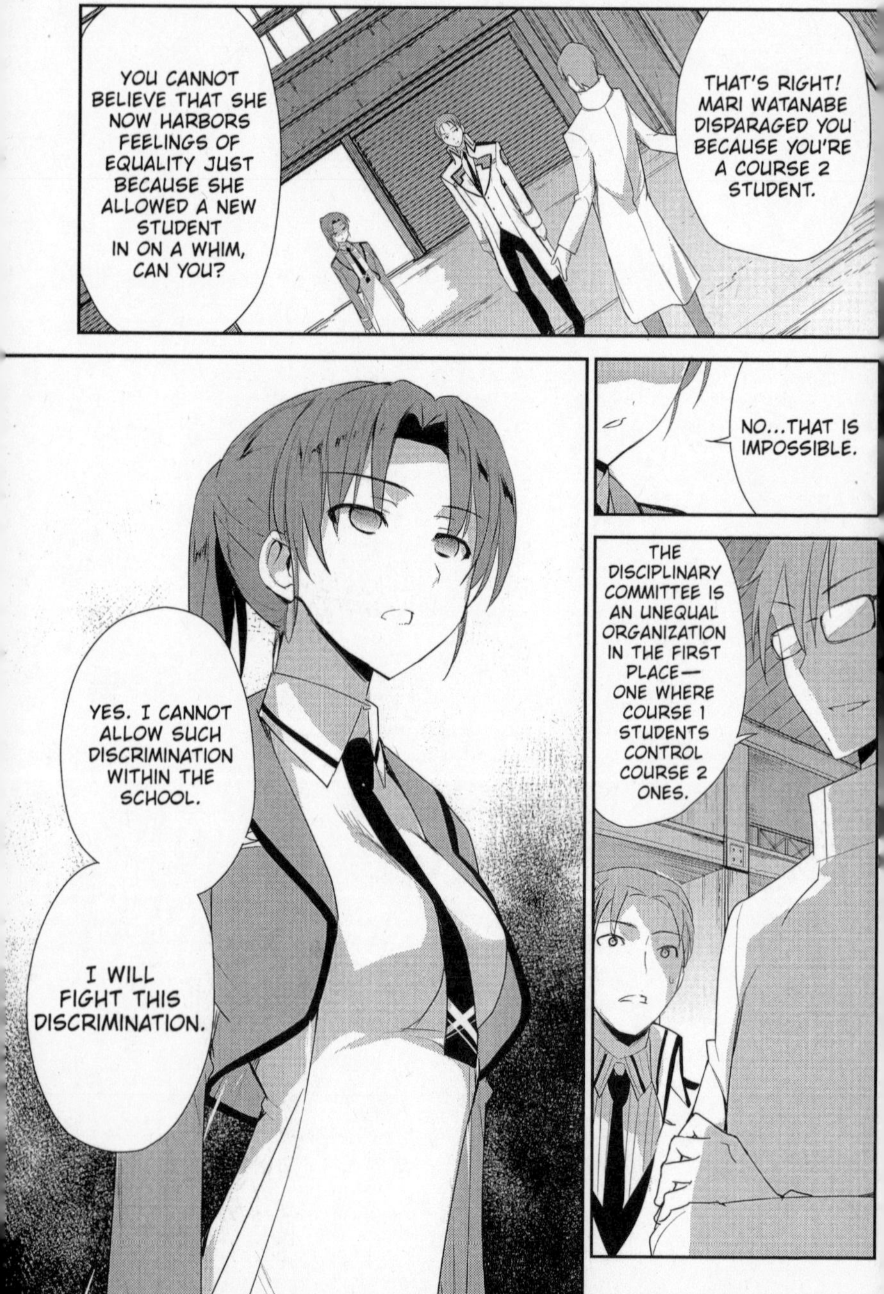
THAT'S RIGHT! MARI WATANABE DISPARAGED YOU BECAUSE YOU'RE A COURSE 2 STUDENT.
YOU CANNOT BELIEVE THAT SHE NOW HARBORS FEELINGS OF EQUALITY JUST BECAUSE SHE ALLOWED A NEW STUDENT IN ON A WHIM, CAN YOU?
NO...THAT IS IMPOSSIBLE.
THE DISCIPLINARY COMMITTEE IS AN UNEQUAL ORGANIZATION IN THE FIRST PLACE—ONE WHERE COURSE 1 STUDENTS CONTROL COURSE 2 ONES.
YES. I CANNOT ALLOW SUCH DISCRIMINATION WITHIN THE SCHOOL.
I WILL FIGHT THIS DISCRIMINATION.

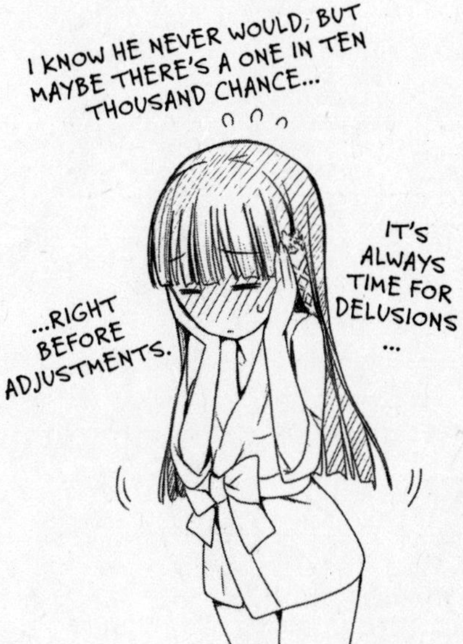
I KNOW HE NEVER WOULD, BUT MAYBE THERE'S A ONE IN TEN THOUSAND CHANCE...
IT'S ALWAYS TIME FOR DELUSIONS...
...RIGHT BEFORE ADJUSTMENTS.

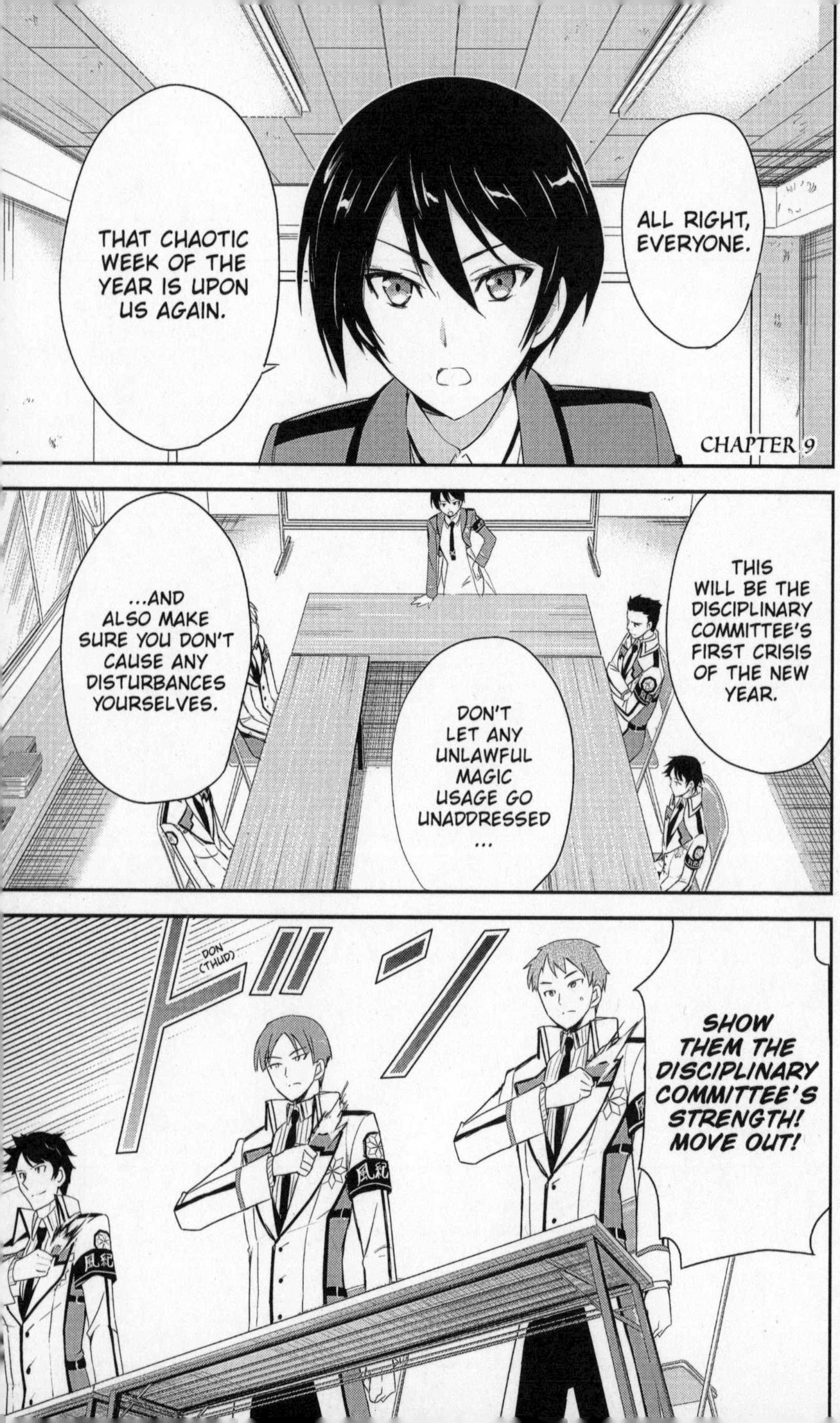
ALL RIGHT, EVERYONE.
THAT CHAOTIC WEEK OF THE YEAR IS UPON US AGAIN.
CHAPTER 9
THIS WILL BE THE DISCIPLINARY COMMITTEE'S FIRST CRISIS OF THE NEW YEAR.
DON'T LET ANY UNLAWFUL MAGIC USAGE GO UNADDRESSED ...
...AND ALSO MAKE SURE YOU DON'T CAUSE ANY DISTURBANCES YOURSELVES.
SHOW THEM THE DISCIPLINARY COMMITTEE'S STRENGTH! MOVE OUT!
DON (THUD)

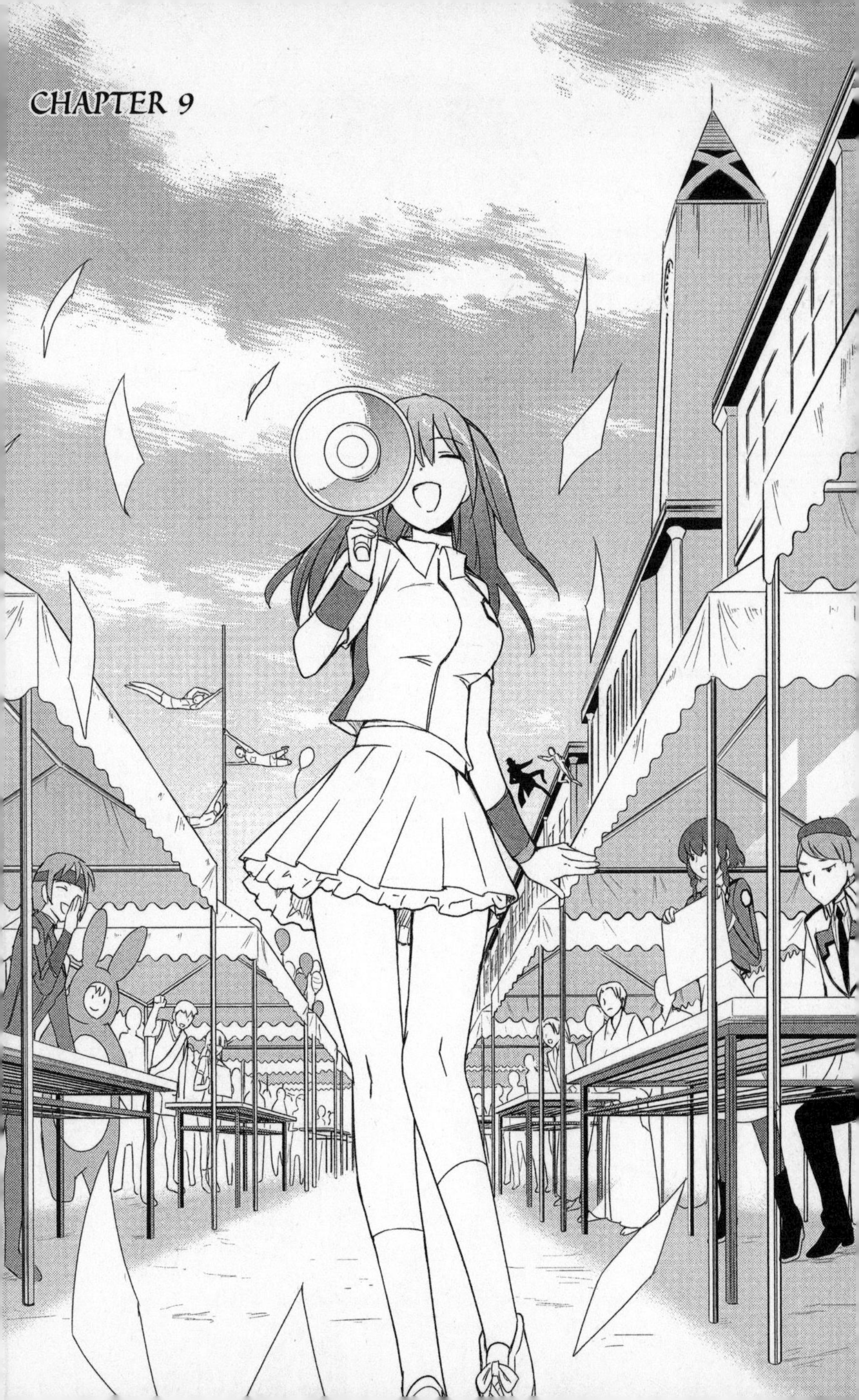
CHAPTER 9

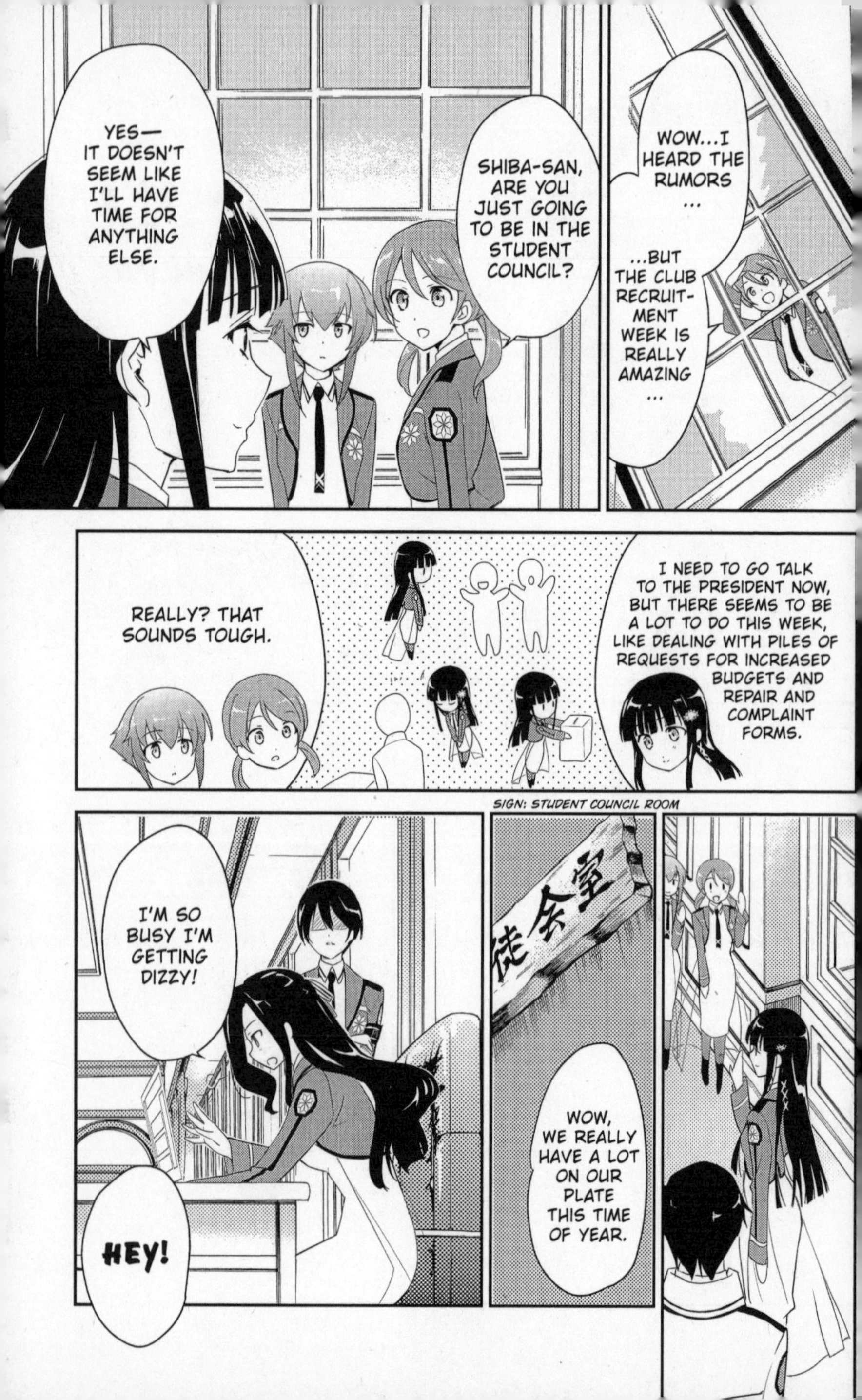
WOW...I HEARD THE RUMORS ...
...BUT THE CLUB RECRUIT-MENT WEEK IS REALLY AMAZING ...
SHIBA-SAN, ARE YOU JUST GOING TO BE IN THE STUDENT COUNCIL?
YES— IT DOESN'T SEEM LIKE I'LL HAVE TIME FOR ANYTHING ELSE.
I NEED TO GO TALK TO THE PRESIDENT NOW, BUT THERE SEEMS TO BE A LOT TO DO THIS WEEK, LIKE DEALING WITH PILES OF REQUESTS FOR INCREASED BUDGETS AND REPAIR AND COMPLAINT FORMS.
REALLY? THAT SOUNDS TOUGH.
SIGN: STUDENT COUNCIL ROOM
徒会室
WOW, WE REALLY HAVE A LOT ON OUR PLATE THIS TIME OF YEAR.
I'M SO BUSY I'M GETTING DIZZY!
HEY!

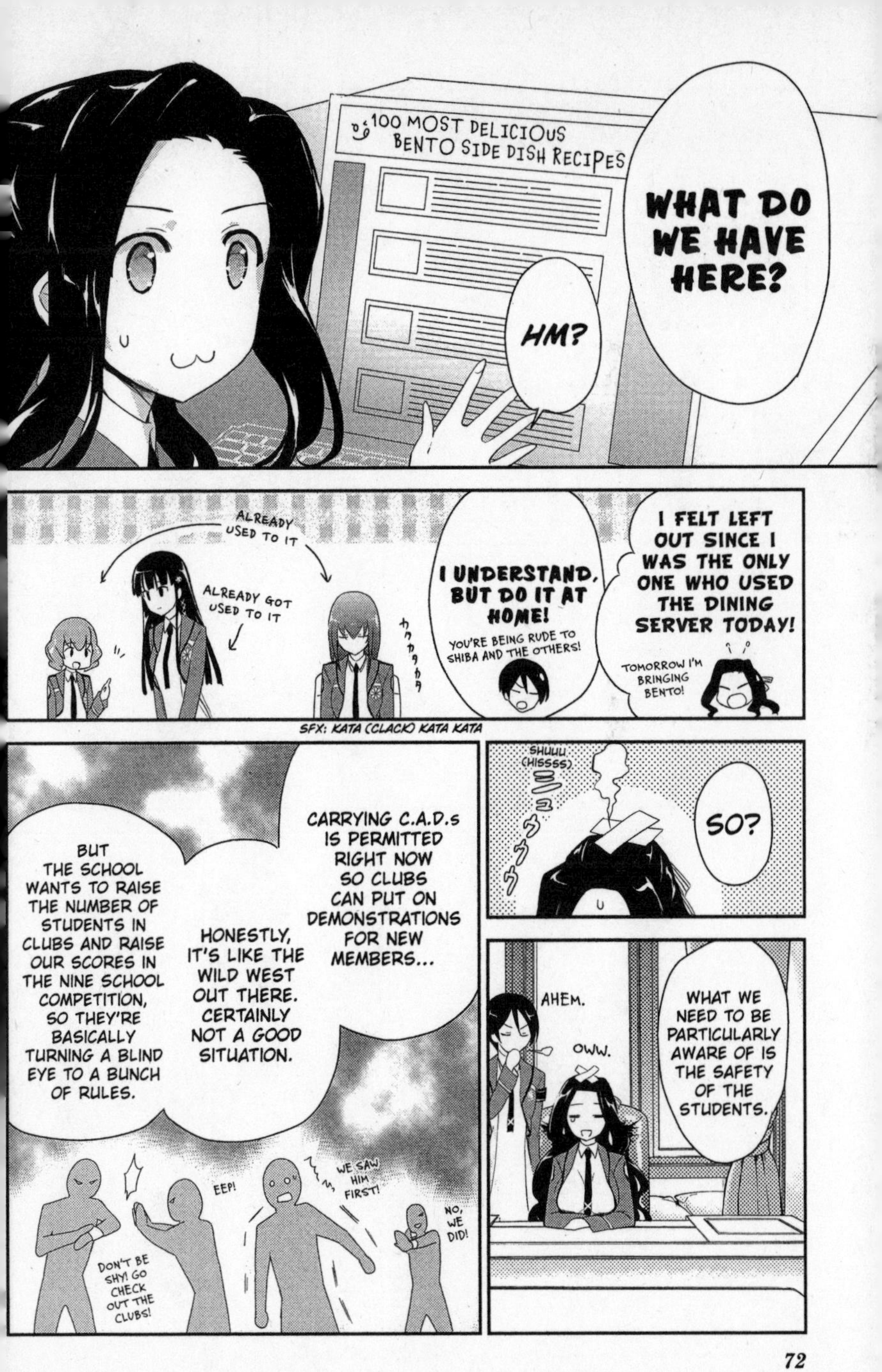
100 MOST DELICIOUS BENTO SIDE DISH RECIPES
WHAT DO WE HAVE HERE?
HM?
I FELT LEFT OUT SINCE I WAS THE ONLY ONE WHO USED THE DINING SERVER TODAY!
TOMORROW I'M BRINGING BENTO!
I UNDERSTAND, BUT DO IT AT HOME!
YOU'RE BEING RUDE TO SHIBA AND THE OTHERS!
ALREADY USED TO IT
ALREADY GOT USED TO IT
SFX: KATA (CLACK) KATA KATA
SHUUU (HISSSS)
SO?
WHAT WE NEED TO BE PARTICULARLY AWARE OF IS THE SAFETY OF THE STUDENTS.
AHEM.
OWW.
CARRYING C.A.D.s IS PERMITTED RIGHT NOW SO CLUBS CAN PUT ON DEMONSTRATIONS FOR NEW MEMBERS...
HONESTLY, IT'S LIKE THE WILD WEST OUT THERE. CERTAINLY NOT A GOOD SITUATION.
BUT THE SCHOOL WANTS TO RAISE THE NUMBER OF STUDENTS IN CLUBS AND RAISE OUR SCORES IN THE NINE SCHOOL COMPETITION, SO THEY'RE BASICALLY TURNING A BLIND EYE TO A BUNCH OF RULES.
WE SAW HIM FIRST!
NO, WE DID!
EEP!
DON'T BE SHY! GO CHECK OUT THE CLUBS!

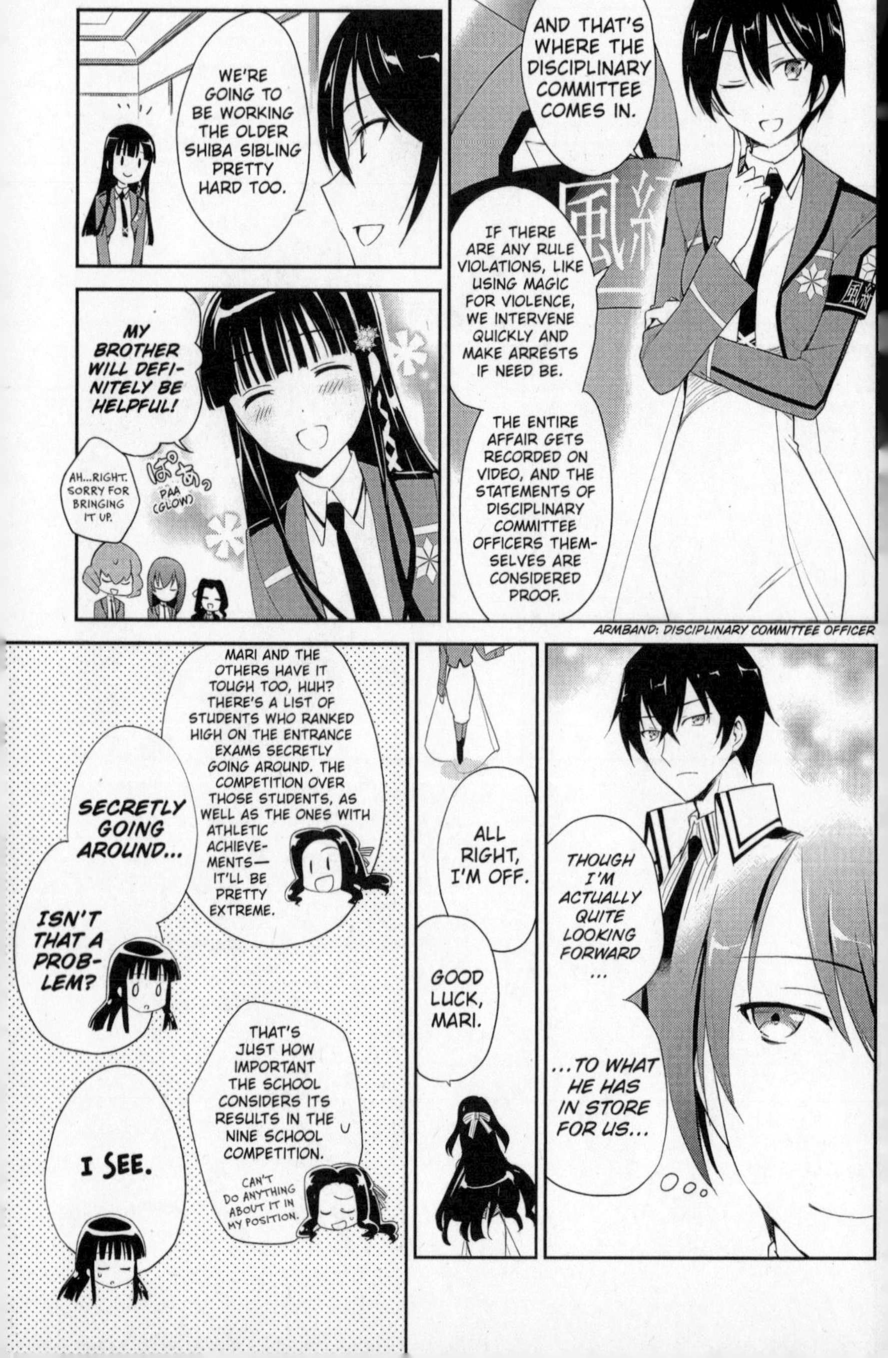
AND THAT'S WHERE THE DISCIPLINARY COMMITTEE COMES IN.
IF THERE ARE ANY RULE VIOLATIONS, LIKE USING MAGIC FOR VIOLENCE, WE INTERVENE QUICKLY AND MAKE ARRESTS IF NEED BE.
THE ENTIRE AFFAIR GETS RECORDED ON VIDEO, AND THE STATEMENTS OF DISCIPLINARY COMMITTEE OFFICERS THEMSELVES ARE CONSIDERED PROOF.
WE'RE GOING TO BE WORKING THE OLDER SHIBA SIBLING PRETTY HARD TOO.
MY BROTHER WILL DEFINITELY BE HELPFUL!
ぱぁっ
PAA (GLOW)
AH...RIGHT. SORRY FOR BRINGING IT UP.
ARMBAND: DISCIPLINARY COMMITTEE OFFICER
THOUGH I'M ACTUALLY QUITE LOOKING FORWARD ...
...TO WHAT HE HAS IN STORE FOR US...
ALL RIGHT, I'M OFF.
GOOD LUCK, MARI.
MARI AND THE OTHERS HAVE IT TOUGH TOO, HUH? THERE'S A LIST OF STUDENTS WHO RANKED HIGH ON THE ENTRANCE EXAMS SECRETLY GOING AROUND. THE COMPETITION OVER THOSE STUDENTS, AS WELL AS THE ONES WITH ATHLETIC ACHIEVEMENTS—IT'LL BE PRETTY EXTREME.
SECRETLY GOING AROUND...
ISN'T THAT A PROBLEM?
THAT'S JUST HOW IMPORTANT THE SCHOOL CONSIDERS ITS RESULTS IN THE NINE SCHOOL COMPETITION.
I SEE.
CAN'T DO ANYTHING ABOUT IT IN MY POSITION.

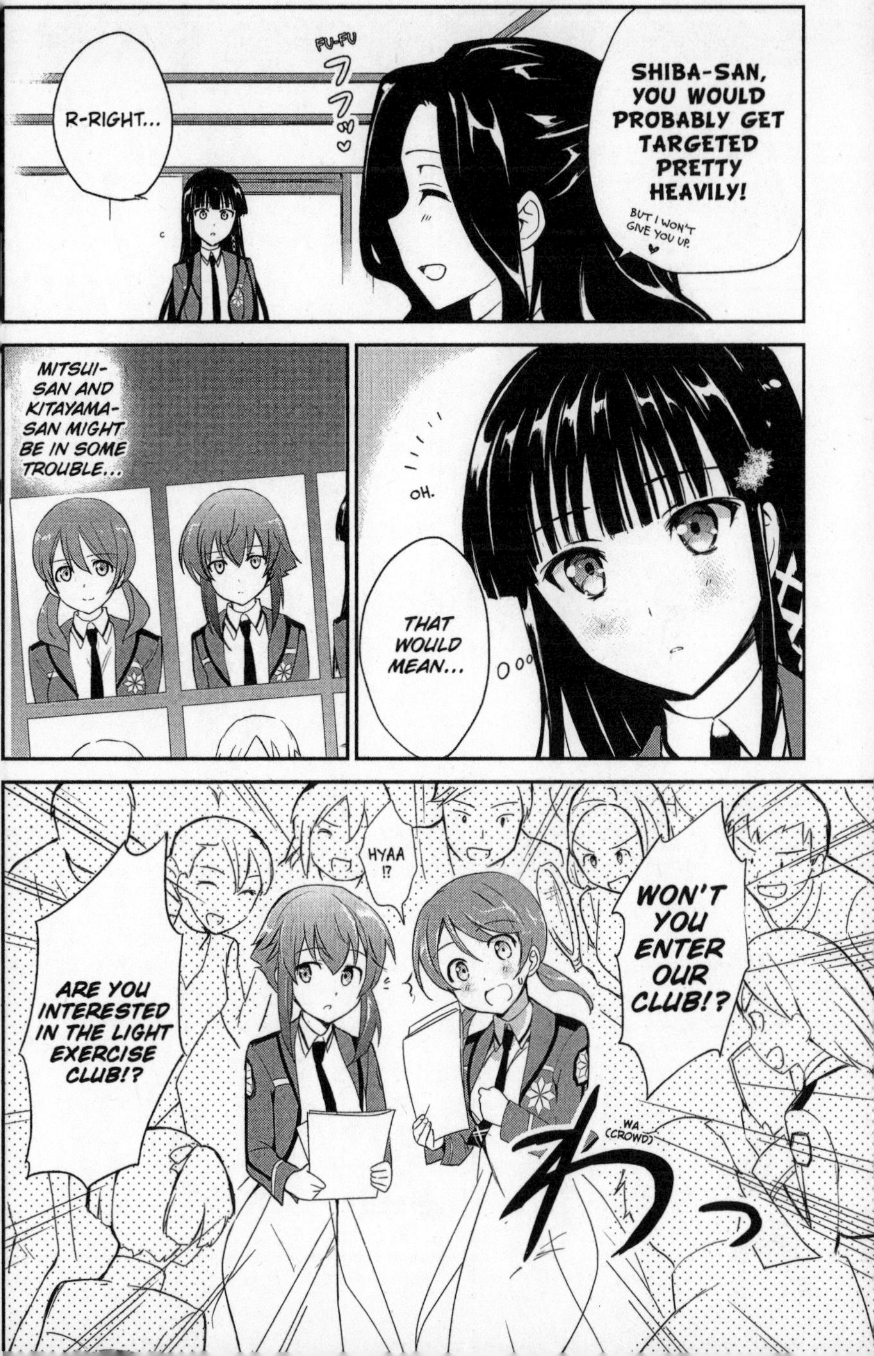
SHIBA-SAN, YOU WOULD PROBABLY GET TARGETED PRETTY HEAVILY!
BUT I WON'T GIVE YOU UP.
FU-FU
R-RIGHT...
OH.
THAT WOULD MEAN...
MITSUI-SAN AND KITAYAMA-SAN MIGHT BE IN SOME TROUBLE...
WON'T YOU ENTER OUR CLUB!?
WA (CROWD)
HYAA!?
ARE YOU INTERESTED IN THE LIGHT EXERCISE CLUB!?

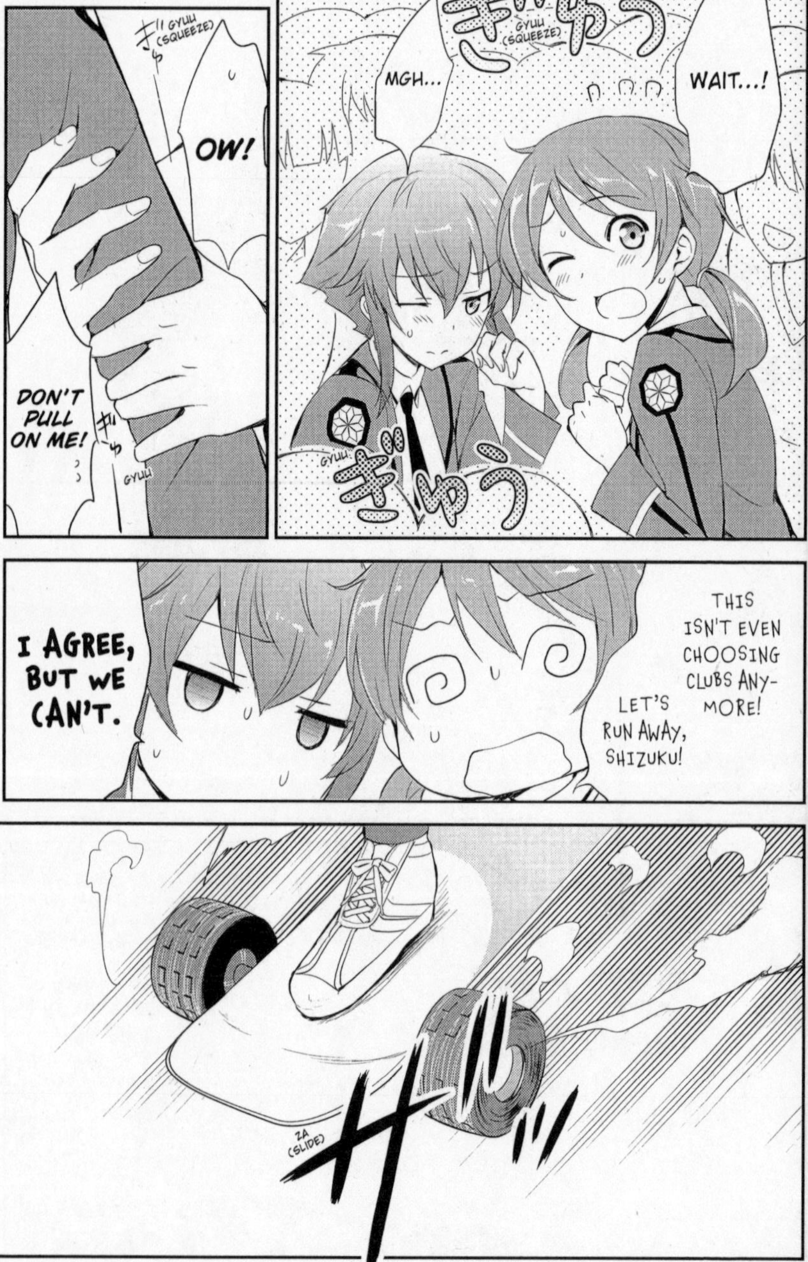
WAIT...!
ぎゅう
GYUU (SQUEEZE)
MGH...
ぎゅう
GYUU
OW!
ぎゅ
GYUU (SQUEEZE)
DON'T PULL ON ME!
ぎゅ
GYUU
THIS ISN'T EVEN CHOOSING CLUBS ANY-MORE!
LET'S RUN AWAY, SHIZUKU!
I AGREE, BUT WE CAN'T.
ザッ
ZA (SLIDE)

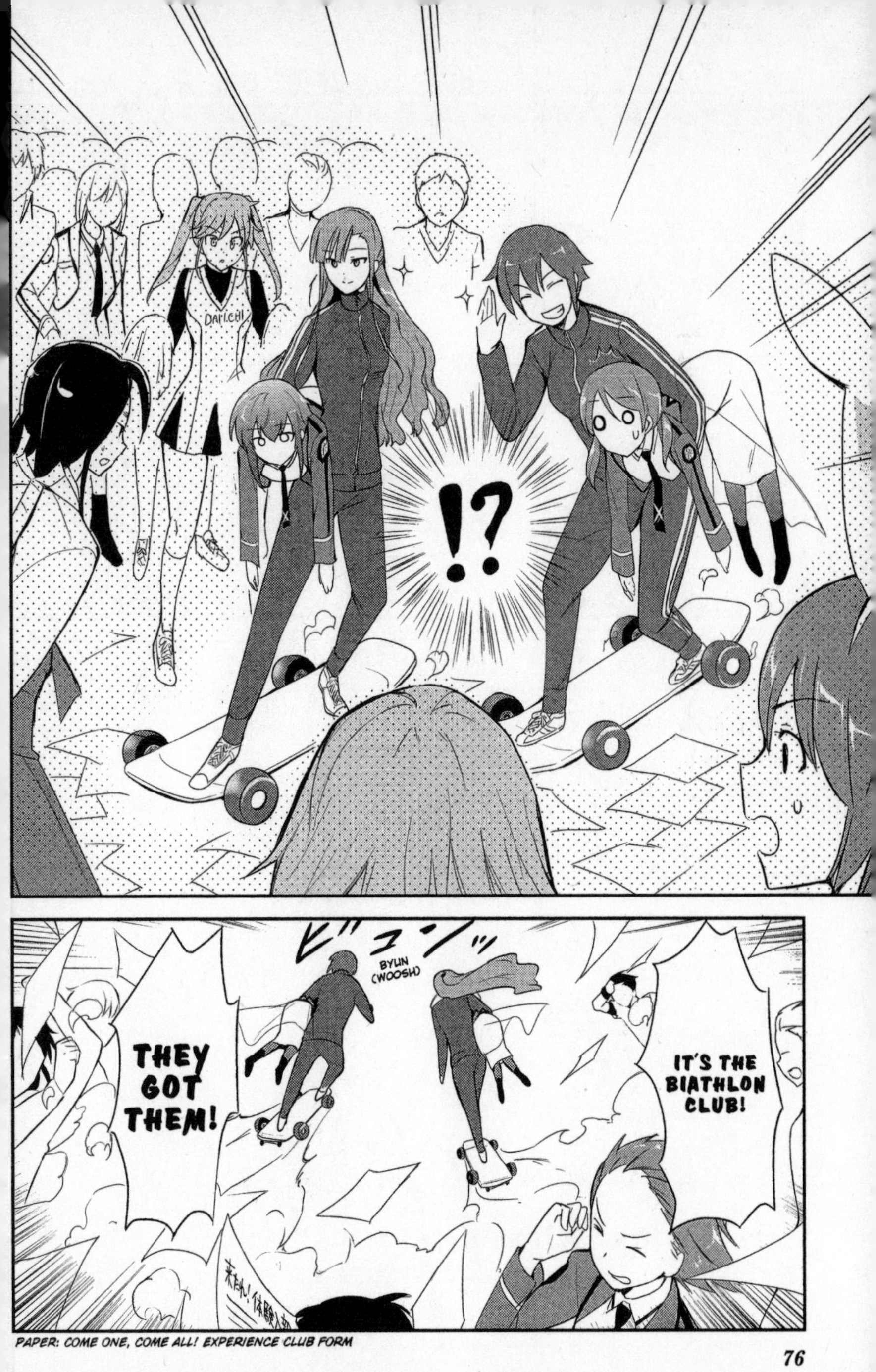
!?
IT'S THE BIATHLON CLUB!
BYUN (WOOSH)
THEY GOT THEM!
PAPER: COME ONE, COME ALL! EXPERIENCE CLUB FORM

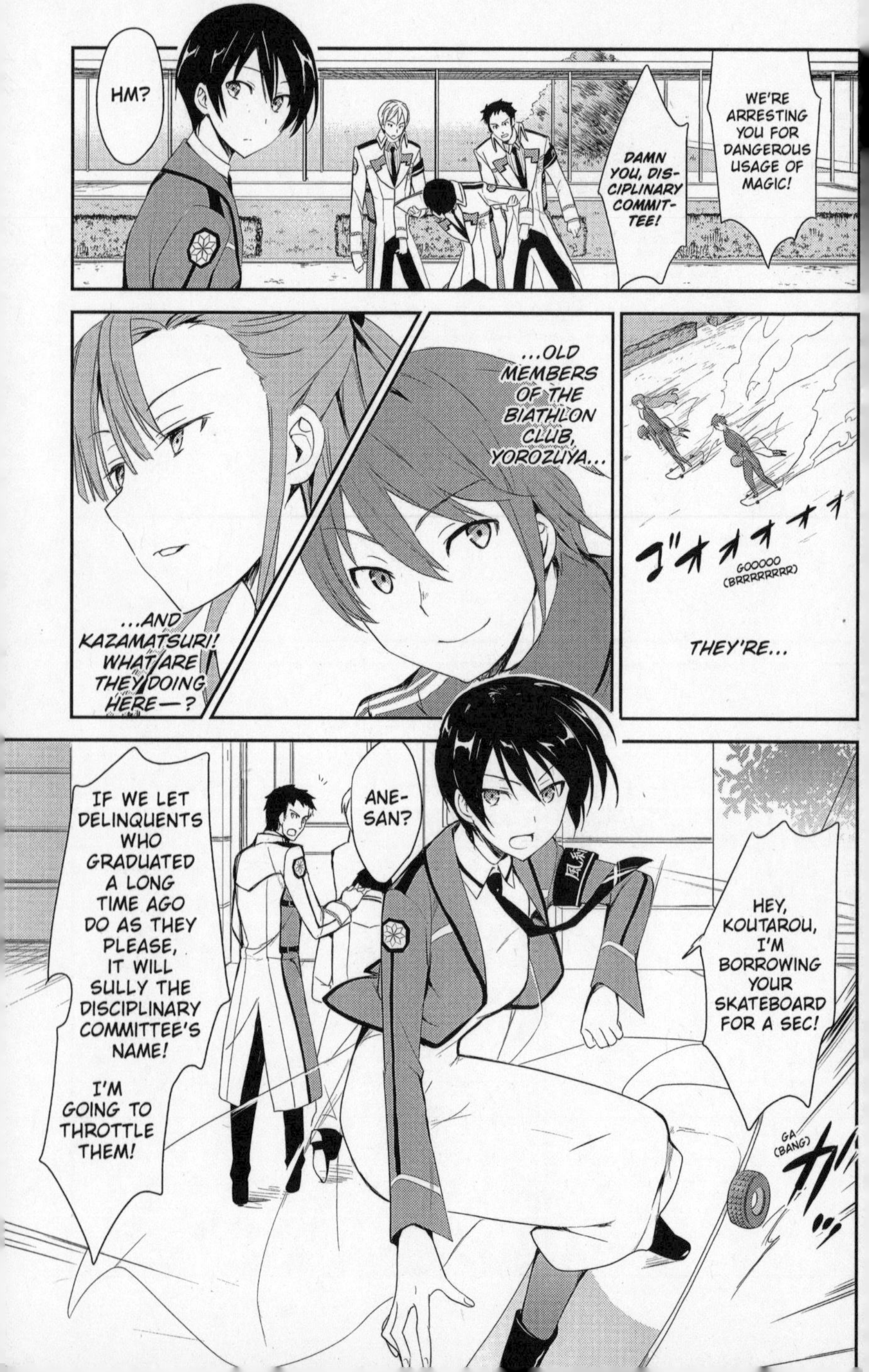
WE'RE ARRESTING YOU FOR DANGEROUS USAGE OF MAGIC!
DAMN YOU, DISCIPLINARY COMMITTEE!
HM?
ゴオオオオオ
GOOOOO (BRRRRRRRR)
THEY'RE...
...OLD MEMBERS OF THE BIATHLON CLUB, YOROZUYA...
...AND KAZAMATSURI! WHAT ARE THEY DOING HERE—?
HEY, KOUTAROU, I'M BORROWING YOUR SKATEBOARD FOR A SEC!
ガッ
GA (BANG)
ANE-SAN?
IF WE LET DELINQUENTS WHO GRADUATED A LONG TIME AGO DO AS THEY PLEASE, IT WILL SULLY THE DISCIPLINARY COMMITTEE'S NAME!
I'M GOING TO THROTTLE THEM!

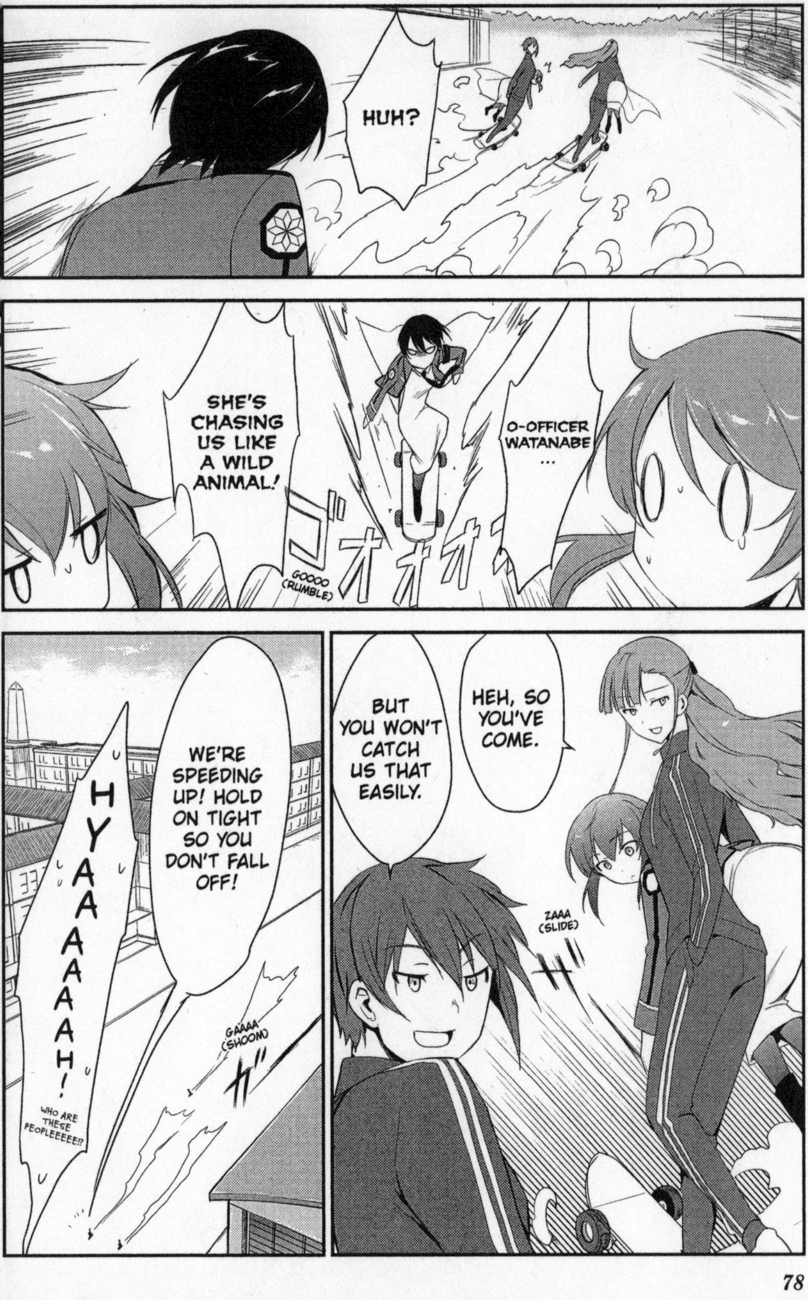
HUH?
O-OFFICER WATANABE ...
SHE'S CHASING US LIKE A WILD ANIMAL!
GOOOO (RUMBLE)
HEH, SO YOU'VE COME.
BUT YOU WON'T CATCH US THAT EASILY.
ZAAA (SLIDE)
WE'RE SPEEDING UP! HOLD ON TIGHT SO YOU DON'T FALL OFF!
HYAAAAAAAH!
WHO ARE THESE PEOPLEEEEE!?
GAAAA (SHOOM)

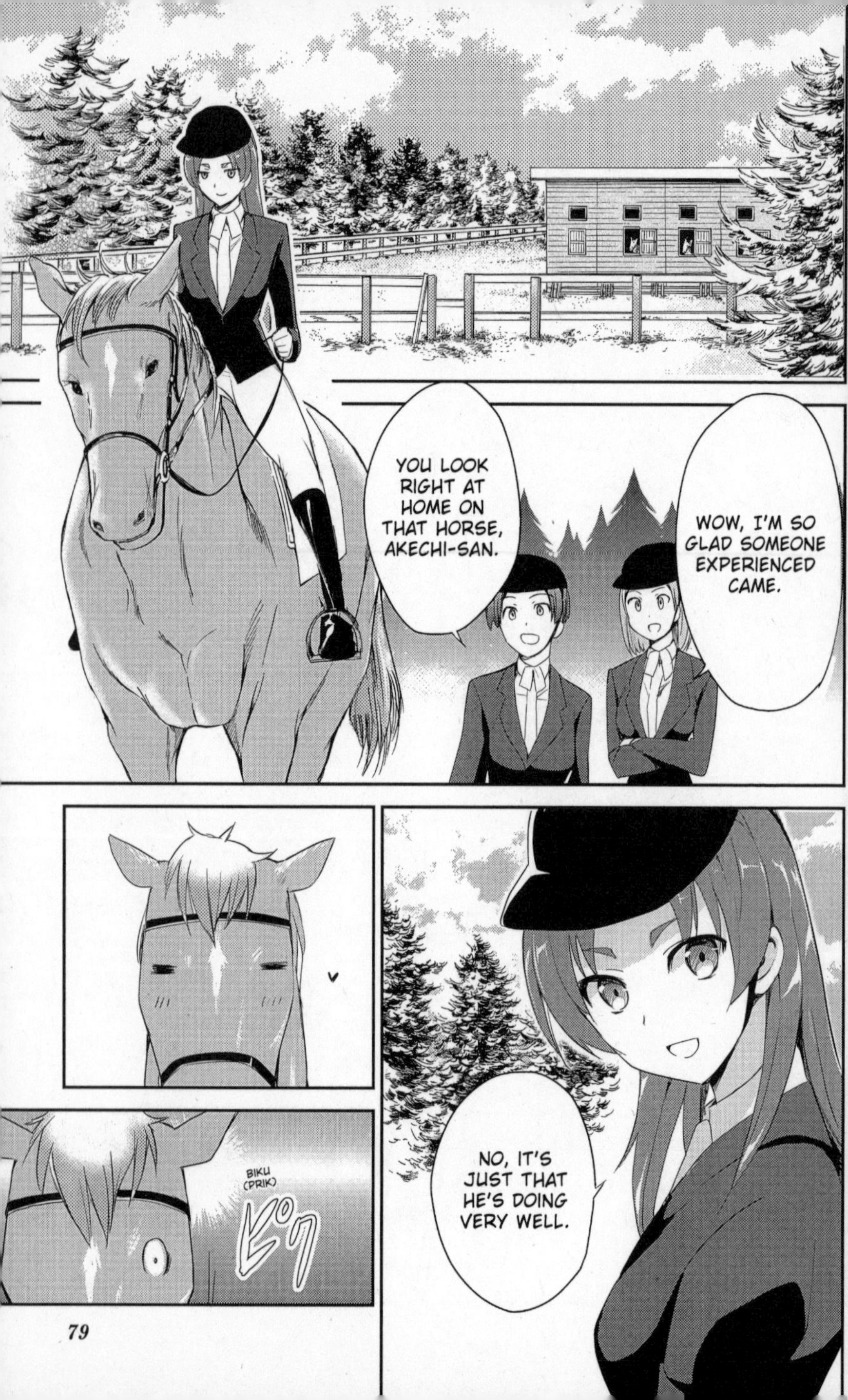
WOW, I'M SO GLAD SOMEONE EXPERIENCED CAME.
YOU LOOK RIGHT AT HOME ON THAT HORSE, AKECHI-SAN.
NO, IT'S JUST THAT HE'S DOING VERY WELL.
BIKU (PRIK)

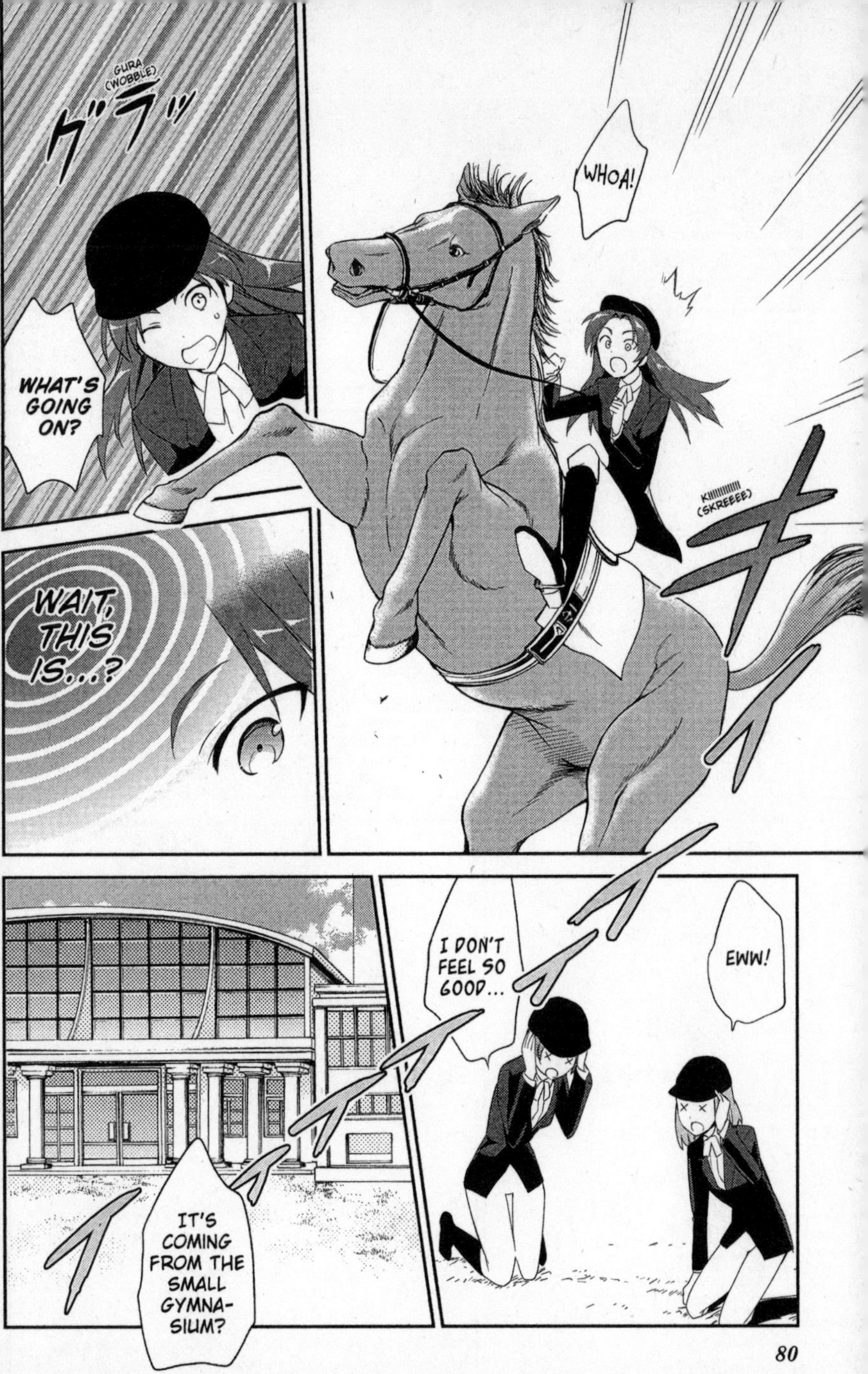
WHOA!
KIIIIIIIIIII (SKREEEE)
GURA (WOBBLE)
WHAT'S GOING ON?
WAIT, THIS IS...?
EWW!
I DON'T FEEL SO GOOD...
IT'S COMING FROM THE SMALL GYMNASIUM?

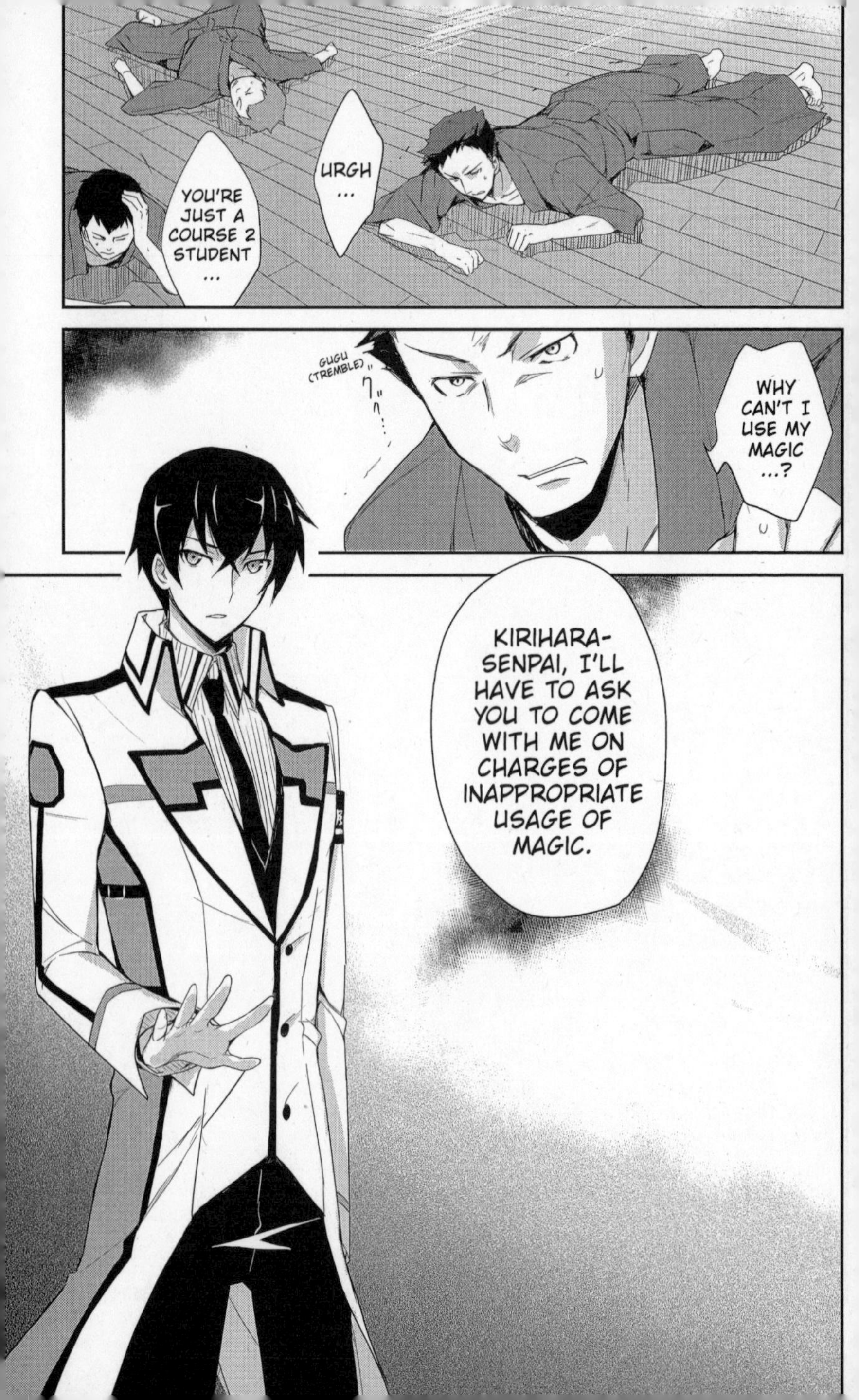
URGH ...
YOU'RE JUST A COURSE 2 STUDENT ...
WHY CAN'T I USE MY MAGIC ...?
GUGU (TREMBLE)
KIRIHARA-SENPAI, I'LL HAVE TO ASK YOU TO COME WITH ME ON CHARGES OF INAPPROPRIATE USAGE OF MAGIC.

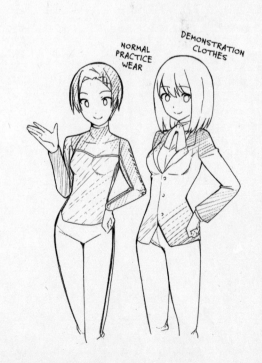

NORMAL
PRACTICE
WEAR

DEMONSTRATION
CLOTHES

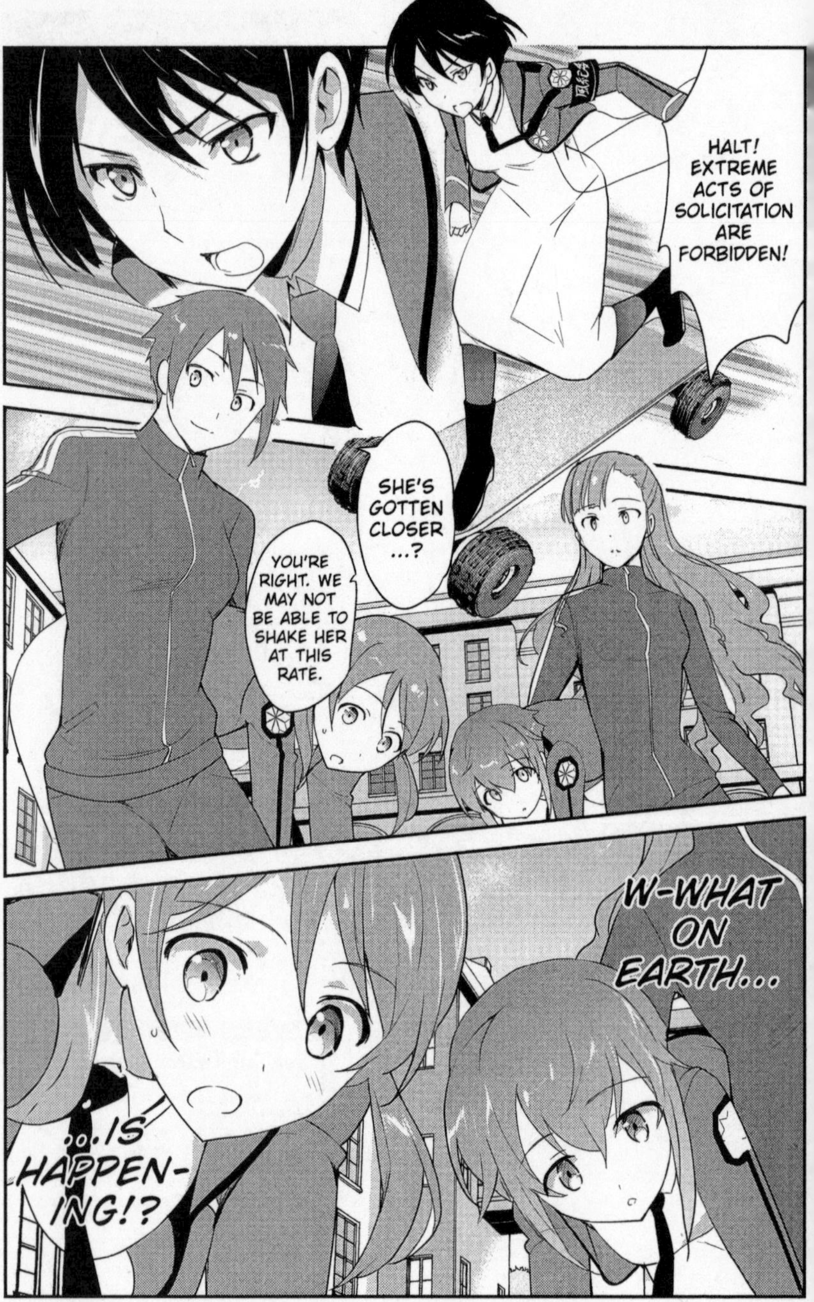
HALT! EXTREME ACTS OF SOLICITATION ARE FORBIDDEN!
SHE'S GOTTEN CLOSER ...?
YOU'RE RIGHT. WE MAY NOT BE ABLE TO SHAKE HER AT THIS RATE.
W-WHAT ON EARTH...
...IS HAPPEN-ING!?

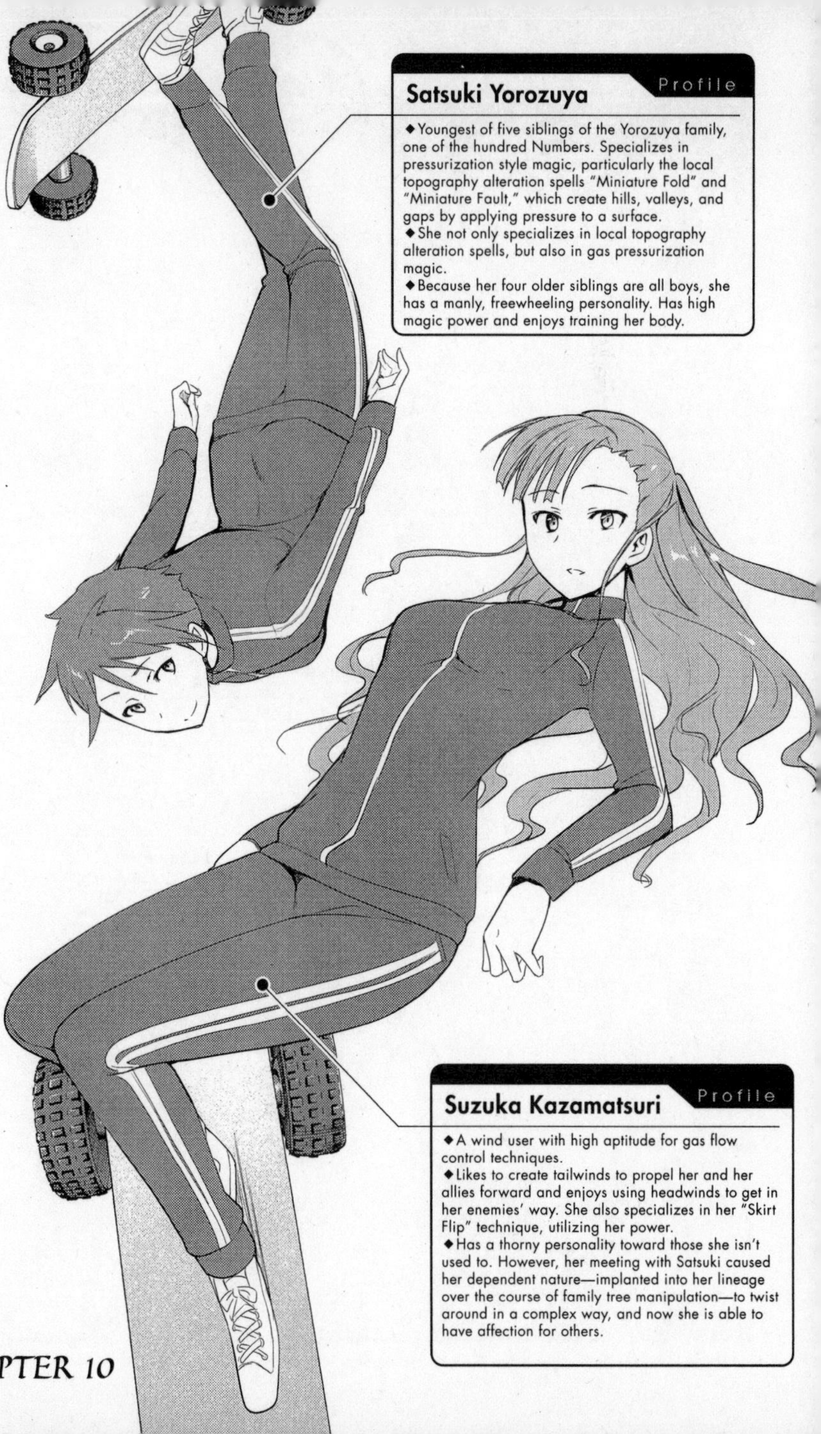

Satsuki Yorozuya

Profile

◆Youngest of five siblings of the Yorozuya family, one of the hundred Numbers. Specializes in pressurization style magic, particularly the local topography alteration spells "Miniature Fold" and "Miniature Fault," which create hills, valleys, and gaps by applying pressure to a surface.
◆She not only specializes in local topography alteration spells, but also in gas pressurization magic.
◆Because her four older siblings are all boys, she has a manly, freewheeling personality. Has high magic power and enjoys training her body.

Suzuka Kazamatsuri

Profile

◆A wind user with high aptitude for gas flow control techniques.
◆Likes to create tailwinds to propel her and her allies forward and enjoys using headwinds to get in her enemies' way. She also specializes in her "Skirt Flip" technique, utilizing her power.
◆Has a thorny personality toward those she isn't used to. However, her meeting with Satsuki caused her dependent nature—implanted into her lineage over the course of family tree manipulation—to twist around in a complex way, and now she is able to have affection for others.

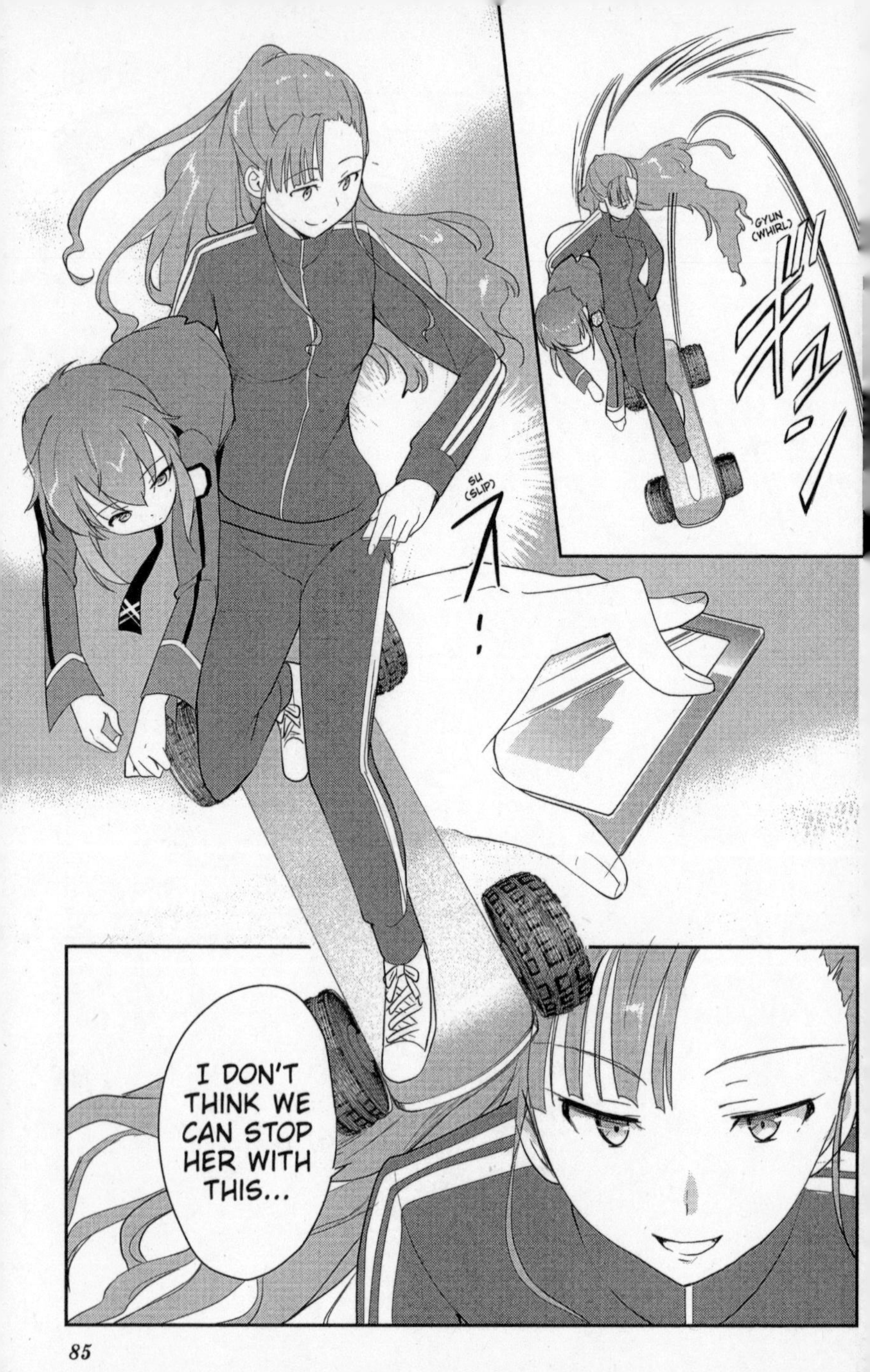
GYUN (WHIRL)
ギュン
SU (SLIP)
I DON'T THINK WE CAN STOP HER WITH THIS...

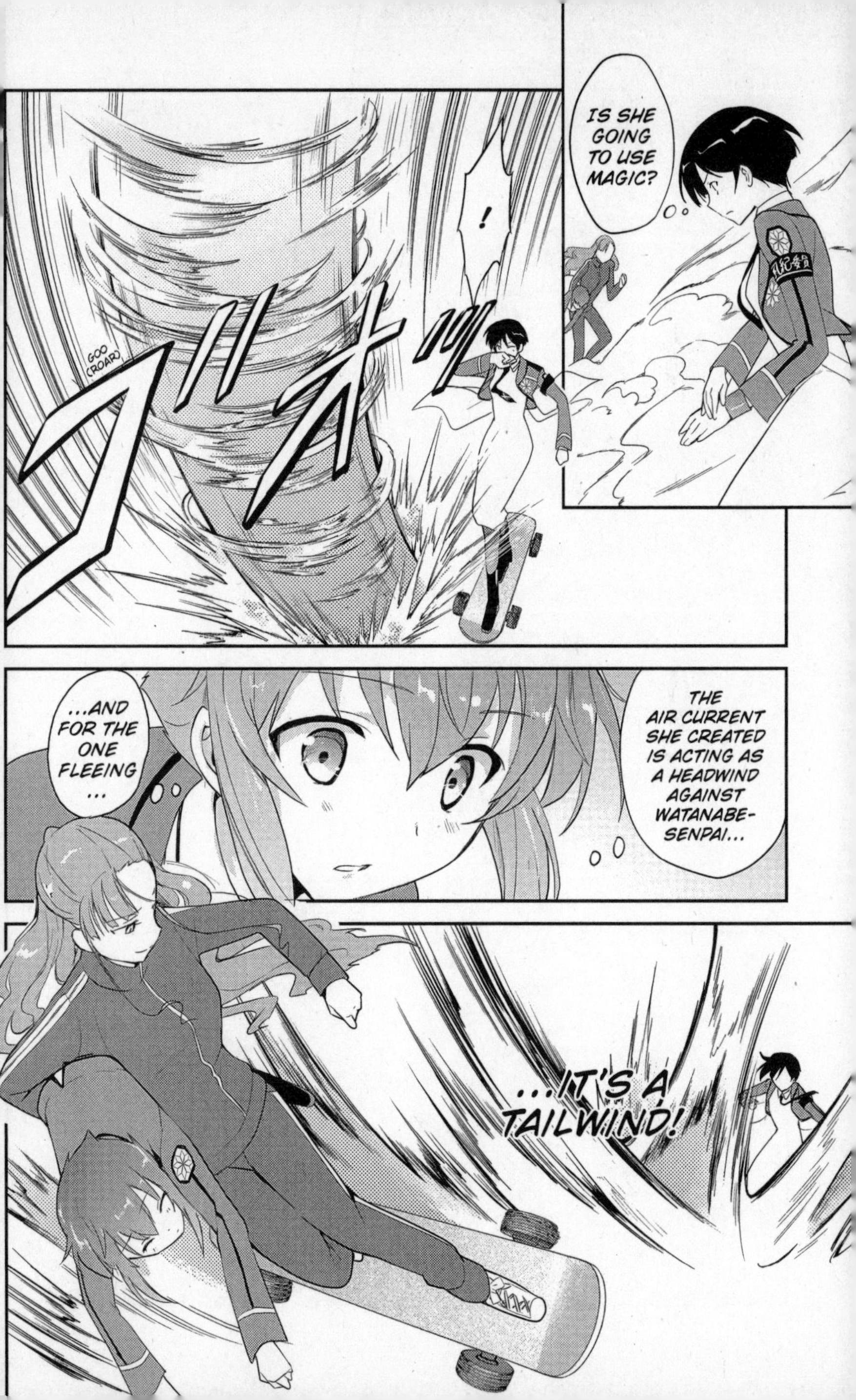
IS SHE GOING TO USE MAGIC?
!
GOO (ROAR)
グオッ
THE AIR CURRENT SHE CREATED IS ACTING AS A HEADWIND AGAINST WATANABE-SENPAI...
...AND FOR THE ONE FLEEING...
...IT'S A TAILWIND!

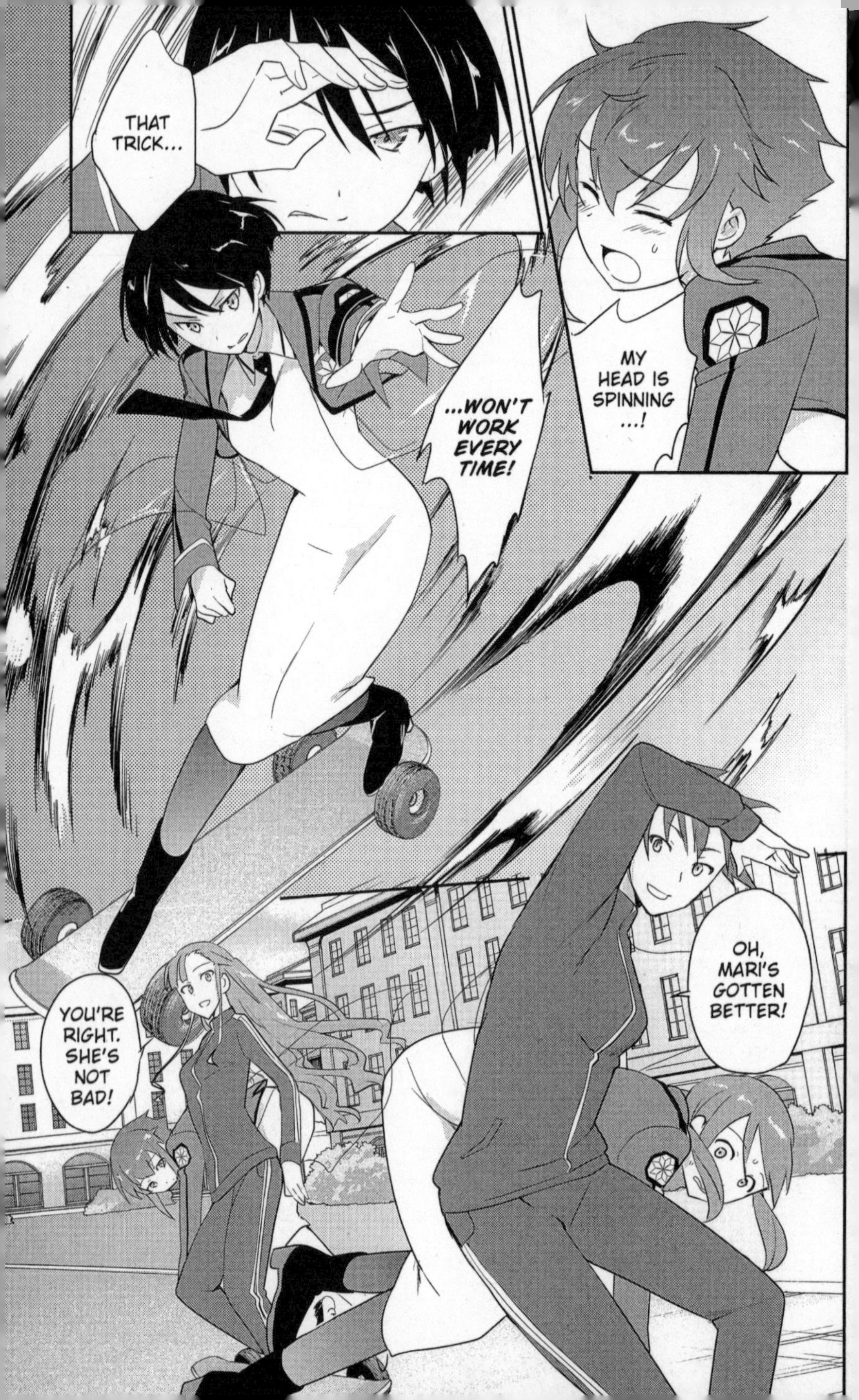
MY HEAD IS SPINNING ...!
THAT TRICK...
...WON'T WORK EVERY TIME!
OH, MARI'S GOTTEN BETTER!
YOU'RE RIGHT. SHE'S NOT BAD!

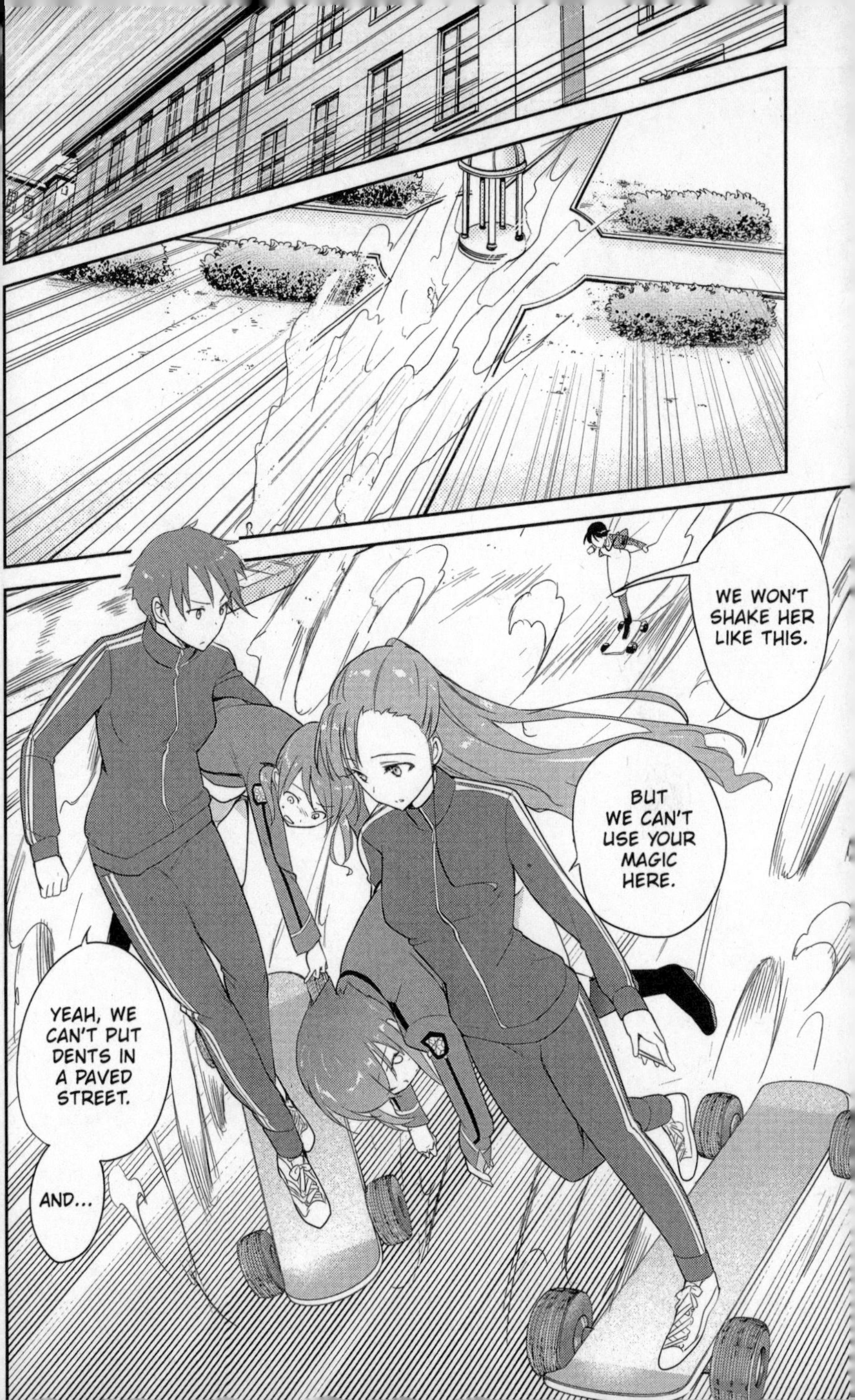
WE WON'T SHAKE HER LIKE THIS.
BUT WE CAN'T USE YOUR MAGIC HERE.
YEAH, WE CAN'T PUT DENTS IN A PAVED STREET.
AND...

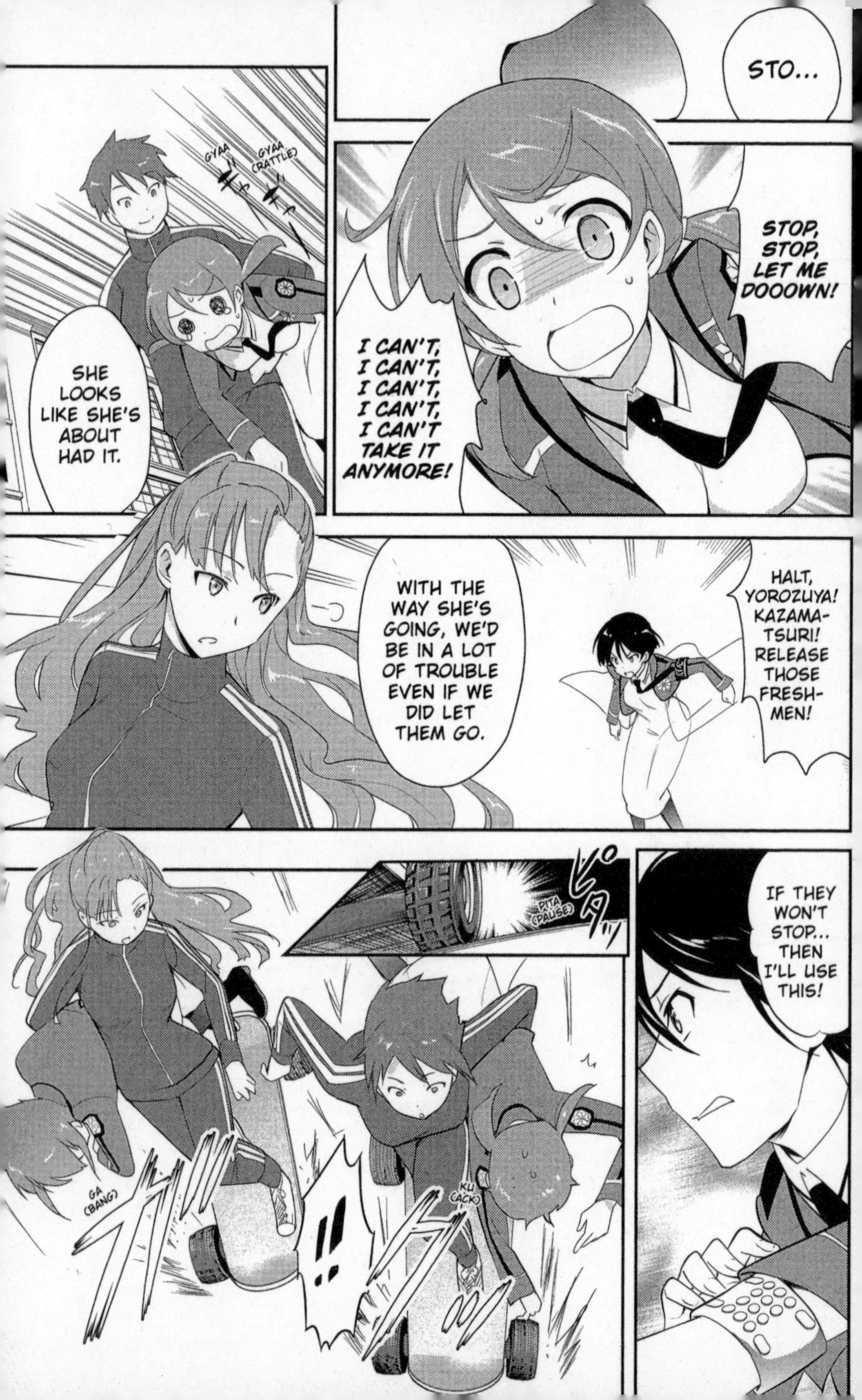
STO...
STOP, STOP, LET ME DOOOWN!
I CAN'T, I CAN'T, I CAN'T, I CAN'T, I CAN'T TAKE IT ANYMORE!
GYAA (RATTLE)
GYAA
SHE LOOKS LIKE SHE'S ABOUT HAD IT.
HALT, YOROZUYA! KAZAMA-TSURI! RELEASE THOSE FRESH-MEN!
WITH THE WAY SHE'S GOING, WE'D BE IN A LOT OF TROUBLE EVEN IF WE DID LET THEM GO.
IF THEY WON'T STOP... THEN I'LL USE THIS!
PITA (PAUSE)
KU (ACK)
!!
GA (BANG)

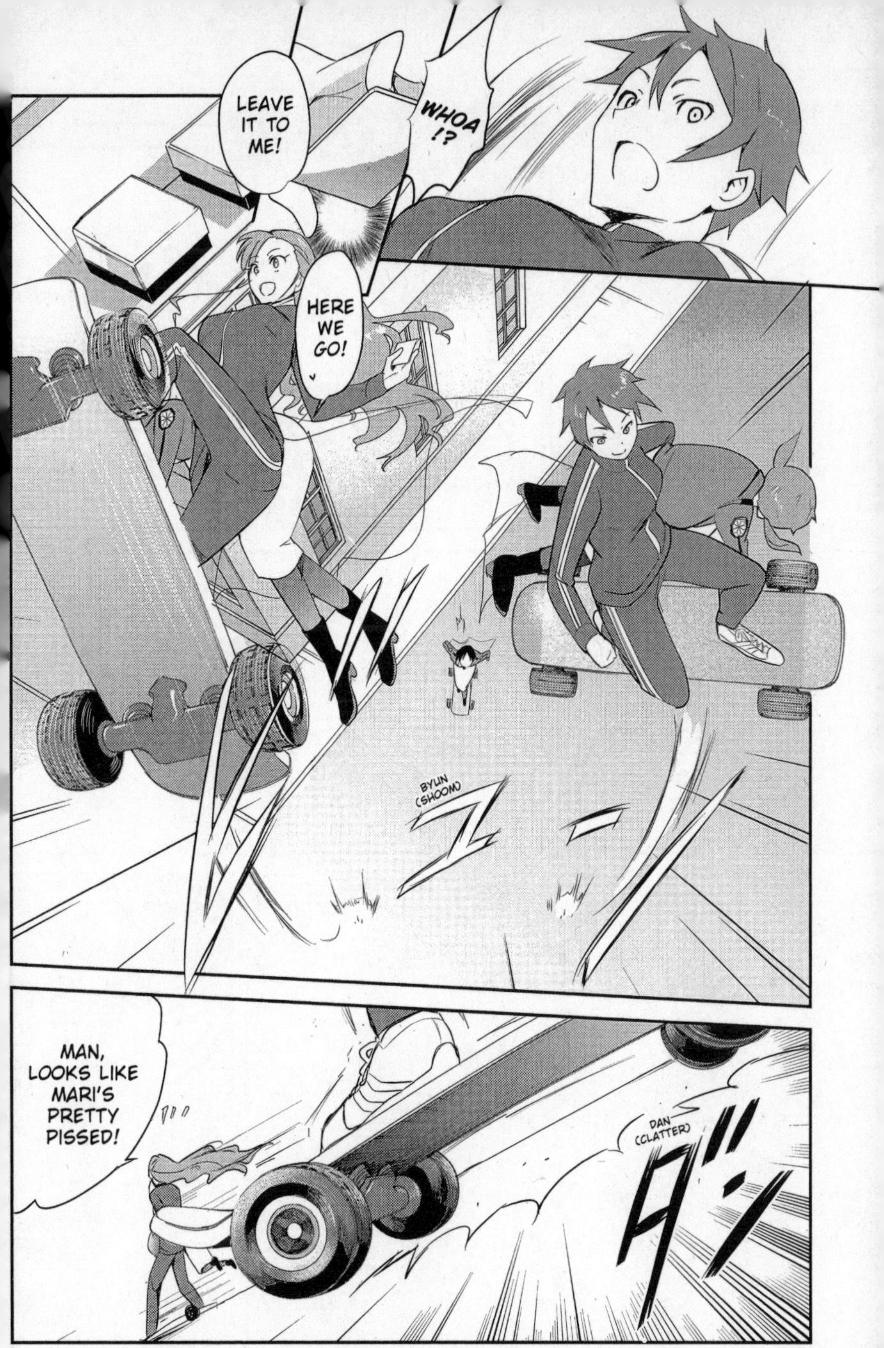
WHOA !?
LEAVE IT TO ME!
HERE WE GO!
BYUN (SHOOM)
DAN (CLATTER)
MAN, LOOKS LIKE MARI'S PRETTY PISSED!

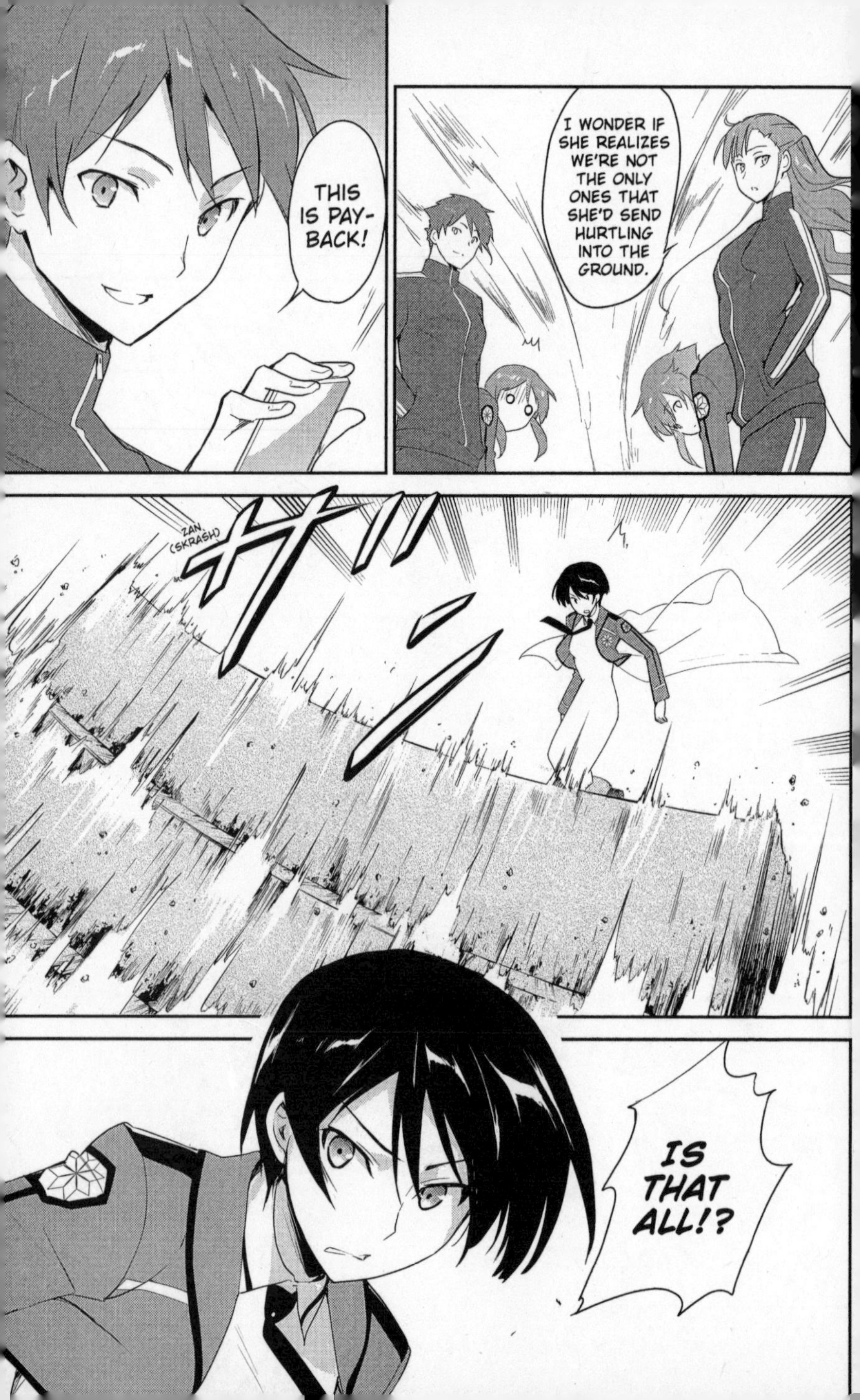
I WONDER IF SHE REALIZES WE'RE NOT THE ONLY ONES THAT SHE'D SEND HURTLING INTO THE GROUND.
THIS IS PAY-BACK!
ZAN (SKRASH)
IS THAT ALL!?

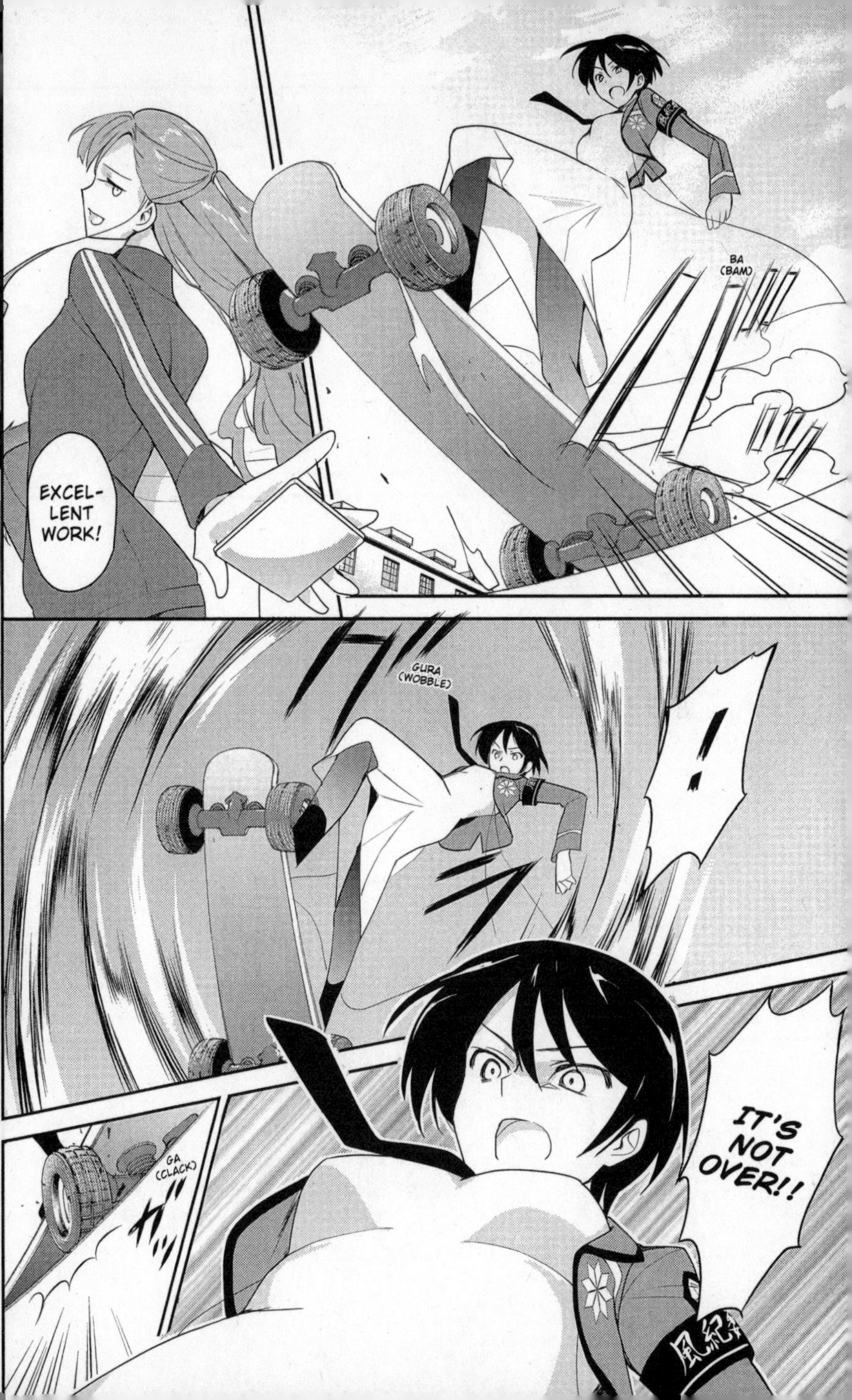
BA (BAM)
EXCEL-LENT WORK!
GURA (WOBBLE)
!
IT'S NOT OVER!!
GA (CLACK)

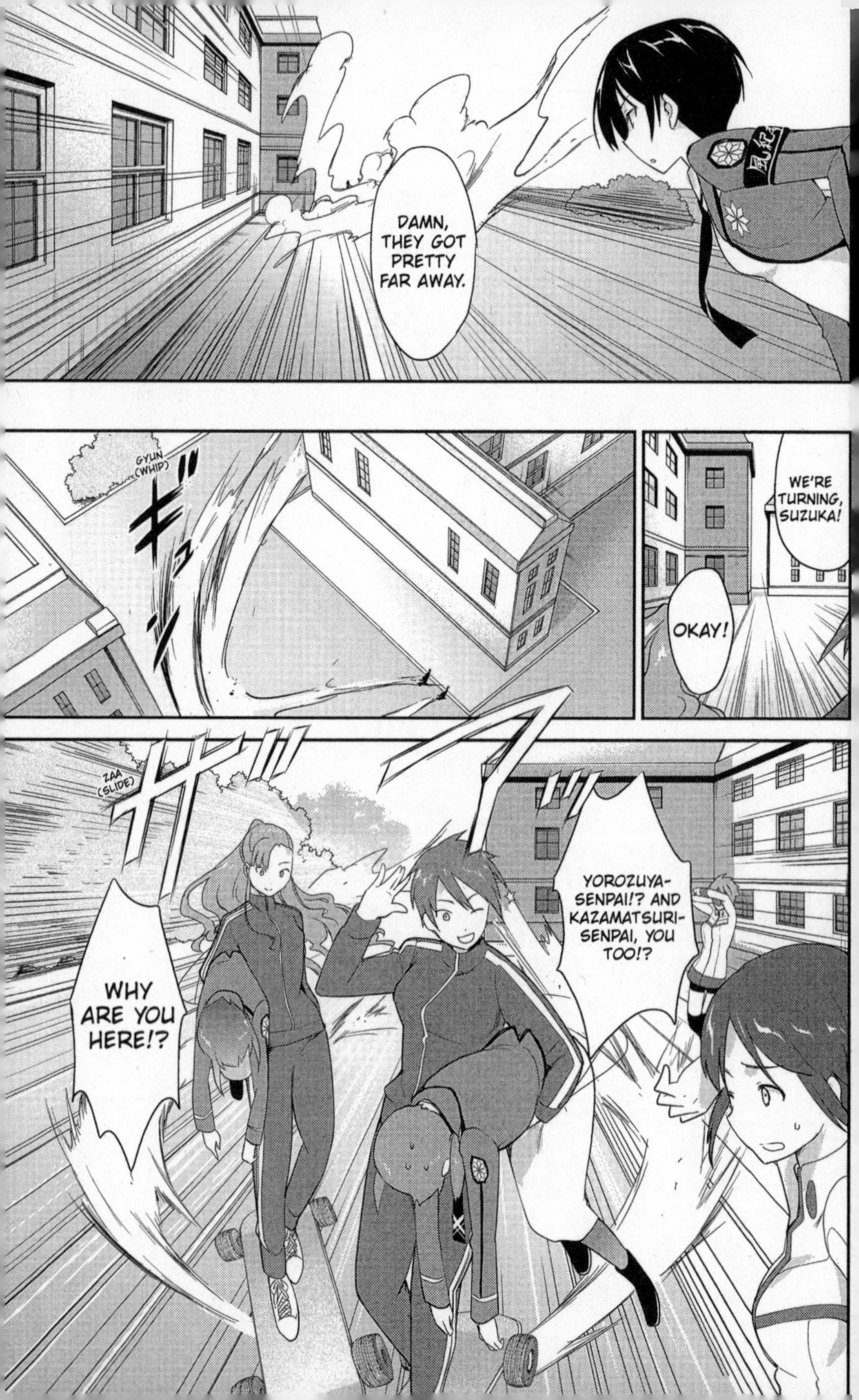
DAMN, THEY GOT PRETTY FAR AWAY.
WE'RE TURNING, SUZUKA!
OKAY!
GYUN (WHIP)
YOROZUYA-SENPAI!? AND KAZAMATSURI-SENPAI, YOU TOO!?
ZAA (SLIDE)
WHY ARE YOU HERE!?

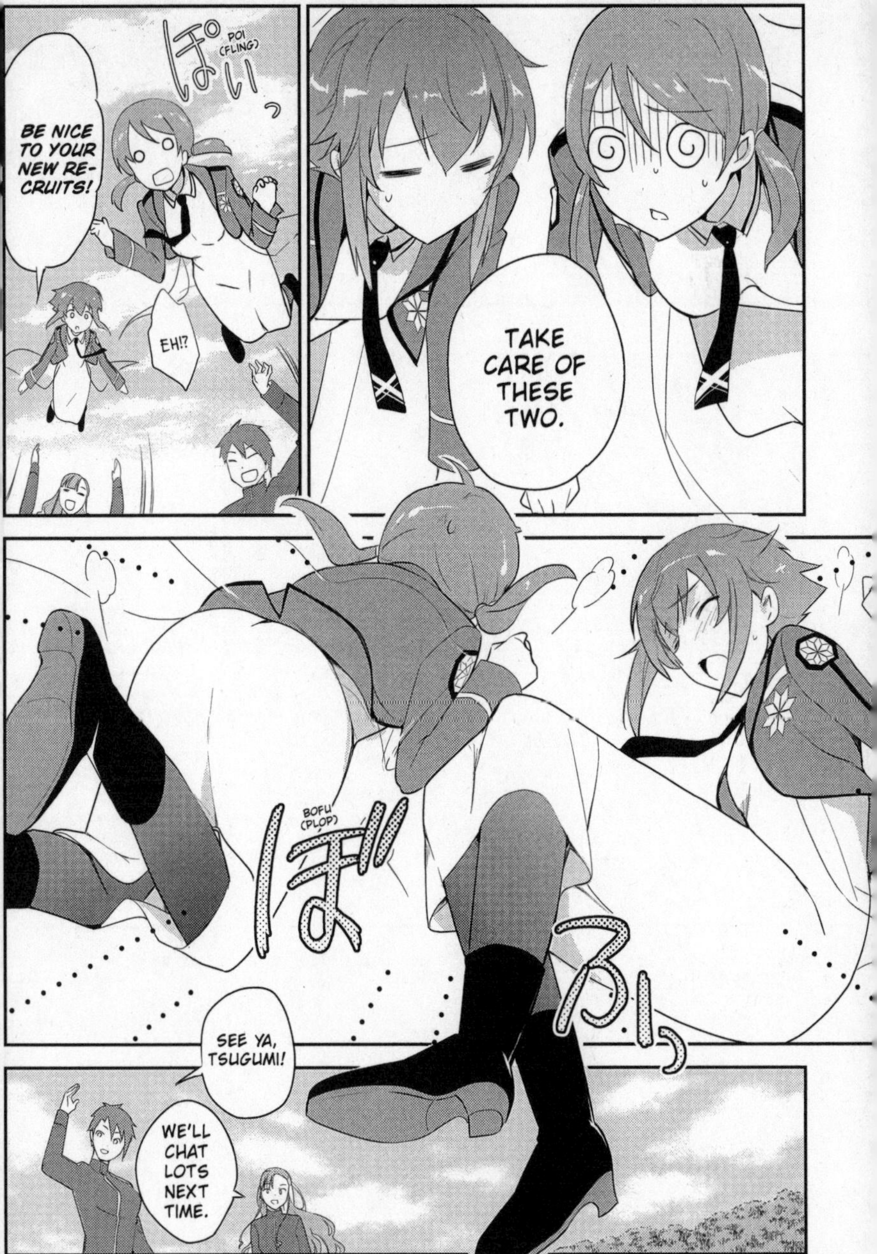
TAKE CARE OF THESE TWO.
ぽいっ
POI (FLING)
BE NICE TO YOUR NEW RE-CRUITS!
EH!?
ぼふっ
BOFU (PLOP)
SEE YA, TSUGUMI!
WE'LL CHAT LOTS NEXT TIME.

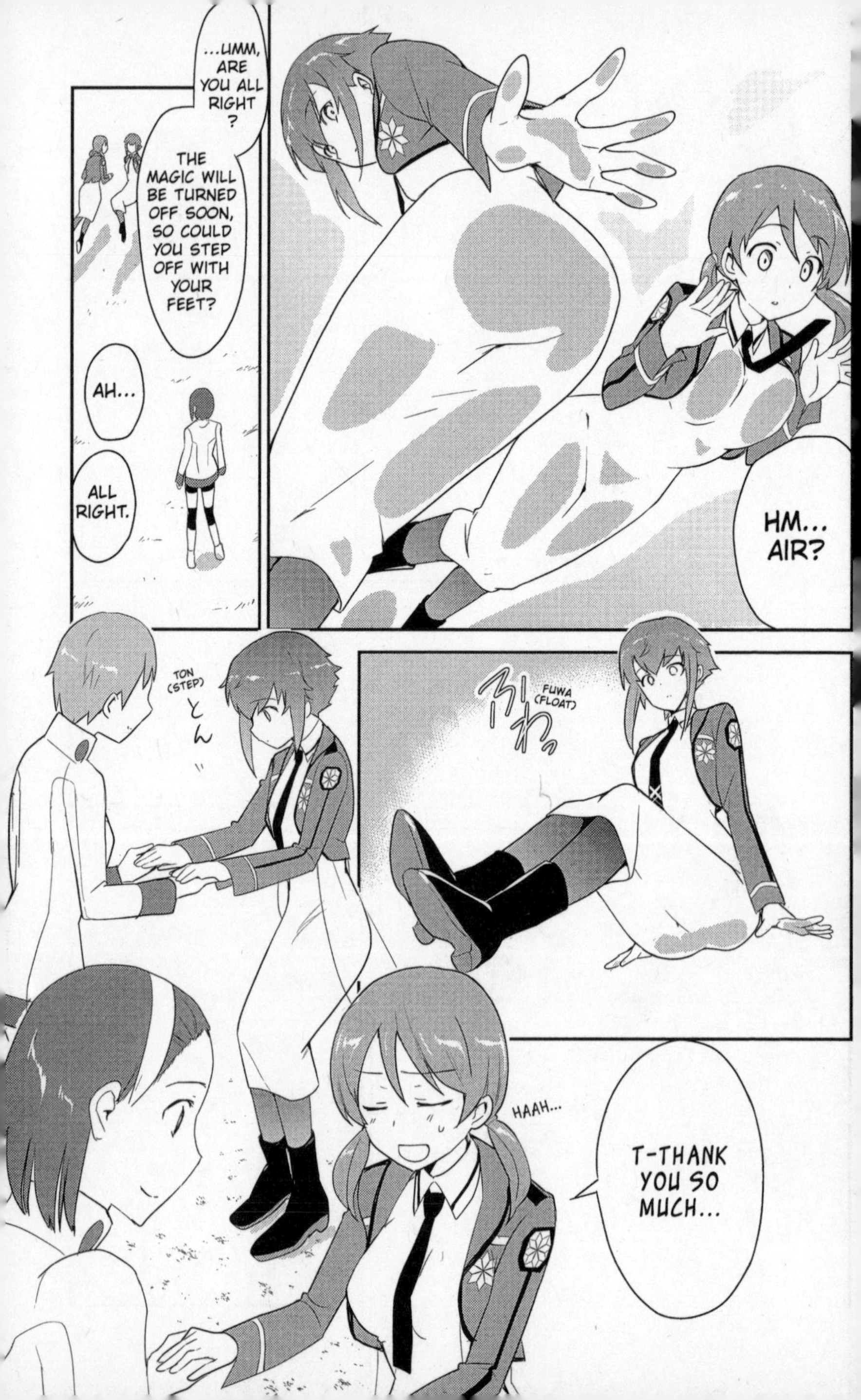
HM... AIR?
...UMM, ARE YOU ALL RIGHT?
THE MAGIC WILL BE TURNED OFF SOON, SO COULD YOU STEP OFF WITH YOUR FEET?
AH...
ALL RIGHT.
FUWA (FLOAT)
ふわっ
TON (STEP)
とん
T-THANK YOU SO MUCH...
HAAH...

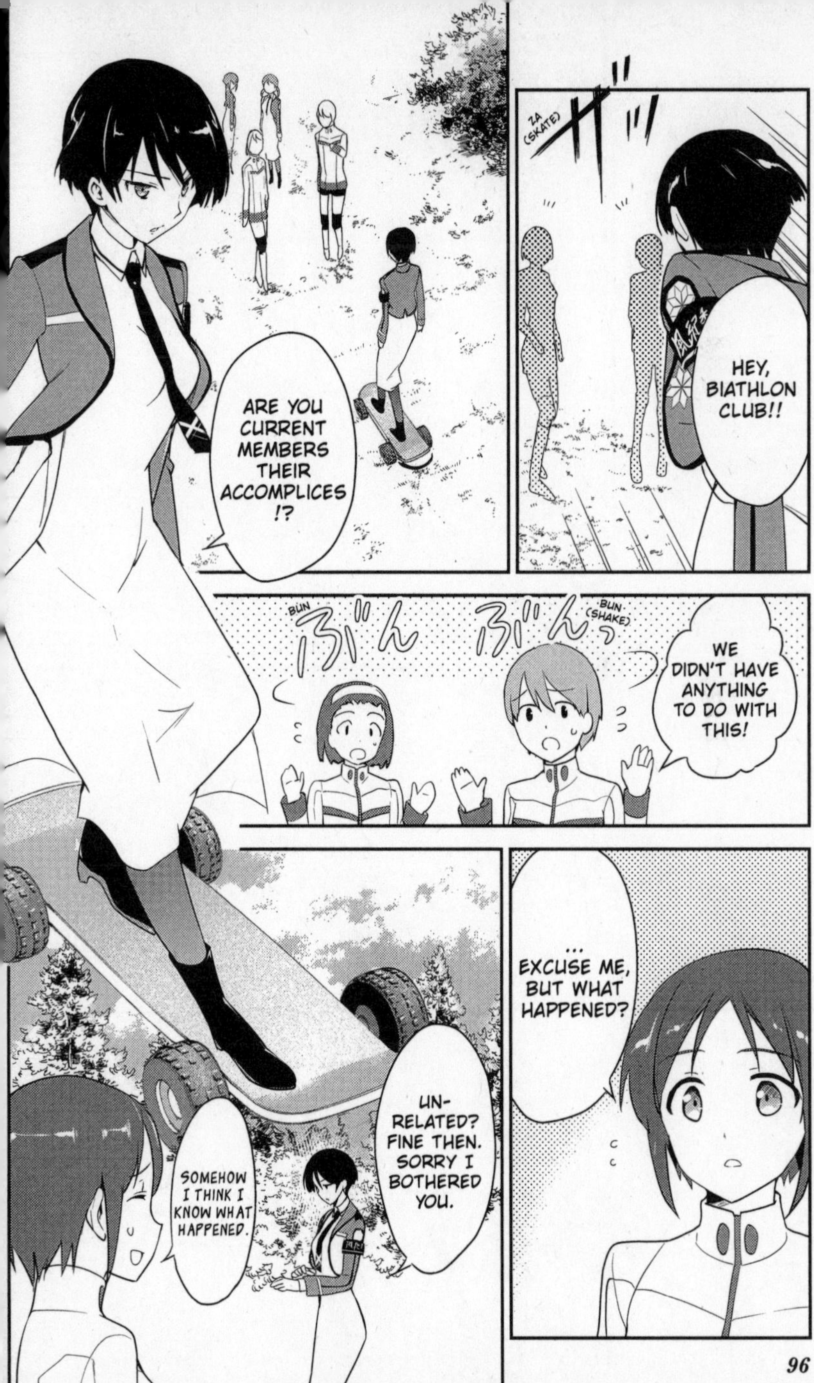

ZA (SKATE)
HEY, BIATHLON CLUB!!
ARE YOU CURRENT MEMBERS THEIR ACCOMPLICES!?
BUN
BUN (SHAKE)
WE DIDN'T HAVE ANYTHING TO DO WITH THIS!
... EXCUSE ME, BUT WHAT HAPPENED?
UN-RELATED? FINE THEN. SORRY I BOTHERED YOU.
SOMEHOW I THINK I KNOW WHAT HAPPENED.

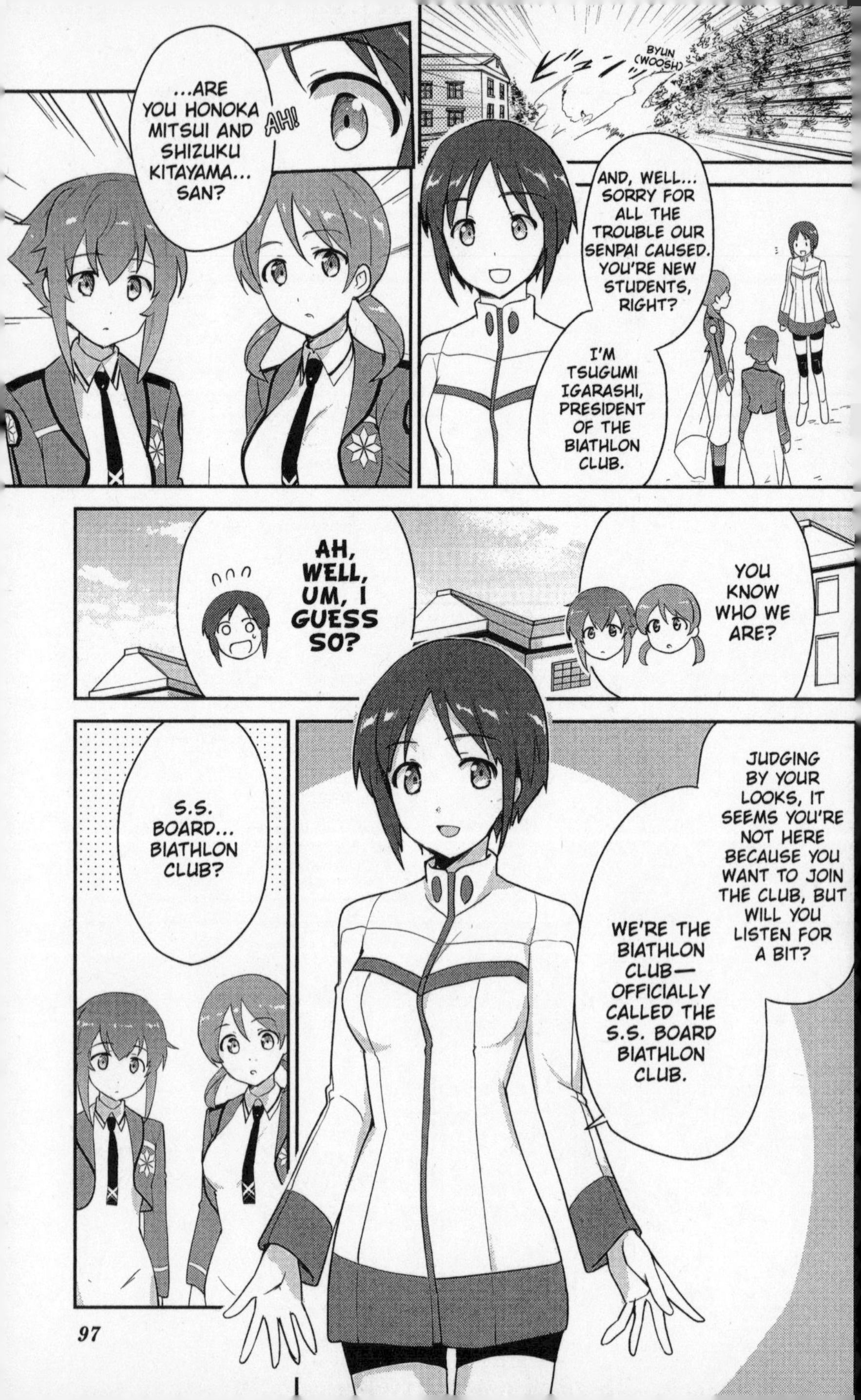
BYUN (WOOSH)
AND, WELL... SORRY FOR ALL THE TROUBLE OUR SENPAI CAUSED. YOU'RE NEW STUDENTS, RIGHT?
I'M TSUGUMI IGARASHI, PRESIDENT OF THE BIATHLON CLUB.
...ARE YOU HONOKA MITSUI AND SHIZUKU KITAYAMA... SAN?
AH!
YOU KNOW WHO WE ARE?
AH, WELL, UM, I GUESS SO?
JUDGING BY YOUR LOOKS, IT SEEMS YOU'RE NOT HERE BECAUSE YOU WANT TO JOIN THE CLUB, BUT WILL YOU LISTEN FOR A BIT?
WE'RE THE BIATHLON CLUB—OFFICIALLY CALLED THE S.S. BOARD BIATHLON CLUB.
S.S. BOARD... BIATHLON CLUB?

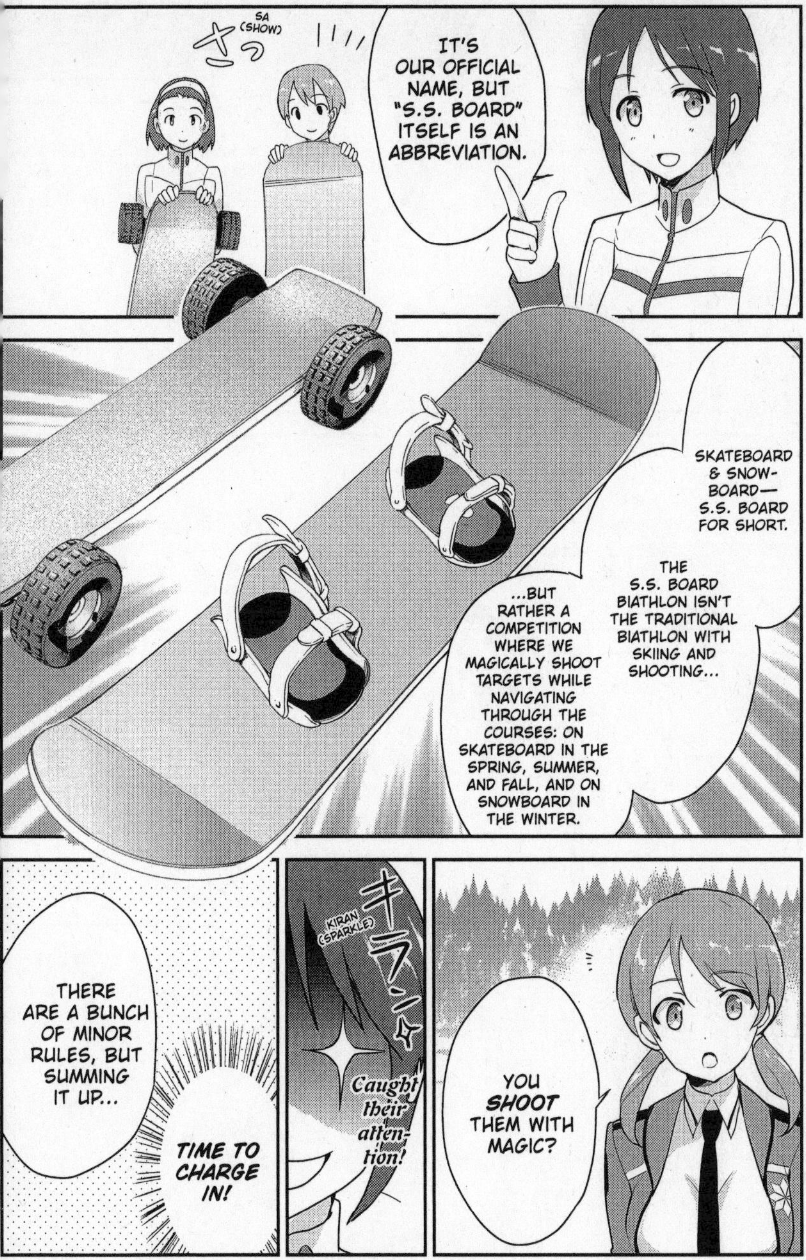
IT'S OUR OFFICIAL NAME, BUT "S.S. BOARD" ITSELF IS AN ABBREVIATION.
さっ
SA (SHOW)
SKATEBOARD & SNOW-BOARD—S.S. BOARD FOR SHORT.
THE S.S. BOARD BIATHLON ISN'T THE TRADITIONAL BIATHLON WITH SKIING AND SHOOTING...
...BUT RATHER A COMPETITION WHERE WE MAGICALLY SHOOT TARGETS WHILE NAVIGATING THROUGH THE COURSES: ON SKATEBOARD IN THE SPRING, SUMMER, AND FALL, AND ON SNOWBOARD IN THE WINTER.
YOU *SHOOT* THEM WITH MAGIC?
キラン
KIRAN (SPARKLE)
Caught their attention!
THERE ARE A BUNCH OF MINOR RULES, BUT SUMMING IT UP...
TIME TO CHARGE IN!

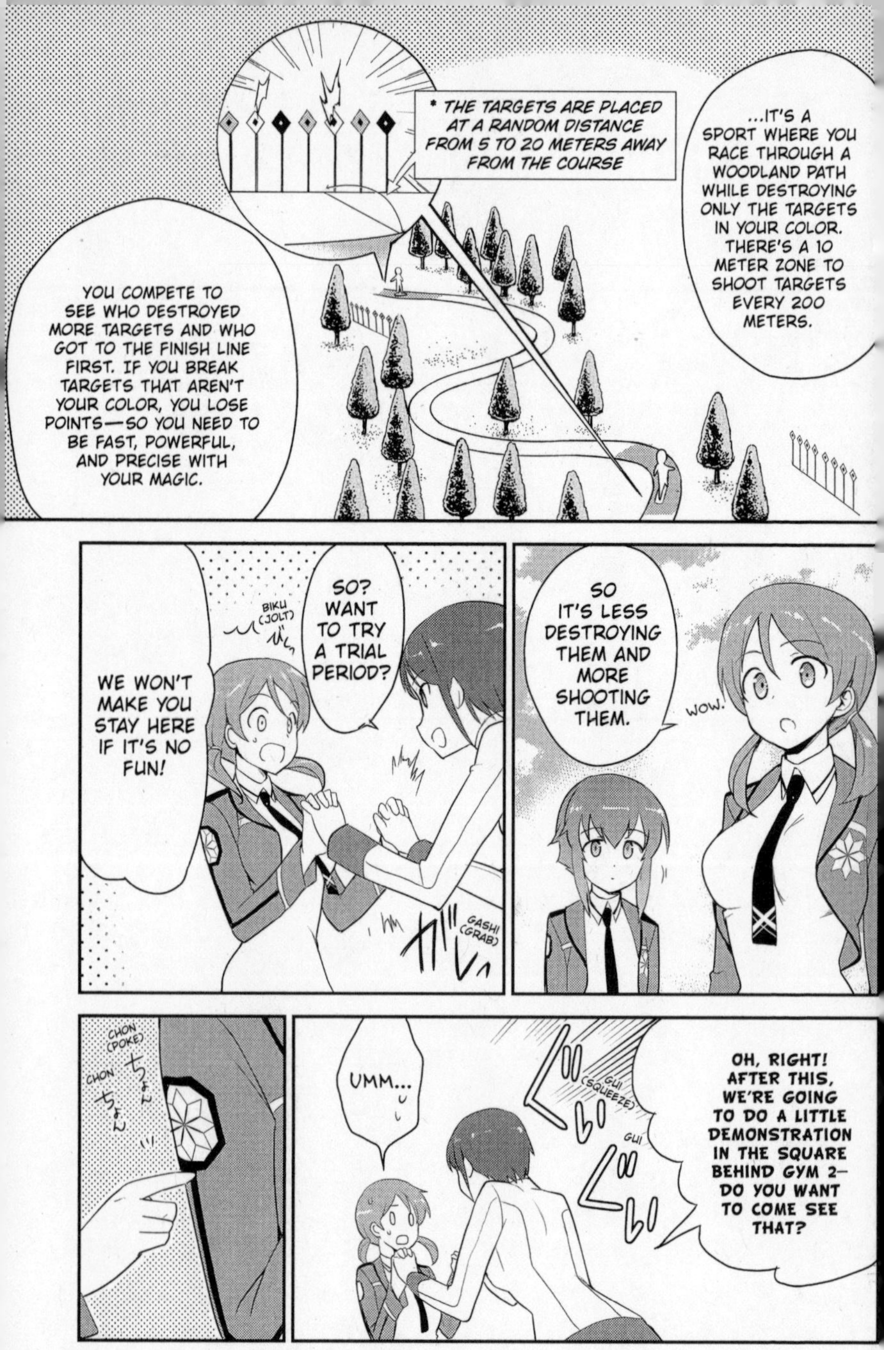
...IT'S A SPORT WHERE YOU RACE THROUGH A WOODLAND PATH WHILE DESTROYING ONLY THE TARGETS IN YOUR COLOR. THERE'S A 10 METER ZONE TO SHOOT TARGETS EVERY 200 METERS.
* THE TARGETS ARE PLACED AT A RANDOM DISTANCE FROM 5 TO 20 METERS AWAY FROM THE COURSE
YOU COMPETE TO SEE WHO DESTROYED MORE TARGETS AND WHO GOT TO THE FINISH LINE FIRST. IF YOU BREAK TARGETS THAT AREN'T YOUR COLOR, YOU LOSE POINTS—SO YOU NEED TO BE FAST, POWERFUL, AND PRECISE WITH YOUR MAGIC.
SO IT'S LESS DESTROYING THEM AND MORE SHOOTING THEM.
WOW.
SO? WANT TO TRY A TRIAL PERIOD?
BIKU (JOLT)
WE WON'T MAKE YOU STAY HERE IF IT'S NO FUN!
GASHI (GRAB)
OH, RIGHT! AFTER THIS, WE'RE GOING TO DO A LITTLE DEMONSTRATION IN THE SQUARE BEHIND GYM 2—DO YOU WANT TO COME SEE THAT?
GUI (SQUEEZE)
GUI
UMM...
CHON (POKE)
CHON

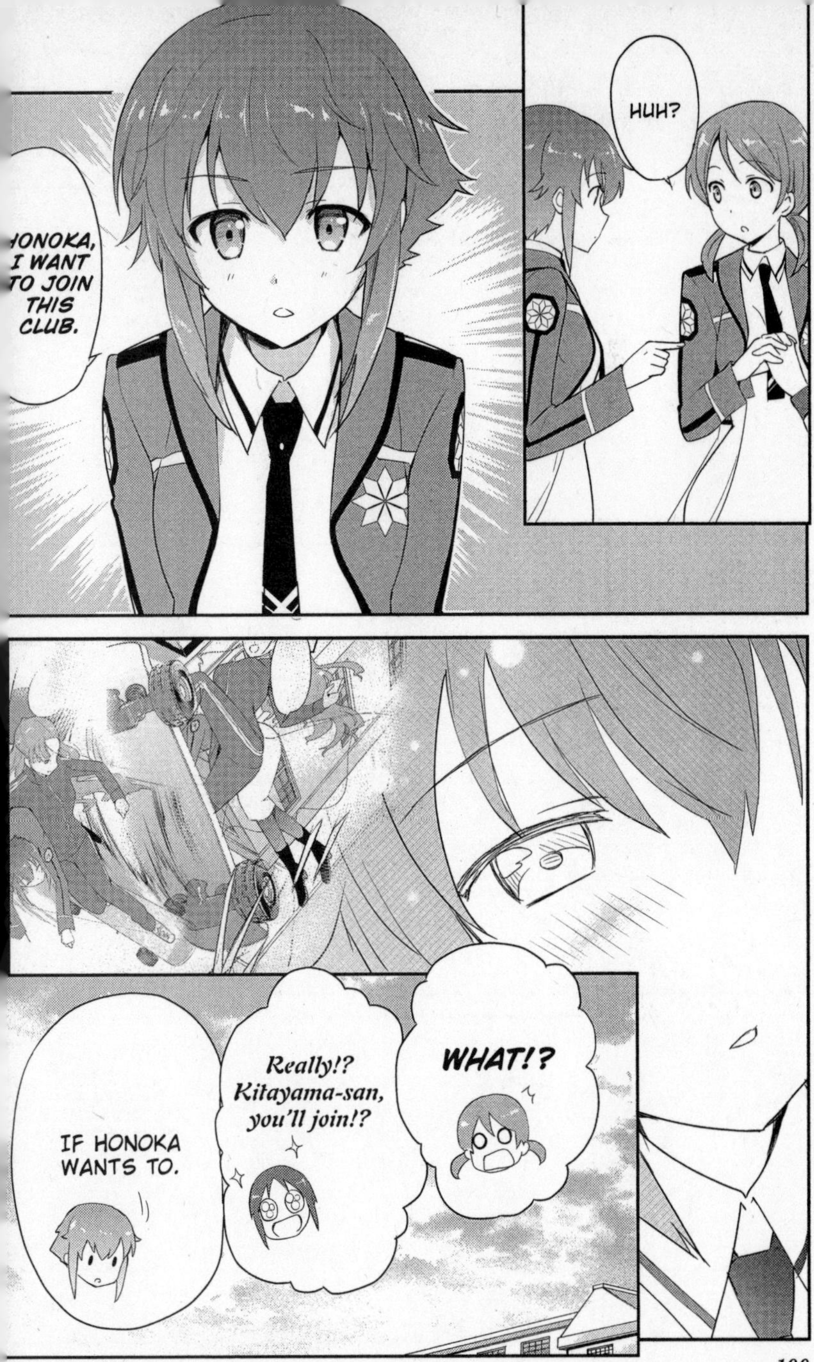
HUH?
HONOKA, I WANT TO JOIN THIS CLUB.
WHAT!?
Really!? Kitayama-san, you'll join!?
IF HONOKA WANTS TO.

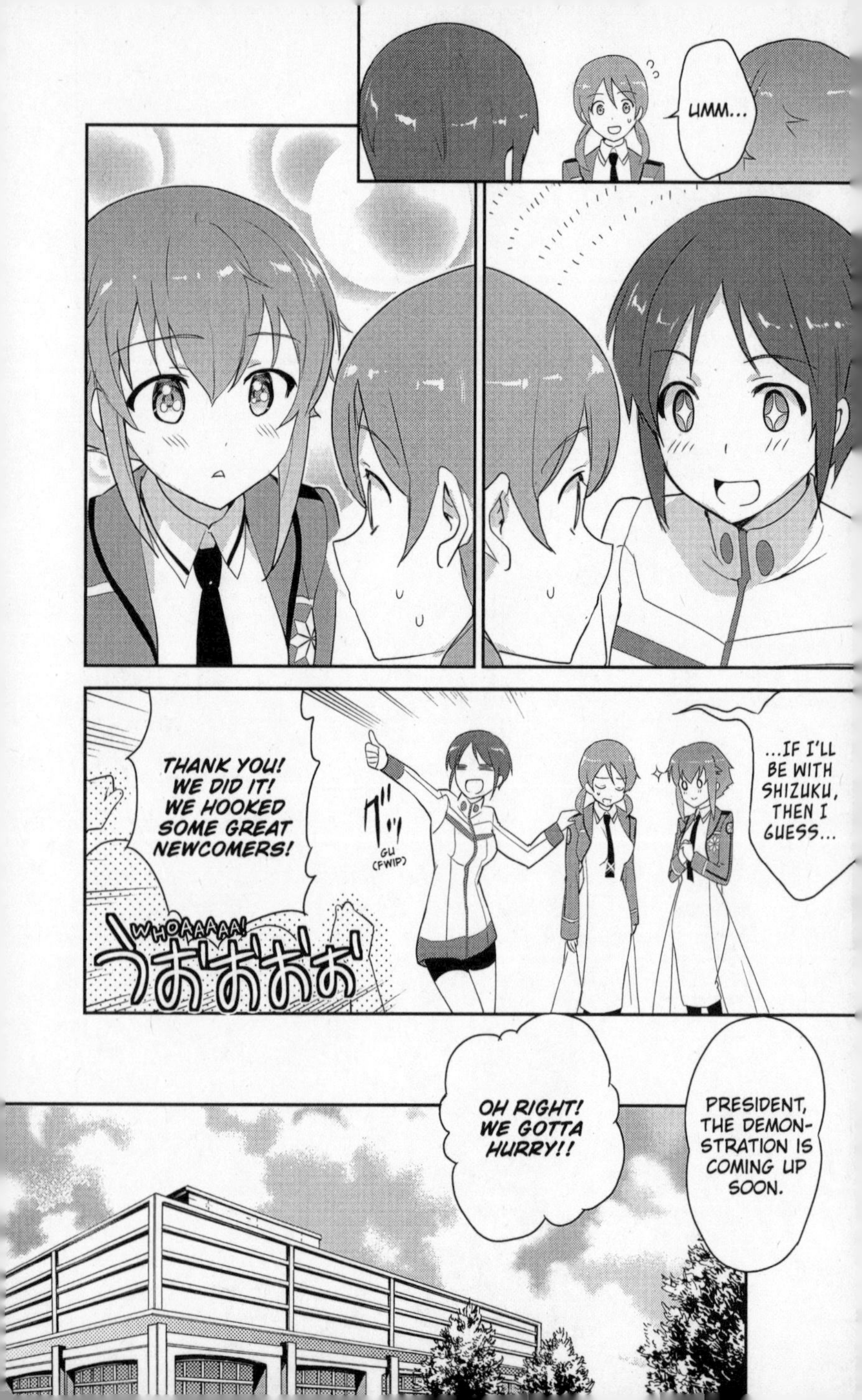
UMM...
...IF I'LL BE WITH SHIZUKU, THEN I GUESS...
THANK YOU! WE DID IT! WE HOOKED SOME GREAT NEWCOMERS!
GU (FWIP)
うおおおお
WHOAAAAA!
PRESIDENT, THE DEMON-STRATION IS COMING UP SOON.
OH RIGHT! WE GOTTA HURRY!!

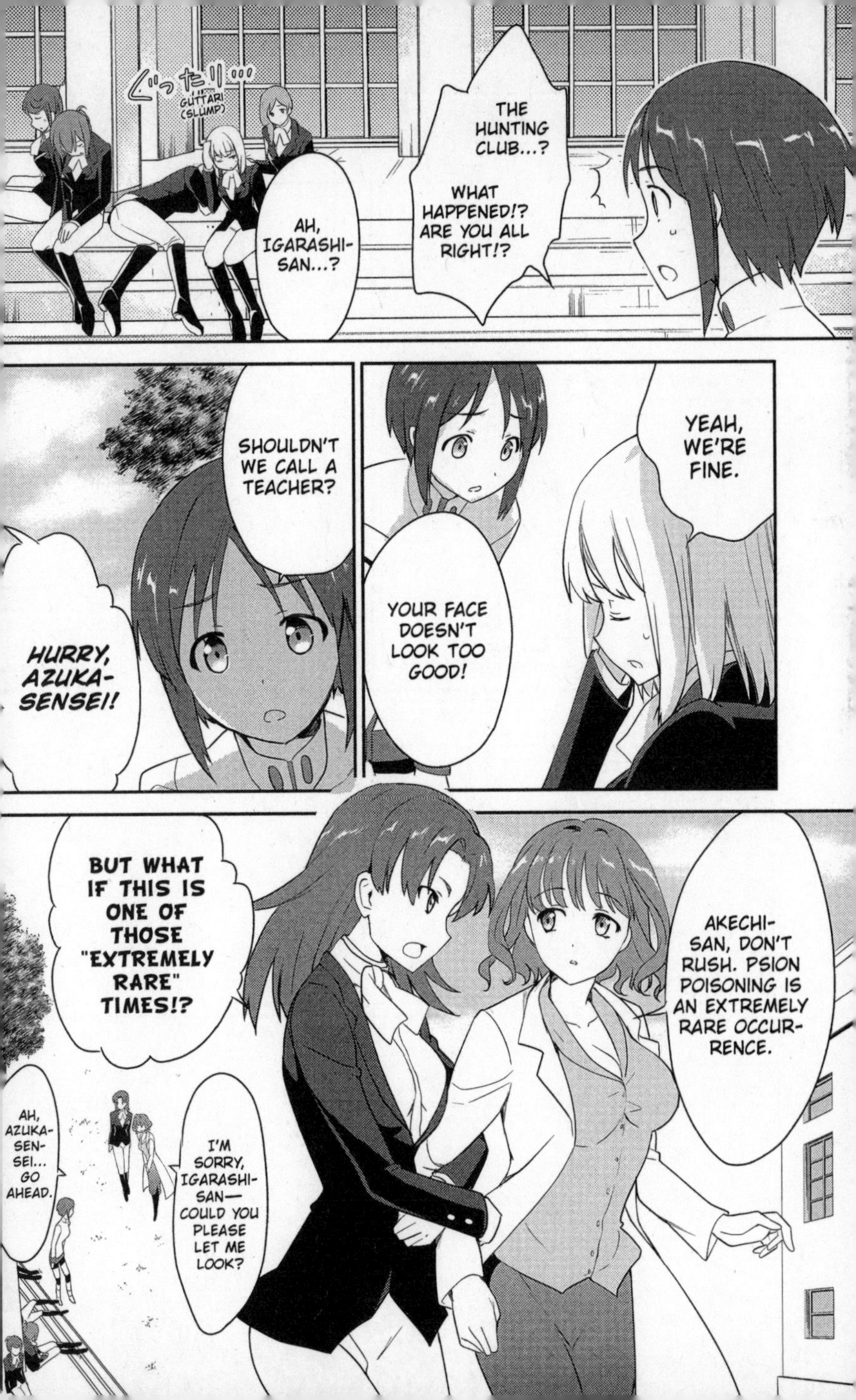
THE HUNTING CLUB...? WHAT HAPPENED!? ARE YOU ALL RIGHT!?
AH, IGARASHI-SAN...?
ぐったり…
GUTTARI (SLUMP)
YEAH, WE'RE FINE.
YOUR FACE DOESN'T LOOK TOO GOOD!
SHOULDN'T WE CALL A TEACHER?
HURRY, AZUKA-SENSEI!
AKECHI-SAN, DON'T RUSH. PSION POISONING IS AN EXTREMELY RARE OCCURRENCE.
BUT WHAT IF THIS IS ONE OF THOSE "EXTREMELY RARE" TIMES!?
I'M SORRY, IGARASHI-SAN—COULD YOU PLEASE LET ME LOOK?
AH, AZUKA-SENSEI... GO AHEAD.

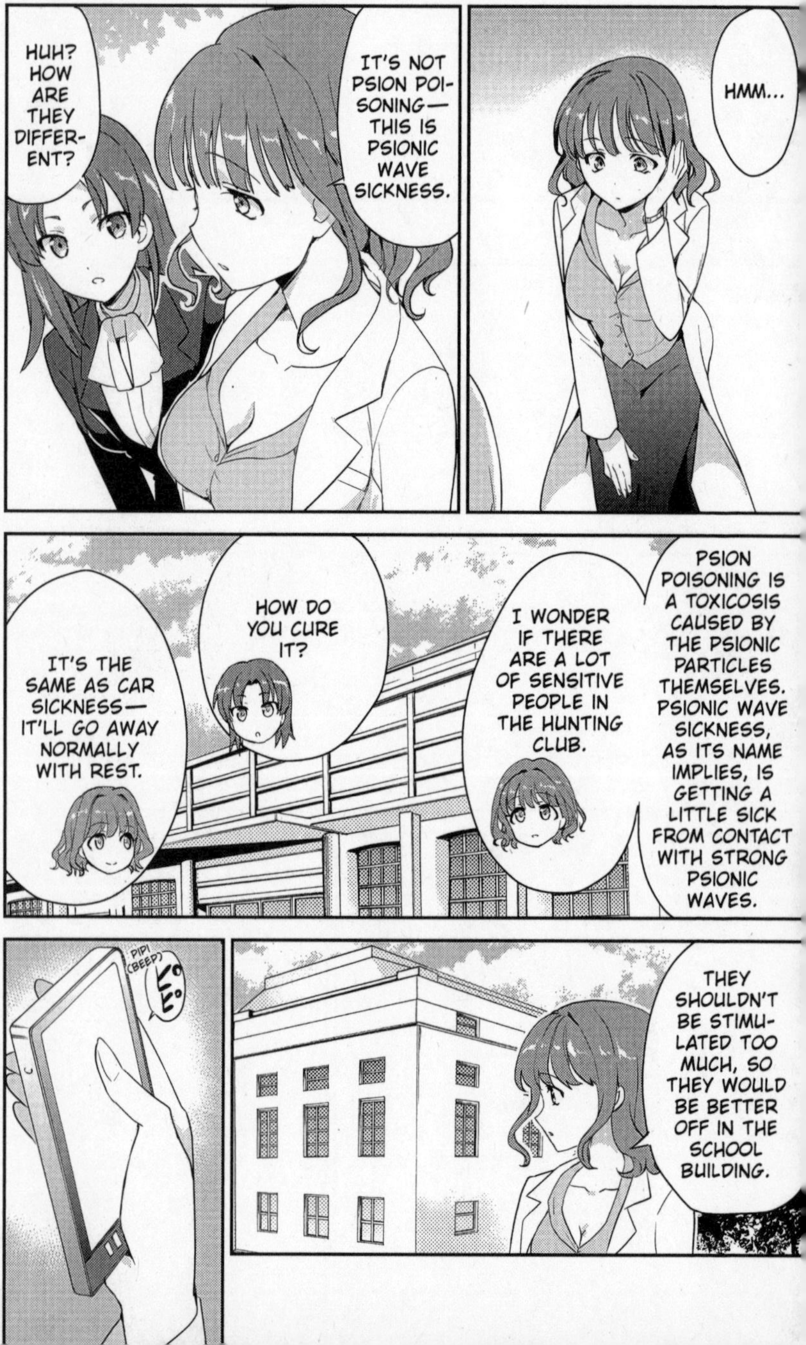
HMM...
IT'S NOT PSION POISONING—THIS IS PSIONIC WAVE SICKNESS.
HUH? HOW ARE THEY DIFFERENT?
PSION POISONING IS A TOXICOSIS CAUSED BY THE PSIONIC PARTICLES THEMSELVES. PSIONIC WAVE SICKNESS, AS ITS NAME IMPLIES, IS GETTING A LITTLE SICK FROM CONTACT WITH STRONG PSIONIC WAVES.
I WONDER IF THERE ARE A LOT OF SENSITIVE PEOPLE IN THE HUNTING CLUB.
HOW DO YOU CURE IT?
IT'S THE SAME AS CAR SICKNESS—IT'LL GO AWAY NORMALLY WITH REST.
THEY SHOULDN'T BE STIMULATED TOO MUCH, SO THEY WOULD BE BETTER OFF IN THE SCHOOL BUILDING.
PIPI (BEEP)

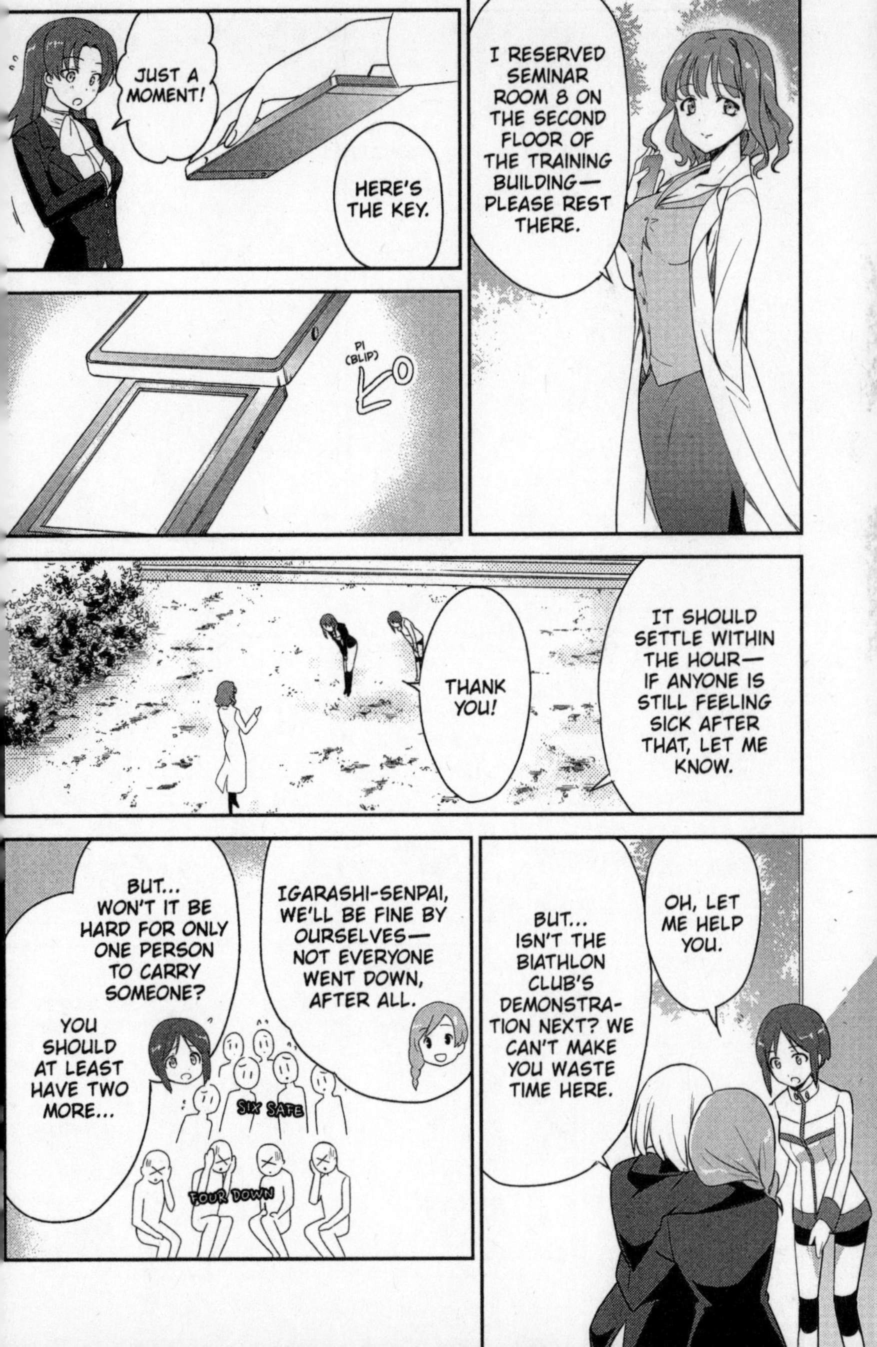

I RESERVED SEMINAR ROOM 8 ON THE SECOND FLOOR OF THE TRAINING BUILDING—PLEASE REST THERE.
HERE'S THE KEY.
JUST A MOMENT!
PI (BLIP)
IT SHOULD SETTLE WITHIN THE HOUR—IF ANYONE IS STILL FEELING SICK AFTER THAT, LET ME KNOW.
THANK YOU!
OH, LET ME HELP YOU.
BUT... ISN'T THE BIATHLON CLUB'S DEMONSTRATION NEXT? WE CAN'T MAKE YOU WASTE TIME HERE.
IGARASHI-SENPAI, WE'LL BE FINE BY OURSELVES—NOT EVERYONE WENT DOWN, AFTER ALL.
BUT... WON'T IT BE HARD FOR ONLY ONE PERSON TO CARRY SOMEONE?
YOU SHOULD AT LEAST HAVE TWO MORE...
SIX SAFE
FOUR DOWN

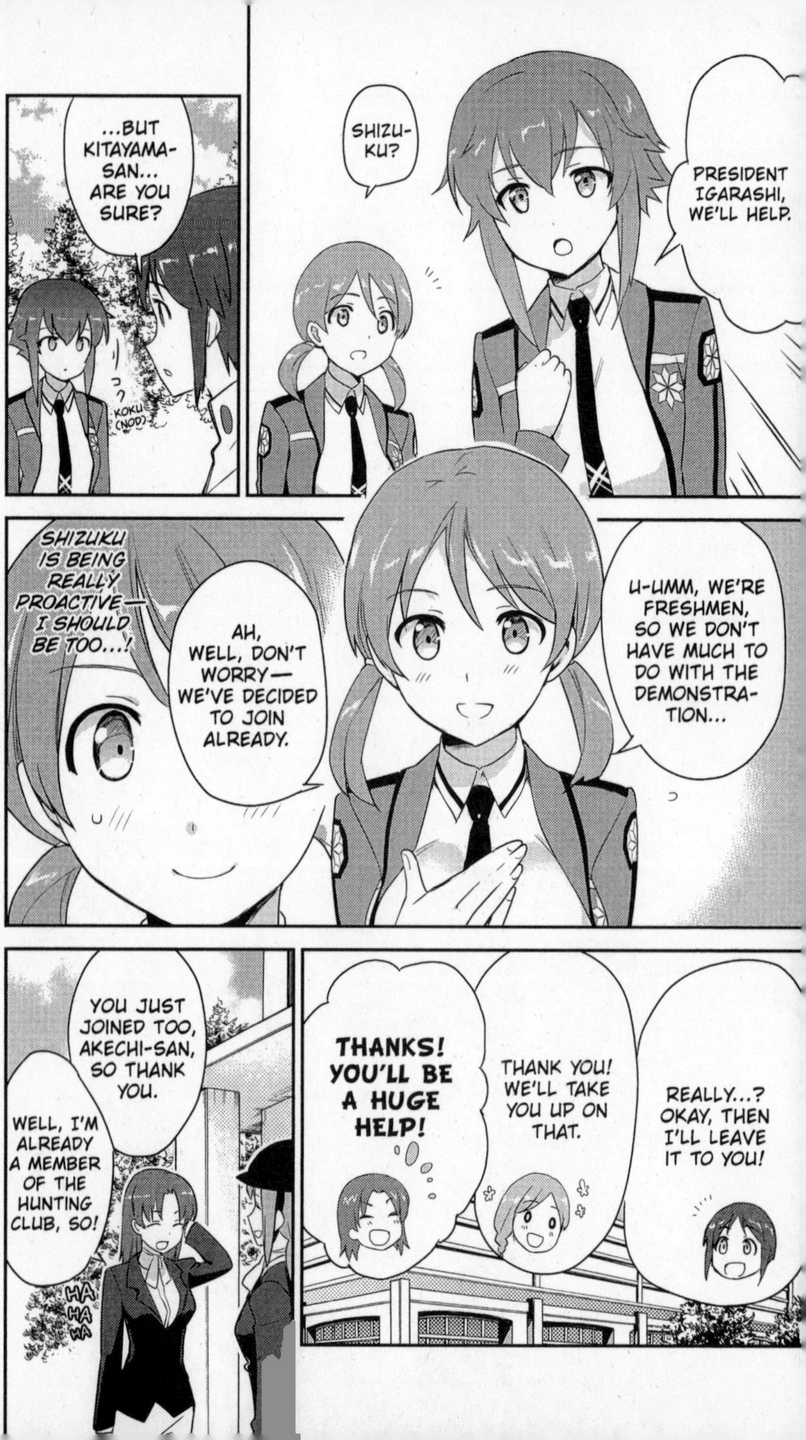
PRESIDENT IGARASHI, WE'LL HELP.
SHIZU-KU?
...BUT KITAYAMA-SAN... ARE YOU SURE?
KOKU (NOD)
U-UMM, WE'RE FRESHMEN, SO WE DON'T HAVE MUCH TO DO WITH THE DEMONSTRA-TION...
AH, WELL, DON'T WORRY— WE'VE DECIDED TO JOIN ALREADY.
SHIZUKU IS BEING REALLY PROACTIVE— I SHOULD BE TOO...!
REALLY...? OKAY, THEN I'LL LEAVE IT TO YOU!
THANK YOU! WE'LL TAKE YOU UP ON THAT.
THANKS! YOU'LL BE A HUGE HELP!
YOU JUST JOINED TOO, AKECHI-SAN, SO THANK YOU.
WELL, I'M ALREADY A MEMBER OF THE HUNTING CLUB, SO!
HA HA HA HA

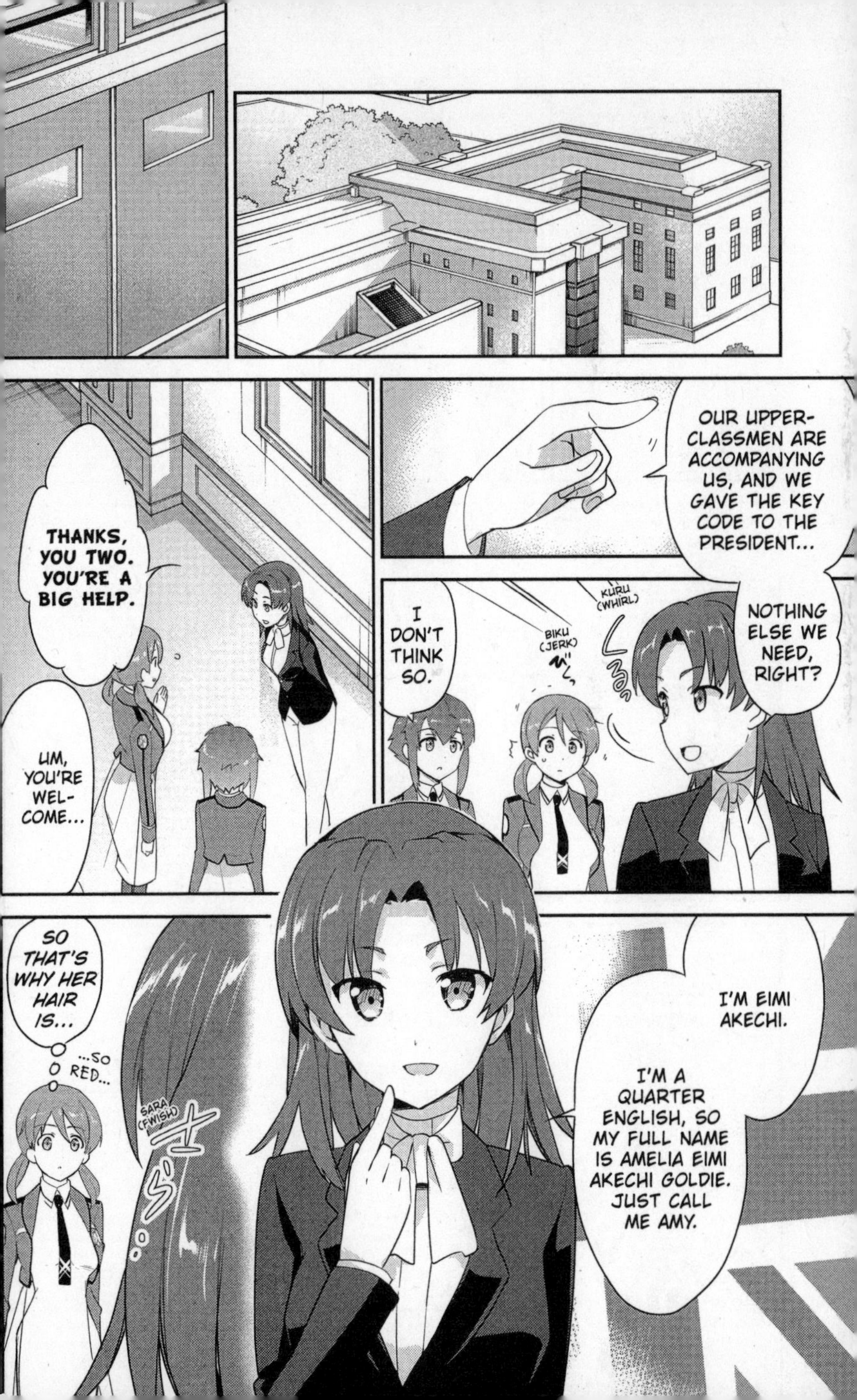
OUR UPPER-CLASSMEN ARE ACCOMPANYING US, AND WE GAVE THE KEY CODE TO THE PRESIDENT...
NOTHING ELSE WE NEED, RIGHT?
KURU (WHIRL)
BIKU (JERK)
I DON'T THINK SO.
THANKS, YOU TWO. YOU'RE A BIG HELP.
UM, YOU'RE WEL-COME...
I'M EIMI AKECHI.
I'M A QUARTER ENGLISH, SO MY FULL NAME IS AMELIA EIMI AKECHI GOLDIE. JUST CALL ME AMY.
SARA (FWISH)
SO THAT'S WHY HER HAIR IS...
...SO RED...

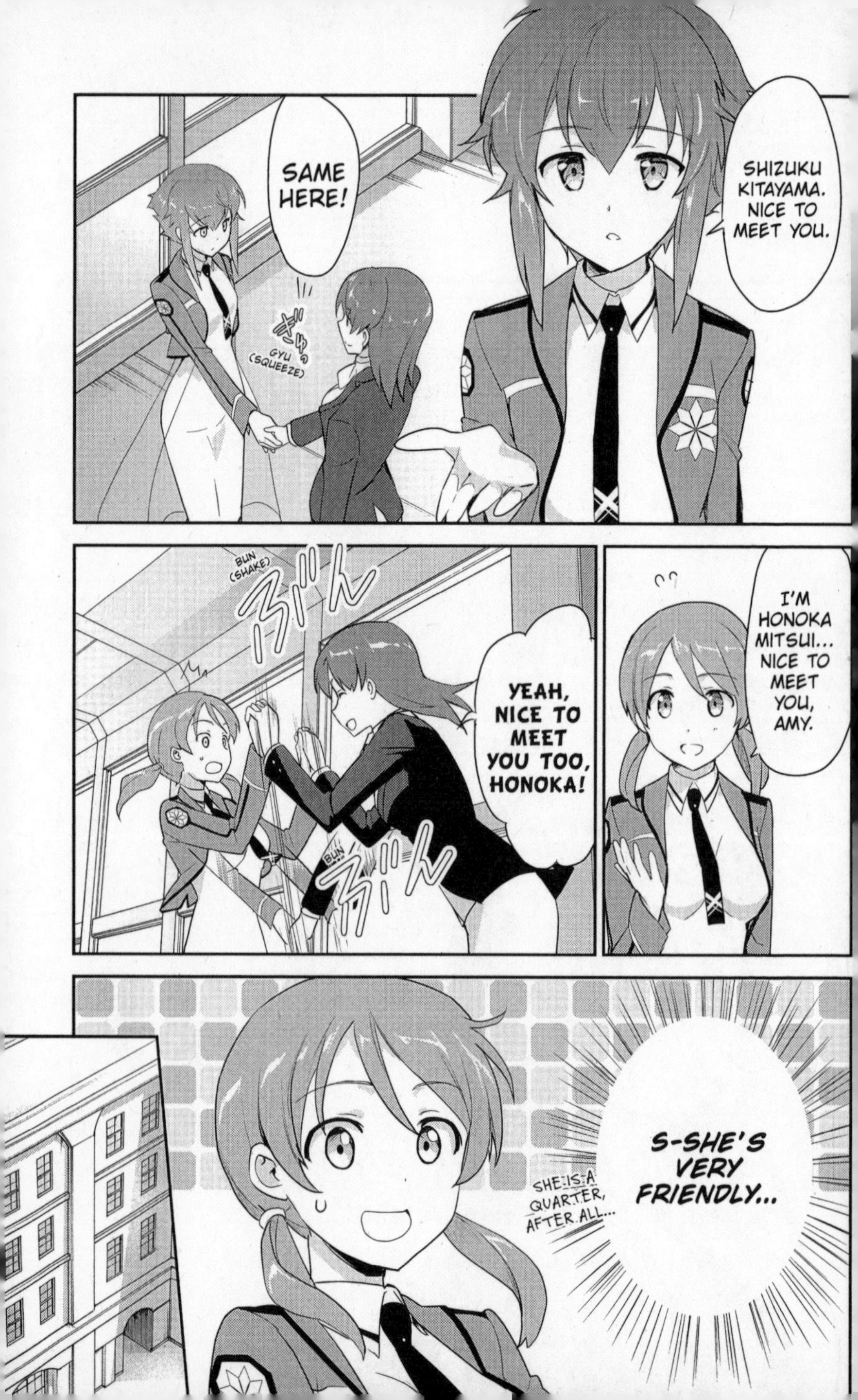
SHIZUKU KITAYAMA. NICE TO MEET YOU.
SAME HERE!
ぎゅっ
GYU (SQUEEZE)
I'M HONOKA MITSUI... NICE TO MEET YOU, AMY.
BUN (SHAKE)
ぶん
YEAH, NICE TO MEET YOU TOO, HONOKA!
BUN
ぶん
S-SHE'S VERY FRIENDLY...
SHE IS A QUARTER, AFTER ALL...

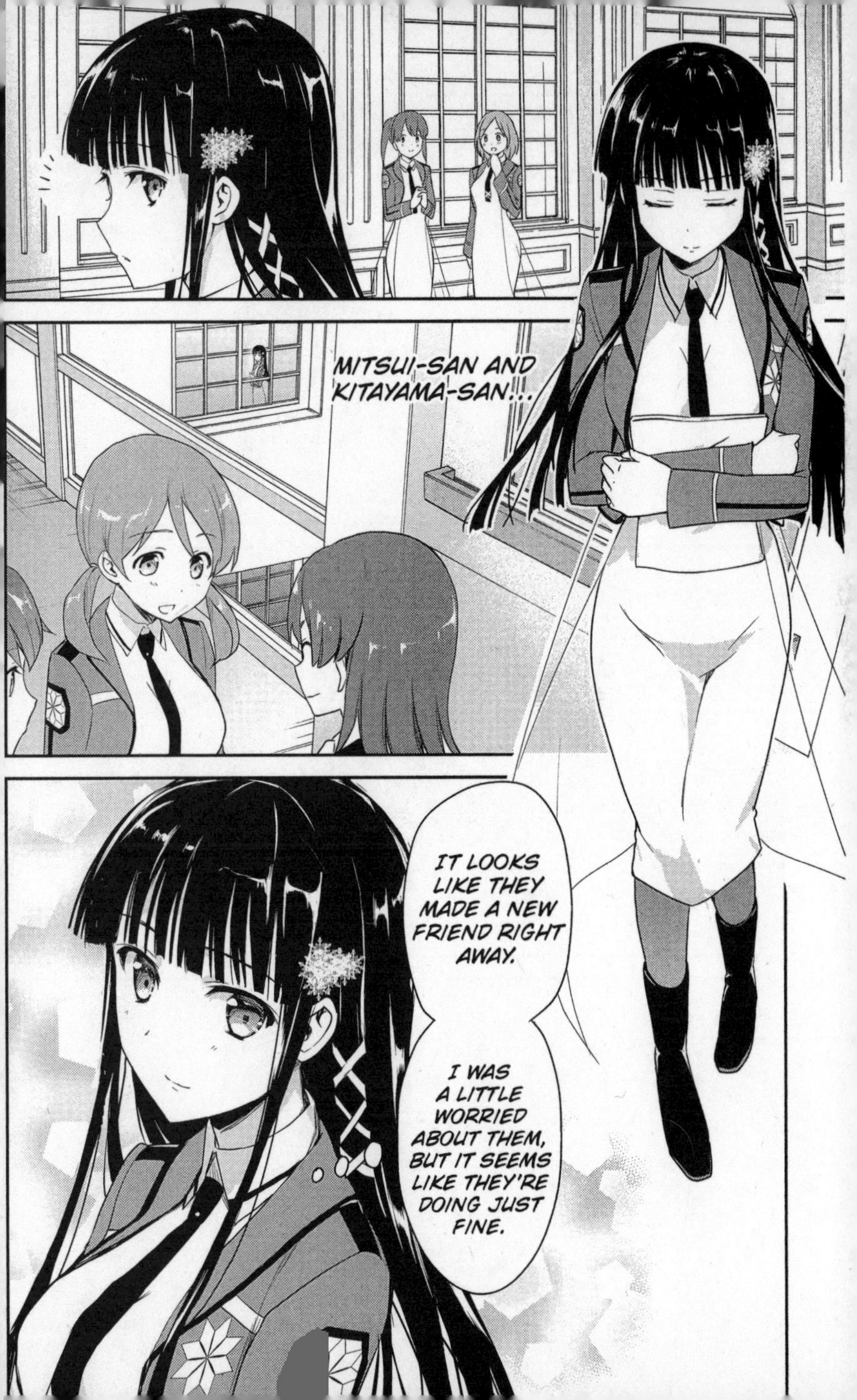
MITSUI-SAN AND KITAYAMA-SAN...
IT LOOKS LIKE THEY MADE A NEW FRIEND RIGHT AWAY.
I WAS A LITTLE WORRIED ABOUT THEM, BUT IT SEEMS LIKE THEY'RE DOING JUST FINE.

CHAPTER 11

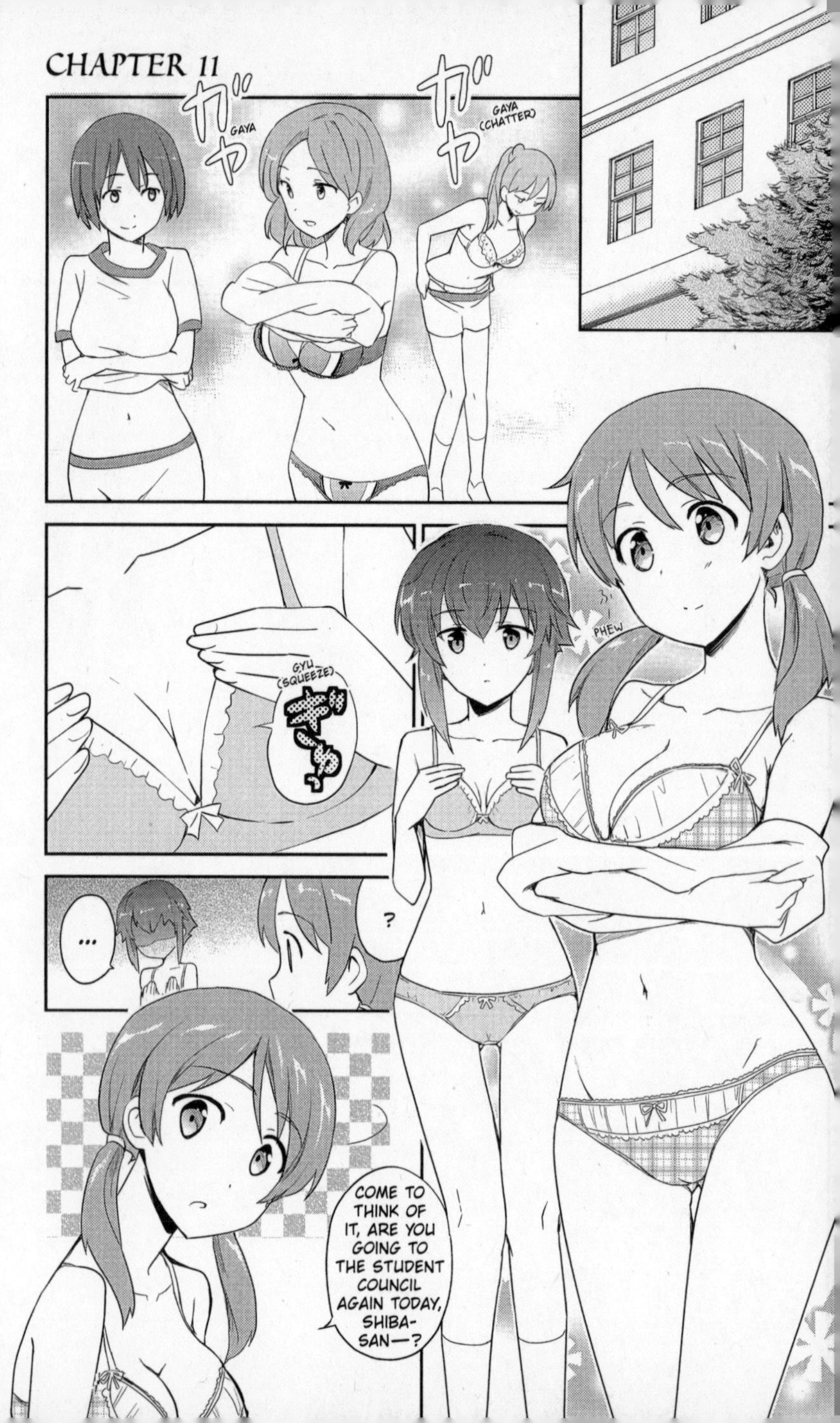

ガヤ
GAYA (CHATTER)
ガヤ
GAYA
PHEW
GYU (SQUEEZE)
?
...
COME TO THINK OF IT, ARE YOU GOING TO THE STUDENT COUNCIL AGAIN TODAY, SHIBA-SAN—?

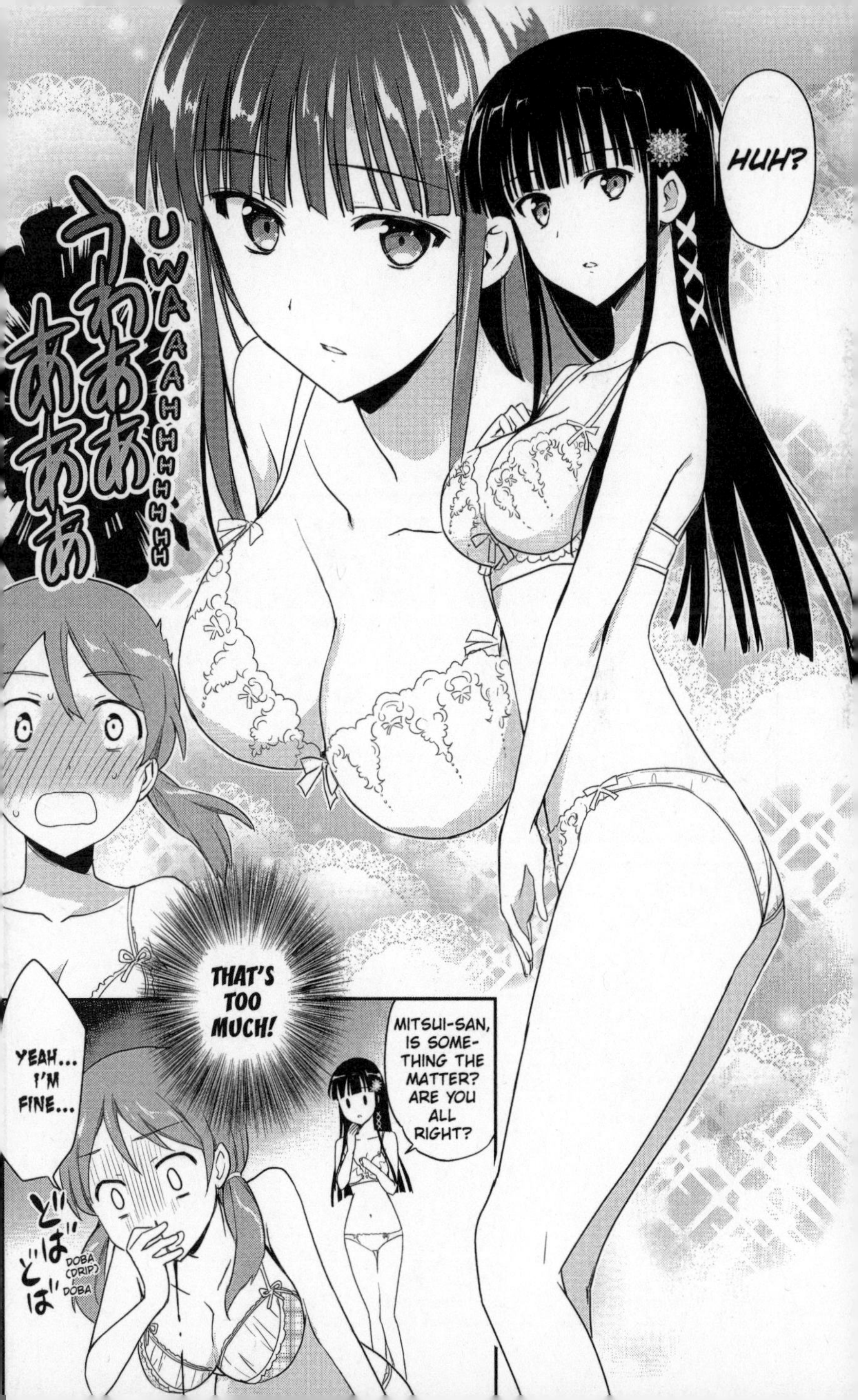
HUH?
うわあああああ
UWAAAHHHHHHH
THAT'S TOO MUCH!
MITSUI-SAN, IS SOME-THING THE MATTER? ARE YOU ALL RIGHT?
YEAH... I'M FINE...
どばどば
DOBA (DRIP) DOBA

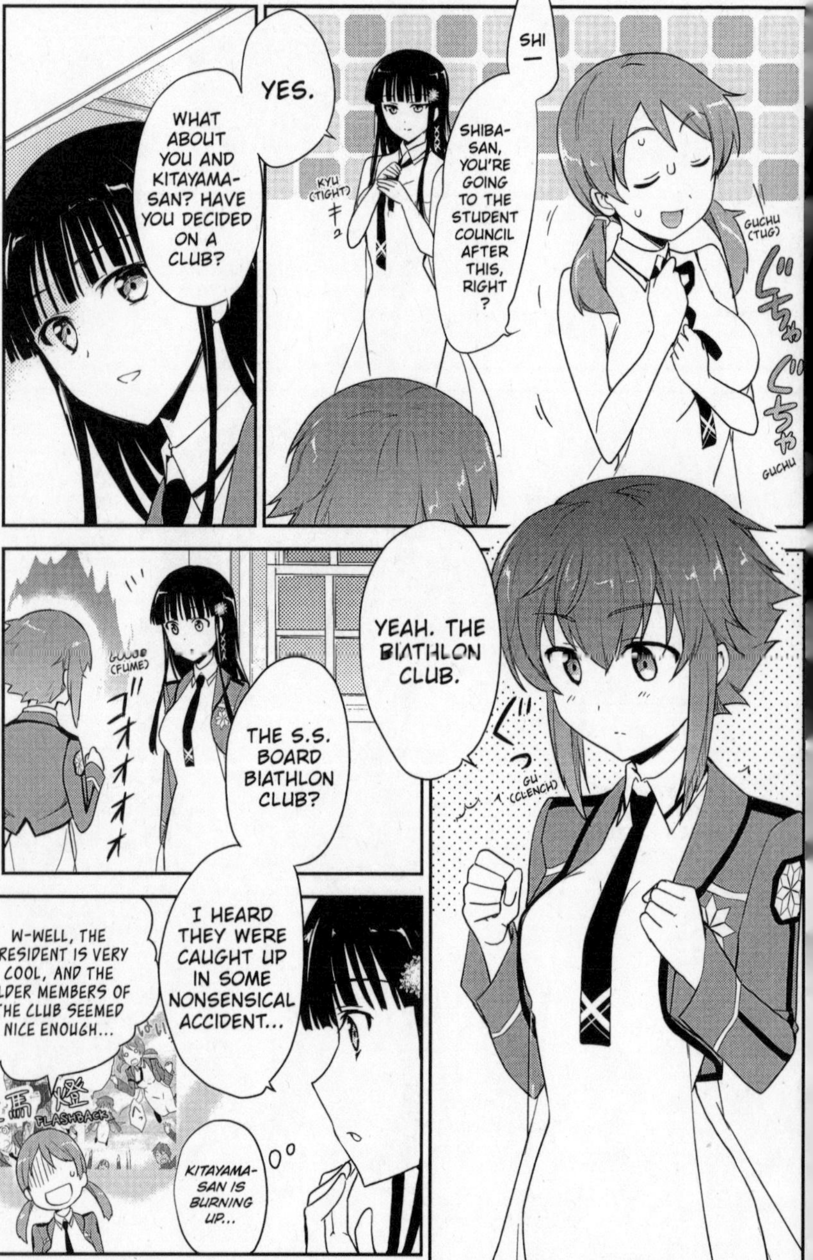
SHI—
SHIBA-SAN, YOU'RE GOING TO THE STUDENT COUNCIL AFTER THIS, RIGHT?
GUCHU (TUG)
GUCHU
KYU (TIGHT)
YES.
WHAT ABOUT YOU AND KITAYAMA-SAN? HAVE YOU DECIDED ON A CLUB?
YEAH. THE BIATHLON CLUB.
GU (CLENCH)
THE S.S. BOARD BIATHLON CLUB?
GUOOO (FUME)
I HEARD THEY WERE CAUGHT UP IN SOME NONSENSICAL ACCIDENT...
W-WELL, THE PRESIDENT IS VERY COOL, AND THE OLDER MEMBERS OF THE CLUB SEEMED NICE ENOUGH...
FLASHBACK
KITAYAMA-SAN IS BURNING UP...

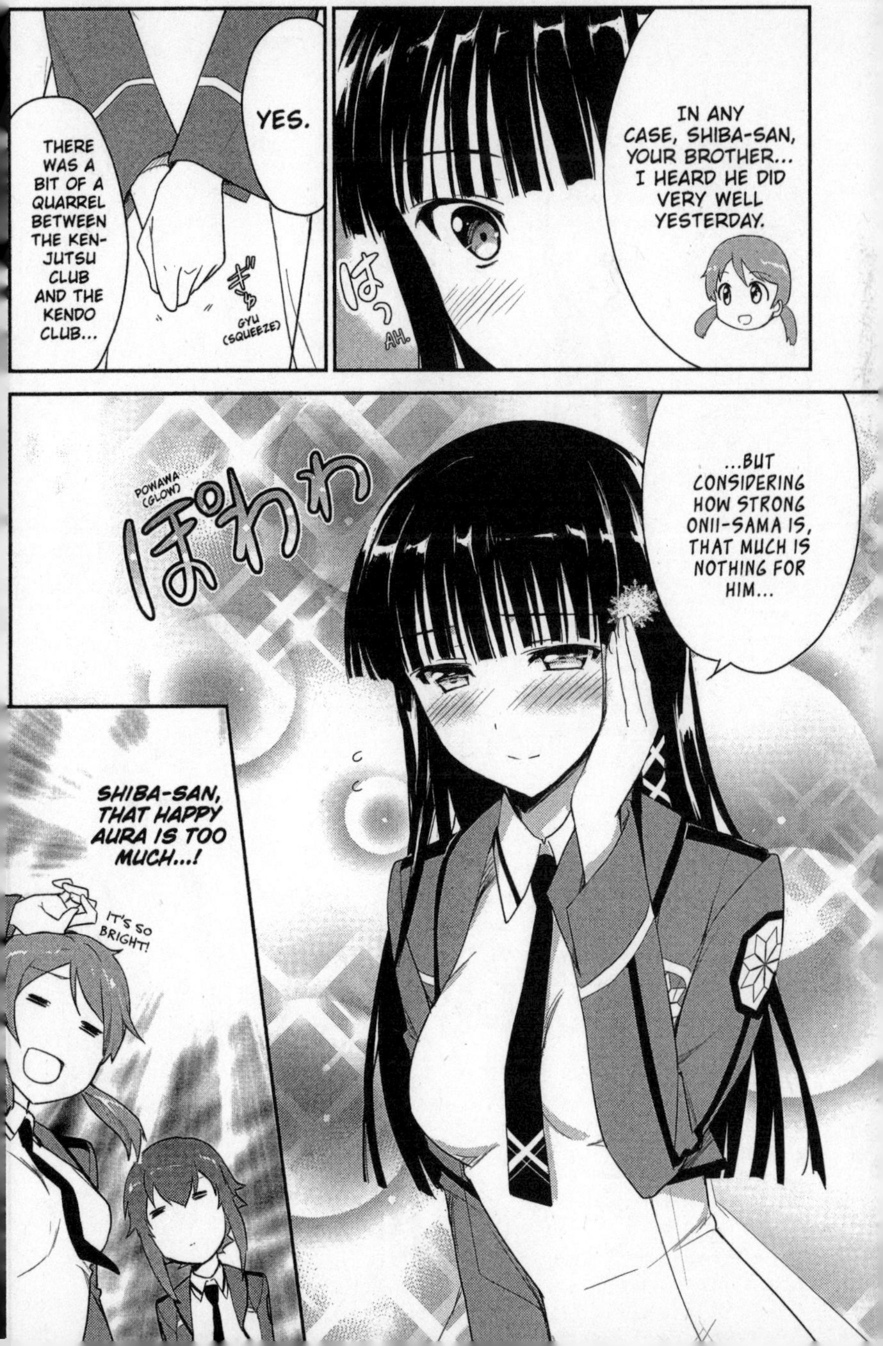
IN ANY CASE, SHIBA-SAN, YOUR BROTHER... I HEARD HE DID VERY WELL YESTERDAY.
はっ
AH.
YES.
THERE WAS A BIT OF A QUARREL BETWEEN THE KEN-JUTSU CLUB AND THE KENDO CLUB...
ぎゅ
GYU (SQUEEZE)
...BUT CONSIDERING HOW STRONG ONII-SAMA IS, THAT MUCH IS NOTHING FOR HIM...
ぽわわ
POWAWA (GLOW)
SHIBA-SAN, THAT HAPPY AURA IS TOO MUCH...!
IT'S SO BRIGHT!

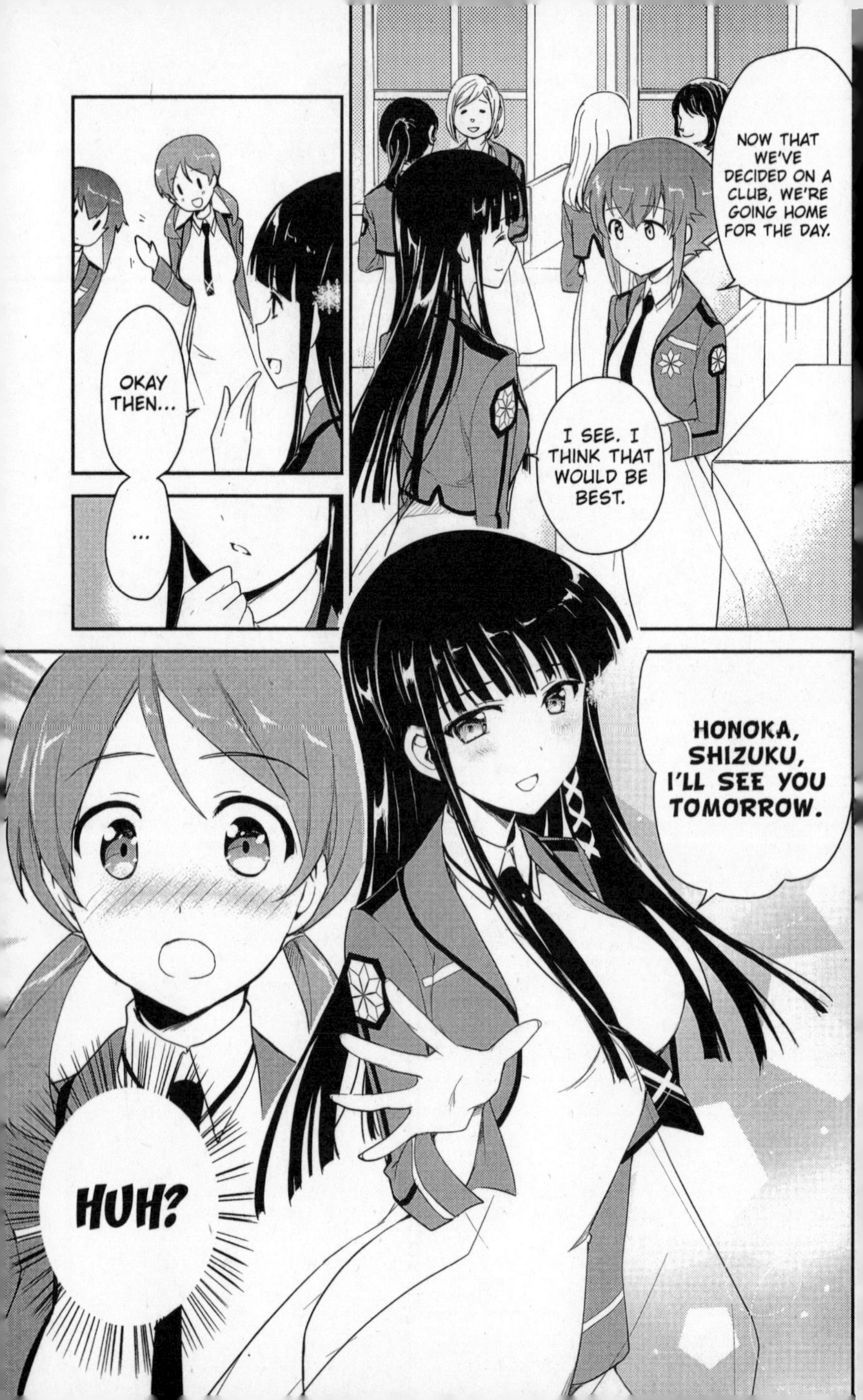
NOW THAT WE'VE DECIDED ON A CLUB, WE'RE GOING HOME FOR THE DAY.
I SEE. I THINK THAT WOULD BE BEST.
OKAY THEN...
...
HONOKA, SHIZUKU, I'LL SEE YOU TOMORROW.
HUH?

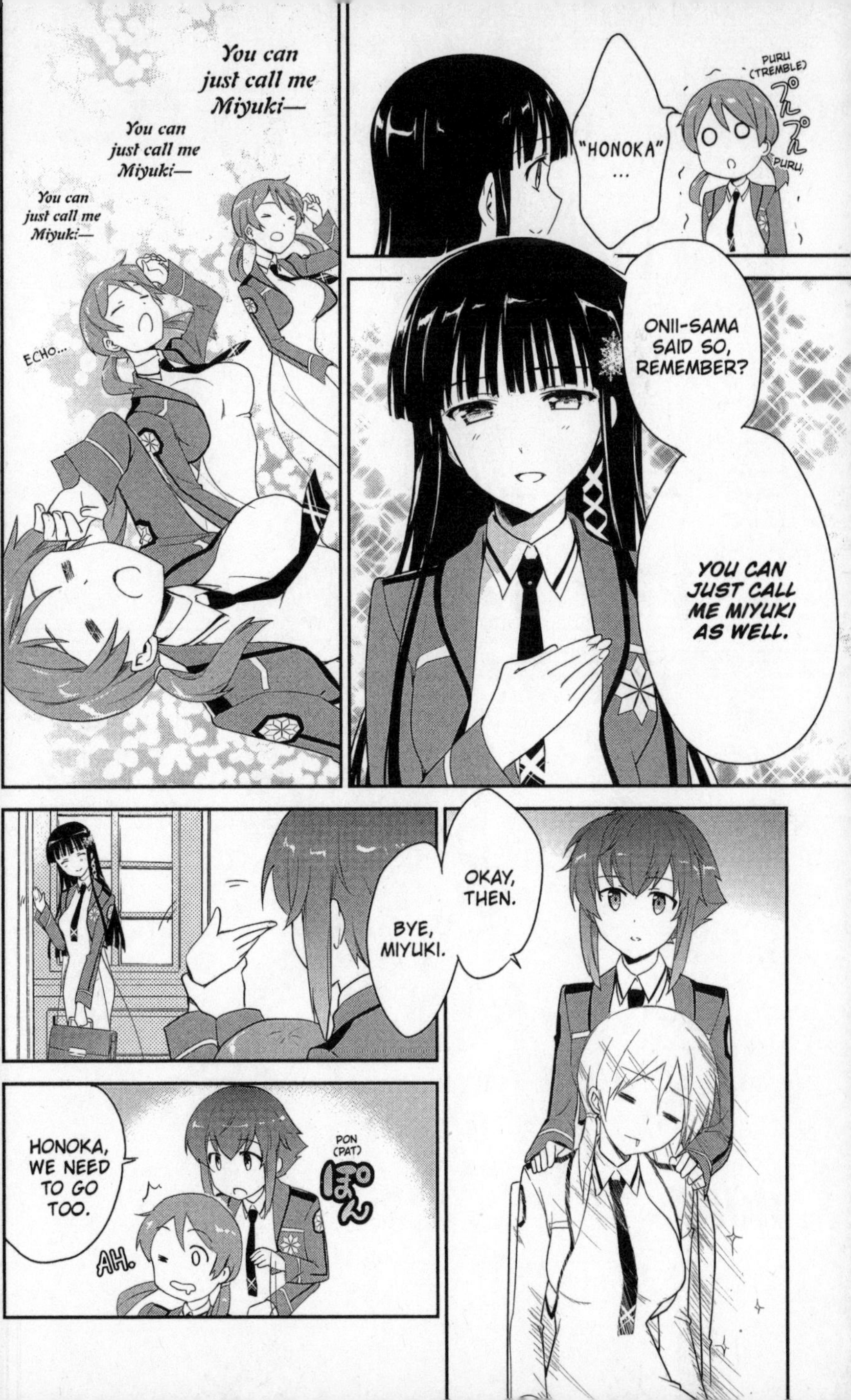
"HONOKA"
...
PURU (TREMBLE)
ぷるぷる
PURU
ONII-SAMA SAID SO, REMEMBER?
YOU CAN JUST CALL ME MIYUKI AS WELL.
You can just call me Miyuki—
You can just call me Miyuki—
You can just call me Miyuki—
ECHO...
OKAY, THEN.
BYE, MIYUKI.
HONOKA, WE NEED TO GO TOO.
PON (PAT)
ぽん
AH.

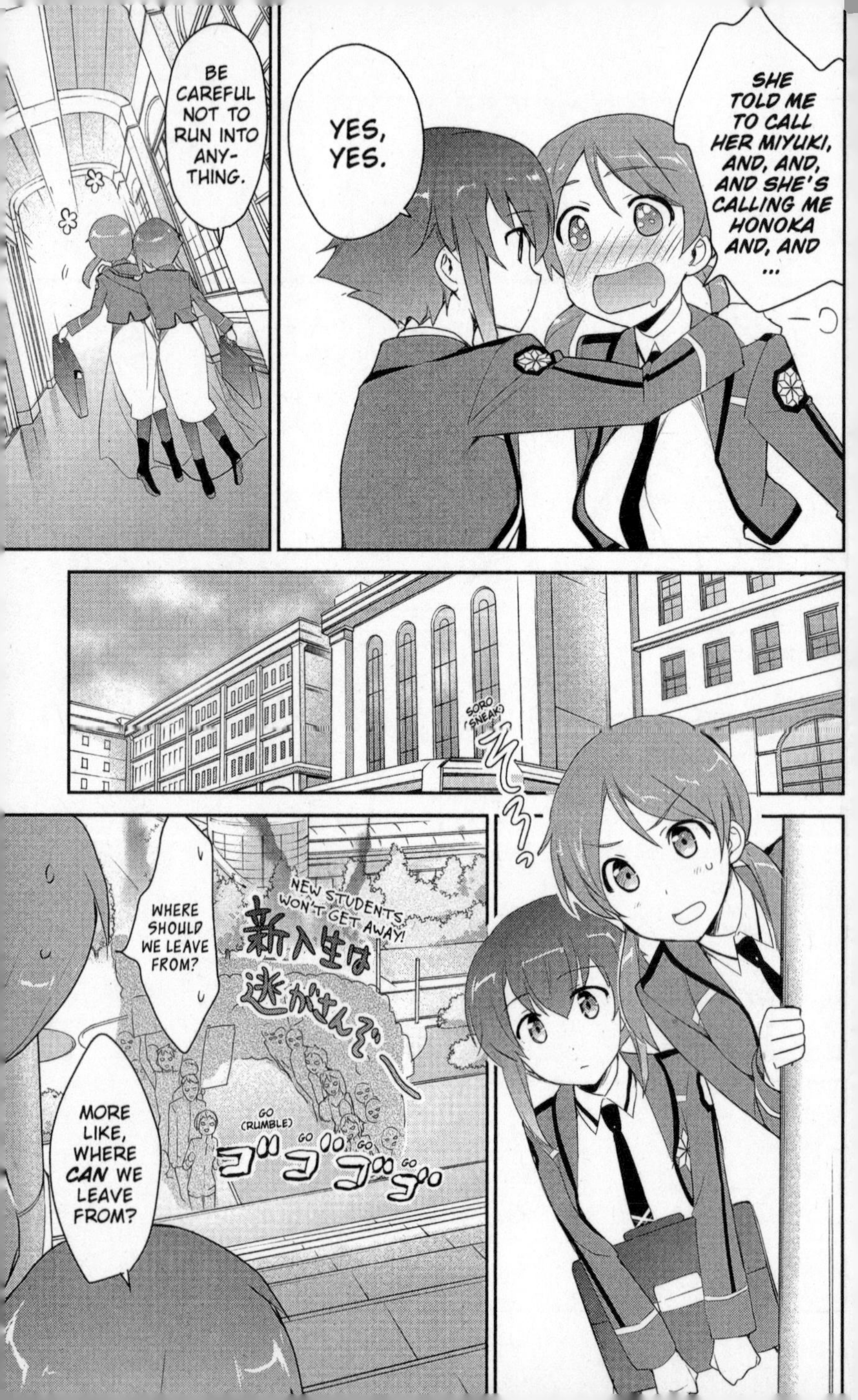
SHE TOLD ME TO CALL HER MIYUKI, AND, AND, AND SHE'S CALLING ME HONOKA AND, AND ...
YES, YES.
BE CAREFUL NOT TO RUN INTO ANY-THING.
SORO (SNEAK)
そろ～
WHERE SHOULD WE LEAVE FROM?
新入生は逃がさんぞ～
NEW STUDENTS WON'T GET AWAY!
GO (RUMBLE)
GO GO
ゴゴゴゴ
MORE LIKE, WHERE CAN WE LEAVE FROM?

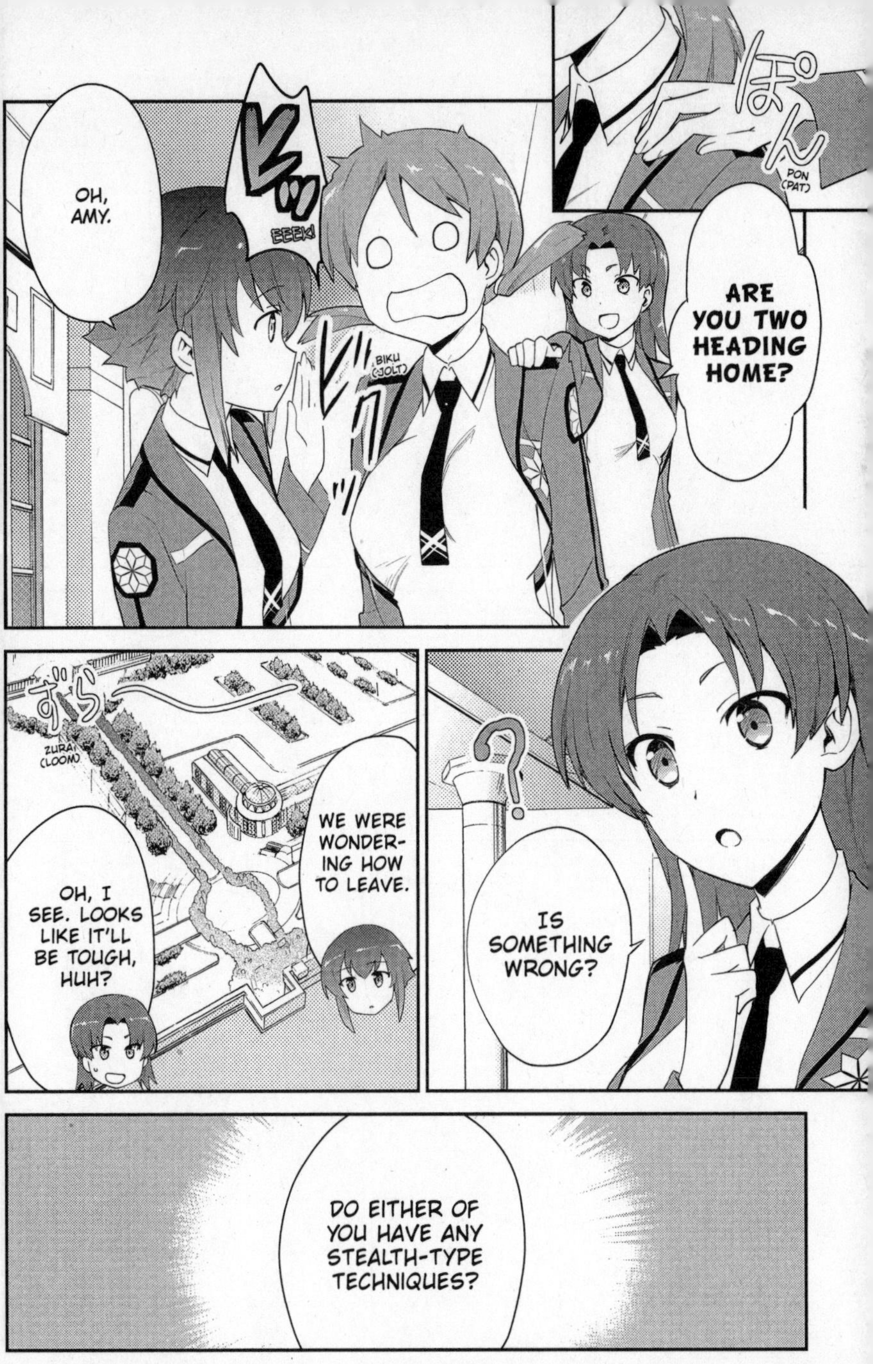
PON (PAT)
ARE YOU TWO HEADING HOME?
EEEK!
BIKU (JOLT)
OH, AMY.
IS SOMETHING WRONG?
ZURA (LOOM)
WE WERE WONDERING HOW TO LEAVE.
OH, I SEE. LOOKS LIKE IT'LL BE TOUGH, HUH?
DO EITHER OF YOU HAVE ANY STEALTH-TYPE TECHNIQUES?

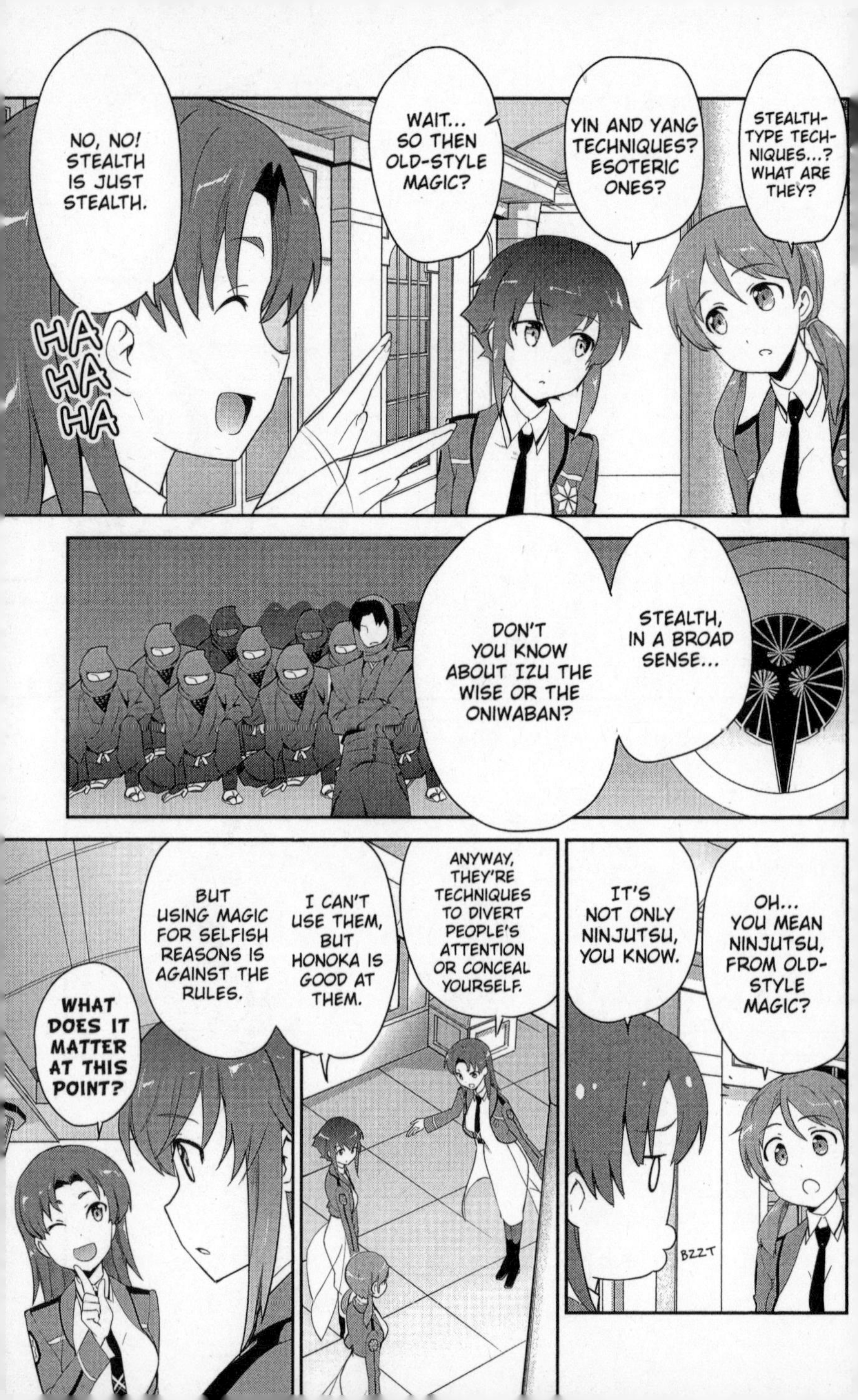
STEALTH-TYPE TECHNIQUES...? WHAT ARE THEY?
YIN AND YANG TECHNIQUES? ESOTERIC ONES?
WAIT... SO THEN OLD-STYLE MAGIC?
NO, NO! STEALTH IS JUST STEALTH.
HA HA HA
STEALTH, IN A BROAD SENSE...
DON'T YOU KNOW ABOUT IZU THE WISE OR THE ONIWABAN?
OH... YOU MEAN NINJUTSU, FROM OLD-STYLE MAGIC?
IT'S NOT ONLY NINJUTSU, YOU KNOW.
BZZT
ANYWAY, THEY'RE TECHNIQUES TO DIVERT PEOPLE'S ATTENTION OR CONCEAL YOURSELF.
I CAN'T USE THEM, BUT HONOKA IS GOOD AT THEM.
BUT USING MAGIC FOR SELFISH REASONS IS AGAINST THE RULES.
WHAT DOES IT MATTER AT THIS POINT?

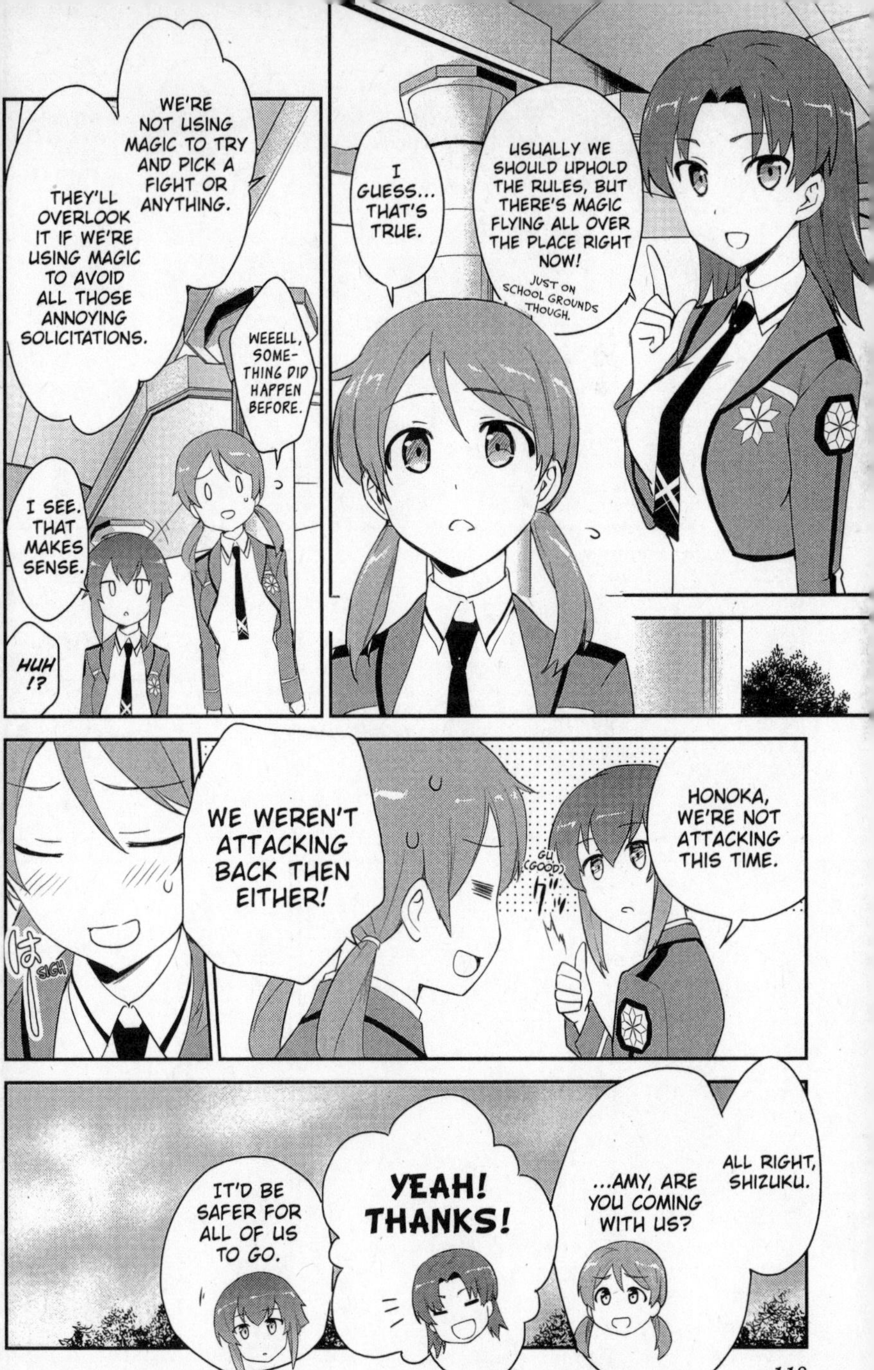
USUALLY WE SHOULD UPHOLD THE RULES, BUT THERE'S MAGIC FLYING ALL OVER THE PLACE RIGHT NOW!
JUST ON SCHOOL GROUNDS THOUGH.
I GUESS... THAT'S TRUE.
WE'RE NOT USING MAGIC TO TRY AND PICK A FIGHT OR ANYTHING.
THEY'LL OVERLOOK IT IF WE'RE USING MAGIC TO AVOID ALL THOSE ANNOYING SOLICITATIONS.
WEEELL, SOMETHING DID HAPPEN BEFORE.
I SEE. THAT MAKES SENSE.
HUH!?
HONOKA, WE'RE NOT ATTACKING THIS TIME.
GU (GOOD)
WE WEREN'T ATTACKING BACK THEN EITHER!
SIGH
ALL RIGHT, SHIZUKU.
...AMY, ARE YOU COMING WITH US?
YEAH! THANKS!
IT'D BE SAFER FOR ALL OF US TO GO.

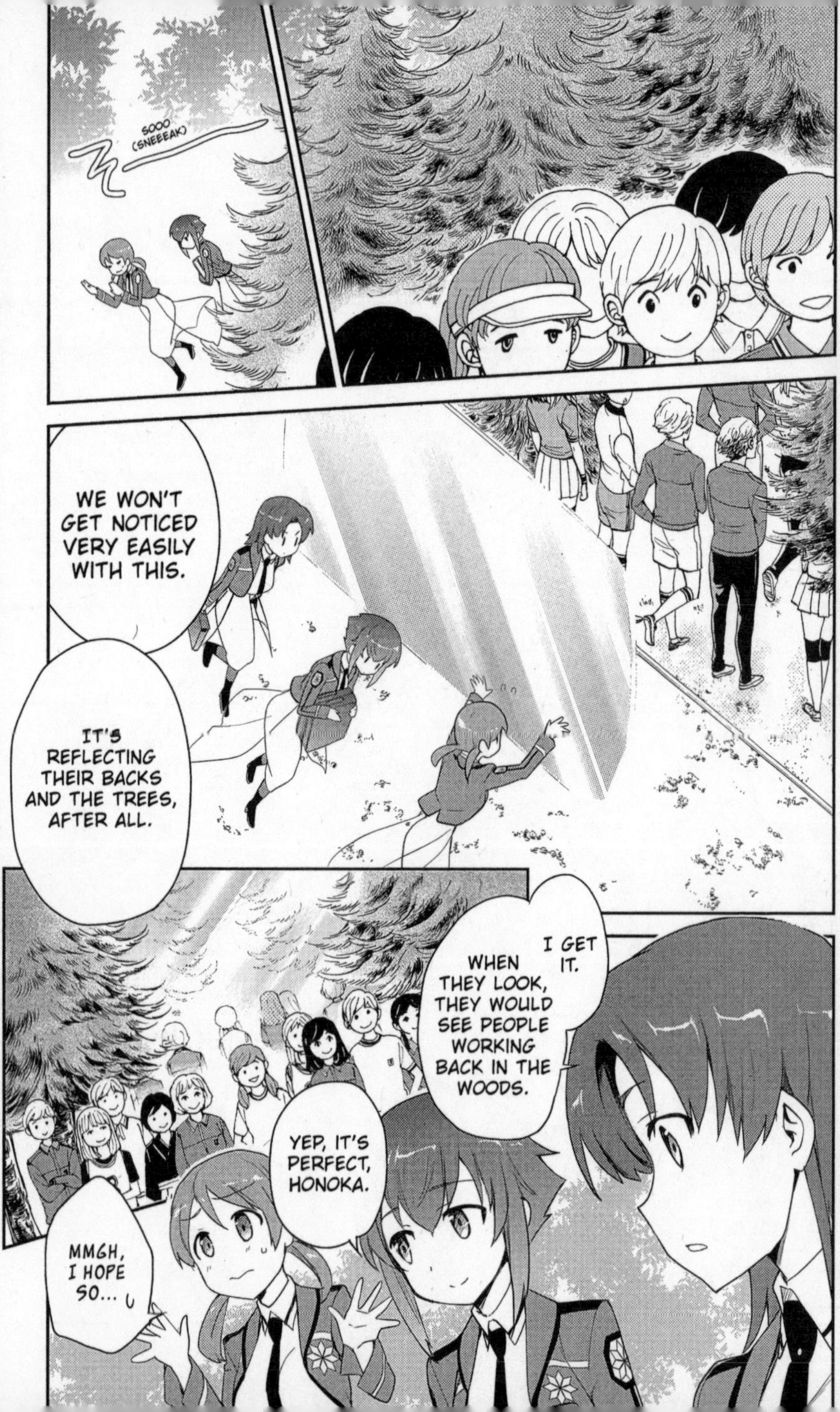
SOOO (SNEEEAK)
WE WON'T GET NOTICED VERY EASILY WITH THIS.
IT'S REFLECTING THEIR BACKS AND THE TREES, AFTER ALL.
I GET IT.
WHEN THEY LOOK, THEY WOULD SEE PEOPLE WORKING BACK IN THE WOODS.
YEP, IT'S PERFECT, HONOKA.
MMGH, I HOPE SO...

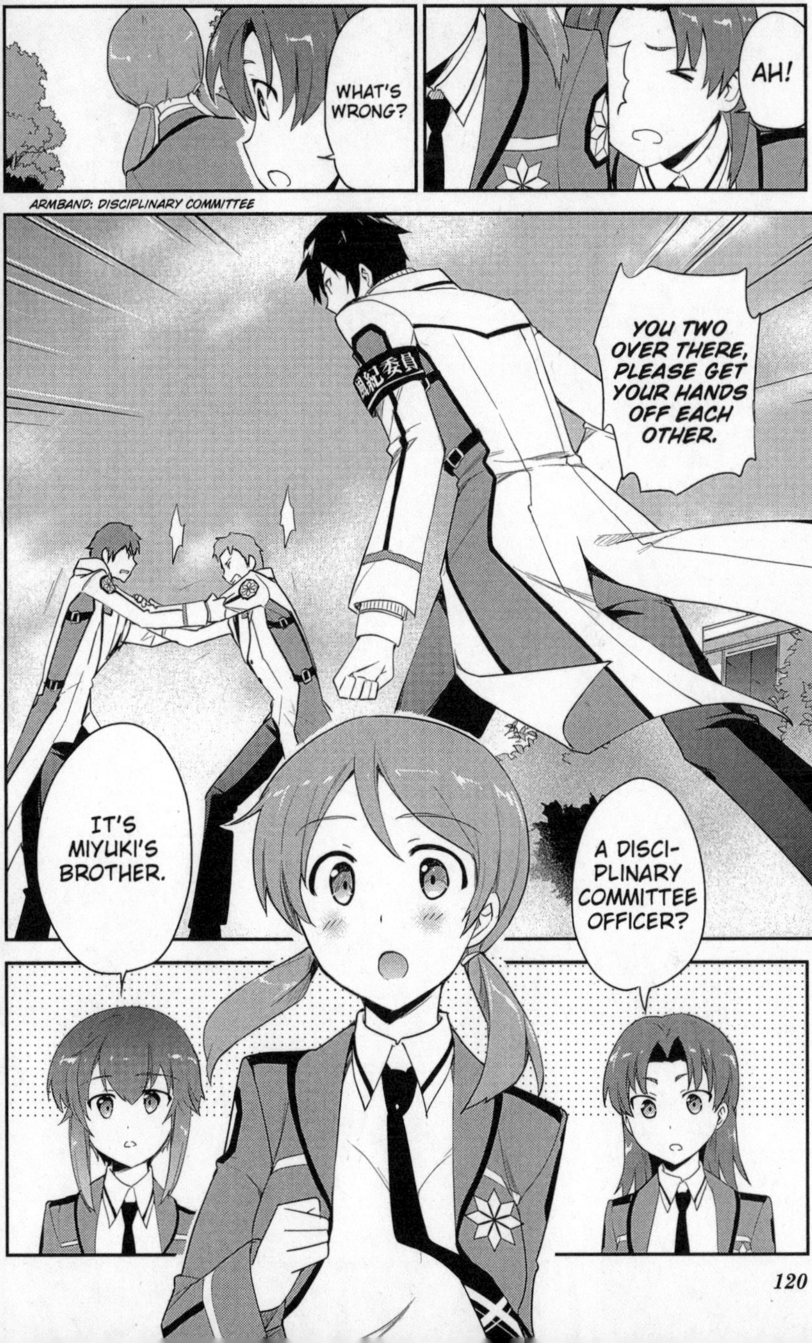
AH!
WHAT'S WRONG?
ARMBAND: DISCIPLINARY COMMITTEE
YOU TWO OVER THERE, PLEASE GET YOUR HANDS OFF EACH OTHER.
A DISCIPLINARY COMMITTEE OFFICER?
IT'S MIYUKI'S BROTHER.

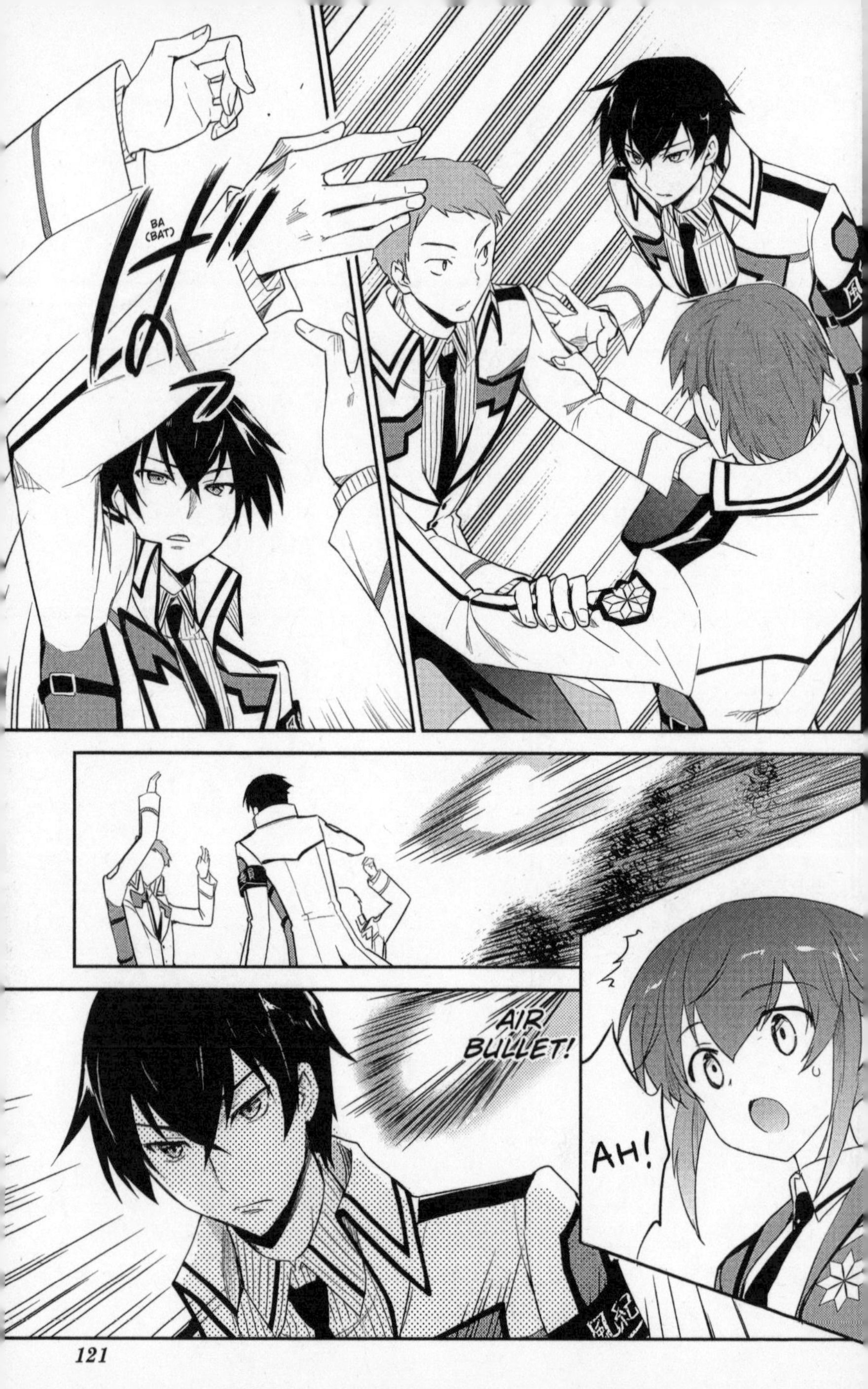
BA (BAT)
AH!
AIR BULLET!

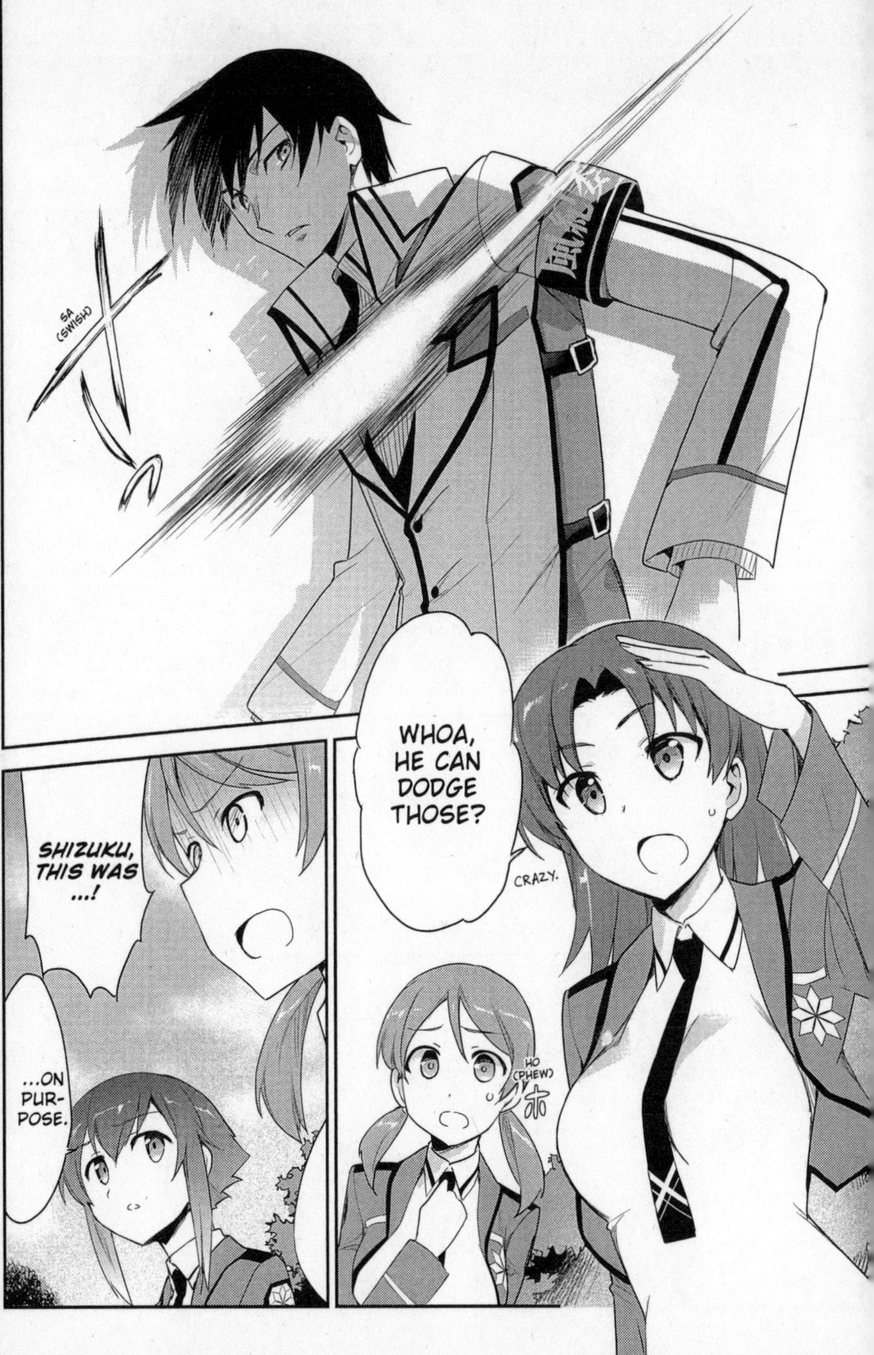
SA (SWISH)
WHOA, HE CAN DODGE THOSE?
CRAZY.
HO (PHEW)
SHIZUKU, THIS WAS ...!
...ON PURPOSE.

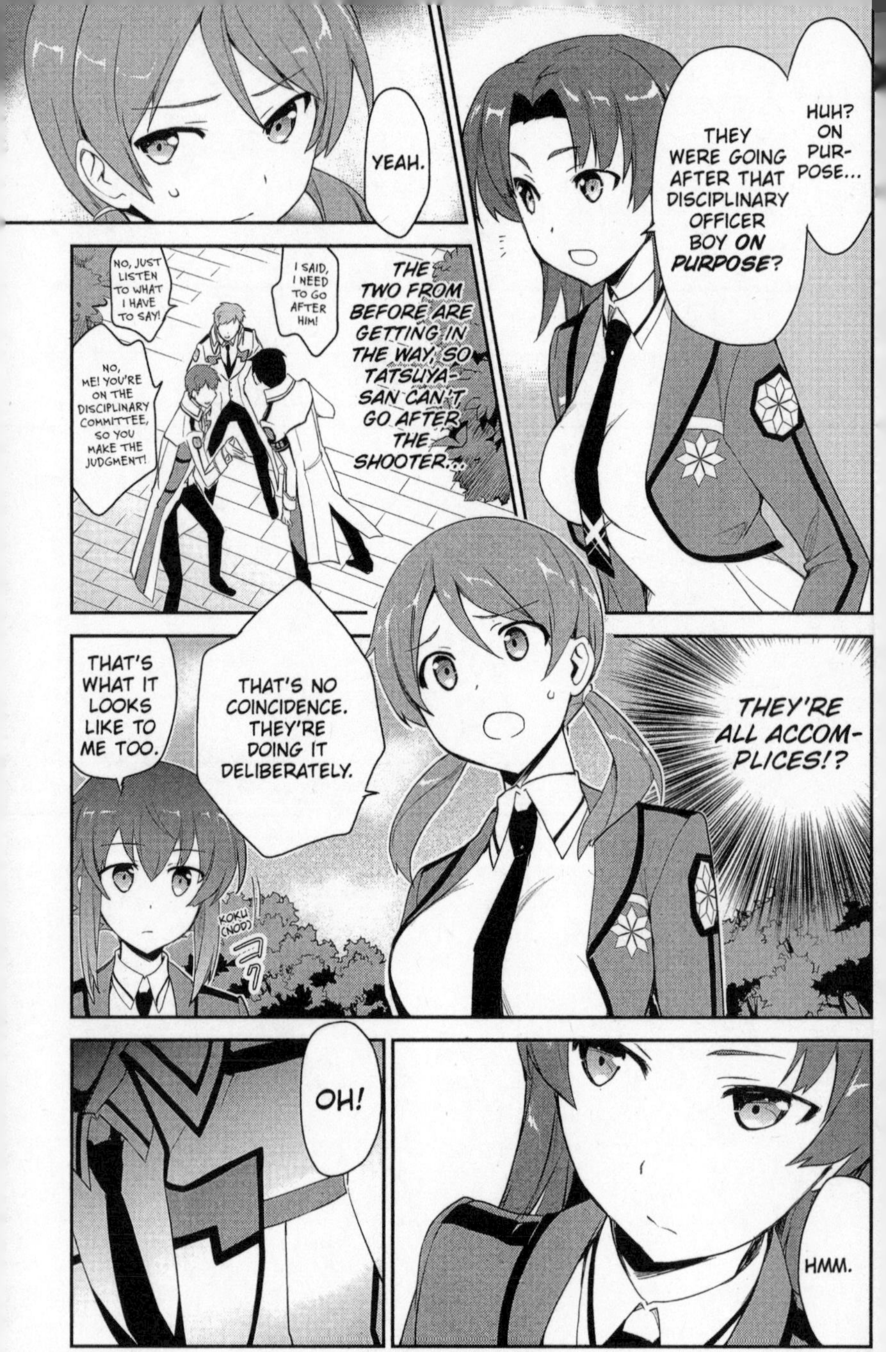
HUH? ON PUR-POSE...
THEY WERE GOING AFTER THAT DISCIPLINARY OFFICER BOY **ON PURPOSE**?
YEAH.
THE TWO FROM BEFORE ARE GETTING IN THE WAY, SO TATSUYA-SAN CAN'T GO AFTER THE SHOOTER...
I SAID, I NEED TO GO AFTER HIM!
NO, JUST LISTEN TO WHAT I HAVE TO SAY!
NO, ME! YOU'RE ON THE DISCIPLINARY COMMITTEE, SO YOU MAKE THE JUDGMENT!
THEY'RE ALL ACCOM-PLICES!?
THAT'S NO COINCIDENCE. THEY'RE DOING IT DELIBERATELY.
THAT'S WHAT IT LOOKS LIKE TO ME TOO.
KOKU (NOD)
HMM.
OH!

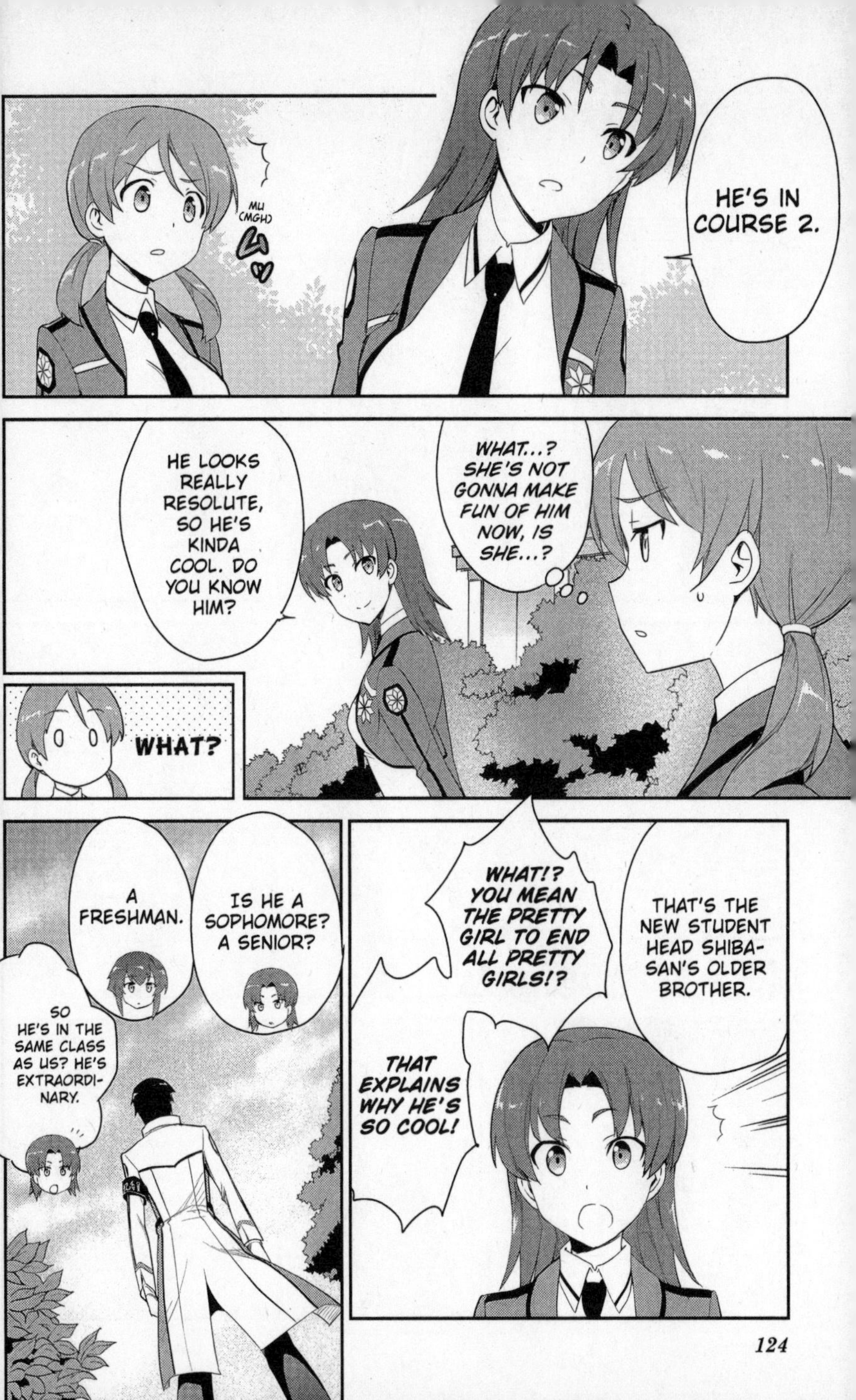
HE'S IN COURSE 2.
MU (MGH)
WHAT...? SHE'S NOT GONNA MAKE FUN OF HIM NOW, IS SHE...?
HE LOOKS REALLY RESOLUTE, SO HE'S KINDA COOL. DO YOU KNOW HIM?
WHAT?
THAT'S THE NEW STUDENT HEAD SHIBA-SAN'S OLDER BROTHER.
WHAT!? YOU MEAN THE PRETTY GIRL TO END ALL PRETTY GIRLS!?
THAT EXPLAINS WHY HE'S SO COOL!
IS HE A SOPHOMORE? A SENIOR?
A FRESHMAN.
SO HE'S IN THE SAME CLASS AS US? HE'S EXTRAORDI-NARY.

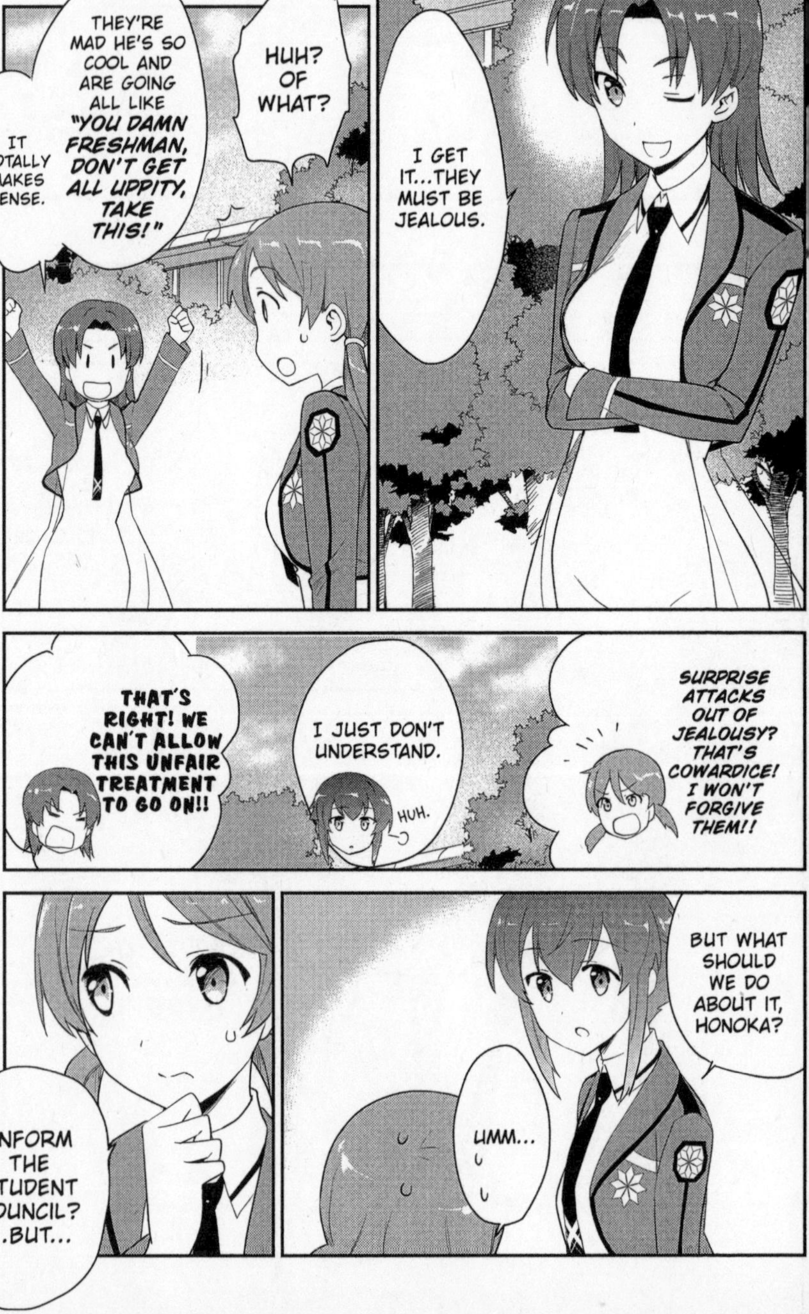
I GET IT...THEY MUST BE JEALOUS.
HUH? OF WHAT?
THEY'RE MAD HE'S SO COOL AND ARE GOING ALL LIKE "YOU DAMN FRESHMAN, DON'T GET ALL UPPITY, TAKE THIS!"
IT TOTALLY MAKES SENSE.
SURPRISE ATTACKS OUT OF JEALOUSY? THAT'S COWARDICE! I WON'T FORGIVE THEM!!
I JUST DON'T UNDERSTAND.
HUH.
THAT'S RIGHT! WE CAN'T ALLOW THIS UNFAIR TREATMENT TO GO ON!!
BUT WHAT SHOULD WE DO ABOUT IT, HONOKA?
UMM...
INFORM THE STUDENT COUNCIL? ...BUT...

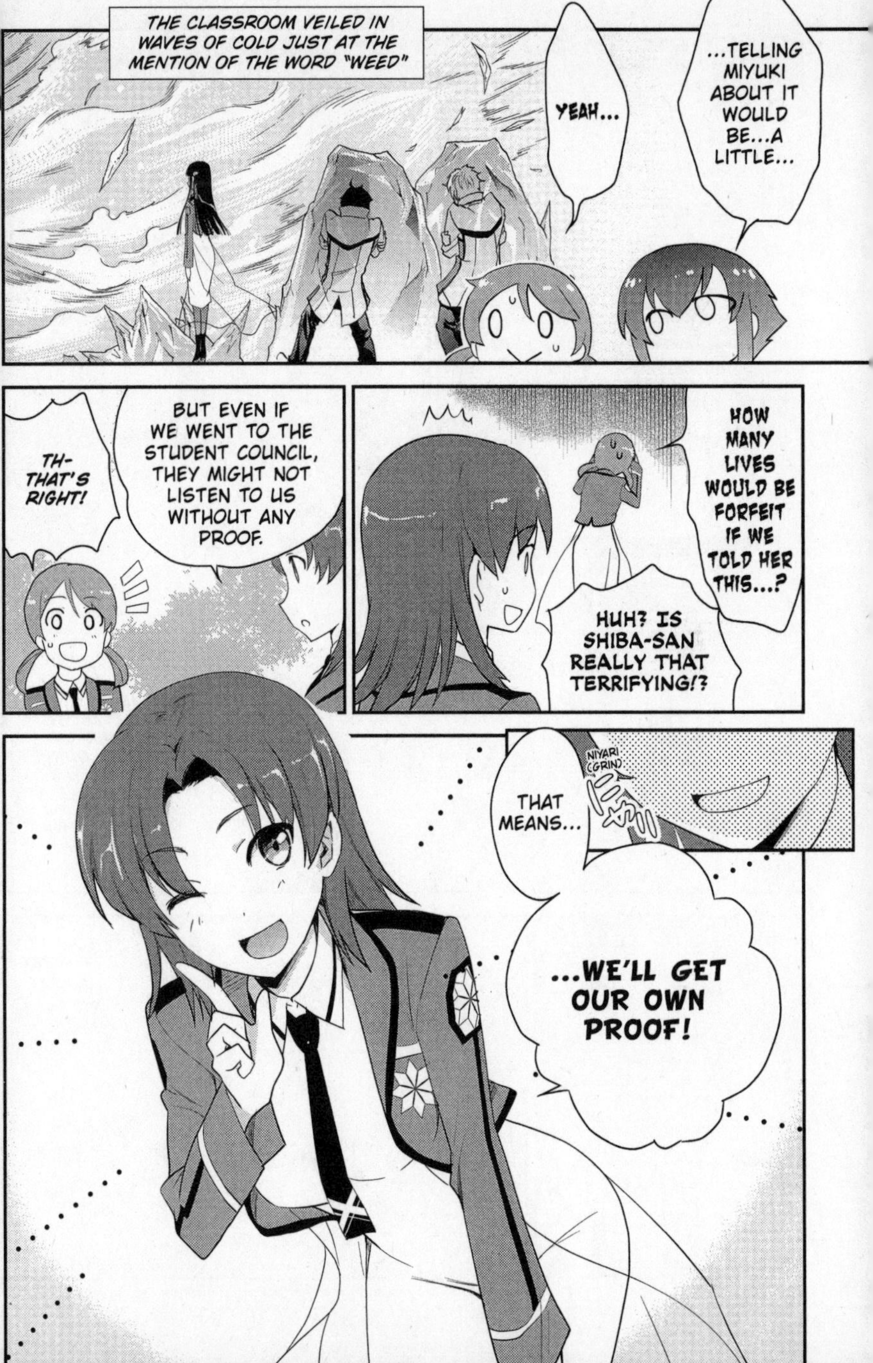
...TELLING MIYUKI ABOUT IT WOULD BE...A LITTLE...
YEAH...
THE CLASSROOM VEILED IN WAVES OF COLD JUST AT THE MENTION OF THE WORD "WEED"
HOW MANY LIVES WOULD BE FORFEIT IF WE TOLD HER THIS...?
HUH? IS SHIBA-SAN REALLY THAT TERRIFYING!?
BUT EVEN IF WE WENT TO THE STUDENT COUNCIL, THEY MIGHT NOT LISTEN TO US WITHOUT ANY PROOF.
TH-THAT'S RIGHT!
NIYARI (GRIN)
THAT MEANS...
...WE'LL GET OUR OWN PROOF!

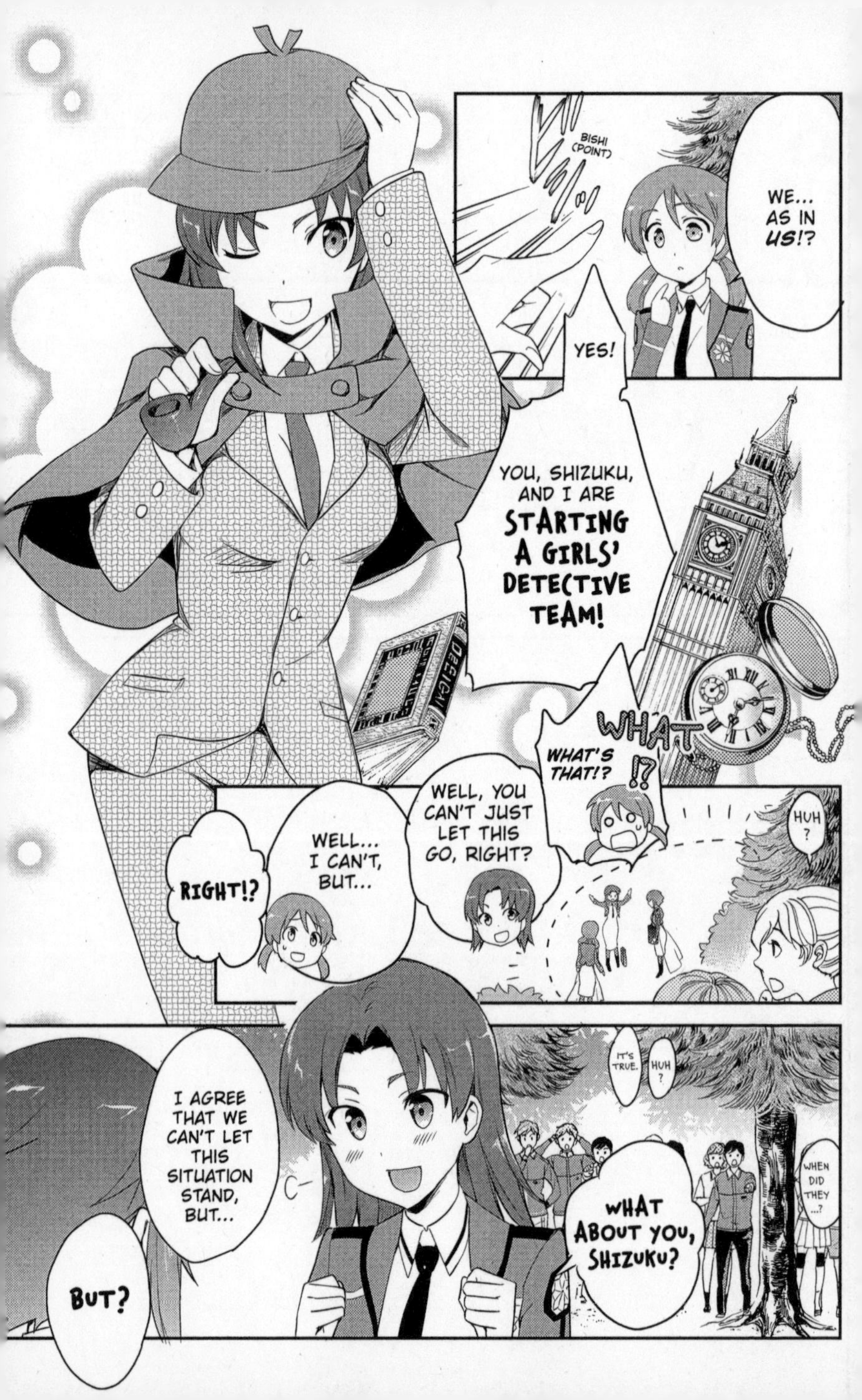
BISHI (POINT)
WE... AS IN US!?
YES!
YOU, SHIZUKU, AND I ARE STARTING A GIRLS' DETECTIVE TEAM!
WHAT
WHAT'S THAT!?
!?
HUH?
WELL, YOU CAN'T JUST LET THIS GO, RIGHT?
WELL... I CAN'T, BUT...
RIGHT!?
WHEN DID THEY ...?
HUH?
IT'S TRUE.
WHAT ABOUT YOU, SHIZUKU?
I AGREE THAT WE CAN'T LET THIS SITUATION STAND, BUT...
BUT?

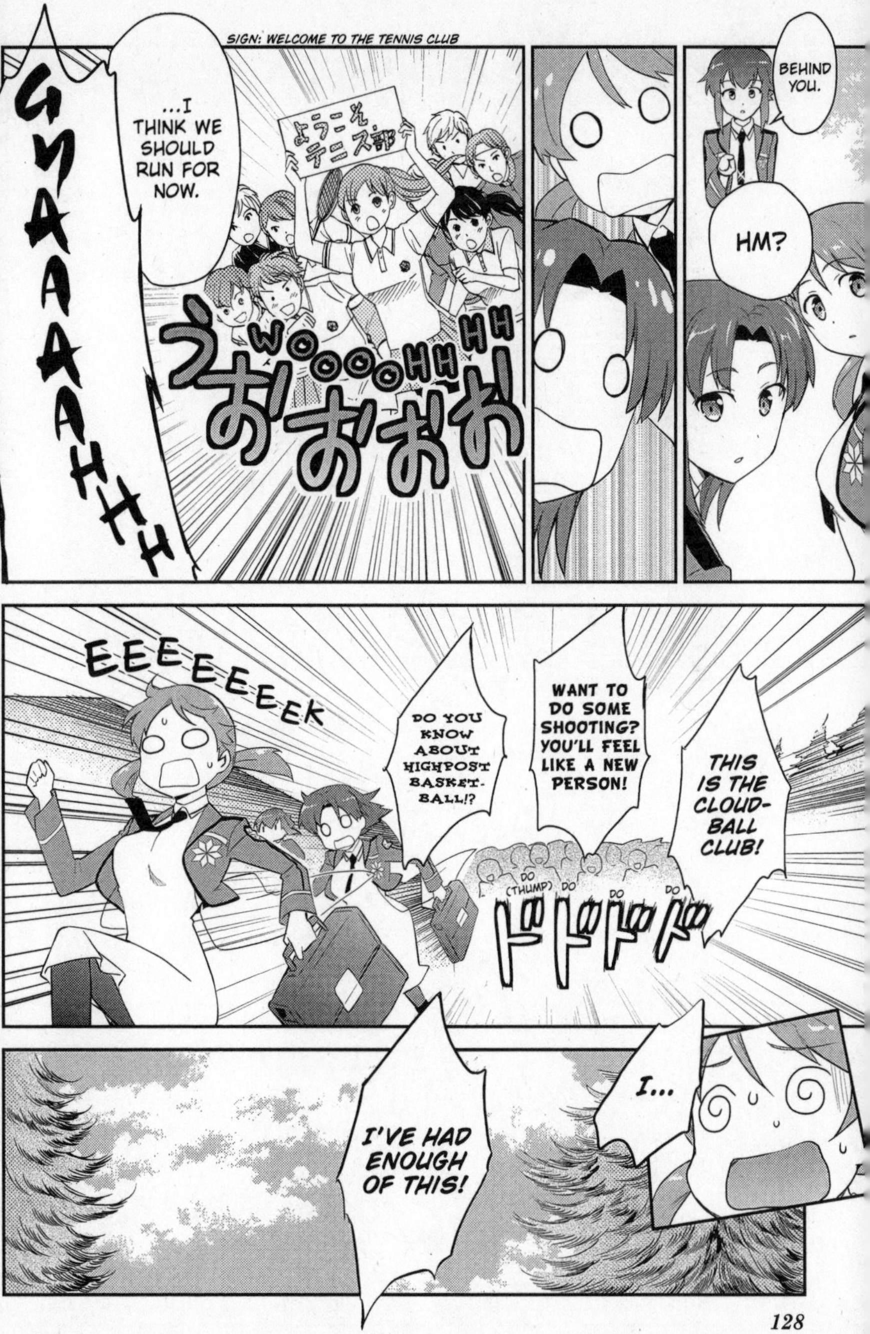
BEHIND YOU.
HM?
SIGN: WELCOME TO THE TENNIS CLUB
ようこそ テニス部
...I THINK WE SHOULD RUN FOR NOW.
うおおおお
WOOOOOHHHHH
GYAAAAAHHHH
THIS IS THE CLOUD-BALL CLUB!
WANT TO DO SOME SHOOTING? YOU'LL FEEL LIKE A NEW PERSON!
DO YOU KNOW ABOUT HIGHPOST BASKET-BALL!?
ドドドドド
DO (THUMP) DO DO DO
EEEEEEEEEK
I...
I'VE HAD ENOUGH OF THIS!

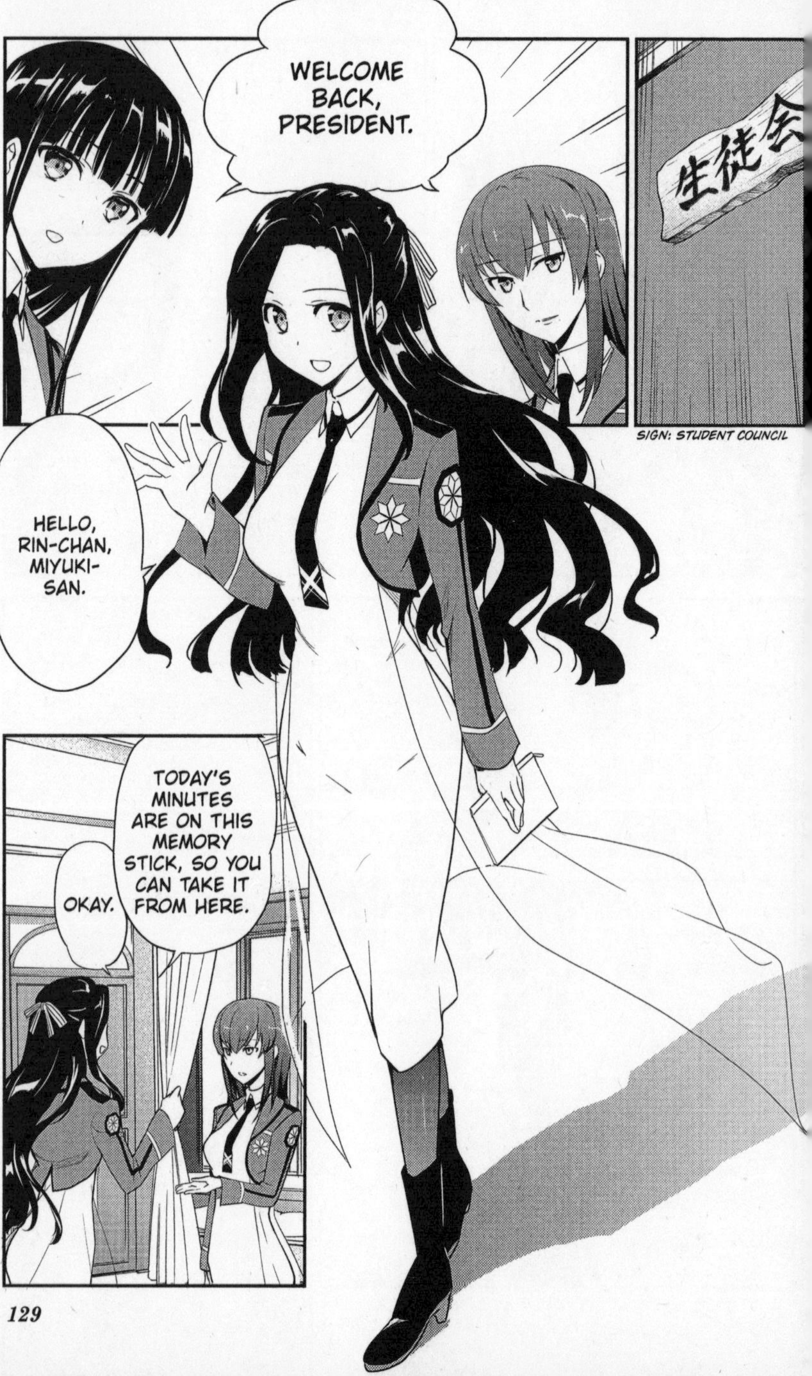
生徒会
WELCOME BACK, PRESIDENT.
SIGN: STUDENT COUNCIL
HELLO, RIN-CHAN, MIYUKI-SAN.
TODAY'S MINUTES ARE ON THIS MEMORY STICK, SO YOU CAN TAKE IT FROM HERE.
OKAY.

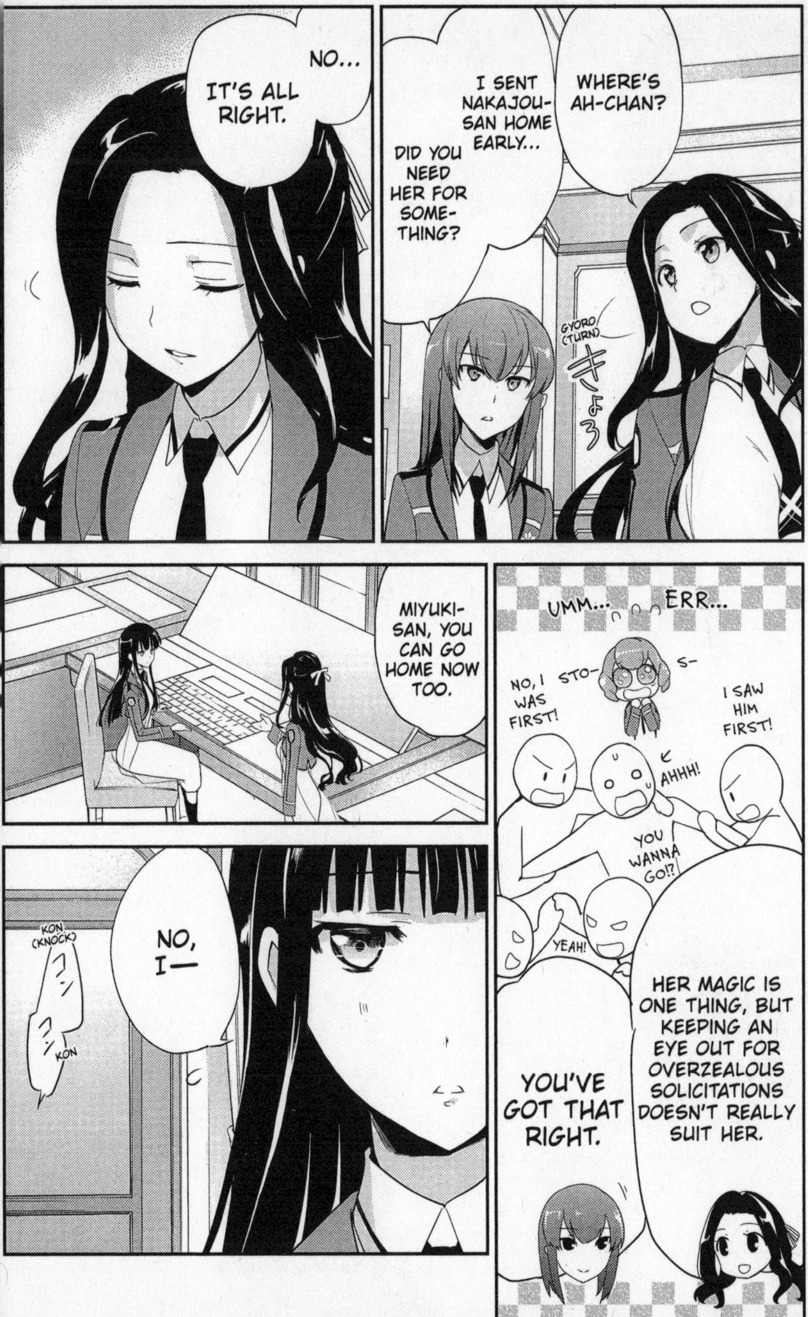
WHERE'S AH-CHAN?
I SENT NAKAJOU-SAN HOME EARLY...
DID YOU NEED HER FOR SOMETHING?
GYORO (TURN)
きょろ
NO...
IT'S ALL RIGHT.
UMM... ERR...
S-
STO-
I SAW HIM FIRST!
NO, I WAS FIRST!
AHHH!
YOU WANNA GO!?
YEAH!
HER MAGIC IS ONE THING, BUT KEEPING AN EYE OUT FOR OVERZEALOUS SOLICITATIONS DOESN'T REALLY SUIT HER.
YOU'VE GOT THAT RIGHT.
MIYUKI-SAN, YOU CAN GO HOME NOW TOO.
NO, I—
KON (KNOCK)
コン
コン
KON

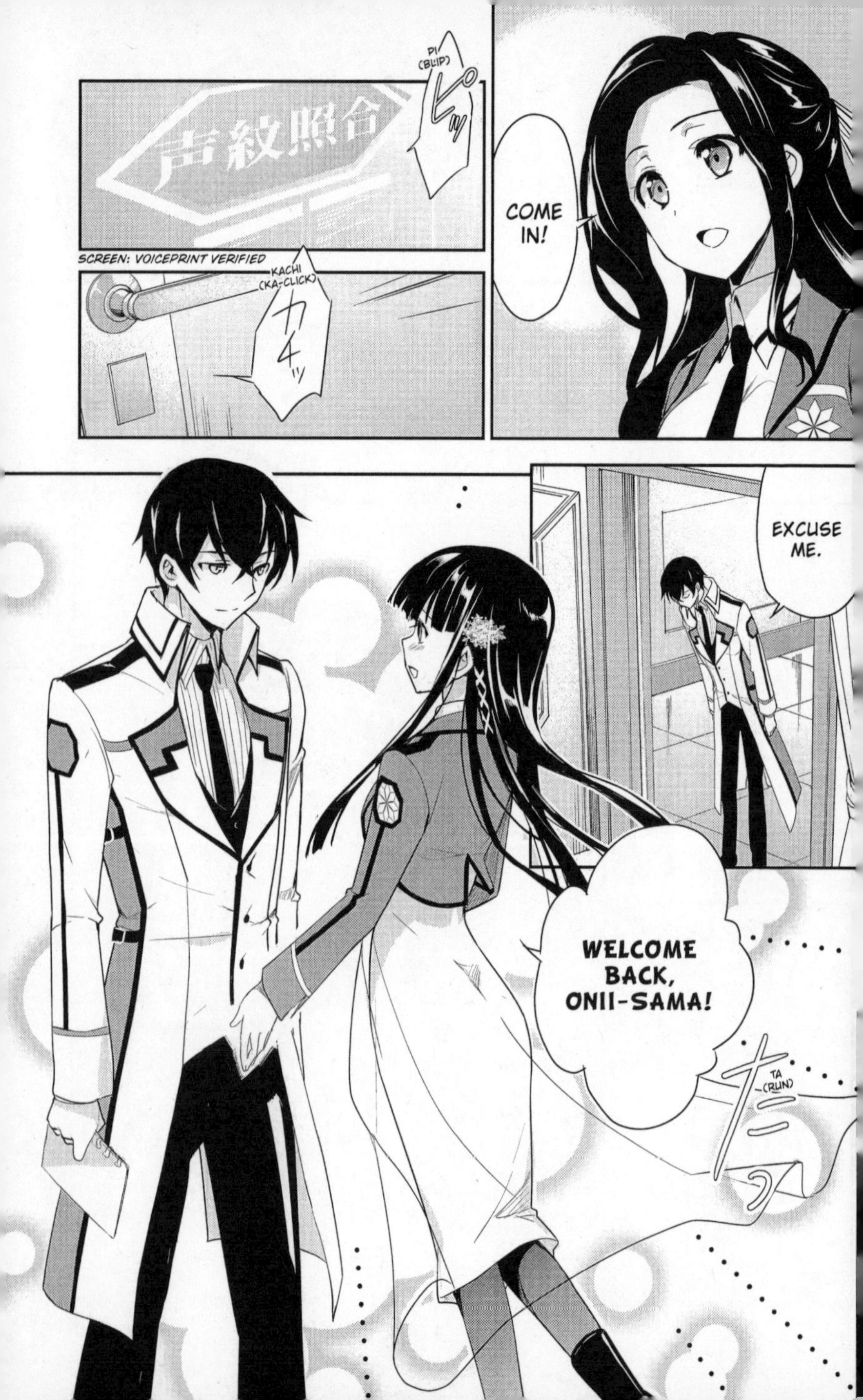
COME IN!
PI (BLIP)
ピッ
声紋照合
SCREEN: VOICEPRINT VERIFIED
KACHI (KA-CLICK)
カチッ
EXCUSE ME.
WELCOME BACK, ONII-SAMA!
TA (RUN)
タッ

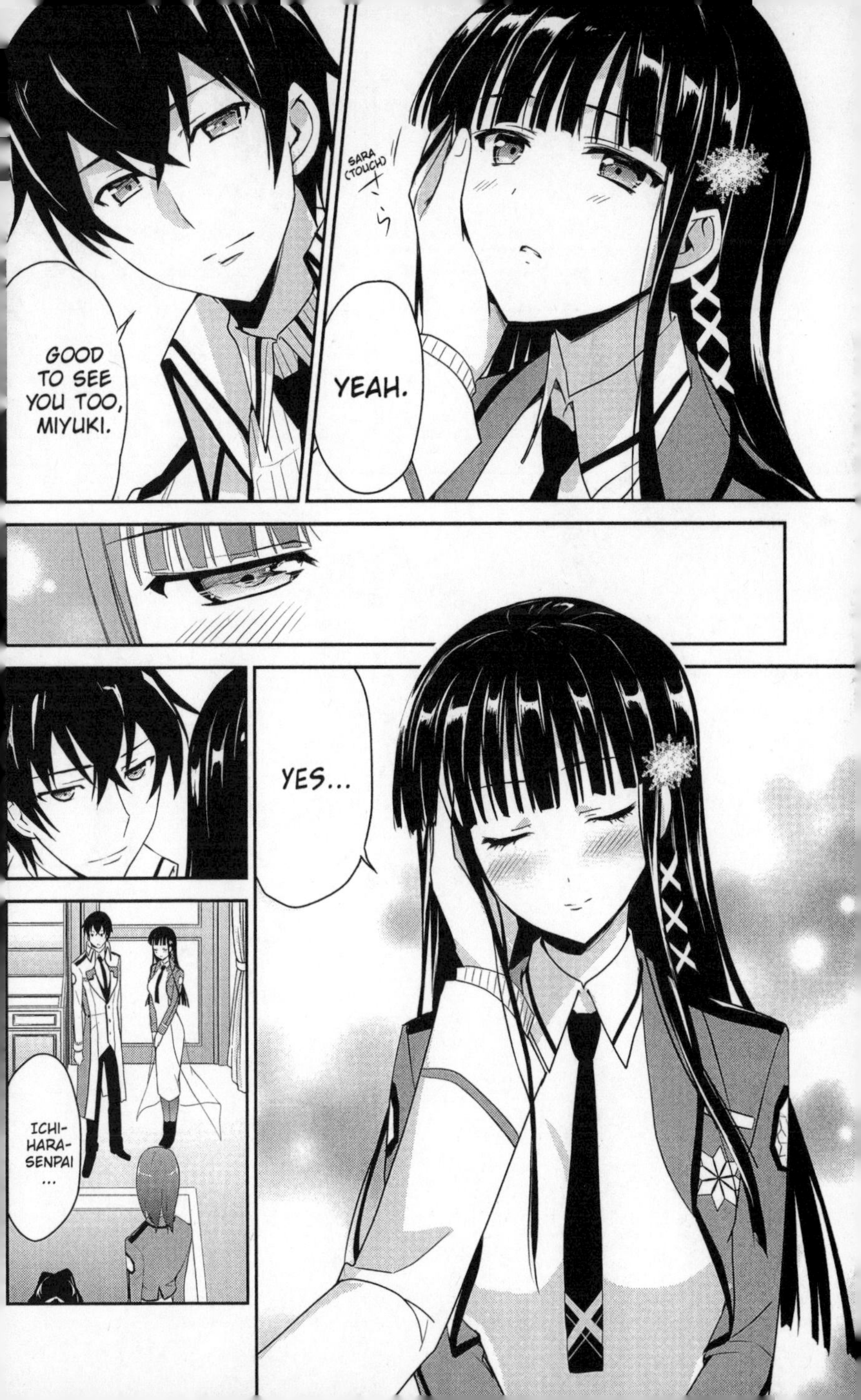
SARA (TOUCH)
さら
YEAH.
GOOD TO SEE YOU TOO, MIYUKI.
YES...
ICHI-HARA-SENPAI ...

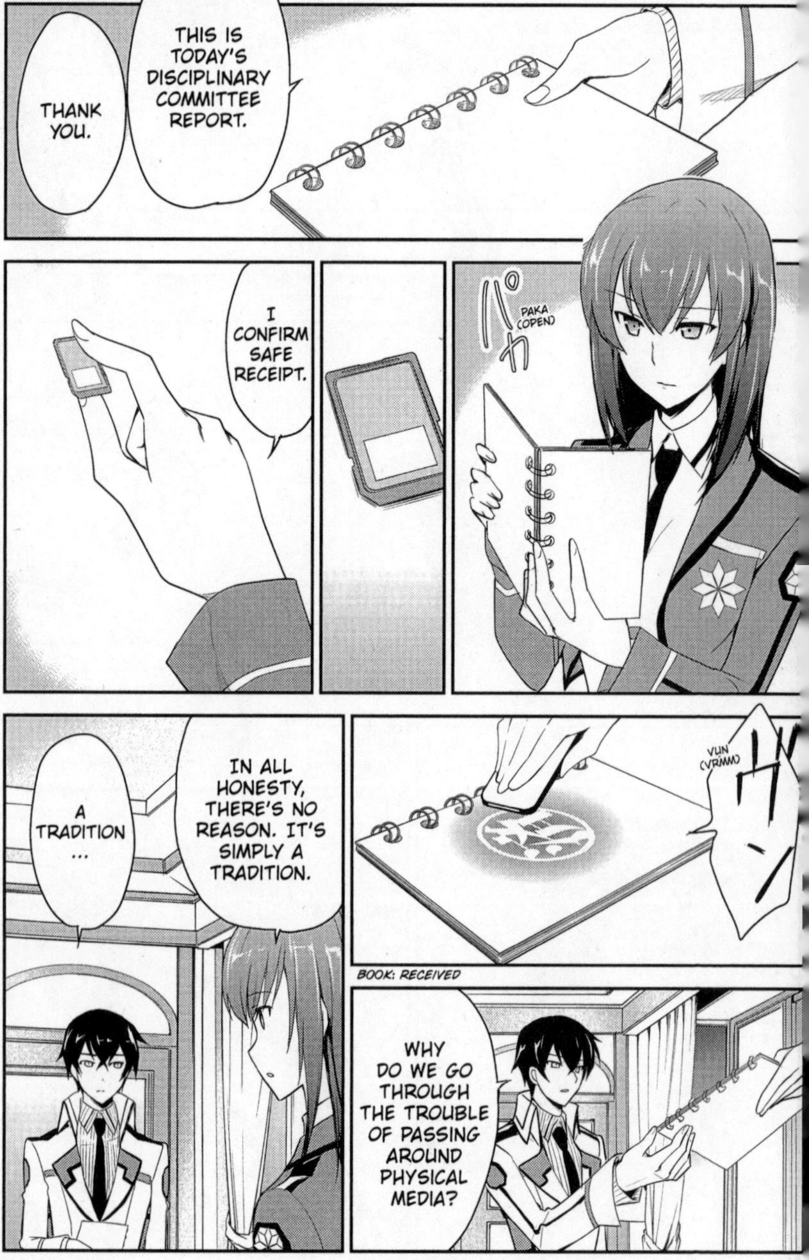
THIS IS TODAY'S DISCIPLINARY COMMITTEE REPORT.
THANK YOU.
パカ
PAKA (OPEN)
I CONFIRM SAFE RECEIPT.
VUN (VRMM)
BOOK: RECEIVED
WHY DO WE GO THROUGH THE TROUBLE OF PASSING AROUND PHYSICAL MEDIA?
IN ALL HONESTY, THERE'S NO REASON. IT'S SIMPLY A TRADITION.
A TRADITION ...

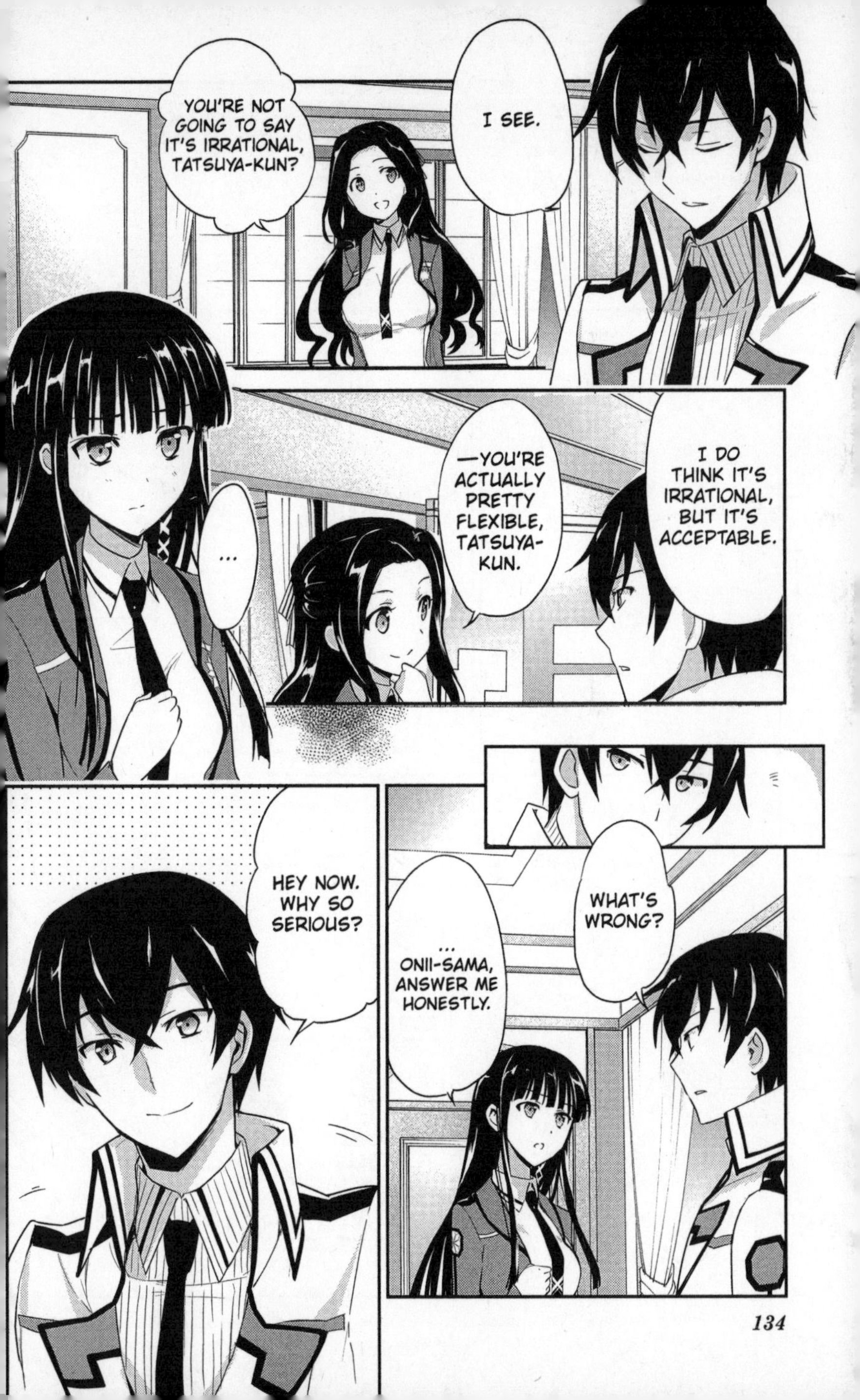
I SEE.
YOU'RE NOT GOING TO SAY IT'S IRRATIONAL, TATSUYA-KUN?
I DO THINK IT'S IRRATIONAL, BUT IT'S ACCEPTABLE.
—YOU'RE ACTUALLY PRETTY FLEXIBLE, TATSUYA-KUN.
...
WHAT'S WRONG?
... ONII-SAMA, ANSWER ME HONESTLY.
HEY NOW. WHY SO SERIOUS?

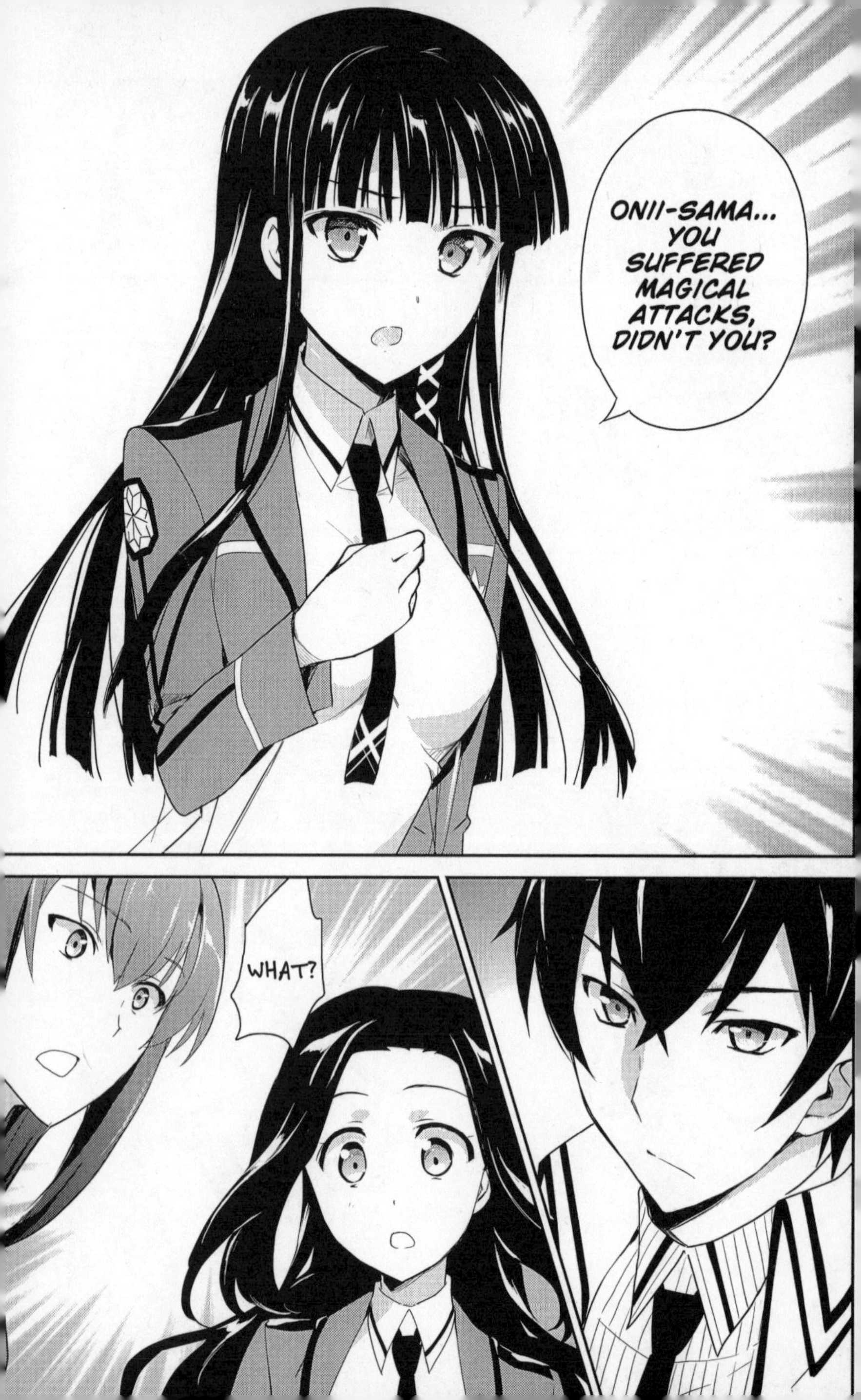
ONII-SAMA... YOU SUFFERED MAGICAL ATTACKS, DIDN'T YOU?
WHAT?

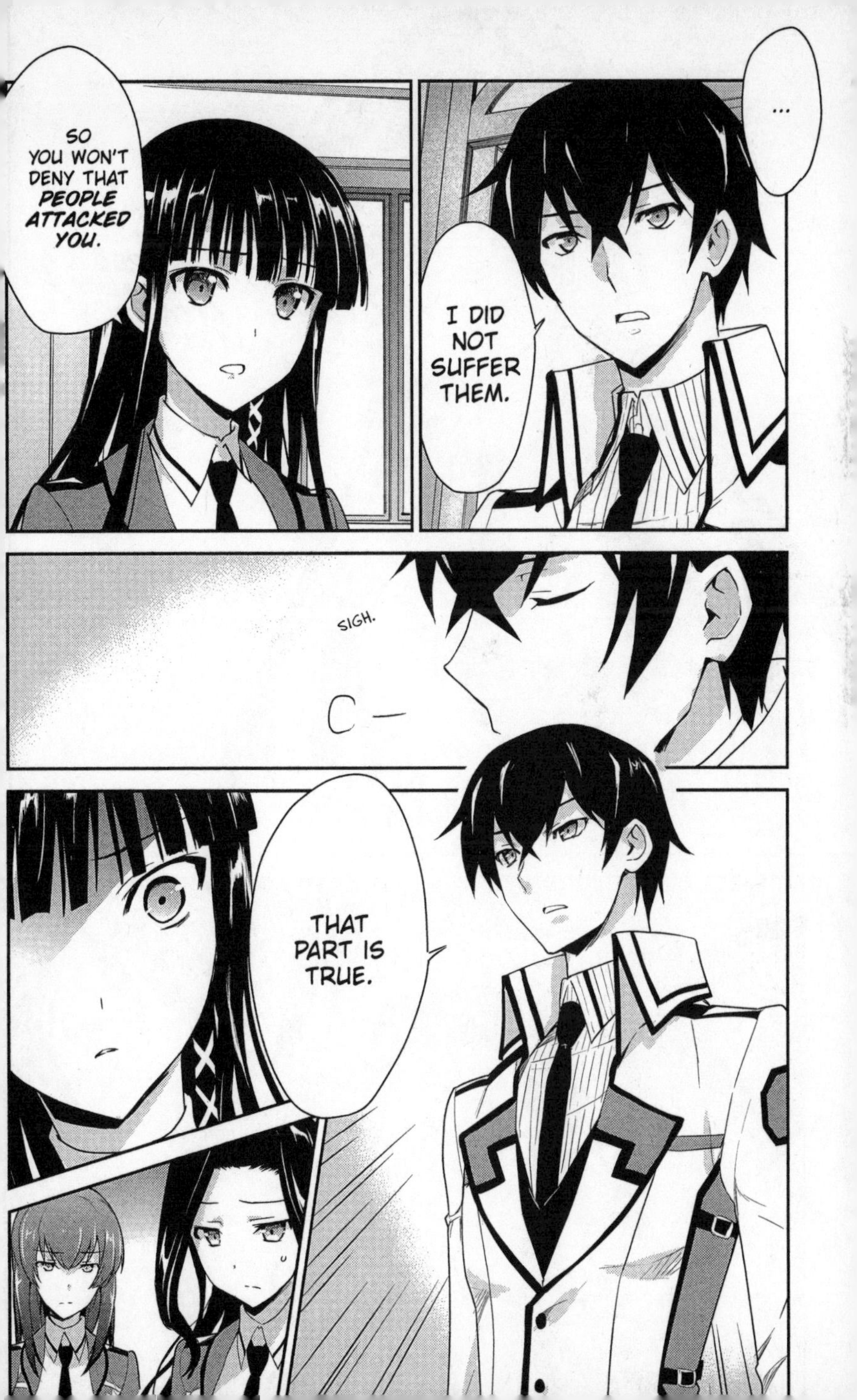
...
I DID NOT SUFFER THEM.
SO YOU WON'T DENY THAT PEOPLE ATTACKED YOU.
SIGH.
THAT PART IS TRUE.

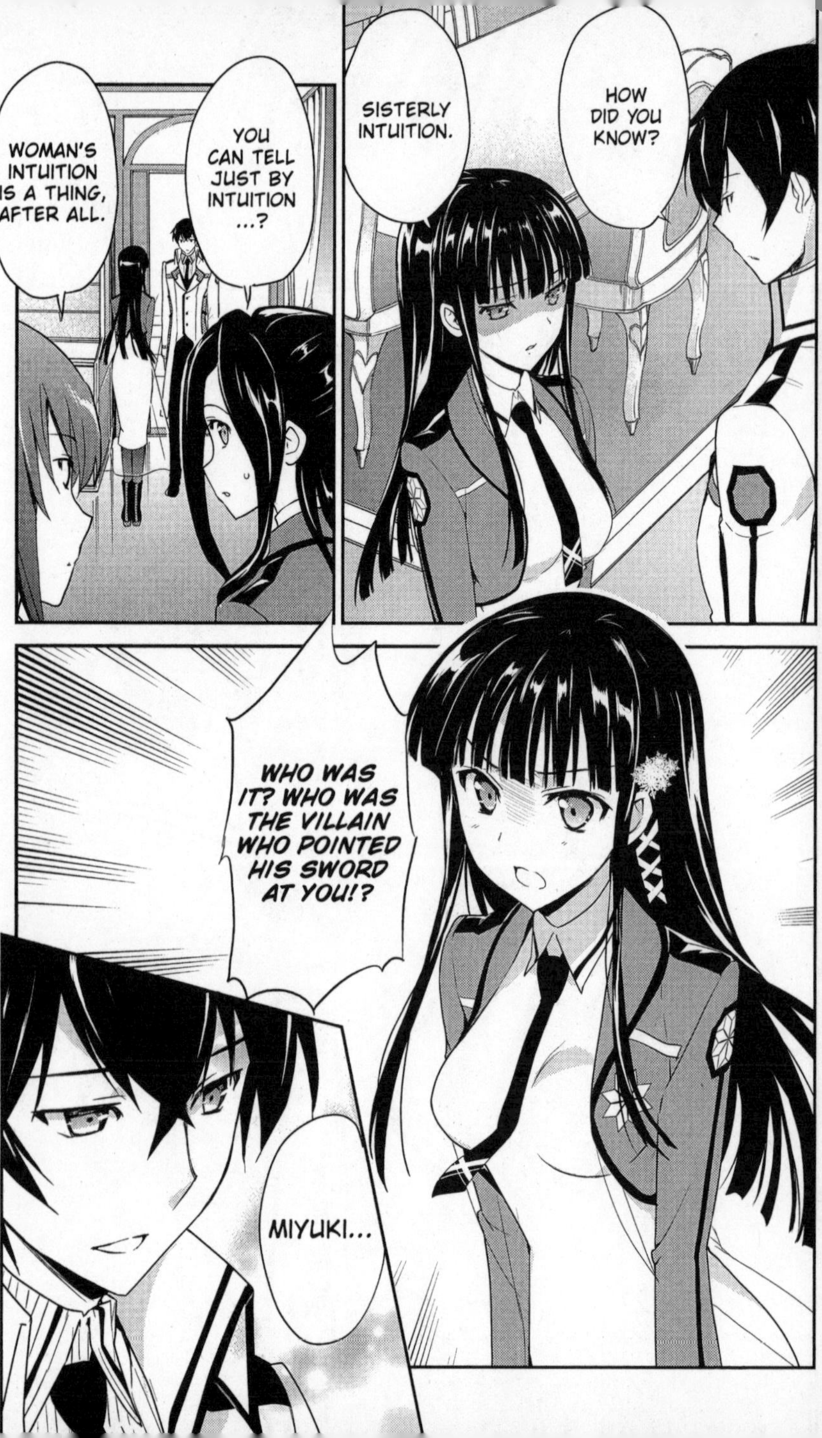
HOW DID YOU KNOW?
SISTERLY INTUITION.
YOU CAN TELL JUST BY INTUITION ...?
WOMAN'S INTUITION IS A THING, AFTER ALL.
WHO WAS IT? WHO WAS THE VILLAIN WHO POINTED HIS SWORD AT YOU!?
MIYUKI...

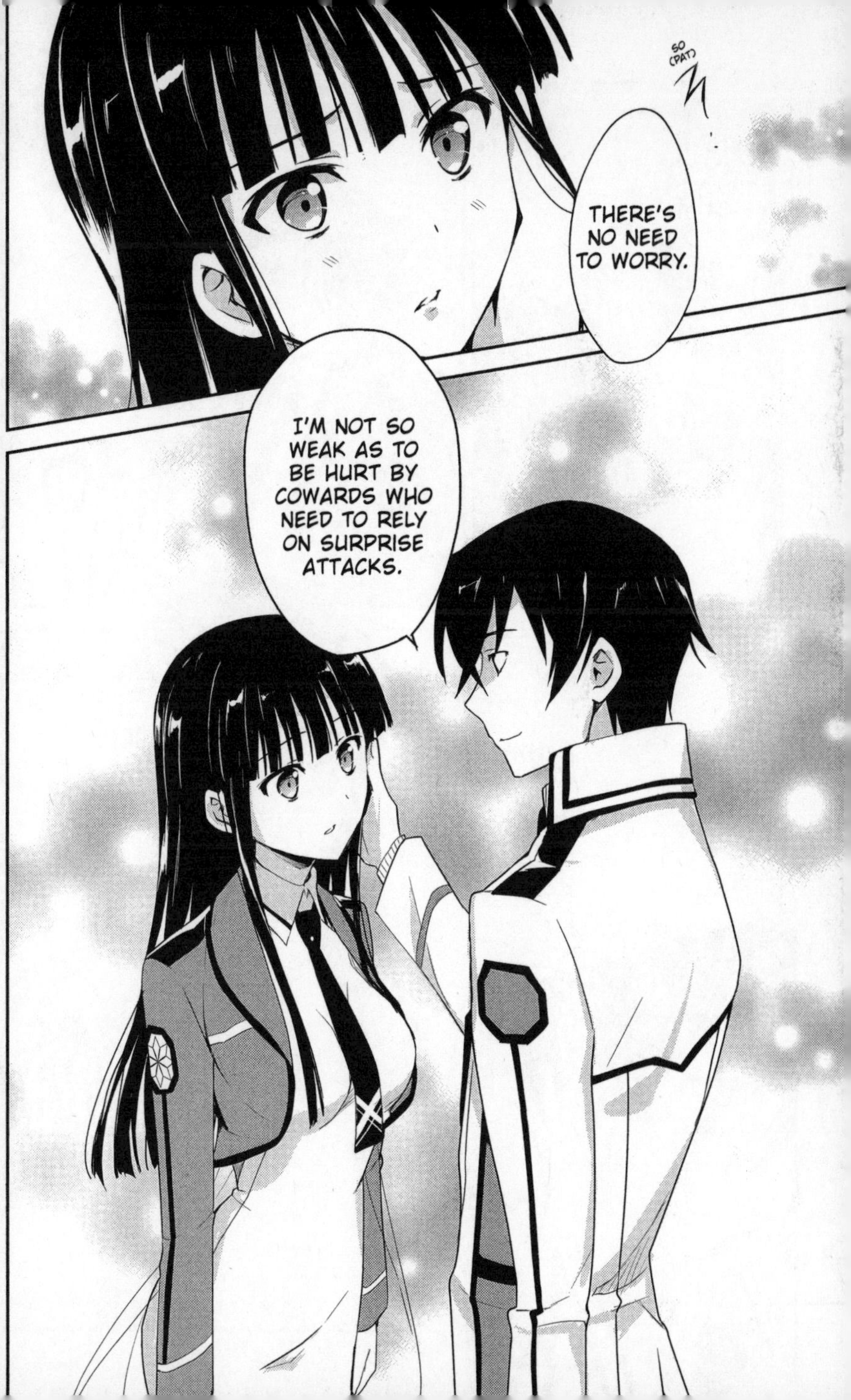
SO (PAT)
THERE'S NO NEED TO WORRY.
I'M NOT SO WEAK AS TO BE HURT BY COWARDS WHO NEED TO RELY ON SURPRISE ATTACKS.

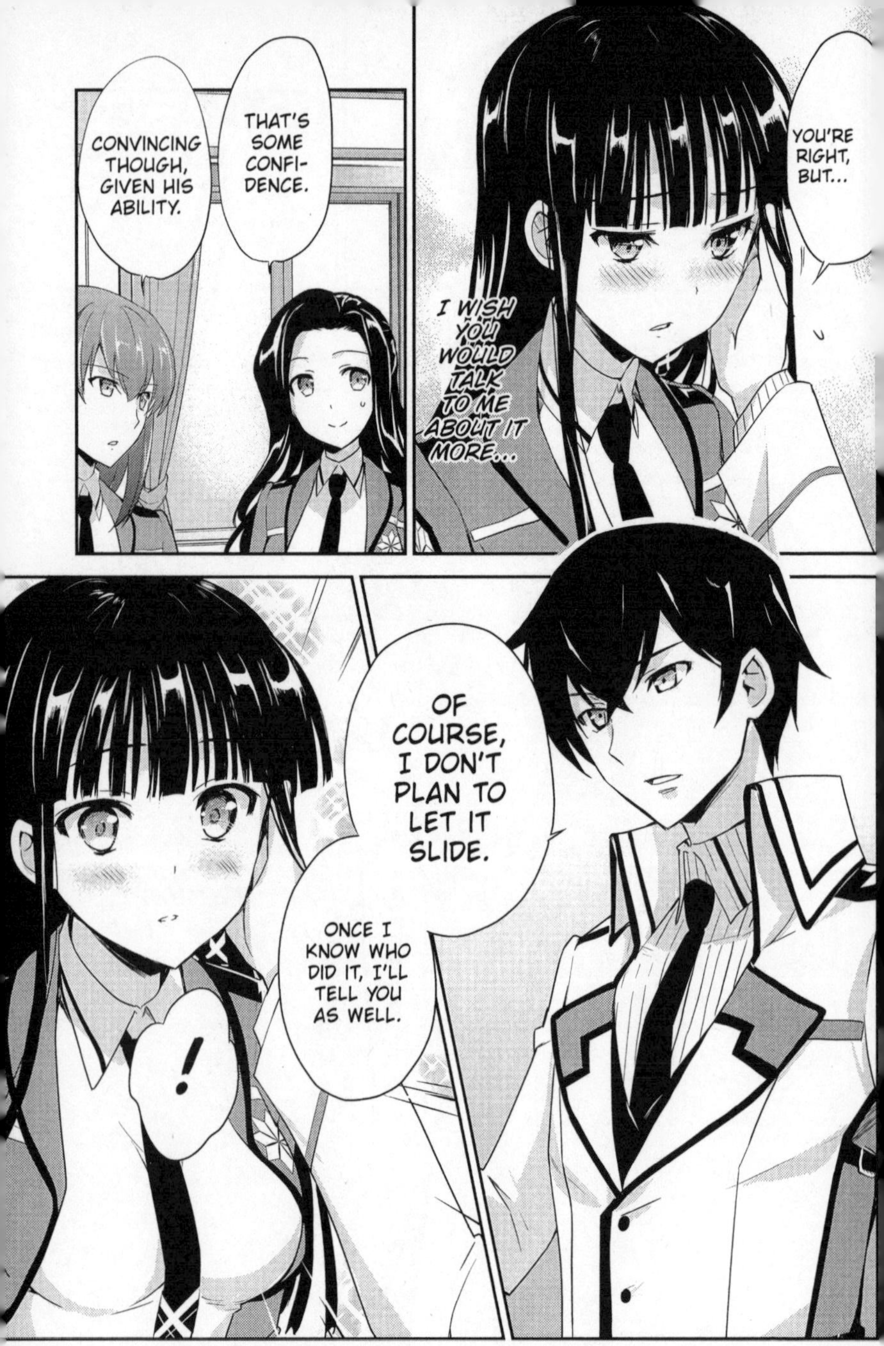
YOU'RE RIGHT, BUT...
I WISH YOU WOULD TALK TO ME ABOUT IT MORE...
THAT'S SOME CONFI-DENCE.
CONVINCING THOUGH, GIVEN HIS ABILITY.
OF COURSE, I DON'T PLAN TO LET IT SLIDE.
ONCE I KNOW WHO DID IT, I'LL TELL YOU AS WELL.
!

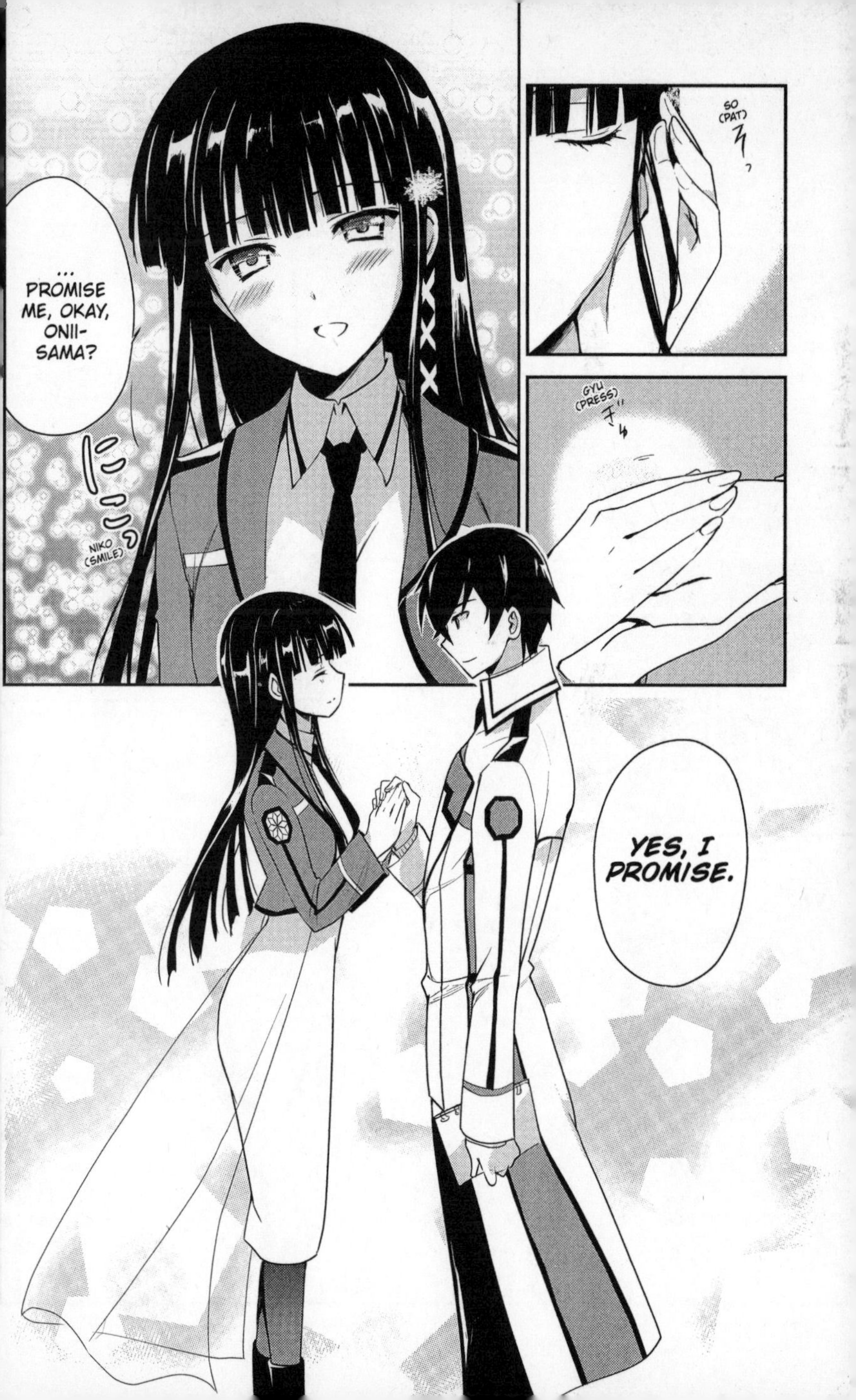
SO (PAT)
GYU (PRESS)
... PROMISE ME, OKAY, ONII-SAMA?
NIKO (SMILE)
YES, I PROMISE.

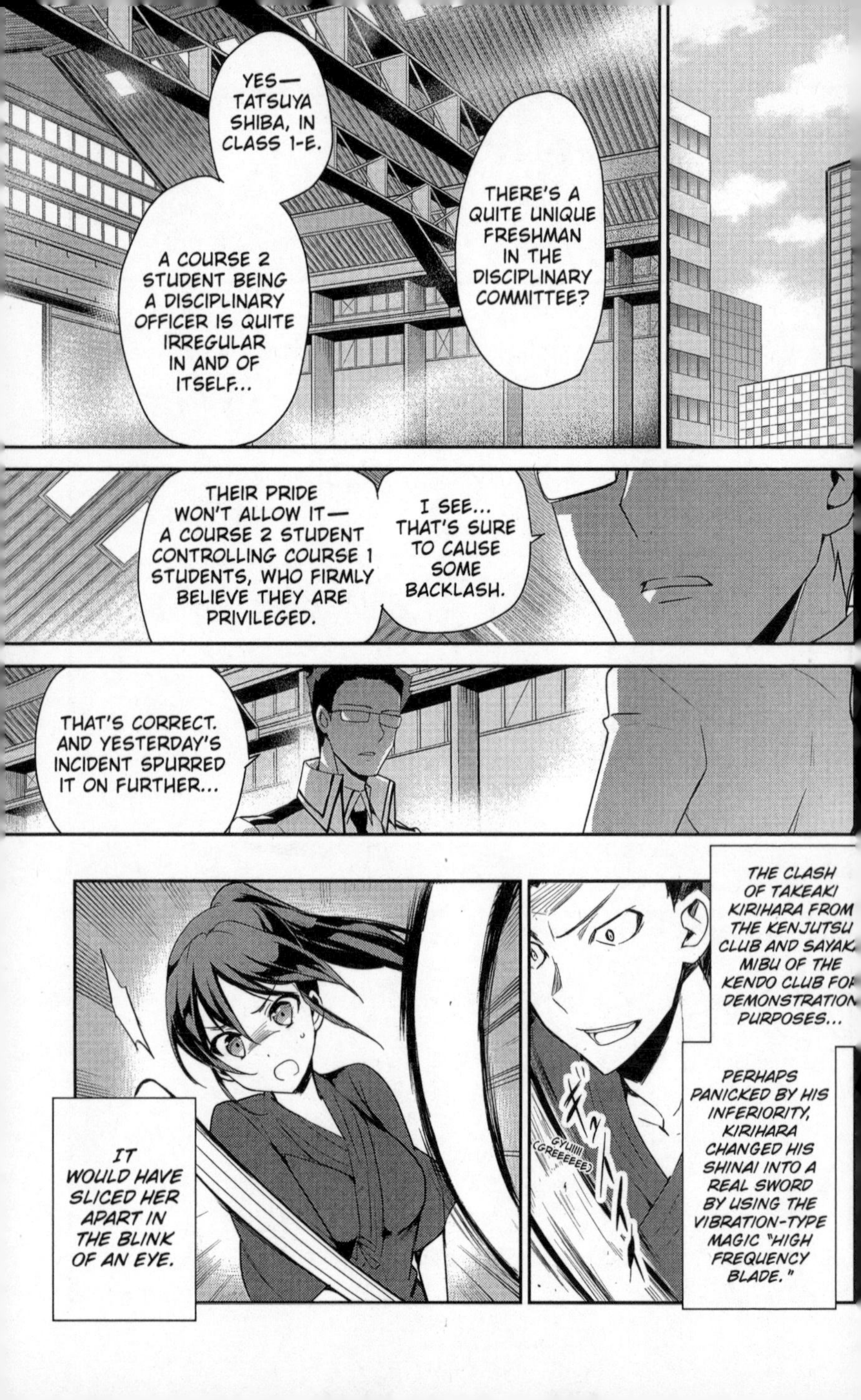
THERE'S A QUITE UNIQUE FRESHMAN IN THE DISCIPLINARY COMMITTEE?
YES— TATSUYA SHIBA, IN CLASS 1-E.
A COURSE 2 STUDENT BEING A DISCIPLINARY OFFICER IS QUITE IRREGULAR IN AND OF ITSELF...
I SEE... THAT'S SURE TO CAUSE SOME BACKLASH.
THEIR PRIDE WON'T ALLOW IT— A COURSE 2 STUDENT CONTROLLING COURSE 1 STUDENTS, WHO FIRMLY BELIEVE THEY ARE PRIVILEGED.
THAT'S CORRECT. AND YESTERDAY'S INCIDENT SPURRED IT ON FURTHER...
THE CLASH OF TAKEAKI KIRIHARA FROM THE KENJUTSU CLUB AND SAYAK MIBU OF THE KENDO CLUB FO DEMONSTRATIO PURPOSES...
PERHAPS PANICKED BY HIS INFERIORITY, KIRIHARA CHANGED HIS SHINAI INTO A REAL SWORD BY USING THE VIBRATION-TYPE MAGIC "HIGH FREQUENCY BLADE."
GYUIIII (GREEEEEEE)
IT WOULD HAVE SLICED HER APART IN THE BLINK OF AN EYE.

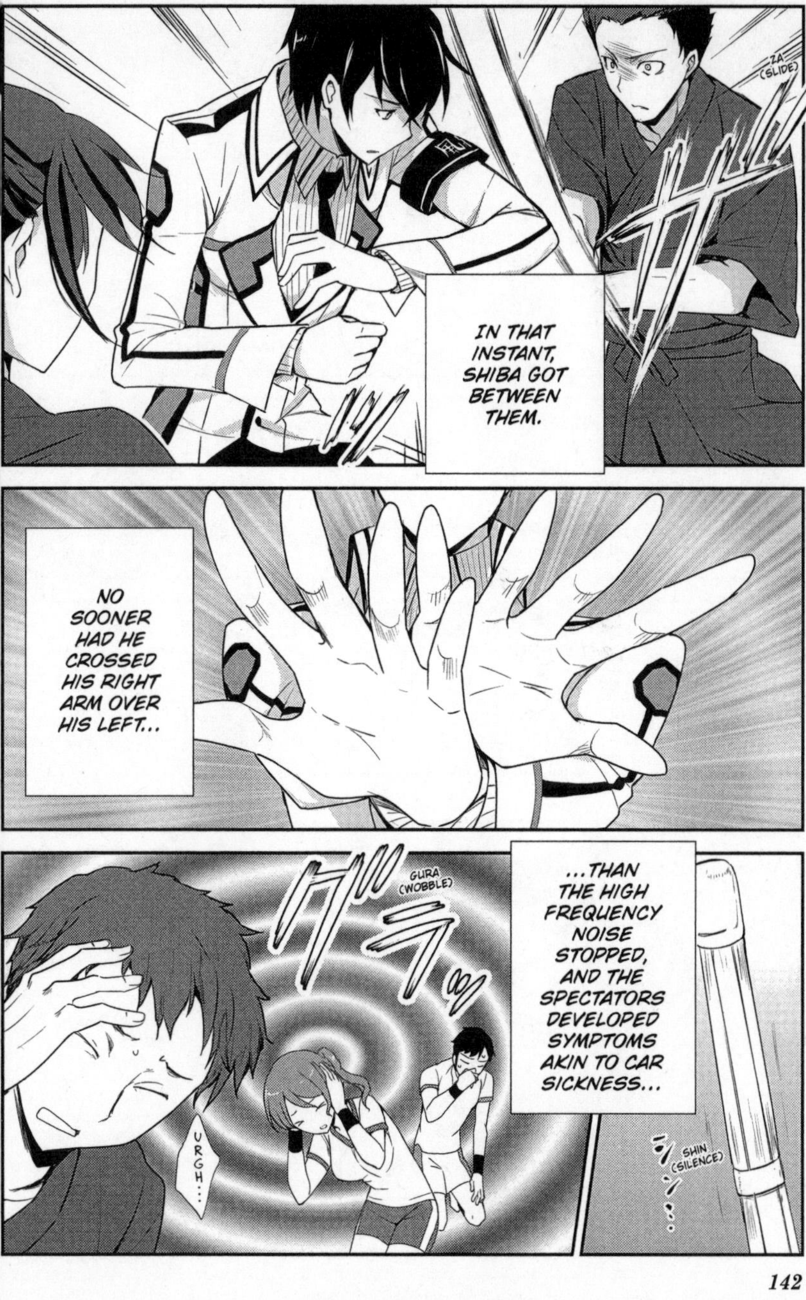
ZA (SLIDE)
IN THAT INSTANT, SHIBA GOT BETWEEN THEM.
NO SOONER HAD HE CROSSED HIS RIGHT ARM OVER HIS LEFT...
...THAN THE HIGH FREQUENCY NOISE STOPPED, AND THE SPECTATORS DEVELOPED SYMPTOMS AKIN TO CAR SICKNESS...
GURA (WOBBLE)
SHIN (SILENCE)
URGH...

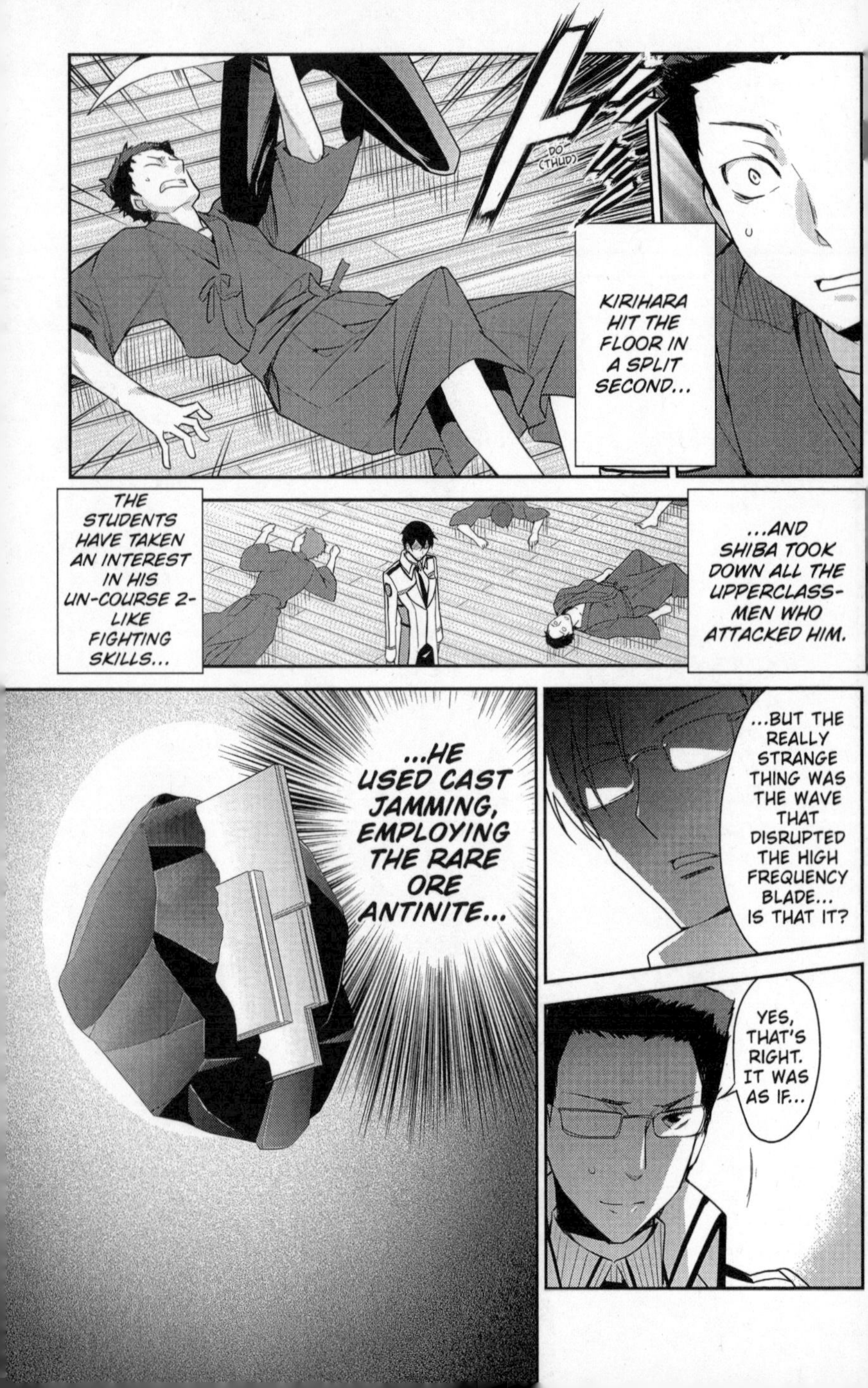
DO (THUD)
KIRIHARA HIT THE FLOOR IN A SPLIT SECOND...
...AND SHIBA TOOK DOWN ALL THE UPPERCLASSMEN WHO ATTACKED HIM.
THE STUDENTS HAVE TAKEN AN INTEREST IN HIS UN-COURSE 2-LIKE FIGHTING SKILLS...
...BUT THE REALLY STRANGE THING WAS THE WAVE THAT DISRUPTED THE HIGH FREQUENCY BLADE... IS THAT IT?
YES, THAT'S RIGHT. IT WAS AS IF...
...HE USED CAST JAMMING, EMPLOYING THE RARE ORE ANTINITE...

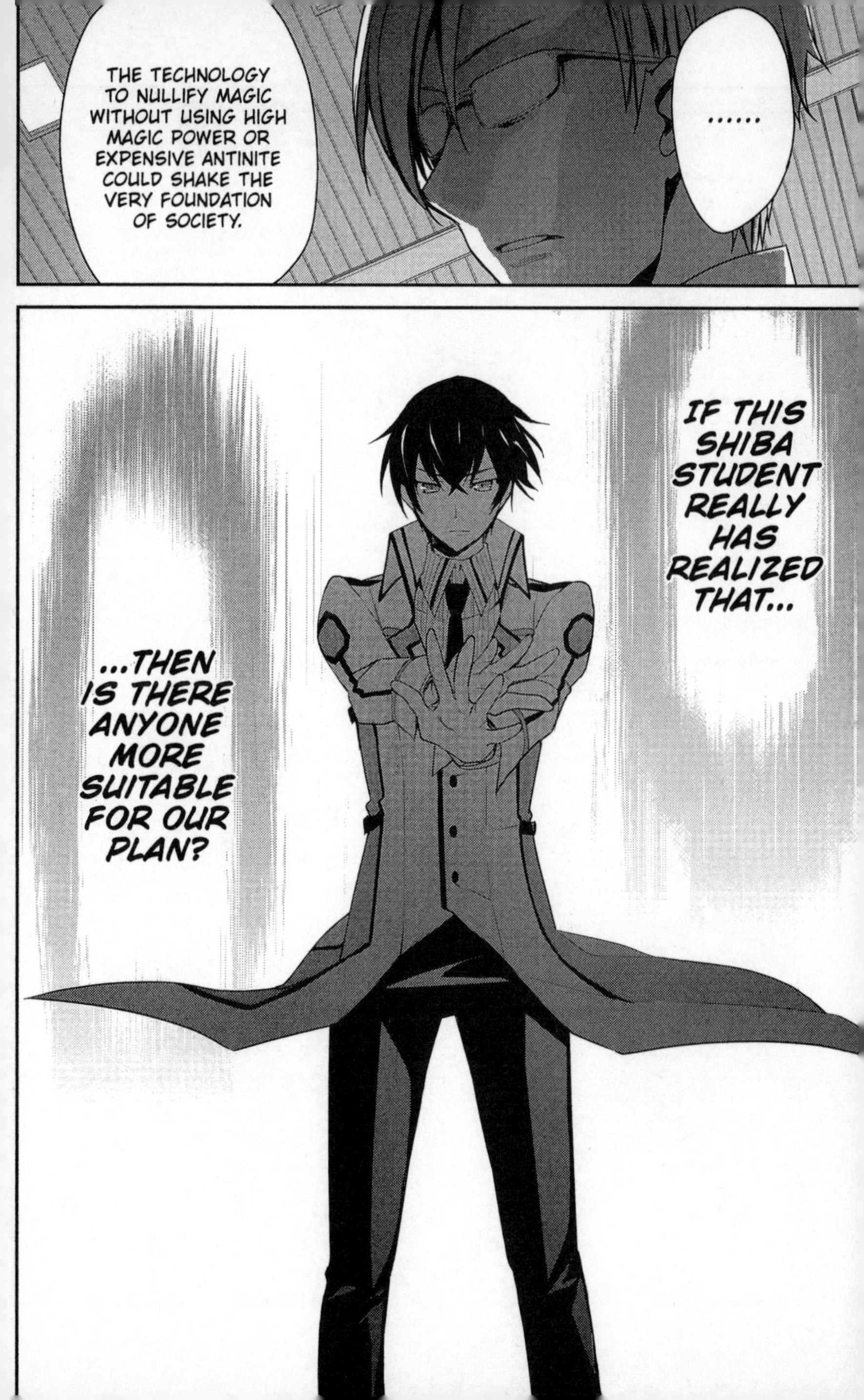
......
THE TECHNOLOGY TO NULLIFY MAGIC WITHOUT USING HIGH MAGIC POWER OR EXPENSIVE ANTINITE COULD SHAKE THE VERY FOUNDATION OF SOCIETY.
IF THIS SHIBA STUDENT REALLY HAS REALIZED THAT...
...THEN IS THERE ANYONE MORE SUITABLE FOR OUR PLAN?

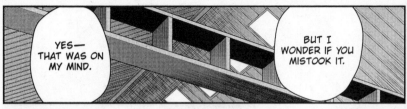

BUT I WONDER IF YOU MISTOOK IT.
YES— THAT WAS ON MY MIND.
SHIBA WAS ON THE RECEIVING END OF A LOT OF BULLYING WHILE MAKING HIS ROUNDS FOR THE DISCIPLINARY COMMITTEE ...
I THOUGHT HE MIGHT USE THAT JAMMING PLOY AGAIN, SO I KEPT HIM UNDER OBSERVATION...
...BUT I COULDN'T PERCEIVE THE DECISIVE MOMENT...
SO IF YOU DON'T ATTACK HIM YOURSELF, YOU CAN'T BE SURE...
CAN YOU DO IT?
YES.
AND IF YOU CAN MAKE HIM OUR ALLY, THAT WOULD BE SPLENDID.
AND FOR THAT ROLE...

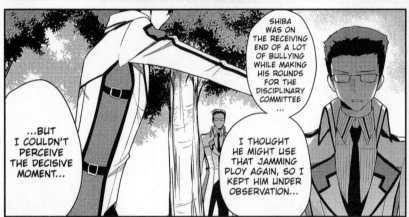

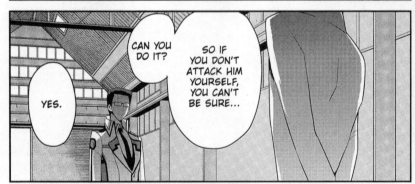

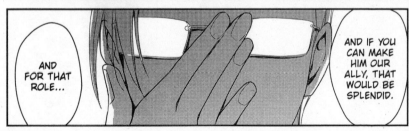

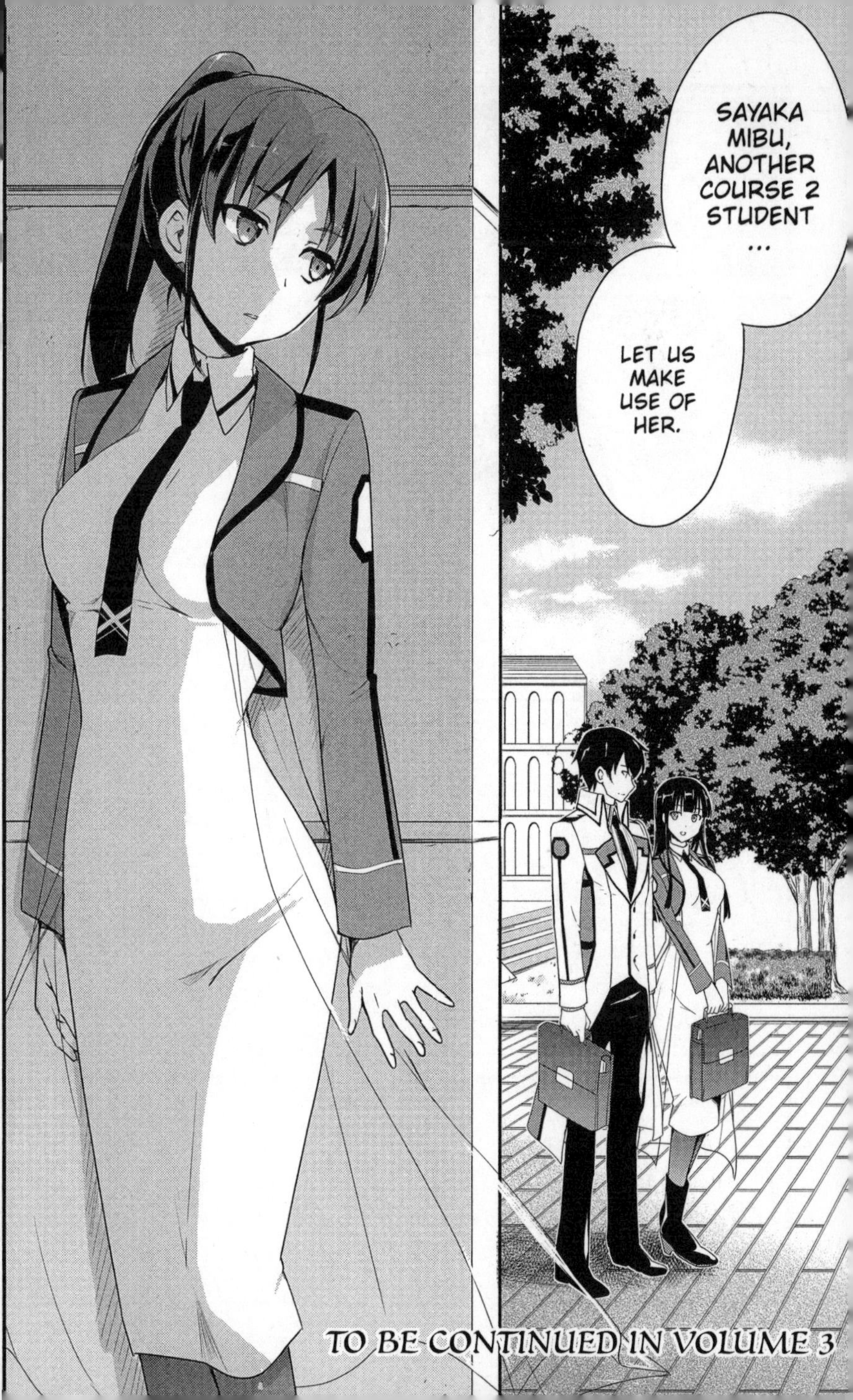
SAYAKA MIBU, ANOTHER COURSE 2 STUDENT ...
LET US MAKE USE OF HER.
TO BE CONTINUED IN VOLUME 3

EXTRA CHAPTER

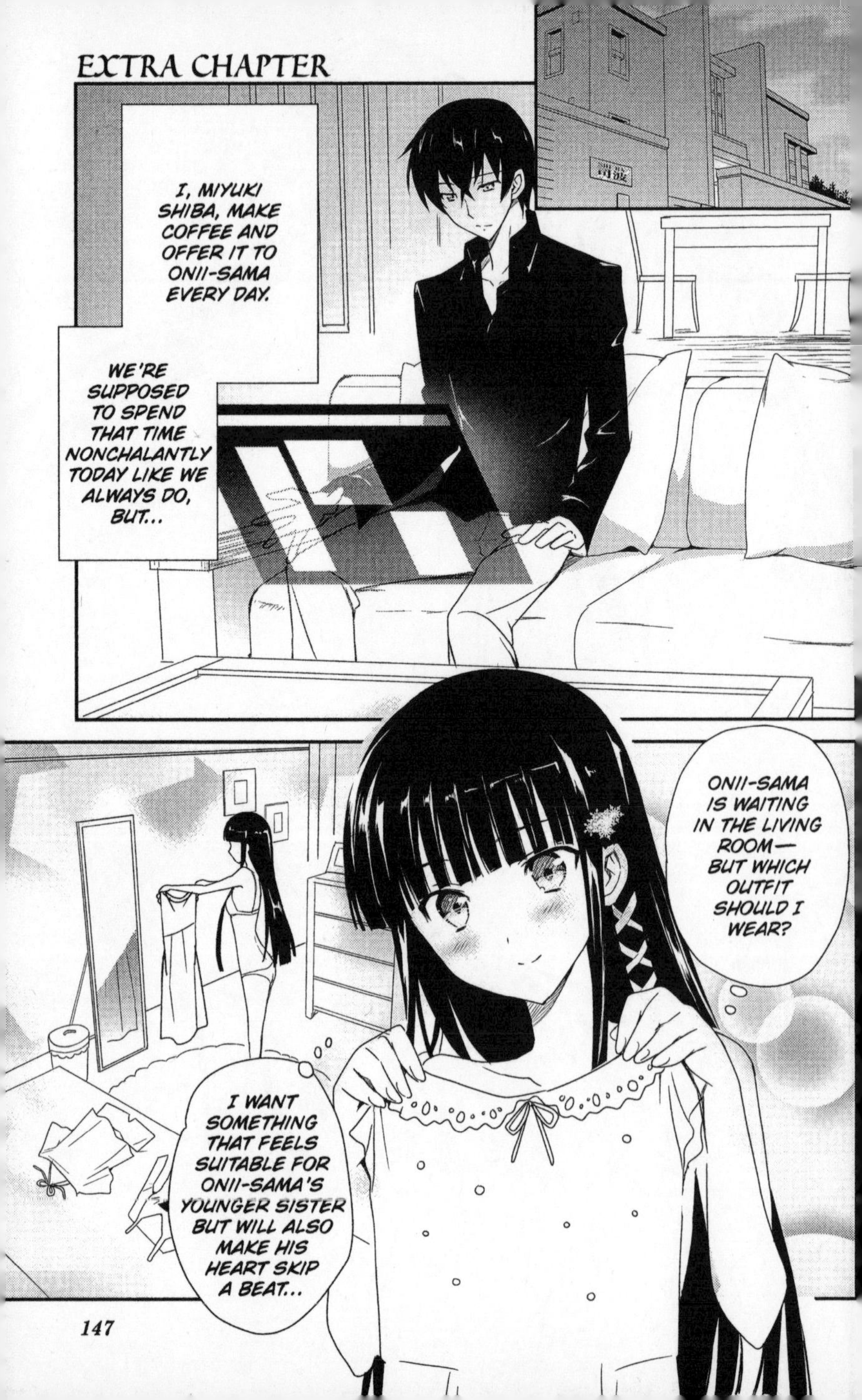
I, MIYUKI SHIBA, MAKE COFFEE AND OFFER IT TO ONII-SAMA EVERY DAY.
WE'RE SUPPOSED TO SPEND THAT TIME NONCHALANTLY TODAY LIKE WE ALWAYS DO, BUT...
ONII-SAMA IS WAITING IN THE LIVING ROOM—BUT WHICH OUTFIT SHOULD I WEAR?
I WANT SOMETHING THAT FEELS SUITABLE FOR ONII-SAMA'S YOUNGER SISTER BUT WILL ALSO MAKE HIS HEART SKIP A BEAT...

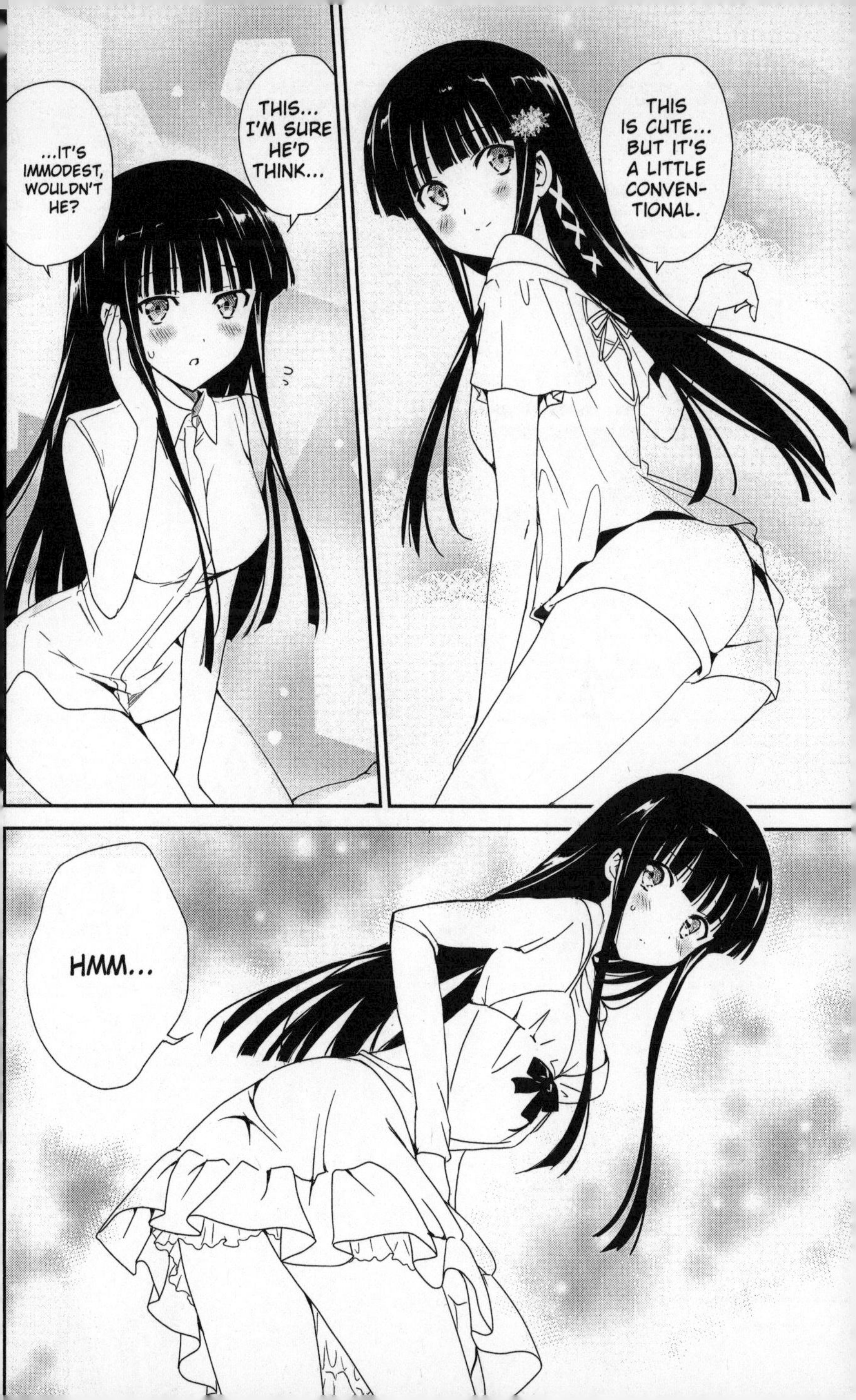
THIS IS CUTE... BUT IT'S A LITTLE CONVEN-TIONAL.
THIS... I'M SURE HE'D THINK...
...IT'S IMMODEST, WOULDN'T HE?
HMM...

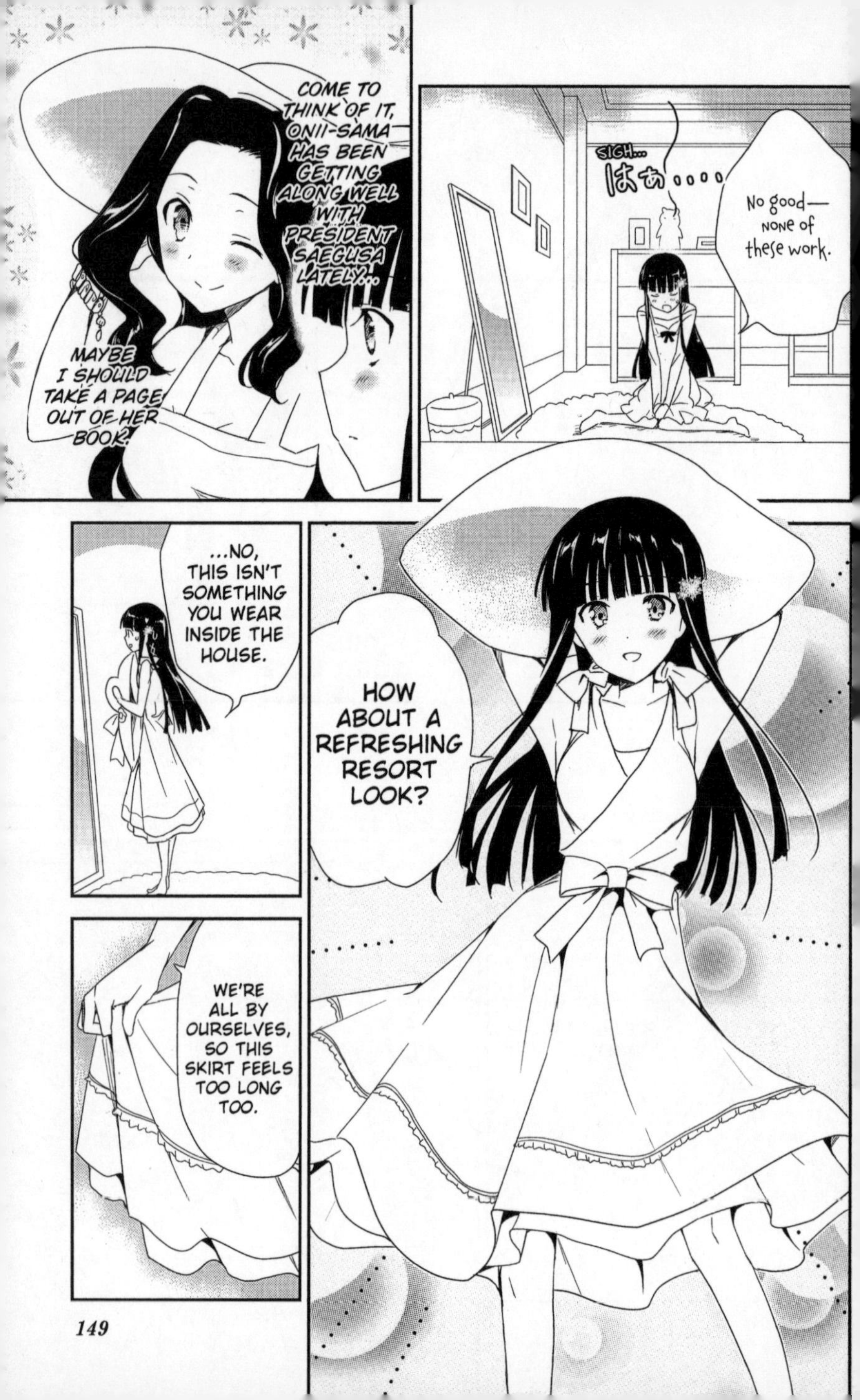
SIGH...
はぁ....
No good— none of these work.
COME TO THINK OF IT, ONII-SAMA HAS BEEN GETTING ALONG WELL WITH PRESIDENT SAEGUSA LATELY...
MAYBE I SHOULD TAKE A PAGE OUT OF HER BOOK!
HOW ABOUT A REFRESHING RESORT LOOK?
...NO, THIS ISN'T SOMETHING YOU WEAR INSIDE THE HOUSE.
WE'RE ALL BY OURSELVES, SO THIS SKIRT FEELS TOO LONG TOO.

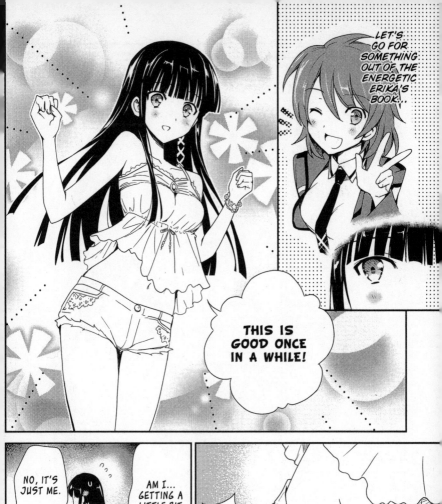

LET'S GO FOR SOMETHING OUT OF THE ENERGETIC ERIKA'S BOOK...

THIS IS GOOD ONCE IN A WHILE!

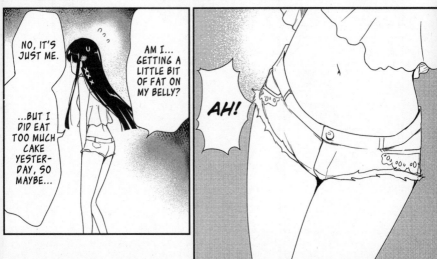

NO, IT'S JUST ME.

AM I... GETTING A LITTLE BIT OF FAT ON MY BELLY?

...BUT I DID EAT TOO MUCH CAKE YESTERDAY, SO MAYBE...

AH!

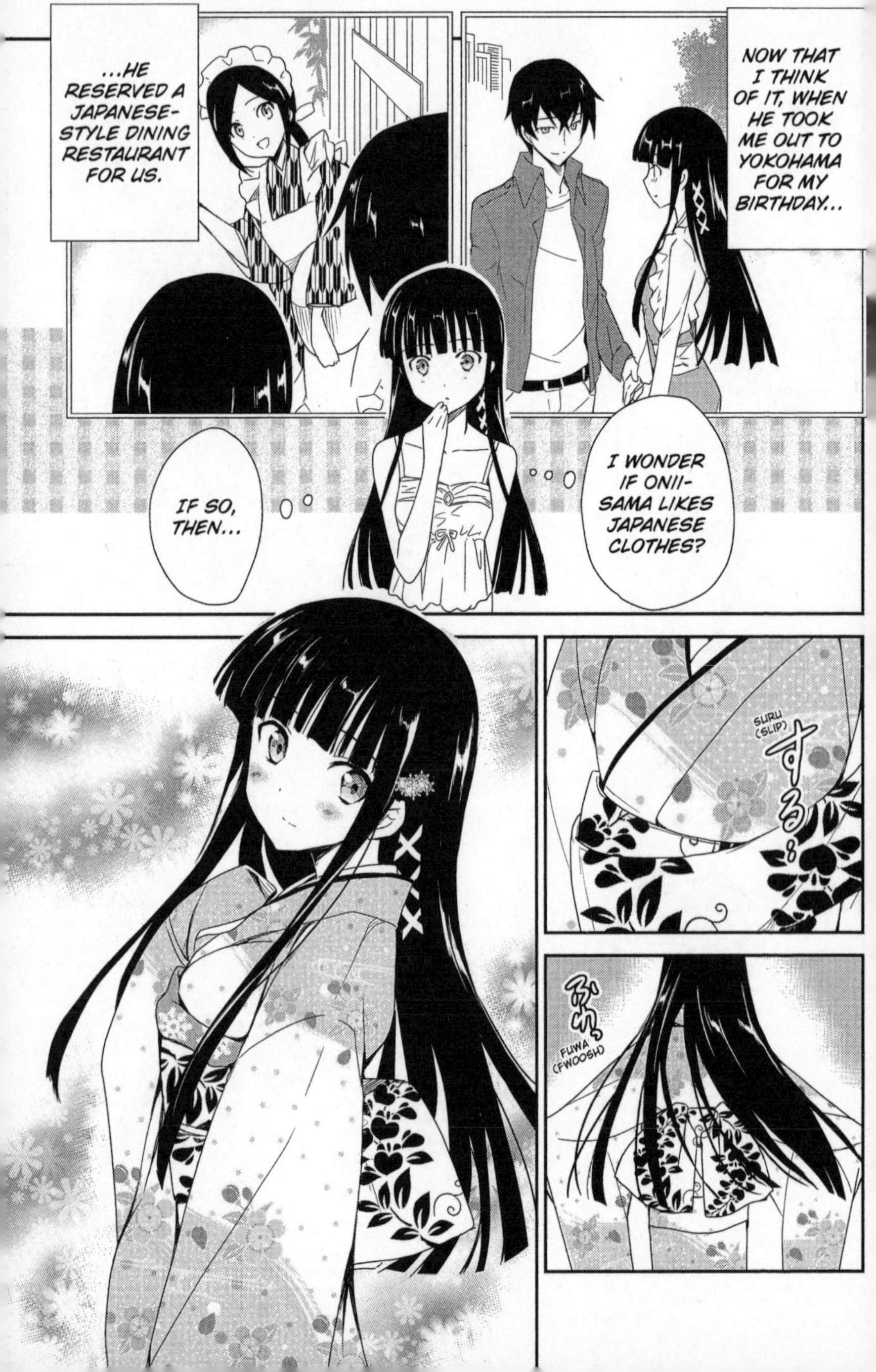
NOW THAT I THINK OF IT, WHEN HE TOOK ME OUT TO YOKOHAMA FOR MY BIRTHDAY...
...HE RESERVED A JAPANESE-STYLE DINING RESTAURANT FOR US.
I WONDER IF ONII-SAMA LIKES JAPANESE CLOTHES?
IF SO, THEN...
SURU (SLIP)
する
ふわ
FUWA (FWOOSH)

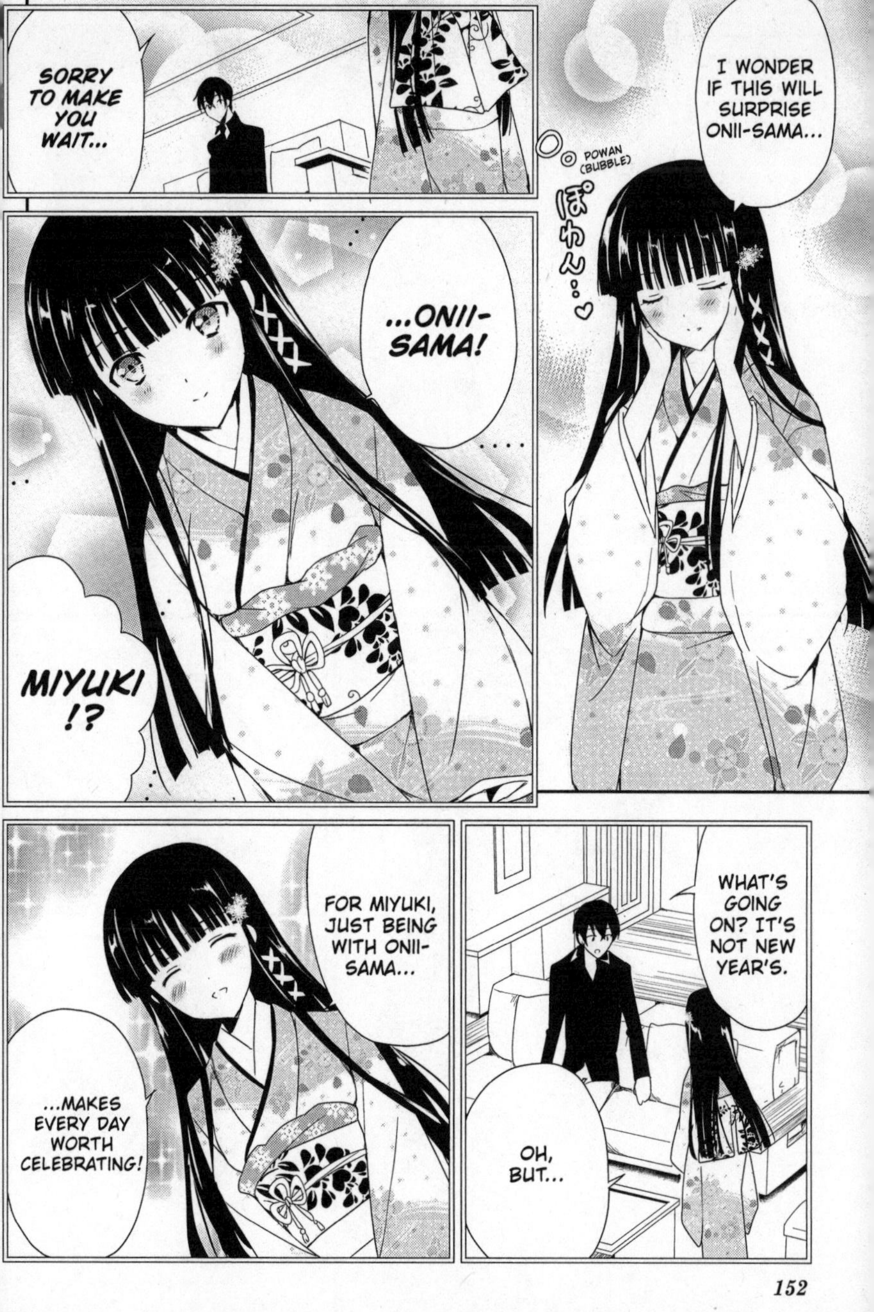
I WONDER IF THIS WILL SURPRISE ONII-SAMA...
POWAN (BUBBLE)
ぽわん♡
SORRY TO MAKE YOU WAIT...
...ONII-SAMA!
MIYUKI !?
WHAT'S GOING ON? IT'S NOT NEW YEAR'S.
OH, BUT...
FOR MIYUKI, JUST BEING WITH ONII-SAMA...
...MAKES EVERY DAY WORTH CELEBRATING!

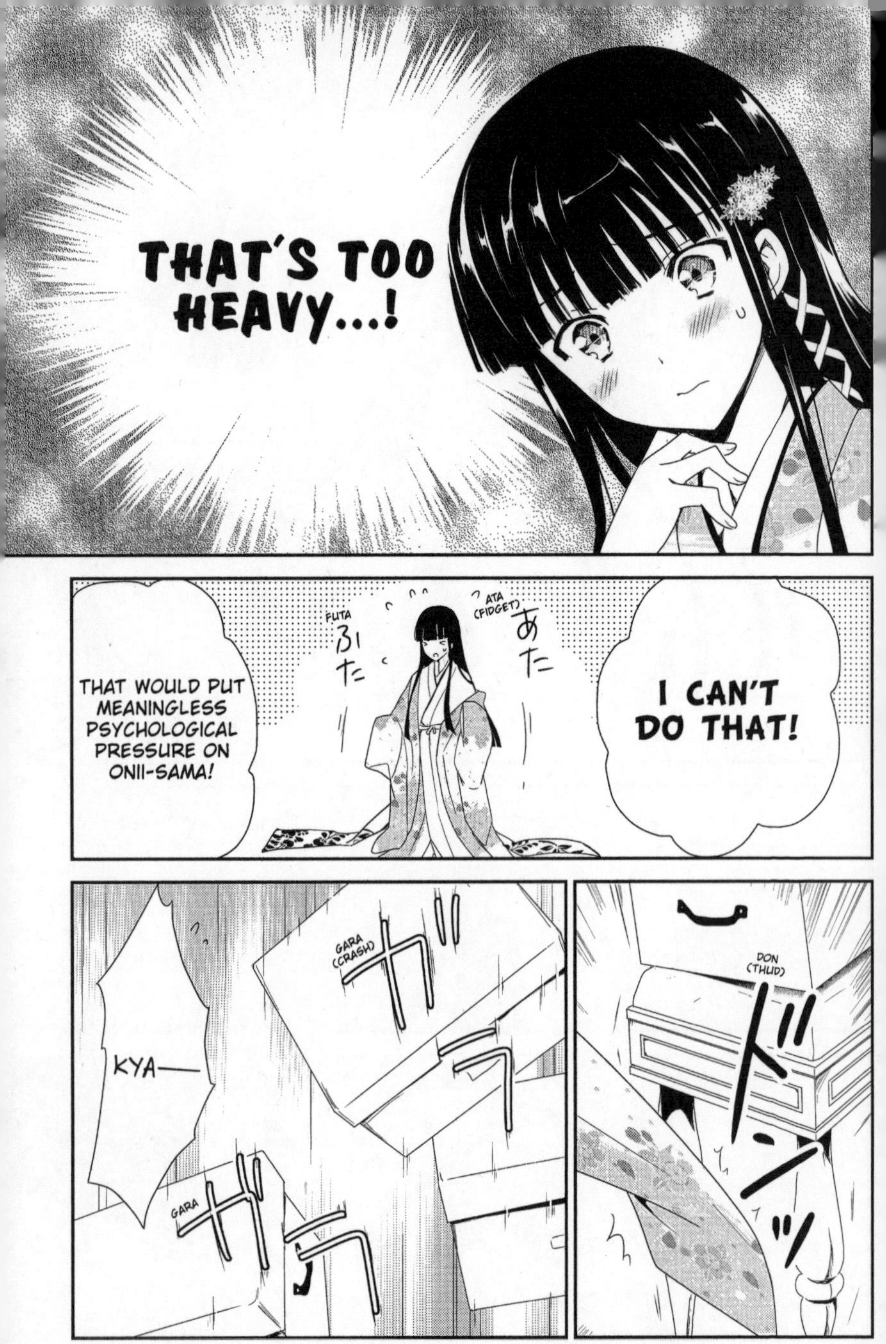
THAT'S TOO HEAVY...!
I CAN'T DO THAT!
ATA (FIDGET)
あた
FUTA
ふた
THAT WOULD PUT MEANINGLESS PSYCHOLOGICAL PRESSURE ON ONII-SAMA!
DON (THUD)
ドン
GARA (CRASH)
ガラ
KYA—
GARA
ガラ

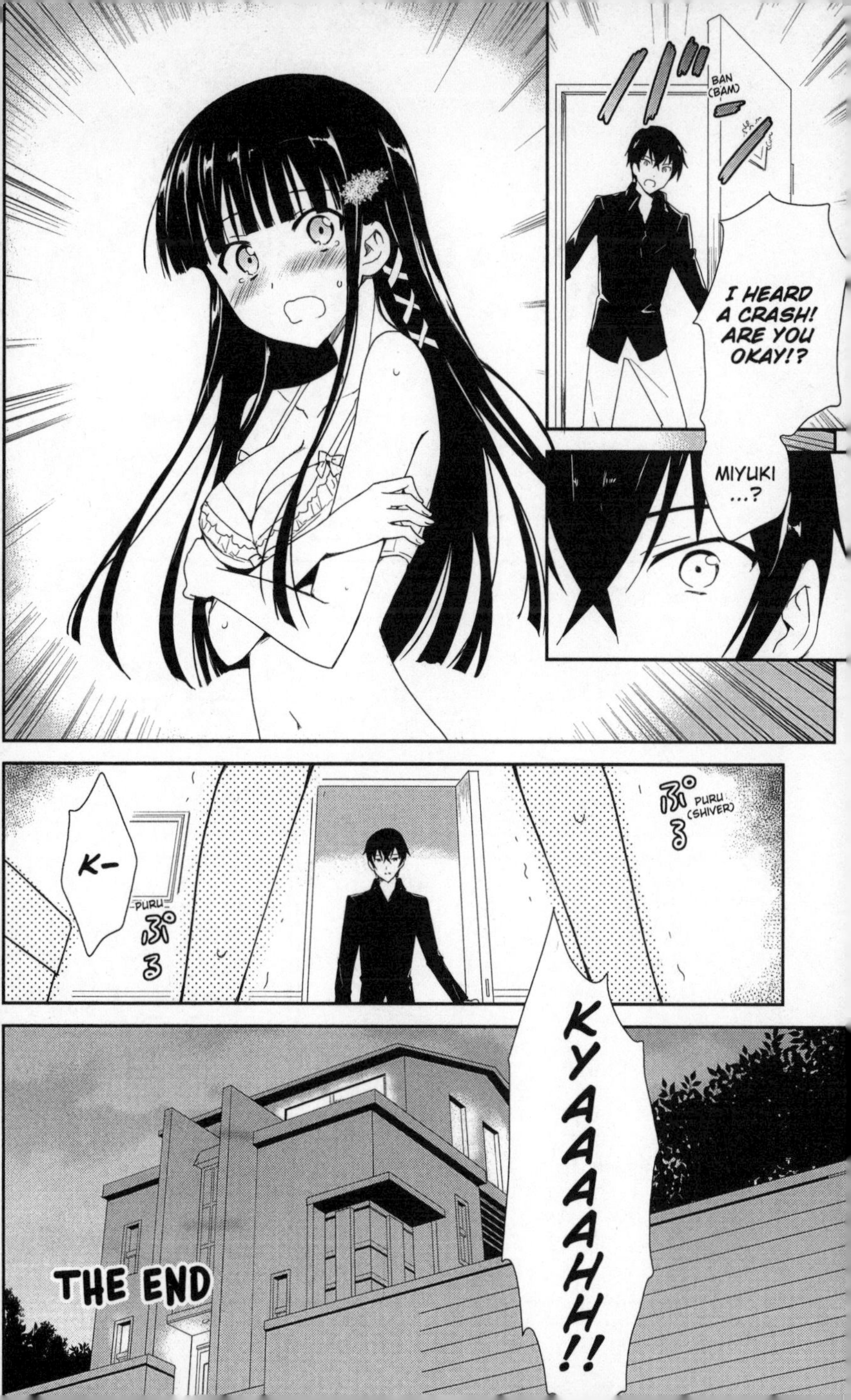
BAN (BAM)
I HEARD A CRASH! ARE YOU OKAY!?
MIYUKI ...?
ぷる PURU (SHIVER)
K-
ぷる PURU
KYAAAAAHH!!
THE END

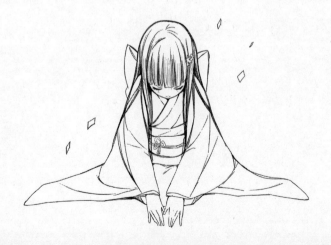

● Activation sequence

The blueprints for magic and the programs used to construct it. Activation sequence data is stored in a compressed format in C.A.D.s. Design waves are sent from the magician to the device, where they are converted into a signal according to the decompressed data and returned to the magician.

● Blooms, Weeds

Terms displaying the gap between Course 1 students and Course 2 students in the First Affiliated High School. The left breast of Course 1 student uniforms is emblazoned with an eight-petaled emblem, but it is absent from the Course 2 uniforms.

● C.A.D. (Casting Assistant Device)

A device that simplifies the activation of magic. Magical programming is recorded inside. The main types are specialized and all-purpose.

● Eidos (Individual information body)

Originally a term from Greek philosophy. In modern magic, "Eidos" are the bodies of information that accompany phenomena. They record the existence of those phenomena on the world, so they can also be called the footprints that phenomena leave on the world. The definition of "magic" in modern magic refers to the technology which modifies these phenomena by modifying Eidos.

● Idea (Information body dimension)

Pronounced "ee-dee-ah." Originally a term from Greek philosophy. In modern magic, "Idea" refers to the platform on which Eidos are recorded. Magic's primary form is a technology wherein a magic program is output onto this platform, thus rewriting the Eidos recorded within.

● Loopcast system

Activation sequences made so that the magician can continually execute a spell as many times as their calculation capacity will permit. Normally one must re-expand activation sequences from the C.A.D. every time one executes the same spell, but the loopcast system makes it possible to avoid this time-consuming repetition by automatically duplicating the activation program's final state in the magician's magic calculation region.

● Magic Association of Japan

A social group of Japanese magicians, with its headquarters in Kyoto. The Kantou branch location is established within Yokohama Bay Hills Tower.

● Magic calculation region

A mental region for the construction of magic sequences. The substance, so to speak, of magical talent. It exists in a magician's unconscious, and even if a magician is normally aware of using his or her magic calculation region, he or she cannot be aware of the processes being conducted within. The magic calculation region can be called a "black box" for the magician himself.

Magic engineer
Refers to engineers who design, develop, and maintain apparatus that assists, amplifies, and strengthens magic. Their reputation in society is slightly worse than that of magicians. However, magic engineers are indispensable for tuning the C.A.D.s, indispensable tools for magicians, so in the industrial world, they're in higher demand than normal magicians. A first-rate magic engineer's earnings surpass even that of first-rate magicians.

Magic High School
The nickname for the high schools affiliated with the National Magic University. There are nine established throughout the country. Of them, the first through the third have two hundred students per grade, and use the Course 1/Course 2 system.

Magic sequence
An information body for the purpose of temporarily altering information attached to phenomena. They are constructed from the psions possessed by magicians.

Magician
An abbreviation of "magical technician." A magical technician is the name for anyone with the skill to use magic at a practical level.

Nine School Competition
Abbreviation of "National Magic High School Goodwill Magic Competition Tournament." Magic high school students from First through Ninth High across the country are gathered to compete with their schools in fierce magic showdowns. There are six events: Speed Shooting, Cloudball, Battle Board, Ice Pillars Break, Mirage Bat, and Monolith Code.

Psions
Non-physical particles belonging to the dimension of psychic phenomena. Psions are elements that record information onconsciousness and thought products. Eidos—the theoretical basis for modern magic—as well as activation sequences and magic sequences—supporting its main framework—are all bodies of information constructed from Psions.

Pushions
Non-physical particles belonging to the dimension of psychic phenomena. Their existence has been proven, but their true form and functions have yet to be elucidated. Magicians are generally only able to "feel" the pushions being activated through magic.

The Ten Master Clans
The strongest group of magicians in Japan. Ten families from a list of twenty-eight are chosen during the Ten Master Clans Selection Conference that happens every four years and are named as the Ten Master Clans. The twenty-eight families are Ichijou, Ichinokura, Isshiki, Futatsugi, Nikaidou, Nihei, Mitsuya, Mikazuki, Yotsuba, Itsuwa, Gotou, Itsumi, Mutsuzuka, Rokkaku, Rokugou, Roppongi, Saegusa, Shippou, Tanabata, Nanase, Yatsushiro, Hassaku, Hachiman, Kudou, Kuki, Kuzumi, Juumonji, and Tooyama.

TRANSLATION NOTES

PAGE 117
Izu the Wise was a feudal lord of the early Edo period whose real name was Matsudaira Nobutsuna. He received his nickname for the wit and intelligence he displayed from an early age.

The **Oniwaban** was a group of undercover agents working for the Tokugawa government in the late 1600s–early 1700s tasked with spying on feudal lords and acting as security guards. They are often imagined as ninja.

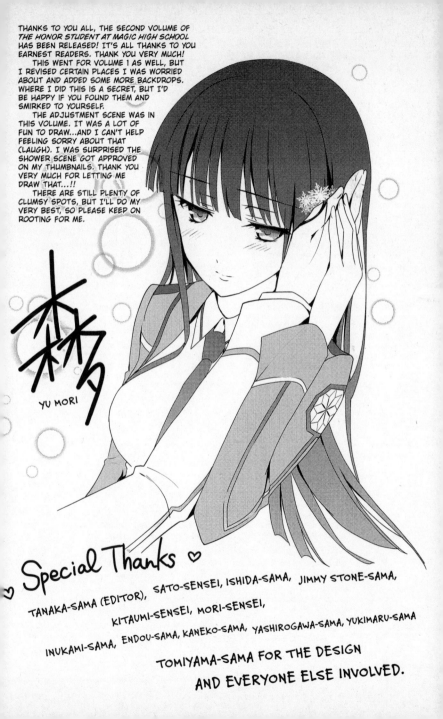

THANKS TO YOU ALL, THE SECOND VOLUME OF *THE HONOR STUDENT AT MAGIC HIGH SCHOOL* HAS BEEN RELEASED! IT'S ALL THANKS TO YOU EARNEST READERS. THANK YOU VERY MUCH!

THIS WENT FOR VOLUME 1 AS WELL, BUT I REVISED CERTAIN PLACES I WAS WORRIED ABOUT AND ADDED SOME MORE BACKDROPS. WHERE I DID THIS IS A SECRET, BUT I'D BE HAPPY IF YOU FOUND THEM AND SMIRKED TO YOURSELF.

THE ADJUSTMENT SCENE WAS IN THIS VOLUME. IT WAS A LOT OF FUN TO DRAW...AND I CAN'T HELP FEELING SORRY ABOUT THAT (LAUGH). I WAS SURPRISED THE SHOWER SCENE GOT APPROVED ON MY THUMBNAILS. THANK YOU VERY MUCH FOR LETTING ME DRAW THAT...!!

THERE ARE STILL PLENTY OF CLUMSY SPOTS, BUT I'LL DO MY VERY BEST, SO PLEASE KEEP ON ROOTING FOR ME.

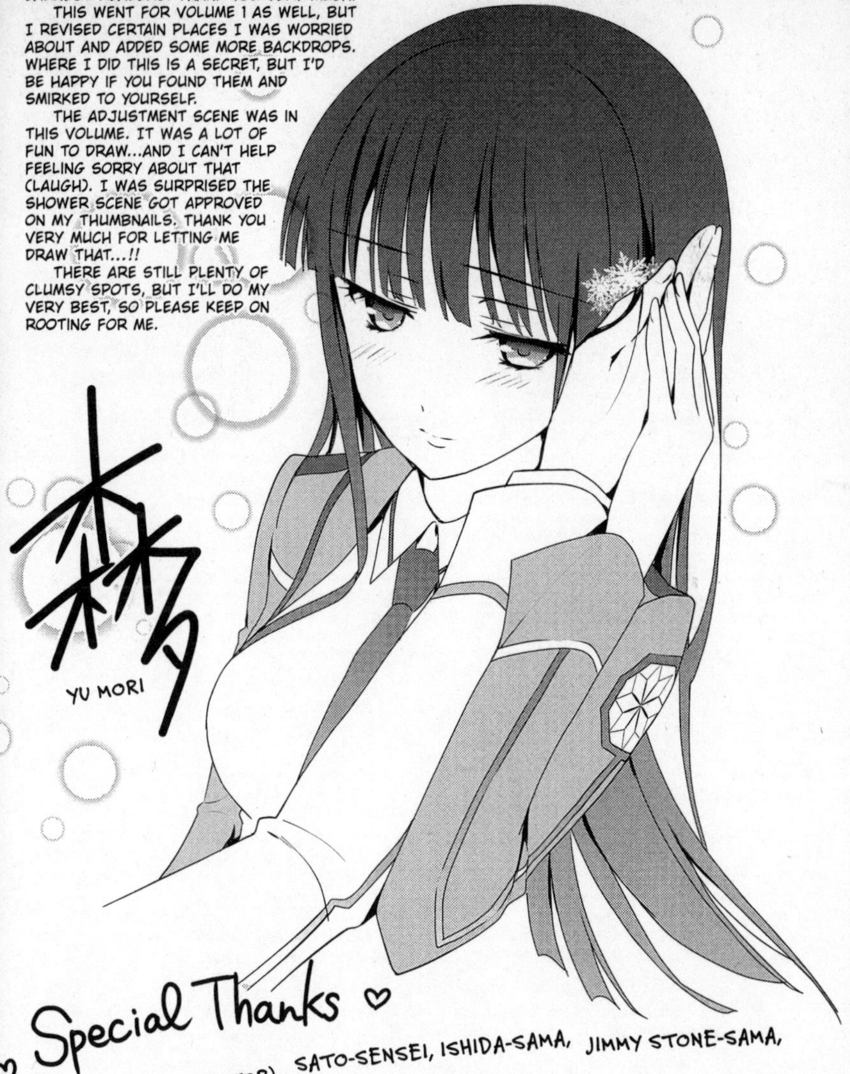

YU MORI

Special Thanks ♡

♡ TANAKA-SAMA (EDITOR), SATO-SENSEI, ISHIDA-SAMA, JIMMY STONE-SAMA,

KITAUMI-SENSEI, MORI-SENSEI,

INUKAMI-SAMA, ENDOU-SAMA, KANEKO-SAMA, YASHIROGAWA-SAMA, YUKIMARU-SAMA

TOMIYAMA-SAMA FOR THE DESIGN

AND EVERYONE ELSE INVOLVED.

Mori-sensei, congratulations on the second volume of *The Honor Student at Magic High School*. It includes that particular scene—the climax of the first half of the Enrollment arc—and it has all sorts of highlights! Well, no, I'm referring to *that* scene. The duel between Tatsuya and Hattori. ...I'm sorry, that was a lie. Thank you for even increasing the amount of fanservice for me. I don't seem to be very good at depictions of *moe*.

Not only does manga have a charm that doesn't exist in novels, but Sensei's individuality shines through in his drawings of his interpretations of the characters and their thoughts, allowing the reader a fresh sense of enjoyment. His "I'm fine, I just took a shower" line was right on the dot.

The Honor Student at Magic High School is placed as a spinoff—a side story, if you will—of the original novels, but Volume 2 portrays the different episodes in the same places and times as the originals, even more than Volume 1 does. They don't appear in the original novels, but in any school there are always club seniors and graduates, and they appear here as well (though they're not quite normal). That's another one of the points I'd like all the fans to pay attention to. The title page with the new student recruitment scene had a circus-like atmosphere too, and those little details deserve attention as well.

I look forward to the world of *Magic High School* that couldn't be fit into the novels expanding greatly from here on out.

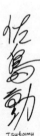

Tsutomu
Sato

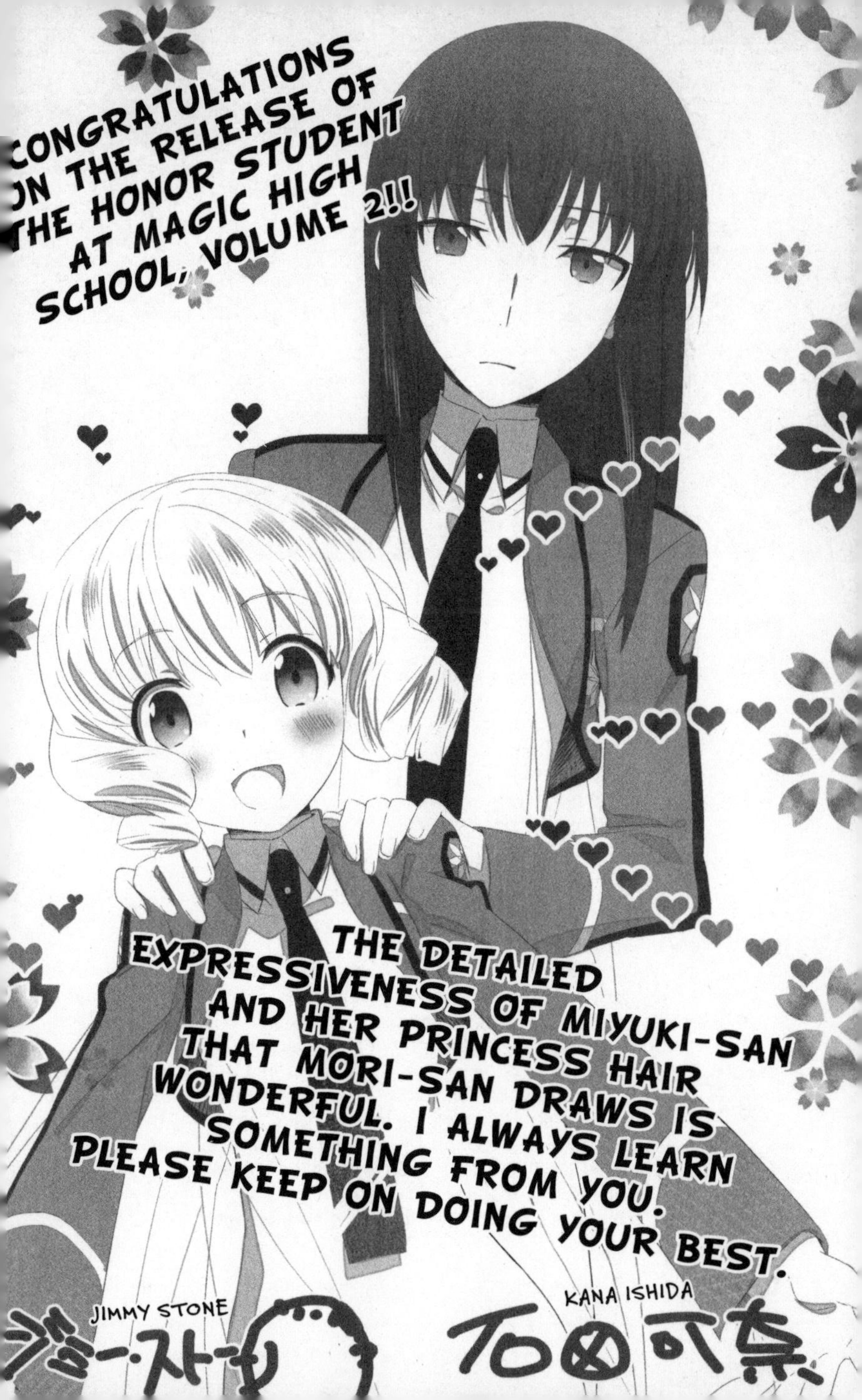
CONGRATULATIONS ON THE RELEASE OF THE HONOR STUDENT AT MAGIC HIGH SCHOOL, VOLUME 2!!
THE DETAILED EXPRESSIVENESS OF MIYUKI-SAN AND HER PRINCESS HAIR THAT MORI-SAN DRAWS IS WONDERFUL. I ALWAYS LEARN SOMETHING FROM YOU.
PLEASE KEEP ON DOING YOUR BEST.
JIMMY STONE
KANA ISHIDA

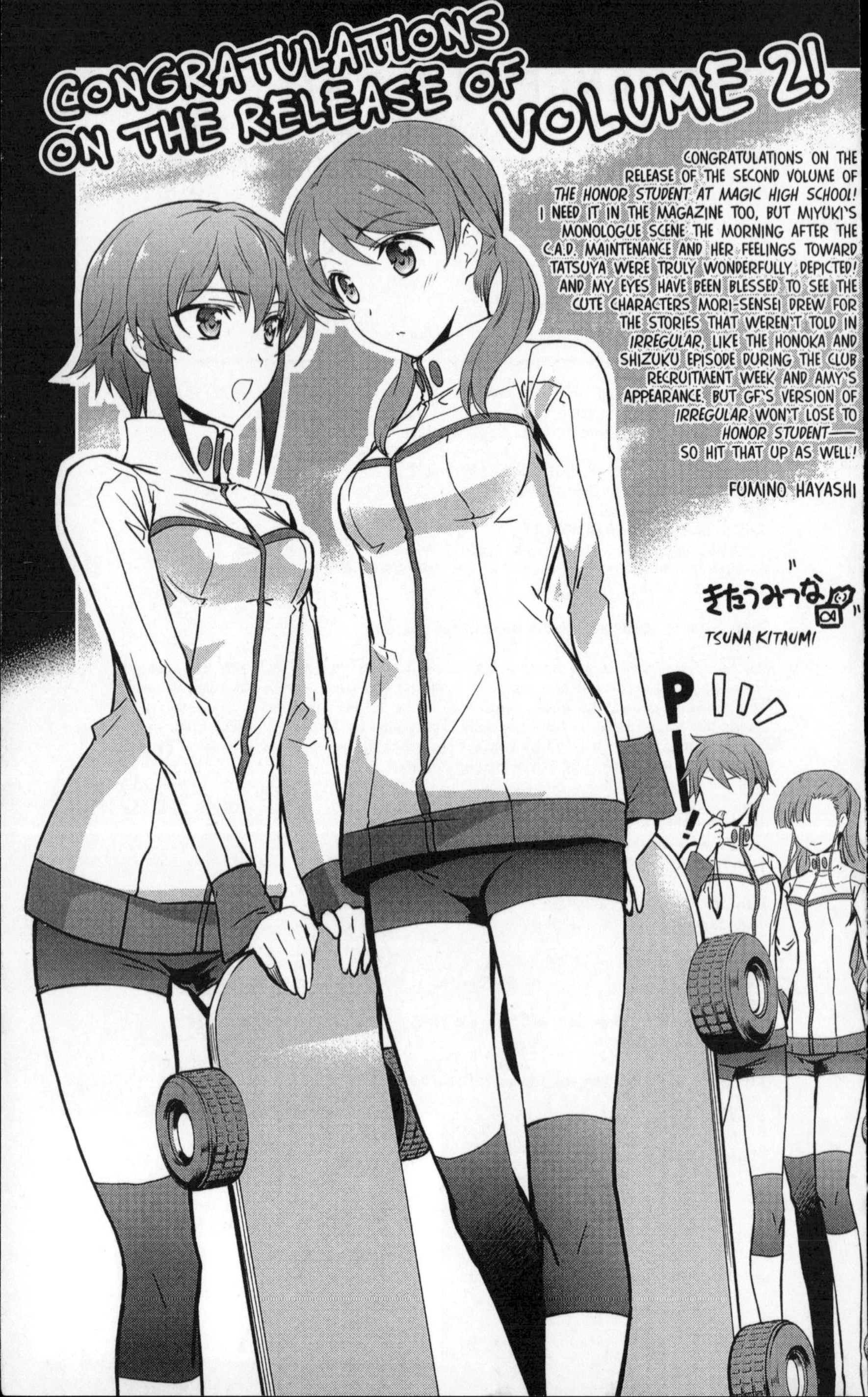
CONGRATULATIONS ON THE RELEASE OF VOLUME 2!
CONGRATULATIONS ON THE RELEASE OF THE SECOND VOLUME OF *THE HONOR STUDENT AT MAGIC HIGH SCHOOL!* I NEED IT IN THE MAGAZINE TOO, BUT MIYUKI'S MONOLOGUE SCENE THE MORNING AFTER THE C.A.D. MAINTENANCE AND HER FEELINGS TOWARD TATSUYA WERE TRULY WONDERFULLY DEPICTED! AND MY EYES HAVE BEEN BLESSED TO SEE THE CUTE CHARACTERS MORI-SENSEI DREW FOR THE STORIES THAT WEREN'T TOLD IN *IRREGULAR*, LIKE THE HONOKA AND SHIZUKU EPISODE DURING THE CLUB RECRUITMENT WEEK AND AMY'S APPEARANCE. BUT GF'S VERSION OF *IRREGULAR* WON'T LOSE TO *HONOR STUDENT*—SO HIT THAT UP AS WELL!
FUMINO HAYASHI
きたうみつな
TSUNA KITAUMI
PI!

THE HONOR STUDENT
AT MAGIC HIGH SCHOOL ❷

YU MORI
Original Story: TSUTOMU SATO
Character Design: KANA ISHIDA

Translation: Andrew Prowse
Lettering: Lys Blakeslee

MAHOUKA KOUKOU NO YUUTOUSEI Volume 2
© TSUTOMU SATO / YU MORI 2013
All rights reserved.
Edited by ASCII MEDIA WORKS
First published in Japan in 2013 by KADOKAWA CORPORATION, Tokyo.
English translation rights arranged with KADOKAWA CORPORATION, Tokyo, through Tuttle-Mori Agency, Inc., Tokyo.

Translation © 2016 by Hachette Book Group, Inc.

Yen Press
Hachette Book Group
1290 Avenue of the Americas
New York, NY 10104

www.hachettebookgroup.com
www.yenpress.com

Yen Press is an imprint of Hachette Book Group, Inc.
The Yen Press name and logo are trademarks of Hachette Book Group, Inc.

The publisher is not responsible for websites (or their content) that are not owned by the publisher.

Library of Congress Control Number: 2015956860

First Yen Press Edition: March 2016

ISBN: 978-0-316-39034-7

10 9 8 7 6 5 4 3 2 1

BVG

Printed in the United States of America